Aaron Burr in Exile

Aaron Burr in Exile

A Pariah in Paris, 1810–1811

Jane Merrill *and*
John Endicott

McFarland & Company, Inc., Publishers
Jefferson, North Carolina

LIBRARY OF CONGRESS CATALOGUING-IN-PUBLICATION DATA

Names: Merrill, Jane, author. | Endicott, John, 1946– author.
Title: Aaron Burr in exile : a pariah in Paris, 1810–1811 /
Jane Merrill and John Endicott.
Description: Jefferson, North Carolina : McFarland & Company, Inc.,
Publishers, 2016. | Includes bibliographical references and index.
Identifiers: LCCN 2015048994 | ISBN 9780786494910
(softcover : acid free paper) ∞
Subjects: LCSH: Burr, Aaron, 1756–1836—Travel—France—Paris. | Statesmen—
United States—Biography. | Vice-Presidents—United States—Biography.
Classification: LCC E302.6.B9 M48 2016 | DDC 973.4/6092—dc23
LC record available at http://lccn.loc.gov/2015048994

BRITISH LIBRARY CATALOGUING DATA ARE AVAILABLE

ISBN 978-0-7864-9491-0 (print)
ISBN 978-1-4766-2130-2 (ebook)

© 2016 Jane Merrill and John Endicott. All rights reserved

*No part of this book may be reproduced or transmitted in any form
or by any means, electronic or mechanical, including photocopying
or recording, or by any information storage and retrieval system,
without permission in writing from the publisher.*

On the cover: *Passage des Panoramas*, Paris, France,
c. 1810 watercolor (Gianni Dagli Orti/
The Art Archive at Art Resource, New York)

Printed in the United States of America

*McFarland & Company, Inc., Publishers
Box 611, Jefferson, North Carolina 28640*
www.mcfarlandpub.com

Table of Contents

Acknowledgments vi
Preface by Jane Merrill 1

One. Journal Keeping 5
Two. Persona Non Grata 11
Three. New Year's Eve, Paris, 1810 17
Four. Acquaintances 22
Five. Money Matters 43
Six. Lifestyle 57
Seven. Exploring the Capital 76
Eight. Cultural Diversions 103
Nine. Dining In and Out 124
Ten. Perambulation 141
Eleven. Female Companions 152
Twelve. Sex and Sanguinity 162
Thirteen. Julie 178
Fourteen. Saga of a Passport 182

Epilogue 187
Appendix A—Reading Burr 191
Appendix B—Aaron Burr and His Protégé John Vanderlyn in Paris, 1810–1811 (by Katherine Woltz) 194
Chapter Notes 219
Bibliography 227
Index 231

Acknowledgments

First of all, we are grateful to Peter J. Tavino, who precipitated this study by communicating his own lively interest in Aaron Burr. We are indebted to many libraries, especially the public libraries of Weston, Massachusetts, and Westport, Connecticut, and to the library of Wellesley College. We have many scholars to thank who have not only helped with sources but by speaking personally, and thereby making writing the book all the more agreeable: Dr. Pierre Baron, president of the French Society of the History of Dental Art; Dr. Valerio Burello, president of the Italian Society of Odontological History; Andrew McClellan, art historian at Tufts University; Jean-Luc Chappey, professor at the Institute of Modern and Contemporary History (Paris); Meghan Constantino of the Grolier Club; Denise Z. Davidson of Georgia State University; Priscilla Parkhurst Ferguson, cultural historian at Columbia University; Chris Filstrup, reference librarian, Stony Brook University; Thomas A. Foster of DePaul University; Peter Hicks, historian at the Foundation Napoleon; Claire A. Lyons, professor at the University of Maryland; David Lubin of Wake Forest University; Jeri Quinzio, culinary historian; Brenda Rosseau and Al Saguto of the Colonial Williamsburg Foundation; Sabine Kegel, head of the department of watches and wristwatches, Christie's; and Dr. Francisco Javier Sanz-Serrulla, historian of medicine. We thank Katherine Woltz, director of the Vanderlyn Catalogue Raisonné, for being a bright light and for contributing her essay as Appendix B to this book; Rosalind Parry for peeping around Paris and for conversation; and among all the museums, especially Yale's Walpole Library and British Art Library, the Lilly Library, McGill University Library, and the Walters Museum for their "open" policy of aid to writers and scholars. Amy Imhof and David L. Arnheim did selfless readings of the manuscript. Thank you, both of you, for your alacrity and enthusiasm for the subject.

Preface

Jane Merrill

> Paris has huge depth, so much behind it, so many meanings. Perhaps it intimidates a little: I mean the image of Paris, not the city itself; on the contrary, it is the city where as soon as you set foot in it you immediately find it familiar.—Italo Calvino, *Hermit in Paris*[1]

The Founding Fathers were not insular, and statistics attest that sailing across the ocean in vessels of the day was actually not as risky as one might imagine. However, Aaron Burr was the only American of note who lived in Paris before the mid–19th century who was not insulated by wealth and means—the one who saw the city from arguably the best angle: down and out. This book is based on the candid journal he kept while abroad, focusing on the fifteen months he settled in one place.

The United States Lines at one time gave unused staterooms to military officers and their dependents. This is how my family traveled to France, with only a few days' notice, in their flagship, the SS *United States*. Our suite was filled with bouquets for the movie star who had canceled and there was a steward who wore white gloves and walked our dog. When I came down with the measles on the fourth day, I was disguised in headscarf, sunglasses and trench coat, and secreted off the ship.

Our first afternoon in Paris, my 15-year-old brother, Tom, and I explored the hotel room where we would be living for several months. He unlatched the French doors and called me to the balcony.

"Look," he said with awe.

"What is it?"

"It must be an oil well," said Tom.

Our first sight of the Eiffel Tower. I include this personal recollection because hidden in most every book is the "why" of the narrative.

My brother and I had less foreknowledge of Paris in 1958 than Aaron Burr had in 1810. Burr had read French literature in the original, spoke some French, and had French acquaintances in New York, while my father was advised to pack an inflatable kiddie pool, in case France had no bathing facilities. The first time my parents ordered for us in a restaurant the waiter brought a platter of well-done haricots verts (green beans) under a bell-shaped cover instead of a well-done entrecôte (steak). That long-ago initial encounter with

Paris showed me three things that bear on this book: what it is like to come upon the city untutored; what the city was like when most neighborhoods were quiet; and how to appreciate the underside.

Candor and vivacity make Burr's journal, which he intended as an aide-memoire to one day share his experiences with his daughter. It's as good reading as the diary of Samuel Pepys. In Paris, where the journal becomes nearly continuous, Burr noted everyday details, including his sexual assignations; sprinkled throughout, they lend a you-are-there quality to the whole. To Burr, these intimate markers were a way of waving his hat—"See, I'm hale and hearty"—though it can shock the reader who imagines his daughter—to whom the journal is addressed—reading them.

"I think one travels more usefully when they travel alone, because they reflect more," wrote Thomas Jefferson in a letter. In my late twenties, my life fell away (if not apart) on American shores and I was back in Paris, alone, and with a nationality issue like Burr's, in search of a job but having no worker's permit. Fortune smiled when I got a job at an international research institute headed by an ex–U.S. ambassador who phoned the U.S. ambassador to France who in turn said something to the effect that authorities would look the other way so long as I was paid in cash. By 1975, Paris had many cultural references for me, as for most expatriates. An old friend had even advised me that Paris was the place to mend a broken heart.

Aaron Burr by John Vanderlyn or after Vanderlyn's original portrait painted in 1802 in New York City during a brief return from Paris. Burr was probably aged 46, six years before he departed for Europe. The beribboned queue was an intermediary style between powdering the hair and a "Roman" cut that he could have adopted in Paris. Oil on canvas, 22-¼ in. × 16-½ in. (collection of The New-York Historical Society, negative #6227; object #1931.58).

For Burr there was little of the inner landscape, the prior knowledge, which explains why his journal entries have such dash. He isn't reflecting on Enlightenment ideas about the moral life (although he is interested in technology and indifferent to organized religion) and he doesn't wax romantic either. For him, England was hyper-real, a country he fought against as a younger man, while Paris was simply real, not received. On his miles and miles of walks through Paris he was going somewhere, exploring mercantile products, having his boots repaired, his books bound, or shopping for the perfect gift. Only incidentally was he a flâneur. Burr would have endorsed what Italo Calvino said of the City of Light: "It is a giant reference work, a city which you can consult like an encyclopaedia: whatever page is open gives you a complete list of information that is richer than that offered by any other city."

New insight into Burr's state of mind comes from Katherine Woltz's essay (Appendix B) on Burr and American painter John Vanderlyn. Burr's friend, protégé and portraitist, Vanderlyn knew his most intimate secrets and sought to restore public esteem of his friend.

Naturally, Burr came with notions of Napoleon

and the French but engaged the city on his own terms. Why did he write about repairing his umbrella instead of ruminating on Gothic architecture? Because he was not reading Paris as history but recording his shifting perspectives on the contemporary city he traversed, mirroring it as autobiographical souvenir. In Paris, I collected antique earrings and drew them, also drawing them in shops and from portraits in museums. They filled my journal with the same purpose as Burr's, to remember and to tell the story back home (which I did in *I Love Those Earrings* a long time afterward).

My lodging in the mid–1970s was a short walk from where Burr first lived, a *chambre de bonne* at the top of a luxurious old building with a creamy stone façade and a princely marble staircase that stopped just short of the floor with the servants' quarters (upstairs being downstairs), where I lived. The view from our attic rooms rivaled that of any hotel. They had low curved ceilings and a very dark W.C. with a shower stall down the hall. Being a complete outsider, I felt light and temporary, invisible, yet also open to external stimuli and new experiences and people. Every night after work I went out with friends or by myself, and one Friday I came home from the institute, fell asleep … and woke up Sunday. Who was I? Who was this disordered person?

This is what Burr asked over and over, about his sleep, his love/hate relationship with his little rooms, his struggles for food, warmth, adequate clothing, dental care, income, and connections. Until he returned to New York he also had a lot of free time to hang out with his friends, as expatriates tend to do. It was a time of loss of living connections and no clear future, more like what Eva Hoffman in her émigré memoir, *Lost in Translation* (1990), describes as she explores the meaning of exile: "I don't know. I don't see what I've seen, don't comprehend what's in front of me." Yet, choosing Paris in this state of anguish, Burr chose particularly well (as did I).

Paris was then governed by, and beginning to slough off, an artful and disastrous ideology of empire; but Burr never met Napoleon and stayed away from politics. Instead, he carried out a cultural foray, and with rather enforced leisure regrouped his energy unperturbed before returning to New York.

A span of expatriate life creates pinpoints of memory, and making a life when you have next to none is like balancing on a ball or riding a bicycle, a skill you never forget.

One

Journal Keeping

Aaron Burr, third vice president of the United States, Revolutionary War hero, and the most disputed figure in the history of the early republic, spent fifteen months in Paris between 1810 and 1811 that contrasted with any other period of his eventful past. Buttressing his Paris journal with other sources then and now, this book tells the story of his sojourn there. Most important, Burr was adrift. In this state, he attended and adapted to the world around—a "moveable feast," as Ernest Hemingway would write—to make his way in the great capital.

The Parisian expatriate experience, such as that of Ernest Hemingway, Henry Miller, Gertrude Stein and George Orwell in the 1920s, abounds in legend. Scholars have also lately begun to take a closer look. Many readers have now read Julie Flavell's *When London Was the Capital of America* (2011) and learned about the relations of the old and new countries during the early republic. They have become immersed in the complex storytelling of David McCullough's *The Greater Journey: Americans in Paris* (2010), covering diplomats, artists, young doctors and others who absorbed culture in Paris from the 1830s to 1900. Aaron Burr's sojourn falls exactly between these two time periods. His journal notations show the redirection he found from his disrupted American life, in the most exciting city in the world of his time.

Most everyone knows that Aaron Burr won the 1804 duel with Alexander Hamilton. They also may know about Burr's 1807 treason trial. Fewer people know that, tied with Thomas Jefferson in 1800 in the electoral college voting, Burr had it in his power to be elected president, rather than vice president, by the Federalist-controlled Congress. He has a continuing allure as the dark figure in American history, described by Gordon Wood in *Empire of Liberty* (2009) as "the most romanticized and vilified character in American literature." Utilizing Burr's self-portraiture, *Aaron Burr in Exile* presents readers with the real person.

Like several famous American expatriates of the 1920s, Burr had a "down and out" existence in Paris, living on hope and handouts, pawning clothes, dreaming schemes, and enjoying the nightlife. He eventually did return to New York and a successful career in real estate law. He was a survivor who in early childhood lost his parents and his grandparents (both his father and grandfather were presidents of Princeton) in the course of two years, later lost his beloved wife, and then his only child and grandchild. He was in good spirits abroad, sometimes disoriented but never despondent, gathering the inner force for his return.

Burr's Paris stay marked the end of a tumultuous decade in his life, beginning with the voting in the House of Representatives in 1801 to break the Jefferson-Burr tie in the electoral college. As Jefferson's vice president from 1801 to 1805, Burr had little power or influence. Deciding that his political future lay in New York, he ran unsuccessfully for governor in 1804. In the course of that election, Alexander Hamilton, Burr's political opponent for many years, disparaged Burr's personal character one too many times. Burr was the survivor of their duel fought on the banks of the Hudson in July 1804. A month later, while still vice president, Burr was in touch with the British minister plenipotentiary in Washington, who wrote to London of Burr's offer to assist His Majesty's government "to effect a separation of the Western part of the United States from that which lies between the Atlantic and the Appalachian mountains." In early 1805—just after presiding over the Senate impeachment trial of Justice Chase—Burr wrote his son-in-law that "in New York I am to be disfranchised and in New Jersey hanged. Having substantial objections to both, I shall not, for the present, hazard either, but shall seek another country."[1]

The most recent historical verdict on Burr's subsequent adventures in the West is that no one will ever know what he was really up to. The jury in Burr's 1807 trial in Richmond, Virginia, for another capital offence—treason—acquitted him, despite Jefferson's best efforts to see him hang. Burr lay low for several months after his treason trial, dodging both creditors and a lesser criminal charge in Ohio, before setting sail for Britain under an assumed name in June 1808. It would be four years before he returned to American soil.

Debate continues to the present day between Burr partisans and detractors concerning his conduct in the 1801 election deadlock, the 1804 duel, and the 1805–1807 Western venture. Was he angling to be president? Who fired first in the duel? Did Burr intend to dismember the Union? Was he, as charged in the 1804 New York election, a ravisher of women? The challenge to answering such questions isn't that Burr was duplicitous but that he was secretive. Gordon Wood notes, "Burr's correspondence is full of Burn this letter. You never find Thomas Jefferson saying, Burn this letter."[2] Roger G. Kennedy, director emeritus of the National Museum of American History, devoted a book to proving that Burr's character was superior to the characters of Jefferson and Hamilton. Kennedy argues that, while Jefferson was obsessed with leaving a huge collection of self-serving writings to shore up his character for posterity, "the wonder is how little Burr had to say for himself.... If he wished posterity to think well of him, it would have been better had he thought well enough of it to engage it in a conversation."[3]

Yet Burr did engage posterity in a conversation—through a thousand-page journal of his four years in Europe. In a way, the journal was one long letter to Burr's beloved daughter, Theodosia, in contemplation of a reunion that never happened. Nevertheless, Burr decided to leave his journal—which includes many accounts of his sexual escapades—behind for posterity even though, having survived his daughter, he could easily have destroyed it. Shedding a bright light on an obscure period in Burr's life, the journal also gives us insight into his character, especially as we see him struggling in Paris toward rehabilitation and return. As Milton Lomask, the author of a two-volume study, *Aaron Burr*, has stated, the journal is "as graphic a self-portrait as we have of Aaron Burr ... a literary tour de force ... deeply moving at times, especially in the Paris scenes."[4]

Burr met the English political philosopher Jeremy Bentham soon after arriving in London, and sent Theodosia a copy of Bentham's famous treatise on morals and legislation, which Bentham had written in French. Bentham proposed to Burr that Theodosia should translate the treatise into English, whereupon she wrote to Burr that knowing Bentham "seriously sanctions [my translation makes me] feel at once confused, confounded, flattered, and pleased…. I shall commence immediately."[5] Theodosia made a start on the Bentham translation, but her health problems prevented her from making much headway on it.

Midnight in Paris

What a difference a decade can make!

At least so Aaron Burr must have thought in Paris on January 4, 1811. That evening, near midnight, heavy snow was falling, and the wind was tempestuous:

> At intervals of one to two minutes, it blows directly down my chimney, and with such force as to carry ashes and coals over the whole floor…. After various experiments how to weather the gale, I at length discovered that I could exist by lying flat on the floor; for this purpose I laid a blanket; and reposing on my elbows, with a candle at my side, on the floor have been reading L'Espion Anglais [The English Spy]; and thus prostrate, I have the honor to write you this. When I got up just now for pen and ink, I found myself almost buried in ashes and cinders. You would have thought that I had laid a month at the foot of Mount Vesuvius.

Just ten years earlier, Burr had been at the height of his political career, the subject of thirty-six ballots in the House of Representatives to determine whether he or Jefferson would be the third U.S. president. And yet on this January 1811 night our third vice-president found himself strangely positioned on his stomach, amidst the ashes, leading a precarious existence in a self-imposed exile.

People write journals to be or not to be read. A spouse might keep a record of unuttered grievances, plant it a certain way to discover if it is read, and fume if no page is turned. Once, a countrywoman in Maine who had strong political opinions and little paper wrote her diary horizontally, and when she finished each page she turned it and wrote vertically. It represented her musings but the diary was not intended for readers and was unreadable. What Burr recorded was a hybrid—a personal log or exercise to clear his mind and notations to evoke his trip later in conversation with his daughter. The journal would recall inner thoughts, struggles, and observations of life around him that would make his reminiscences with her more vivid. He was circumspect at times because someone could break into his lodging and read what he wrote—he was, after all, the former vice-president of the United States and a famous man. Yet he also must have derived satisfaction from putting thoughts down in an unguarded fashion. He was confident and exuberant and, above all, this record would provide him with a text for storytelling.

By its candor and absence of literary pretension, the journal reveals equally Burr's pragmatism and the habits of a Founding Father transplanted abroad. It is all the more significant because of what the catalog for the "Aaron Burr Returns to New York" exhibition at the Grolier Club in 2012 pointed to as the "autobiographical lack" vis-à-vis Burr: "Burr's popular image devolved largely from the negative accounts of his political opponents and enemies, augmented by sensationalized versions of his infamous duel with Alexander Hamilton. Unlike many of his contemporaries, Burr made little effort to author a written account of his life. This autobiographical lack has left Aaron Burr as one of the most maligned figures of the founding era."

But due to the European journal Burr kept, no time in his eventful life is better documented than when he lived in Paris. His journal gives us the feeling of meeting a real person across the centuries, a sense we are reading about ourselves or someone we know who happened to have lived in an earlier time and a different place. Using the journal as its foundation, this book is the first published work to tell in detail how Burr spent his year in Paris: whom he met, where he went, and how he survived with often not even a penny in his pocket.

One anecdote shows how quickly he blended in with this scene. Shortly after arriving in Paris in February of 1810, Burr went to see his first play at the Théatre Français and made the acquaintance of a lady in the adjoining box. He quotes what may have been his standard pickup line: "Vous paraisses plein de génie; la quelle de tous vos talents vous fier le plus?" To which she replied, "Je n'ai cultivé que celle de plaire." (While Burr's spoken French was good, his written French was by his own admission poor; William Bixby, the 1903 owner, editor, and publisher of the journal, translated this exchange as follows: "You appear to be full of genius; upon which of all your talents do you rely most?" "I have cultivated only that of pleasing.")

Theodosia Burr Alston (1802). The "Nag's Head Portrait," attributed to John Vanderlyn, was found in Nag's Head, North Carolina, in 1869, fifty-six years after Theodosia was lost at sea (courtesy Lewis Walpole Library, Yale University).

The lady invited Burr to call on her the next day. He did but in a "fit of discretion" left her apartment before her return. Like the Country Mouse declining a metropolitan banquet, he congratulated himself in his journal entry "on my escape from a dangerous siren." As one of Burr's earliest biographers wrote in 1858, Burr's interest in women's talents was genuine, not simply feigned for pickup purposes: "He flattered [women] with an adroitness seldom equaled, contriving always to praise those qualities upon the fancied possession of which they most valued themselves. But this habit was, by no means, altogether insincere with Colonel Burr. He really liked women, and all of their lovely ways, and had a great opinion of their taste and capacity."[6]

In terms of Burr's own qualities, two words recur in the Burr literature: "enigmatic" and its near anagram, "magnetic." Men from whom he sought material support as well as the many women in his life were in their different ways receptive to his magnetic appeal. Enigmatic describes him as well, and not only because he often wrote in cipher. As Burr's 1858 biographer stated, "To his contemporaries, no less than to recent writers of political history, the suddenness of his elevation was an enigma. John Adams thought it was owing to the prestige of his father's and grandfather's name. Hamilton attributed it to Burr's unequalled wire-pulling. Some thought it was his military reputation. Others called it luck. His own circle of friends regarded his elevation as the legitimate result of a superiority to most of his rivals in knowledge, culture, and talents."[7]

One. Journal Keeping 9

Sketchbook of Figure Studies (1810–1820) by Thomas Sully. Sully chose a moment of theatricality and mystery: the unidentified pensive young woman in white musing on a beloved person in a faraway place. Drawings in ink, wash and graphite on light brown laid paper with fibers of mixed composition, 8-13/16 in. × 11-½ in. (22.4 cm × 29.2 cm) (Rogers Fund, 1953; image copyright © Metropolitan Museum of Art; image source: Art Resource, New York).

As his European journal reveals, Burr's talents included—in addition to charm and boundless mental, physical and sexual energy—an incisive mind on which his early successful career as a lawyer was based. A New York attorney who practiced law alongside Burr and Alexander Hamilton judged that "as a lawyer, Burr was not inferior to Hamilton.... I used to say of them, when they were rivals at the bar, that Burr would say as much in half an hour as Hamilton in two hours. Burr was terse and convincing, while Hamilton was flowing and rapturous. They were much the greatest men in this State, and perhaps the greatest men in the United States."

Burr in Europe was not practicing law, but he was occasionally called on for legal advice. An excerpt from his journal illustrates his ability to sum up the principal points of a case, a passage which also serves to situate us in that very different time and place. He received a letter requesting "advice about some matters depending on the law of the United States." The author of the letter, Robert Morris, took a full two hours to tell the following "extraordinary story" that Burr chose to encapsulate as follows:

> Miss E.A.C., at 18, married on the Continent an Irishman named M., then about 50, who happened to have then, and now living, another wife in England. E.A. was very beautiful, and the parties became very attached to each other. M. became suspected by the French government, and was taken up and put in prison. She favored his escape, and he got off; on which she was put up in prison, and kept a whole year on black bread and water, and, in prison, and among felons, was brought to bed. Soon after this, and about six months ago, she was released.... M. had gone to sea and was drowned; but he had taken good care of his E.A.; by the most extraordinary villainies, he bought and loaded a ship to the value of 90,000 guineas, which he sent off to Philadelphia, and had there vested in her name. He got the ship there insured for her full value, not in his own name, and procured such full testimony of her total loss that the underwriters paid the amount of the policy without suit, and soon afterward it was discovered that she arrived safe in Philadelphia. But then the ship and cargo appeared never to have belonged to M., but a person of a different name, by whom the assignment was made to E.A., and all without her knowledge. She is now just 21. Am to meet her tomorrow, and then shall know more. From R.M.'s story, her sufferings and her fortitude are the most surprising. He was two hours in relating it.... Now, what they want of me is to show how E.A. may get and keep the 90,000 guineas, about $400,000, which are deposited in Philadelphia. R.M. paid me nothing, and I suppose E.A. is not in a condition to pay, for she and her mother support themselves by making straw hats.

The Robert Morris who told this odd story to Burr was the son of Robert Morris, Senior, the financier of the American Revolution who ended up in debtors' prison for three years and who died near penniless. The Morrises and Burr were involved in the founding of the Holland Land Company, on the speculation in the shares of which, as we shall see, Burr hoped to make a fortune in Paris by trading on information known only to him. The elder Robert Morris left a will closed by words which Aaron Burr might well have adapted to his similar situation at the end of his own life: "I have to express my regret at having lost a very large fortune acquired by honest industry, which I had long hoped and expected to enjoy with my family during my own life and then to distribute amongst those of them that should outlive me. Fate has determined otherwise and we must submit to its decree, which I have done with patience and fortitude."

Unlike Morris, Burr avoided debtors' prison—narrowly. Like Morris, Burr was endowed with a strong reserve of patience and fortitude. Biographer Milton Lomask called Burr's Paris journal a "story of the human spirit transcending tribulation," and it is here we look to become better acquainted with the inner person.

Two

Persona Non Grata

Aaron Burr arrived in Paris in February 1810, ten days after his 54th birthday, and he was unable to leave Paris and the French empire until July 1811. He had desired to return to America a full year earlier, as recorded in his journal entry for July 27, 1810: "Now, Madame, shall tell you a secret. Despairing of any success in my project ["X," Burr's Mexico liberation plan, described in a subsequent chapter], a few days ago asked for a passport to go to the United States, which was refused. Asked one to go to Rouen, to see Madame Langworthy, which was granted. Was told that I could not go out of the empire. Me voilà prisonnier d'état et presque sans sous! [Here I am a prisoner of state and almost penniless!]"

Over the next twelve months, Burr chronicled his failed attempts to secure the passport needed to leave Napoleon's continental empire, run as a police state under the tight control of the emperor. In fact, Burr would never have been allowed to enter France in the first place had he not succeeded in being on cordial terms with Napoleon's minister plenipotentiary in Hamburg, who granted Burr a passport to travel to Paris. That minister, Antoine Favelet de Bourienne, wrote in his 1829 *Memoirs of Napoleon Bonaparte* of his decision to defy orders from Paris to "persecute" Burr:

> At the height of his glory and power, Bonaparte was so suspicious that the veriest trifles sufficed to alarm him. Colonel Burr, formerly vice-president of the United States, was pointed out to me as a dangerous man, and I received orders to watch him very closely, and arrest him on the slightest grounds of suspicion. Colonel Burr was one of those in favor of whom I ventured to disobey the orders I received from the restless police of Paris. [The Paris police commissioner] directed me to adopt towards him those violent measures which are equivalent to persecution. In answer to these instructions, I stated that Colonel Burr conducted himself with much prudence and propriety; that he kept but little company, and was scarcely spoken of. Far from regarding him as a man who required watching, having learned that he wished to go to Paris, I caused a passport to be procured for him; and I never heard that this dangerous citizen had compromised the safety of the state in any way.[1]

Burr, in viewing himself as "a prisoner of state," was probably mistaken if he believed that Napoleon himself was responsible for withholding the French passport required to leave the empire. In fact, Burr may not have been on Napoleon's radar at all, despite Burr's meeting in Paris with Napoleon's brother, the emperor of Westphalia, Jerome Bonaparte, whom Burr had entertained at his estate in New York City several years earlier. Napoleon held his brother Jerome in extreme contempt, although Burr would not have known that. In a series of letters, not published until 1887, Napoleon excoriated Jerome again and again in the harshest of terms: "All your actions bear the stamp of folly," "Your kingdom has no police, no finances, and no organization," "You have no knowledge whatever," "Cease making yourself ridiculous," "I very much fear it is hopeless to expect anything of you." Thus, predictably, King Jerome proved unable to secure Burr an audience with his brother Napoleon.[2]

Napoleon III published many of his uncle Napoleon's letters during the 1852–1870 Third Empire, but he withheld from publication all of the letters critical of Jerome and other members of the Bonaparte family. Léon Lecestre, curator of the French National Archives, later discovered these letters which he published in 1887. An English translation was published in 1897, *New Letters of Napoleon I, Omitted from the Edition Published Under the Auspices of Napoleon III*.

Since in Paris, as in Hamburg, Burr conducted himself with "prudence and propriety," he was not one to register on Napoleon's constant lookout for malcontents. Napoleon instructed his police commissioner that "all elements of discord must be removed from Paris," a leading bête noire of his being Madame de Staël, the heiress and liberal author and political intriguer. Madame de Staël became the target of many of Napoleon's directives: "Do not allow that bitch, Madame de Staël, to come near Paris. I know she is not very far off.... The arrival of this woman, like that of a bird of ill omen, has always been the signal for some trouble.... You are to see my orders being carried out, and not to allow Madame de Staël to come within 40 leagues of Paris. That wicked schemer ought to make up her mind to behave herself, at last.... Madame de Staël has allowed herself to be drawn into the clique of London intriguers. You will let it be known that up until now she has been looked on as a madwoman, but that, from this day forward, she enters into a circle detrimental to the public peace."[3]

In the same year that Burr was getting nowhere with his quest for a passport to leave, Madame de Staël readily acquired passports for herself and her eldest son to leave France for the United States, where she had vast landholdings in upstate New York. Although she never made use of the passports, "the imperial government would have been delighted to get rid of her." Burr, too, might have achieved a speedier exit from the empire had he been viewed by Napoleon as a troublemaker. On the other hand, the emperor's autocratic whims were not always predictable, as an American consul found out: "Give orders to have Mr. Kuhn, the American Consul at Genoa, placed under arrest, for wearing a Cross of Malta given him by the English, and as being an English agent. His papers will be seized, and an abstract of them made, and he will be kept in secret confinement until you [the Duc de Rovigo] have made your report to me. This man, having received a foreign decoration, ceases to be an American. I am sorry, by the way, you should have communicated with the Ambassador of the United States. My police knows no Ambassadors. I am master in my own house. If I suspect a man, I have him arrested."

The French bureaucracy was immobilized, but why? All in all, Burr's prolonged lack of success in obtaining a passport had to have been due to the fear of officials that a former U.S. vice president with a reputation for intrigue must be an individual of special concern to Napoleon and therefore not to be accommodated. Burr's journal contains dozens of entries concerning his frustrating quest for permission to return to America, drafting many letters, plodding from office to office: "Wrote this morning to the Duc de Bassano, again demanding passport. To Roux to press the same demand on the Duc de Cadore. Roux is always civil." He "received no answer" from the Duc ("this is the diplomatic style of negation");

but Roux "promised to state my further reasons and demand." Burr got nowhere for months on end. A week after this flurry of activity, however, Burr felt he actually was making headway. After attending a public audience with 46 other petitioners, mostly women, before the new minister of police, the Duc de Rovigo, he wrote:

> We all went in. The Duc, in full dress, was at the farther end of the room, and we stood, forming a sort of horseshoe, of which the two ends approached him. He began on his right, and so on, hearing and answering, in about one minute. Some of the women kept him three or four minutes, and some talking on after he had given his answer, till he turned his back and addressed the next. His first question was, "Who are you?" Of one very ill-looking fellow he asked, "Are you Colonel Burr?" By which I learned that he had that person in mind. I shifted my place so as to be the last; but some three or four others, with the like design, got after me. At length my turn came. I announced myself, and told him I had been refused a passport, at which I was the more surprised, as he probably knew the nature of the business which had brought me to France [i.e., "X"].

After exchanging chitchat with Burr, Rovigo expressed interest in reading the memorandum on the X project and said they could talk about the passport issue after he had reviewed the memorandum. Several days later, Burr's friend the Duc d'Alberg introduced Burr to Rovigo again during an evening gathering at the latter's home. Then another week went by, and having heard nothing at all from Rovigo, Burr decided to corner Rovigo in his office:

> Was seated with my back to the door of entrance. But the story is too long to write. I will tell it you [when Burr would see Theodosia again, which he never did]. The conclusion is, that after waiting three hours, I got sight of his Excellency by force, and demanded my passport. "I spoke to His Majesty the day before yesterday and he agreed, but I have to speak about it to the Minister of Foreign Relations and then I will inform you," and he turned his back and made his escape. The assurance that His Majesty has consented is something, though I am very sorry to say, not much. Words cost nothing here, and there is often an immensity of time and space between the promise of a courtier and the performance.

A week later, Burr saw Rovigo again and noted, "Had a few words with him. He said that His Majesty had not yet given his signature but that he would procure it in the course of the next week. Perhaps so." Two more weeks went by, and the Duc d'Alberg related to Burr the latest news from Rovigo: "The Minister of Police said that he had made a report to the Emperor of my demand for a passport and had received no answer. Did not know when one might be given; so that I am just where I was four months ago, only with less money, and the fine season gone." All this transpired in September 1810, more than ten months before Burr's passport was finally issued, so Burr proved quite prescient concerning the glacial pace of the French authorities.

In October 1810, the Duc d'Alberg ferreted out for Burr the fact that the only remaining obstacle to issuance of his passport was the lack of a certificate of his American citizenship signed by the American consular authorities. Burr then discovered that he must request this certificate from none other than his old adversary Alexander McRae. McRae, a Virginia lawyer, had been one of the team prosecuting Burr—unsuccessfully—for treason in Richmond, Virginia, in 1807. Speaking at the trial about Burr's Western schemes, McRae declared that he "was not one to pull punches…. Burr, he believed, was one of a highly dangerous breed, who moved mainly by stealth…. The most dangerous traitor of all," he continued, "was the subtle and cautious traitor, a man such as Burr."[4]

Whether Burr had any treasonable intent to separate the western states from the

Union is debated to this day. At any rate, despite there being no love lost between the two men, Burr now needed to apply to McRae, the American consul in Paris, for the certificate of citizenship, which he did in writing on October 29, 1810: "Mr. Burr presents compliments. Having addressed himself to Mr. Russell [the American chargé d'affaires] for a certificate of citizenship, has been informed by him that the business of granting certificates was transferred to the consul. He therefore repeats the request to Mr. McRae. If a personal request be deemed necessary, Mr. Burr will wait on Mr. McRae for that purpose at any hour he may be pleased to appoint." In his journal, Burr noted to Theo: "Wrote Mr. McRae, asking certificate of citizenship. Requested the messenger verbally that he would send an answer. I expect some vulgar impertinence, coupled with a refusal. Have I told you that the Duc d'Alberg says if I can get a certificate from the American consul, I shall have no further difficulty about a passport? Hence my application to Russell and to McRae. If the latter answers insolently, the only revenge I will take, for revenge, you know, is not in my nature, will be to publish his letter." Burr was correct in his prediction of a refusal, and McRae's letter was published, many years later, in Burr's memoirs: "Mr. McRae answers Mr. Burr's note of this morning, that his knowledge of the circumstances under which Mr. Burr left the United States renders it his duty to decline giving Mr. Burr either a passport or a permis de séjour [residence permit]." McRae went on to note that Burr had the right to appeal McRae's decision to his superior, the chargé d'affaires Jonathan Russell, a Rhode Islander also well known to Burr.

With the same note of false politeness as in his letter to McRae, Burr next addressed himself to Russell:

> It cannot be material to inquire what are the "circumstances" referred to by the consul, nor whether true or false. Mr. Burr is ignorant of any statute or instruction which authorizes a foreign minister or agent to inquire into any circumstances other than those which tend to establish the fact of citizen or not. If, however, Mr. Russell should be of a different opinion, Mr. Burr is ready to satisfy him that no circumstances exist which, by any construction, in the slightest degree impair his rights as a citizen, and that the conclusions of the consul are founded in error, either in point of fact or of inference. Yet, conceiving that every citizen has a right to demand a certificate or passport, Mr. Burr is constrained to renew his application to Mr. Russell, to whom the consul has been pleased to refer the decision.

In response to this application, Russell merely closed out the correspondence, answering, on November 4, 1810, "Mr. Russell has no objection to judging the case which Mr. Burr has presented to him. The man who evades the offended laws of his country, abandons, for the time, the right to their protection. This fugitive from justice, during his voluntary exile, has a claim to no other passport than one which shall enable him to surrender himself for trial for the offenses with which he stands charged. Such a passport Mr. Russell will furnish to Burr, but no other." And there matters stood for Burr, through the harsh Paris winter, and spring and early summer of 1811, until—through an expedient bordering on blackmail described in a later chapter—the Duc de Bassano succeeded at last in wresting the required document from Jonathan Russell.

Burr's career as an American politician came to an abrupt end on the morning of July 11, 1804, when, as vice-president of the United States, he mortally wounded his longtime political adversary Alexander Hamilton in a duel on the bank of the Hudson River. After the duel, Burr presciently wrote to his son-in-law: "The event of which you have been advised has driven me into a sort of exile, and may terminate in an actual and permanent ostracism." Under indictment in New York for killing Hamilton, Burr could not return to his New York City law practice, so he decided to embark on a Western adventure, which led to his 1807 trial for treason and will be discussed in Chapter Five. Notwithstanding Burr's subsequent acquittal, Jonathan Russell's description of Burr in 1810 as a "fugitive from justice" in "voluntary exile" in Paris was entirely correct, in that Burr had left America for Europe to escape not only from his creditors but also from an Ohio misdemeanor indictment (which, like his New York murder charge, was never prosecuted). Burr was correct in predicting the "permanent ostracism," which followed him to Europe and, indeed, lingered for many years, up to the day of his death in September 1836 at the age of eighty.[5] Here is Burr, in July 1809 in Hamburg on his way to Paris, noting that his dubious reputation had preceded him to Europe: "I find that, among the great number of Americans here and there, all are hostile to Aaron Burr—all. What a lot of rascals they must be to make war on one whom they do not know; on one who never did harm or wished to do harm to a human being. Yet they, perhaps, ought not to be blamed, for they are influenced by what they hear. I further learn that Aaron Burr is announced in the Paris papers in a manner no way auspicious."

Without a doubt Burr was deluded to claim he never harmed a human being, given his killing of Alexander Hamilton just five years earlier. On the other hand, the 1903 owner, editor, and publisher of Burr's European journal, William Bixby, had this to say about the Burr-Hamilton duel: "The duel was conducted with the utmost propriety, the participants took equal chances of life or death, and, according to the ethics of that age, though not of this, neither was in the slightest degree censurable."[6] So perhaps, in Burr's thinking, Hamilton's killing didn't count; either that, or perhaps Burr was referring in the above passage only to his claim of innocent conduct in the Western adventures which led to his treason trial.

Pertaining to the duel, dueling was not unknown in America and Europe at the time. Two months after Burr wrote the above entry in his journal, a political duel, similar to the Burr-Hamilton duel except in the result, was fought in England:

> It was barely light on Putney heath when on September 21, 1809, the two senior Cabinet ministers cocked their pistols and took aim. The duelists, Lord Castlereagh and George Canning, were two of the best-known politicians in Britain, rising stars of the Tory party and key figures in running the war against Napoleon. [W]hen Castlereagh discovered that his rival was plotting to have him kicked out of the Government, he issued a fateful challenge. "I will cheerfully give to your lordship the satisfaction which you require," Canning wrote in reply. Then he made his will, wrote a last letter to his wife and prepared for the fatal confrontation. Both combatants seem to have been extraordinarily cool: on his way to the appointed spot, Castlereagh even hummed snatches from popular arias of the day. Both missed with their first shots, but Castlereagh insisted on a second round, and this time he hit his opponent in the thigh, while Canning shot a button off Castlereagh's coat lapel. No lasting harm was done.[7]

And in 1806, less than two years after the Burr-Hamilton duel, future president Andrew Jackson shot and killed attorney and horse breeder Charles Dickinson over disputes that started with racetrack betting. Jackson, who shot second, was wounded and carried a bullet in his chest for life.

Whether as a result of his own duel, or because suspicions lingered that he was a traitor to his country, Burr found on his arrival in Paris in 1810 no escape from ostracism by many, but not all, of his fellow Americans: "On my way home, met _____, who invited me to go home with him to communicate something. It is that the Americans here have entered into a combination against Aaron Burr; that every man who speaks to him shall be shunned as unworthy of society; that no master of any vessel, or any other person, shall take any letter or parcel from him, and other like benevolent things. All of which amused me but alarmed my friend.... A Mr. Thompson, of Charleston, S.C., a Scotchman, but naturalized in the United States, now settled here, being asked if he had called on Colonel Burr, said, No, and no good American would call on him." Moreover, from newspapers arriving in Paris, Burr would learn that America had not yet forgotten about him. One day he recorded wryly, "More American papers, from which I learn that I have a pension of 2,000 sterling from his Majesty the Emperor. An extract from an English paper, also, that I am on a project for dismembering the United States." In a similar vein, Burr noted a few days later, "I am about to undertake the translation from English into French of two octavo volumes for 100 louis. It will take me three months hard work. Better than to starve. But the most curious part of the story is that the book in question contains a quantity of abuse and libels on Aaron Burr."

Despite Burr's making light of such "abuse and libels," as he viewed them, when it came time to return to America he was seriously concerned about the reception he would encounter. Sailing from Amsterdam in September 1811 on the vessel he wrongly believed would carry him to the United States, he wrote in his journal, "I have been on board the Vigilant, the ship which is to bear me to thee.... I feel as if I were already on my way to you, and my heart beats with joy. Yet, alas! that country which I am so anxious to revisit will perhaps reject me with horror." Burr expressed similar fears, but also some bravado when, in March 1812, after many false starts, he was finally onboard ship on his way back to America from England:

> And now, at midnight, I repose, smoking my pipe and contemplating the certainty of escaping from this country, the certainty of seeing you! Those are my only pleasing anticipations. For as to my reception in my own country, so far as depends on the government, if I may judge from the conduct of their agents in every part of Europe, I ought to expect all the efforts of the most implacable malice. This, however, does not permit me to despond, not even to doubt. If there be nothing better to be done, I shall set about making money in every lawful and honorable way.... My great and only real anxiety is for your health. If your constitution should be ruined, and you become the victim of disease, I shall have no attachment to life or motive to exertion.

However, that lies ahead of a most compelling part of Aaron Burr's life, namely, how he spent his many months in Paris before being free to go home. During this residency, Burr discovered that in his time (as in ours) few places in which to live are as magical as the City of Light.

Three

New Year's Eve, Paris, 1810

Burr's journal entry for December 31, 1810, describes the last hours of that decade. Future chapters will delve into aspects of his sojourn. For now, here is how he spent his one New Year's Eve in Paris:

> At 5, to Madame Fenwick's, who received me as one cavalier receives another; greatly flattered by this confidence. At 8 we walked together, where Madame had an engagement, and then parted.
>
> I then deliberated whether I should do some, and what, folly for New Year's eve! A certain poet says, "He who deliberates is lost." It did not turn out so this time, for I resolved to go quietly on home, first taking a tour through the Palais Royal to observe how the evening was celebrated. I see nothing done, except that there are rather more people than usual before 9, and more bons-bons and jujus [toys] selling and exhibited.
>
> The last time I shall ever write 1810, but alas! not the last time I shall write Paris. Have great comfort in my little fireplace. Have been drinking cider and smoking cegars, reading a history of the Languedoc Canal. Yesterday was cold, and today colder. Quite winter; the gutters are all froze hard.
>
> Put on my flannel waistcoat this morning, as I wear no overcoat, for a great many philosophic reasons; principally because I have not got one. The old greatcoat which I have brought from America still serves in traveling, if should ever again travel. Happy New Year! Mother and Gampy! Ah! I catched you both! The clock is now striking twelve.

Burr not only addressed his journal to his daughter, but also traveled through Europe with her portrait: "Yesterday opened your picture. It is in perfect order. Since opening it in Stockholm, I have carried it the whole way (two hundred miles) on my lap. Indeed, Madame, you bothered me not a little. You are now hung up in my room, so that I can talk with you.… Done, even the picture; all, all packed, ready for starting at sunrise. I bid you bon soir a dozen times before I shut you up in that dark case. I can never do it without regret. It seems as if I were burying you alive."

Whether on canvas, paper or enamel, a painting being used as a stand-in for the person was usual for the time. The portrait was an aid in the preliminary stage of a royal courtship all the way back to medieval Persian and Indian fairy tales.

Henry VIII asked the court artist Hans Holbein to paint Anne of Cleves, to help him decide whether she would be suitable as his wife, and her sister as accurately as possible when Henry VIII was shopping for a fourth wife. The portrait satisfied the king who proposed marriage. However, on seeing Anne soon after she arrived in the south of England, Henry went to see her and judged that her pleasant appearance did not live up to the portrait. Henry typically overreacted, could not consummate the marriage and soon annulled it.

Other examples come from fairy tales, such as the stories of the Countess d'Aulnoy, originally published in 1697, where the trope of a noble swooning at a portrait appeared repeatedly, e.g., in the stories of Princess Mayblossom, Princess Rosette and The White Doe (*La Biche au Bois*). Andrew Lang translated this last and included in his *Orange Fairy Book*, and the analogy to Burr's feelings for the picture of an absent Theodosia is striking. In The White Doe, a princess named Desirée instead of "coming out" has been enchanted through teenage by a witch and thus sequestered. Desirée's portrait was made and carried to the greatest courts of the world. Gazing on the princess's traveling picture, princes everywhere admired her, but one prince was so affected that he refused to be separated from the portrait. "He put it in his closet, shut himself up with it, and as if it were alive, spoke to it with infinite passion."[1] From Burr's time, artists with the knack cut silhouettes from black paper, which could be kept as romantic souvenirs.

In the months of the Paris winter before and after New Year's Day 1811, Burr encountered frigid temperatures. In early January: "I suffered at Madame R. Her parlor was at 35 [degrees Fahrenheit], though a great fire, but in a chimney on French principles—the principles of stupidity." In December, as the weather turned colder, Burr made a first, failed attempt to overcome these French "principles of stupidity" in chimney design:

> My room is about ten feet square, in which is a bed and a very large table. The fireplace smokes perpetually. Having endured this now more than two months, and finding my eyes worse for it, sent today for one of those scientific men here called fumistes [chimney doctors]. Showed him the evil and proposed a remedy. "But upon what principles, Sir, are your ideas based?" In vain did I offer to pay for his work, and to take on myself the hazard of the result. "No, that is to turn aside from all principles"; and so we parted. Nineteen out of twenty chimneys of Paris (of France, I might say) smoke always, and the other twentieth occasionally. In vain have Franklin and Rumford shown, by fact and experiment, how chimneys should be built. [French] obstinacy and stupidity passes belief. And so I sit enveloped in smoke, or, as you have it, sit like the gods in their clouds.

Count Rumford, mentioned in this passage, was an engineer and illustrious contemporary of Burr's. Born Benjamin Thompson in Woburn, Massachusetts, and serving as lieutenant colonel in the Loyalist forces in the American Revolution, Rumford was a polymath inventor, knighted by George III, and made a Count of the Holy Roman Empire in 1791 by the reigning monarch of Bavaria. During eleven years in Munich (where he founded the beautiful Englischer Garten), Rumford developed the smoke-free fireplace—tall and shallow with a streamlined throat, that became state of the art. He published his designs in London in 1795 in a pamphlet called *Chimney Fireplaces with Proposals for Improving Them to Save Fuel, to Render Dwelling Houses More Comfortable and Salubrious, and Effectually to Prevent Chimneys from Smoking*. Rumford then superintended the correction of hundreds of fireplaces in England in the late 1790s. By November 1810 Rumford was in the village of Auteuil, now Paris XVI, doing scientific research into coffee makers, lamps and other inventions, but according to Burr, Rumford's principles had not crossed the English Channel. Another instance of a Frenchman clinging to his principles in the face of fact occurred twenty years later, when a French engineer "was sent by his king in 1830 to observe the trials of George Stephenson's 'Rocket' on the newly opened Manchester-Liverpool railway line. The Frenchman sat by the tracks taking copious notes as the sturdy little engine faultlessly pulled the world's first railway train back and forth between the two cities. After conscientiously calculating what he had just observed, he reported his findings back to Paris: 'The thing is impossible,' he wrote. 'It cannot work.'"

Burr succeeded when he attempted a second time to improve his own chimney on Rumford's principles: "At 9 came in a young mason, also a fumiste, whom my carpenter recommended to me to cure my chimney. He consented to work under my direction. I directed the laying of every brick, and at every one he paused to remonstrate against the absurdity. Still he obeyed, always remonstrating, 'That won't do, Sir, I won't vouch for it.' 'Sir, that's my business.' The work being done at 12, fire was immediately lighted, and we all watched the effect with great solicitude. It answered perfectly. The fumiste gazed with astonishment and admiration and seemed to conceive a most profound respect for me."

By January, Burr was able to keep warm enough in his lodgings: "Very cold. The little thermometer, which is outdoors, down to 27; the other, which is at my bedside, at 48 … but this evening have got it up to 52, a very sufferable temperature." Having succeeded at home, a week later Burr obliged a lady friend in Paris whose chimneys smoked:

> Rose at 7. At ½ p. 8 to Madame Fenwick's in the character of a fumiste. Every chimney in the house smokes sometimes, and most of them always. I was railing against the stupidity of the Parisians, and quoted this among other instances. She challenged me to cure the evil. Accepted; and she assigned for trial of my American skill the worst in the house. It has

The Poor Poet (1839) by Carl Spitzweg (1808–1885). Burr wrote of the convenience of being able to reach everything from his bed. Oil on canvas, 36.3 cm × 44.7 cm (bpk, Berlin/Nationalgalerie, Staatliche Museen/Joerg P. Anders/Art Resource, New York).

already been in the hands of several scientific fumistes. Some applied their remedies to the top, and others to the bottom, but equally without effect. This morning was assigned for my experiment, and she gave me carte blanche. At ½ p. 8 I found the mason, the brick and the mortar. We went to work. She, in the meantime, made me breakfast (cafe blanc and honey) in the adjoining room. She amused herself at my folly. Several visitors called and all came in to see what was going forward. "Ah! c'est trop etroit. Ca n'a pas assez de profondeur. La gorge est trop petite. [It is too narrow. There is not enough depth. The flue is too small.]" I made no sort of reply. At length, the work was finished at 4. We made a large fire. The chimney drew to perfection. The doors and windows might be open or shut; nothing disturbed the draught. What added greatly to the merit of the result is, that the day was the most unfavorable, a vehement wind from the quarter that had always filled the house with smoke. "Monsieur, si vous énoncierez comme fumiste, vous feriez fortune. [If you set up as a heating engineer you'd make a fortune.]"

Alcohol has been known to take the edge off poverty and cold. During this harsh Paris winter, Burr refers often to a favorite French wine. In the summer he had bought a supply of "a little white Burgundy which pleases me much; 15 sous the bottle." But by late October, he switched his allegiance to a red wine he first encountered while visiting his friend Colonel Swan, who was housed in a French debtors' prison: "Dined with him and drank vin de Roussillon for the first time ... and on my way home bought half a dozen bottles at 36 sous per bottle; a great extravagance. But recollect, Madame, that it is several weeks since I have bought a single bottle of wine, so that you won't grudge me this luxury."

Ten days later, Burr restocked the Roussillon, also buying some cheaper wine. "Thence to Place St. André, to my vin de Roussillon merchant.[2] Took three bottles of the same, 36 sous, and six of an inferior quality at 25 sous per bottle." Two days later he wrote, "My 25 sous wine is detestable, and has no sort of resemblance to the true Roussillon at 36 sous. Indeed, my dear little Theo, you must not scold so damned hard if I take pretty nearly a bottle a day of the true Roussillon. By way of compensation, will drink neither tea nor coffee in the evening, never dine at restaurants, and eke out a pound of brown sugar a fortnight; and when I have no more money, I will drink water." Next, Burr resolved to exchange the 25-sous wine for Roussillon:

> I may as well tell you now of my economy in this wine affair. Eating my bread and cheese, and seeing a half a bottle of the 25 sous wine left, I thought it would be too extravagant to open a bottle of the bon; so I tried my best to get down the mauvaise, constantly thinking of the other, which was in sight, and trying to persuade myself to give Gamp [Burr] some of that; but no, I stuck to the bad, and got it all down. Then to pay myself for this act of heroism, treated him to a large tumbler of the true Roussillon, and sallied forth to my wine merchant to engage him to exchange the residue. You see I am of the opinion that though a man may be a little poorer for drinking good wine, yet he is, under its influence, much more able to bear poverty.

His finances deteriorated, but Burr continued to indulge his taste for Roussillon. On December 9, 1810, he "made a hearty supper on bread, butter, cheese, and baked apples, with a pint of Roussillon." The next day, with "rain, snow, and hard wind," Burr writes he "treated myself to a bottle of cider and a pint of Roussillon, and have smoked half a dozen segars." The wine that Burr preferred may have been the rancio variety of Roussillon, aged to produce notes of candied fruit. "With rancio wine and warm bread," according to a local proverb, "winter is a pleasant time." And, as Burr discovered, for cigar aficionados, rancio wines have a flavor which "recalls the spiciness of tobacco, and they are the ideal accompaniment for cigars, often complementing them better than brandies."

Burr occasionally had the funds to dine at a Paris restaurant, and he often dined at the homes of Paris friends, but as winter came on, he concluded, "I dine better at home than elsewhere." In November 1810, for example, he "took a bouillon gras [a rich, meaty broth] for dinner and eked it out with a roast fowl, a compliment from Julie [a servant about whom more will be told] and excellent potatoes, which with Roussillon and bread, butter, cheese, and grapes has kept me from starving." A few weeks later, he boasted of another feast in his lodgings: "Dinner, potatoes and a bit of that immortal ham (the residue will be given to the cat tomorrow), a good portion of Roussillon, bread, butter, cheese, and baked apples with which Julie provides me daily, made that I dined better than H.M. [His Majesty]." And again, "Home. Julie had by my fire an excellent bouillon gras, a bottle of cider on my table, and I boiled some potatoes, which with bread, butter, and cheese, I dined better than His Majesty."

As he enjoyed his "segars" and homely meals in his relatively cozy room, Burr may have had in mind a poem Robert Burns wrote in 1795:

> What though on hamely fare we dine,
> Wear hoddin [homespun] grey, an' a that;
> Gie fools their silks, and knaves their wine;
> A Man's a Man for a' that:
> For a' that, and a' that,
> Their tinsel show, an' a' that;
> The honest man, tho' e'er sae poor,
> Is king o' men for a' that.

Four

Acquaintances

Describing the same period Burr spent in Paris, in his *Paris: The Biography of a City* (2004), Colin Jones writes: "Paris was both the motor of revolution and the Revolution's most conspicuous setting." It was the time the King of Rome, Napoleon's son, was born and christened to great fanfare, and of the French victory at Wagram, but it was also a time of human losses mounting in the tens of thousands. Another contemporary chronicler of the city, James H.S. McGregor, has written "under Napoleon, the recklessness and rage that the Terror expressed were not subdued but channeled into military campaigns."[1]

For Burr, it was daunting to figure out who had the power and influence. Napoleon's highest military officers and supporters were nobility, and Bourbon aristocrats reclaimed their old properties in many cases. The French Revolution had leveled the old social order but Napoleon's decree of March 1808 founded a new, and partially inherited, nobility, linking merit, wealth and family prominence.

Burr needed to cultivate people of rank and also form bonds because of the absence of an established circle or family. He knew prominent French people from back home to look up and had letters of introduction to others. There were numerous Americans living the good life and engaged in trade and speculation in Paris, but Burr was now unpopular and people didn't want to offend those in power in America by befriending him. He also was unacquainted with the parvenus who had risen under Napoleon's rule. Still, Burr on a daily basis went out on his rounds to interact with Parisians at all levels of society, business and politics.

We will meet a number of Burr's acquaintances in this chapter and subsequent chapters. Several are mentioned in this typical daily entry for December 14, 1810, as Burr makes his rounds despite a swollen foot run over by a carriage. He has lost his watch the day before:

> Restless. Dreaming of the watch. Caught thief; battles. Alas! all dreams; the watch irrevocably gone. Rose at ½ p. 7. At ½ p. 9 to Denon's; received well; interesting conversation. To d'Alberg's few minutes. To Valkenaer's; still abed but cheerful; nothing from Amsterdam. Passed an hour with Albertina. Engaged to teach her English every evening, chez elle. Thence over the river again to Crede's; not at home. To Vanderlyn's; got New York papers, and told him I could not dine with him as had engaged. Home to meet Forbes by appointment. He arrived just after me and sat an hour. At 5 to Madame Fenwick's where tete-a-tete till past 9 when came in an old gentleman.... Off and home. But on the way a rencont. [sexual encounter]; 3 francs and well satisfied. If only I could forget that watch!

The Expatriates

First, what of Burr's fellow Americans abroad? Given the fraught nature of the Atlantic crossing (the challenges of both weather and keeping clear of marauding vessels) and the high-profile visitations of Franklin, Adams and Jefferson, it's often been assumed that few Americans went to France during the Revolutionary period and Napoleonic era. In fact, thousands did, almost all of them hailing from New England and the mid–Atlantic, and mostly merchants, financiers and commercial agents. If mistaken for Englishmen, they might be hounded, to the extent that Americans in Bordeaux wore cockades in their hats in the postrevolutionary period. U.S. citizens exchanged their passports for the permis de séjour at the prefecture of police, so there is a list of them, 8,000 strong, which William L. Chew III, himself a multicultural individual and a professor of history at Vesalius College in Brussels, has studied closely. There is abundant evidence for such research given that Americans in Paris in the postrevolutionary and imperial periods included luminaries like Jefferson (minister to France from August 1784 to September 1789); John Paul Jones, who died in 1792 at 19, rue de Tournon; Thomas Paine, who between 1781 and 1803 stayed in Paris several times and, contemporaneously with Burr, Washington Irving, and Rembrandt Peale, as well as lesser-known people. Sometimes Burr was mildly humorous about French mores, for example, how the cabriolets tore around town.

Upward of 200 American travelers sojourned in Paris for a year during this time period. The number had built up from 100 at the beginning of the empire (1804) and would reach between 300 and 350 per year by 1815. Three-quarters were business travelers, 12 percent were diplomatic or military people, and over 85 percent had considerable means. The American colony frequented status hotels on the right bank, principally the Rue Cerrutti and the Rue Richelieu. Perhaps the only American travelers in France on as shaky economic footing as Burr's were the occasional stranded sailors and those detained in French prisons. From 50 diaries, Professor Chew derived a picture of what these early American tourists looked at and how they viewed the French people: "To the American eye, evidence of Parisian immorality appeared at every turn, but most typically in the display of outright nudity in art, barely masked nudity on stage and the easy availability of prostitutes."[2] Burr's views stand out in greater relief against the backdrop of American attitudes towards France and the French. He had no "hang-ups." He could admire the first nude painting by an American (John Vanderlyn), enjoy a great performance at the theater, dance at the Paris Opera, and comment on acting, scenery or costumes. He was like a duck in water as an 18th century gentleman when it came to the city's fabled *oiseaux de nuit*. He was not a reformer but neither did he come with a set of prejudices.

In general, Americans admired aspects of Paris, its gardens, its cuisine, and its fashions. They saw it as the capital of Europe, but at the same time they censured its frivolity. Burr's attitude of taking the world at face value contrasts with the aura of risqué sexuality which most American travelers of his time reported about Paris. Burr's dispassion can be measured against what Professor Chew found to be the norm among the early American tourists. Burr was concerned about being fleeced and not knowing correct values and pricing, compared the superiority of heating in the U.S. to France, and criticized the bureaucracy and hassles of a police state. However, his sophistication and lack of prejudice is striking. He came from New York where he met many foreigners, he was competent in French—he didn't need to bone up on it as most Americans did (instead he studied a bit of Spanish)—and over and over again his journal entries describe people he met as individuals without stereotyping them. He didn't see the French as less morally upright—that American fallacy—and he acclimated himself to Paris.

How Burr's tolerance of foreign ways contrasts with what Chew terms "American exceptionalism" comes through in the observation of William Lee, a merchant from Mas-

Marriage Ceremony of Napoleon and Marie-Louise at the Louvre Chapel, 2 April 1810, by Charles Percier, Pierre Fontaine, Pauquet and Normand. It was tight quarters for guests in the Salon Carré, which was draped with rich fabrics and festooned with religious paraphernalia in the semblance of an altar (courtesy Napoleon Collection, Rare Books and Special Collections, McGill University).

sachusetts and the U.S. consul in Bordeaux, on first arriving in Paris: "I find I shall pay dear for being an American. A stranger is well known in Paris. If he goes into a shop to buy anything, he is sure to be asked triple the price they would charge a citizen for the same article, and they are so polite, agreeable, and affable, that a person acquainted only with the rough-hewn, honest, natural American manners cannot escape from their impositions."³

Jefferson wrote of the snares of vice—the availability of prostitutes and the temptations

The Emperor and Empress Receiving on the Balcony of the Tuileries the Homage of the Troops on Their Wedding Day, 2 April 1810, by Charles Percier, Pierre Fontaine, Pauquet and Charles Normand. In the foreground, a soldier fences off a portion of the jostling crowd. On the balcony, Marie-Louise is seated and taking the weight off her shoe-pinched feet (courtesy Napoleon Collection, Rare Books and Special Collections, McGill University).

of loose women—to warn his nephew against learning to love the "voluptuary dress and arts of the European women" while despising the "chaste affections and simplicity" of those of his own country.[4] While longing to be home, Burr was not nostalgic for American manners or the virtuousness of the American citizenry, nor did he censure the French for a perceived moral debauchery. Burr took the world as it was. He appreciated the fashionable Parisiennes, even if they were not as beautiful as he had imagined (his credulousness about the southern region of France having the great beauties is his rare "stereotyping" in the journal). He also showed practical realism in his interest in technology and trade. Expatriates proverbially meet one another in Paris. If Burr's boon companion was the artist John Vanderlyn, a compatriot, that is because they were two cultivated individuals having a prior sympathy long before in the U.S. Essentially, Burr's social circle was small.

John Vanderlyn

Burr looked up John Vanderlyn directly when he himself arrived. This proved good luck because he had sponsored the successful painter in the United States and helped fund his first trip to Europe a few years before, to study. (Napoleon awarded Vanderlyn a prize; another of the eminent painter's claims to fame was that he was the first American to paint subjects naked.) When Burr first settled into his lodgings, he did not hear from his former protégé for a few days; Burr had the wrong address and therefore didn't find him home. (All of the houses had been recently renumbered by imperial decree, odd on one side and even on another, and the switch led to some confusion.) Burr was sorely disappointed ("Is it possible that he, too can have turned rascal?"), proving the importance to him of having this friend who was getting along in Europe. In any event, Vanderlyn's allegiance to Burr was well established. They dined and walked together many, if not most, days.

Colonel Swan

Burr encountered an intriguing former business tycoon in Paris, a Scots-Yankee named Colonel Swan, for whom Burr drew up a will. Swan became a friend Burr visited in a most unusual venue, as Swan was housed in the Sainte Pélagie debtors' prison.

James Swan[5] hailed from Scotland (he came to America at the age of 11). He was a year younger than Burr and, like Burr, a Revolutionary War hero. Swan dressed up with other Sons of Liberty as a Mohawk and threw a cargo of tea from East India House into the Boston Harbor. He subsequently was twice wounded in the Battle of Bunker Hill. He also placed his considerable fortune at the service of the Continental Army. After the Revolutionary War, when Massachusetts annexed Maine, many large tracts of land were put up for sale. General Henry Knox, the secretary of war under Washington, and Colonel James Swan had known each other as clerks in the same mercantile firm near Faneuil Hall in Boston and had remained friends. Knox married money and Swan, too, married up. He also inherited a legacy from a rich Scots relative. While Swan bought expansive, dense Maine timberlands for lumbering and set up as a wealthy man to live in the grand style, Knox purchased vast tracts on the coast. Swan located his mansion on Swan's Island, the largest of a cluster of islands formerly known as the Burnt Cote group, between Isle au Haut and Mount Desert Island, which he purchased from the state of Massachusetts in 1789. In the deed from the state was a stricture that the island would have 50 Protestant (Congregational) families within six years; that each family would have a house at least 18 feet square; and that the town should build a meeting house and hire a pastor. Swan complied and brought in his own ships, materials and workers. Soon Swan's Island had two mills and a growing settlement. The mansion is said to have been the model for General Knox's Montpelier, built a few years later in Thomaston, Maine, a replica of which is now a landmark down the coast. Swan's plan to locate a summer home on Swan's Island makes him the first wealthy "sunbird" to have a vacation house in a northern locale.[6]

The lumbering and fishing were lucrative, but Colonel Swan overreached. He bought land in Kentucky and western Virginia as well as confiscated Tory property in Boston and Dorchester, and he was plunged into debt when the land speculations turned out badly. To retrieve his fortune, he left for Paris in 1787, a teach-yourself French grammar in hand, and soon made a new fortune through contracts to supply the French army.

During the French Revolution, Swan tried to save Royalist friends from the guillotine. He persuaded a number of them to emigrate to freedom in America. His partner Stephen Clough of Edgecomb, Maine, loaded his ship *Sally* with tapestries, furniture and clothes belonging to Queen Marie Antoinette. Various aristocrats made it to America, some settling in New Orleans, but the plot to rescue the queen came too late. She was taken from the Conciergerie and beheaded, supposedly with Captain Clough looking on in horror in the crowd. The *Sally* (named after Clough's wife from Wiscasset, Maine) sailed from Le Havre in the middle of the night before Robespierre heard of the mission. Some of the queen's furniture is now in the Museum of Fine Arts in Boston. Clough's third daughter and a granddaughter were given the name Antoinette.

Most American businessmen departed France in the wake of the Terror, but Swan managed to stay on excellent terms with Robespierre's *commission des subsistances*. From 1794 to 1796 he was the official purchasing agent of the French government in the United States and sent more than 200 shiploads of American provisions to France—lumber from Wiscasset, rice from Charleston, fish from Boston, and flour, cornmeal, beef and pork from various ports. Few ships were taken by the British and, for those that were, Swan proudly neutralized the trouble and made an adjustment or restitution in nearly every case. For example, he offered Gouverneur Morris, late minister to Paris, one thousand pounds as reward for each cargo he recovered.

With the credit that the French provided Swan's agency, he bought quantities of luxury goods that were advertised and sold in America. This appears to have been Swan's idea and from the establishments of the flown or executed aristocrats came luxury items like silks and satins, vases and mirrors, valuable books, and pianos, stored in the national warehouses. The *Boston Gazette* for February 16, 1795, announced that an auction house on Foster's Wharf would sell "1000 packages of French Goods as follows—12 cases of Cambrickes, 12 bales of Broadclothes, 14 cases of Looking Glasses. 16 do. Elegant China Ware, 12 do. Millinery, 26 do. Perfumery, 12 do. Feathers and Plumes, 3 do. women's and men's Slippers, 10 do. House Furniture, 8 trunks Leather Gloves."

Swan was also empowered to negotiate a liquidation of the American debt to France for money loaned to the colonies during the American Revolution. Colonel Swan accomplished the repayment, which was used to purchase grain and foodstuffs for France. While Swan was exonerated of debt himself, his partner in Europe went to trial to recover certain funds he alleged were due him—an amount Swan could easily have paid off had he wished to.

Unfortunately, it was claimed Swan had contracted a debt of 2,000,000 francs, which he denied, and he refused to pay it. The French arrested him and sentenced him to Sainte Pélagie Prison, where he was confined from 1808 to 1830—such an extended time because Swan wouldn't secure liberty on an unjust plea. His wife and children went home and Lafayette and other friends argued with him to no avail. Swan gave up much of his life, including the comforts of his Parisian and New England homes, for a perceived principle. When Burr met Swan he had been in prison since 1808 and was growing accustomed to captivity. Burr's journal reads as follows:

> Then on to Pélagie, where dined with Swan. The important concern about Merino sheep. No doubt there is a great deal of money to be made by it, but it is out of my line. [A week later:] I passed an hour with Swan, talking principally of sheep. [The next day:] A note also from Swan. Still sheep!
> Wherever I be, and in whatever situation, if I cannot be acquainted with the first in the place, I make it a rule not to be acquainted at all—as I have said before, I find it much more agreeable and cheaper—and besides, is supporting a character of rank I maintained at home, and I shall again after my return, disencumbered from the shackles and perplexities of deranged business and a want of money.

To Swan's apartments in the Rue de la Clif, opposite Sainte Pélagie, Swan invited his friends and lodged his servants and a mistress. He had stables for his carriages, in which guests drove to the promenade, the ball, the theatre, everywhere in his name. He gave great dinners where there was always a place left for the absent one at the table, as there was in his box at the theater. Swan's obsession that Burr relates was Merino sheep. Today Swans Island Company, founded on Swans Island, makes high-end blankets out of merino wool. Colonel Swan would have been pleased at having been a couple of centuries ahead of his time, as merino wool is now a staple of upscale fashion labels every winter.

Jonathan Russell

Politics is largely proving that the other party is unfit to rule—to paraphrase H.L. Mencken. Such was the situation of Burr and the chargé d'affaires from the U.S. to Paris when Burr was there. Rhode Island-born Jonathan Russell (1771–1832)[7] graduated from Brown University (then Rhode Island College), studied law and was admitted to the bar but did not practice, and became a wealthy merchant and diplomat, ending his career in the U.S. Congress (1821–1823), where he chaired the Committee on Foreign Affairs.

When Theodosia Burr wrote a plea in June 1809 to Dolley Madison to bring her father home, President Madison was urgently trying to stave off what had seemed unimaginable: another war with the British. Negotiating for peace also preoccupied Jonathan Russell, whom Madison had made the U.S chargé d'affaires to France in 1810. That Russell extended no help to procure Burr a passport must be seen in light of the fact that the United States was embroiled in its first international conflict, rather than that it was shunning the survivor of the ill-fated duel with Alexander Hamilton. Befriending Aaron Burr would earn no points from England, and who knew what would strike a match in the Anglo-American antagonisms. Jonathan Russell was, after only a year in Paris, transferred to England, where he was chargé d'affaires when the war of 1812 began. In 1811, Russell arranged for all Burr's communications with home to be intercepted. "Any letter to you would be opened," Burr wrote to Theodosia.

Russell, a distinguished statesman, can be recalled for an unrelated three events that curiously echo Burr's political hassles. First of all, while the British were dallying over how to respond to the official complaints about impressment of American sailors and interference with American trade, Russell was a ready target. This caused him some personal rancor against the British, consequent to which he wrote a rousing patriotic poem about the sea battle between the *Constitution*—"Old Ironsides"—and the British (formerly French) frigate *Guerriere*, off the coast of Massachusetts. The name of the hero who commanded the *Constitution* was, aptly, Captain Hull, and Russell wrote with fire in his pen about the British tyrants: "Confounded—defeated—in terror they flee.... The strong she had vanquished, the weak she had plundered—/And madly proclaimed herself queen of the seas."[8]

Second, in 1822, Russell wrote a tract accusing John Quincy Adams, a fellow negotiator of the treaty to end the War of 1812, of bias in favor of British interests in the talks. Russell intended the pamphlet to support the presidential candidacy of another negotiator at Ghent, Henry Clay, in the 1824 election. Adams wrote back virulently, marshaling facts to refute his accuser. The nasty newspaper exchange that ensued resulted in political slang being adopted at the time in New England: "to Jonathan Russell" someone, or to devastate an opponent in a dispute. After the feud, Russell retired from political life to his home in Mendon, Massachusetts.

The footnote to the feud came in 1824, a year later. August 23, 1824, was a red-letter day on the calendar of the former congressman and ambassador. Russell made plans for a gala celebration to welcome to his home the Marquis de Lafayette on his tour of the United States. Russell's uncle had served under the great general in the American Revolution and Russell had met Lafayette in Paris in 1811. Russell and Lafayette were chummy enough that Lafayette sent Russell a book of Alexander Humboldt's maps of the Western Hemisphere to pass on to Thomas Jefferson. The visit of Lafayette to the Russell home was to be one of the highlights to cap off Russell's career in public service. His house was decorated and fine foods were prepared but Lafayette and his entourage never arrived; instead the dignitaries traveled through central Massachusetts. One of the traveling companions was John Quincy Adams, who intervened to alter the itinerary and reroute the party to bypass the former congressman's home in Mendon and go directly to Providence.[9]

Social Calls

As for Thomas Jefferson or Benjamin Franklin, it was paramount for Burr to socialize, to make rounds of social visits. He liked to exchange ideas and witty conversation and he had his waning political ventures as well. According to the spies following him, should Burr's schemes have found tangible support from a European government, he might have gone into action. Contemporaries and later commentaries criticized Franklin for being such a man-about-town at Versailles. How else could an American survive without influence? And influence came through the visitor's extended social set. Some Americans as well as French officials ignored Burr or turned him away. Gaining reception took patience; some avenues that appeared promising proved useless. Burr's accounts are in several cases funny. For instance, when the Duc de Cadore's porter was sick, wife stood in for him—a lucky stroke for Burr, who was able to appeal to the woman and gain admittance to the antechamber.

Like Montesquieu, the author of *Lettres Persanes*, or Moliere in several of his comedies, Burr had a detached laugh at high society's mores. On March 10, 1810, he had to talk someone into buying a ticket to the Tuileries and prepared letters to be presented to the emperor. In the spring of 1810, dining at the Baron d'Alberg's, "there was a Count Louis (senateur, I think), General Vallance, two ladies, and five other gentlemen. Gamp [Burr refers to himself here] was of so small account that neither chair nor plate was provided for him, and he stood a minute after all were seated."

Before Burr went to France he knew French diplomats and business people in New York, as well as aristocratic émigrés from the French Revolution. When he told Theodosia to have a bath built in South Carolina, he told her to do it as French people did. But in Paris, having a bath became a small luxury. He had others, principally his wine and cigars. He was a person from the American elite, now at the outside of the window looking in.

Dueling had more currency in France in 1810 than in the United States, where it was beginning to go out of fashion, and there is no evidence in Burr's Paris journal that any of the French (other than Talleyrand, a friend of Hamilton's) held Burr's duel against him.[10] An extraordinary duel took place less than two years before Burr arrived when Monsieur de Grandpré and Monsieur Le Pique quarreled over a lady engaged at the Imperial Opera, Mademoiselle Tirevit. To settle their claims the two men agreed to fight a duel and the lady agreed to favor the survivor. Like Agassiz and Federer competing in tennis on a "sky court," the duelists were to fight in the air. Two balloons of the same size and shape were constructed and on the designated day a great crowd of spectators assembled in the Jardin des Tuileries. Each duelist had a second, but they were to fire not at each other but at each other's balloons. The ropes were cut and the balloons ascended in a moderate wind, which kept them at about the original eighty yards apart. Monsieur Le Pique fired but missed. Monsieur de Grandpré fired and punctured his opponent's balloon. Le Pique and his second plunged a half-mile to their deaths.[11]

The New Notables

Burr, from a republican world, found himself in a setting where titles counted for a great deal. This had always been the case for visitors and envoys from the American colonies who went to Europe. They met with courtiers, landed aristocrats whose prestige at court one could inquire about or observe. Burr, on the other hand, was entering a prestige cauldron, where it was hard to tell which administrator was over whom, who had power and who had less, and who was wickedly wealthy and on the rise.

Birds of a feather flock together, yet from our vantage point the plumage of the flock of notables, those who gratefully accepted imperial titles whom Burr encountered, seems an odd assortment. In perspective, the nobility of France, after a thousand years, were on their way out (ending definitively in 1870), but not before the nobility had a new identity and were sitting very prettily on the socioeconomic tree. In 1800, the first full year of the Consulate, over 40,000 families were permitted to return. The *bonnet rouge* came down from steeples; the titles madame and mademoiselle replaced *citoyenne*; the revolutionary calendar was dropped; and people went back to using a seven-day, instead of a ten-day, week and observed Christmas and Easter again.

Beginning in 1802, Napoleon tried to create a "mixed elite," combining members of the traditional aristocracy of the ancien régime and the new elites issuing from the revolution. Napoleon, from small provincial nobility himself, turned his back on the revolution when he created a vehicle for ennobling men called the Legion of Honor. By a single stroke he had a new award of nobility that he controlled, his own cadre. The Legion of Honor revived the Order of Saint Louis, founded by Louis XIV but abolished in 1793, according to Jean-Luc Chappy (personal communication, December 20, 2013).

A new society, Napoleon reasoned, needed a new elite, an aristocracy not of birth but of merit. Boundless in his own ambition, Napoleon derided it in others, remarking disdainfully of his own creation, the Legion, "It is by such baubles that one leads men by the nose!" Under the empire no fewer than 48,000 *rubans rouges* were distributed, including 1,200 to civilians. "Hanging by a thread,"[12] said the cynics, yet the Legion would remain a source of power and influence for republican regimes long after Napoleon's demise.

Napoleon kept certain aristocratic émigrés who had fled during the Terror on an official list of no-entry, but most of them he welcomed back to France and into the heart of his organization. This was a fusion of elites, not an embourgeoisement.[13] It was a conscious regression on the part of Napoleon, but the old nobility went into professions because they had to have money. They were not anymore living off the peasants so they had to compensate by other strategies, principally salaried posts, and also by affirming their identity by manners and display to prevent a plummeting déclassement. They fed into the burgeoning imperial bureaucracy.

The Legion of Honor[14] in 1810 had approximately 30,000 members, one per thousand of population of the empire. The Legion and the imperial nobility were not, however, the ideal homogenous corps the emperor intended, points out historian Pierre Duyre: "[The differences of education, social status and wealth, and the perpetual posting of its military members in the army prevented the hoped-for amalgam; this would in any event have required more than a dozen years to accomplish] *Les différences d'éducation, de situation social et de fortune, et le perpetual séjour a l'armée de ses membres militaires, empêchent l'amalgame souhaité: il aurait en tout cas fallu plus de douze ans pour le réaliser.*"

Some of the most important noble families boycotted the empire, yet they were not rejected. Wanting to integrate all the top people, Napoleon allowed them to participate in social events so long as they subscribed to the prevailing etiquette—and they couldn't wear uniforms, which in a militaristic society must have made some feel poorly.

Would Burr have found the nobles he contacted in Paris ready to talk about the bad old days of revolution? Amnesia was the prevailing etiquette: one did not stray conversationally into the subject of the revolution. The topic was only acceptable if limited to the privations one suffered during that time. Explains J. Willms, "Bonaparte made clever use of this taboo, and by encouraging national reconciliation he consolidated his own position. His political priority was to obtain the allegiance of the former opponents of his tightly controlled central government. And because of the great prestige of his military and civil bureaucracies—which grew to mammoth size along with the Empire itself—nothing was more sought after than a position in this hierarchy, were it ever so humble."[15]

While being a nobleman didn't bring instant income, it usually came with a large purse and source of income from the post. The essential design was that a prince's son would be a duke and a duke's son a count and a count's son a baron. Whether it was actually hereditary or not was a shaky matter. At first it was, and then Napoleon saw too big a proliferation of notables in the future and curbed the inheritance of titles. The leaders and heads of the new industries meanwhile rivaled nobility from both sources. It was very uncouth to have made money from the revolution, but it was fine to have done so as a banker, before or after.

The nobility's loyalty proved provisional. Sanity prevailed and fair-weather friends abandoned Bonaparte after Waterloo. Napoleon confided in a henchman that the new nobility had not lived up to his expectations. The restoration of the monarchy brought the restoration of ancient nobility, who took up their titles again irrespective of how they were oriented to the empire.

Two Ministers of Foreign Affairs

It was Burr's natural error to imagine that achieving an introduction to Talleyrand would lead to Napoleon. Talleyrand had been a guest at Richmond Hill, Burr's New York estate, but when Burr requested an interview, Talleyrand rebuffed him with a haughty note: "General Hamilton's likeness always hangs over my mantle."

Charles-Maurice de Talleyrand, once a cleric present at Louis XVI's inauguration, was Napoleon's advisor in the wake of the revolution and from 1799 to 1808 (the Consulate through the heyday of the empire) his first foreign minister. Talleyrand embodied the rules of Machiavelli's *The Prince*, virtually brushing Napoleon's epaulettes and polishing his crown until, deciding the emperor had betrayed his country in warring against Russia, he dispatched him to die in exile on St. Helena. Talleyrand was a formidable personality and is known as one of the great statesmen of history. His methods were manipulative but his thinking was straight. He wanted to reconstruct France, believed that France needed a constitutional monarchy and Napoleon was the only person strong enough to unite the land, and also believed that he could guide Napoleon and point out his true interests. Thus, Talleyrand initially saw his role as reining in Napoleon's grandiose desire for universal sovereignty over Europe and to be bigger than the Hapsburgs ever had been.

Talleyrand served as Napoleon's foreign minister for eight years. After being dismissed in 1808, he retained a ceremonial rank and the title of Prince of Benevento. He operated

Opposite, top: The Birth of the King of Rome, 20 March 1811, son of Napoleon I and Marie-Louise. An artist re-created the scene from hearsay. The cradle, a gift from the City of Paris now at the Schonbrunn Palace in Vienna, is very different from the depiction here—having a complex iconography wrought in more than 500 pounds of silver. The actual cradle stands on horns of plenty and is decorated with little angels, bees on all sides, and an eaglet representing the infant gazing up from the footboard at the N in a crown overhead. The artist put the bees on the baby blanket and shaped the cradle like a horn of plenty (courtesy Napoleon Collection, Rare Books and Special Collections, McGill University).

Four. Acquaintances 33

Napoleon on Horseback Reviewing Cavalry Troops Passing Behind the Arc de Triomphe du Carrousel. The impressive revue at the newly built Carrousel Arch has a small inset at the bottom of the engraving, representing a balcony of the Tuileries Palace (Library of Congress, Prints and Photographs Division).

on the fringe of the court and began to drift towards friendship with Czar Alexander of Russian and restoration of the Bourbons.

There is no reason to conjecture that Burr knew of the rift between Talleyrand and Napoleon. More likely is that Burr had heard of the friendship Gouverneur Morris had established with Talleyrand—Morris and Talleyrand were cheerfully *à trois* with the coquette Adelaide de Flahaut in 1789. Burr must have known that Talleyrand was a sybarite and gambler and had serial affairs; such a person might receive an American of prestige in disrepute. Nevertheless, Burr didn't hear much of the statesman, as Talleyrand was in semi-retirement until Napoleon was exiled to Elba in 1814.

In 1807 in Berlin, Talleyrand was informed of Napoleon's decision to destroy the Spanish Bourbons. Having always argued for diplomacy and policies that would bring order to Europe, Talleyrand determined to resign from the imperial government. When he returned from Tilsit he did so, to Napoleon's mystification and chagrin. To save face, Napoleon made his former foreign minister a dignitary of the realm with a nongovernmental title of Vice-Grand Elector (Joseph Bonaparte, King of Naples, being the Grand Elector). Since a person couldn't be in the government and also a dignitary, this covered the reality of the split between Talleyrand and the chief. For his part, Talleyrand spoke with irony of his title as an "honorable and lucrative

Decoration commemorating the birth of the "King of Rome" (1811) by Bertrand Andrieu and André Galle. The king of Rome was an infant when this medal was struck. His profile is on the obverse and on the reverse side is a double portrait of his parents, Napoleon and Marie-Louise (courtesy Walters Art Museum).

sinecure." With typical terseness, he explained to his peers why he fell out with Napoleon and then tendered his resignation: "It is quite simple. I do not wish to be the executioner of Europe." He saw the emperor was straying from the path Talleyrand had seen fit to clear.

Grass did not grow under the governmental position. The day following Talleyrand's resignation, on August 10, 1807, Napoleon chose a successor, Jean-Baptiste de Champagny—minister of interior for the previous three years. De Champagny had named his third son Napoleon and was ready, and eager to serve as the new minister of foreign affairs. By all accounts, he was handpicked to be the sort of person to sidestep confrontations with his boss. De Champagny was named Comte de l'Empire (one has the impression Napoleon liked inventing titles). The new foreign minister oversaw the abdication of Charles IV of Spain, which Talleyrand had abjured, and was rewarded with a hereditary hold in Italy and, yes, a new title—the duc de Cadore—which is how Burr referred to him in 1810. From the outside it was sensible to hope for Cadore to be a stepping stone at the center of power, except that all was not as it seemed, and Cadore would not hold firmly to his position and it was all he could do for Napoleon not to take him down with him after Waterloo.

A biographer of Talleyrand, J.F. Bernard,[16] wrote that Champagny was all that Napoleon could have wished: obedient, respectful, and totally innocent of ideas of his own. "The only difference between Champagny and myself," Talleyrand remarked, "is that if the emperor told him to have someone's head cut off, it would be done within the hour, whereas, it would have taken me a month, at the very least, to get around it." So zealous was the new minister that Napoleon, who had been spoiled by Talleyrand's deliberate lack of haste, had to administer a mild reprimand: "You should always keep my letters on your desk for three or four days before sending them out." To this, Talleyrand added advice of his own: "You will find, after you have served the emperor for a while, that it is unwise to carry out his orders too quickly." And years later he was to note, "The emperor compromised himself on the very day that it became possible for him to do fifteen minutes early that which I had always insisted he do fifteen minutes later."

However, quarrels ensued. Clearly Napoleon wanted to conquer Russia, not engage in diplomacy with the tsar. Nobody could disagree with Napoleon and stay in favor. Cadore advised a policy of peaceful trade with Russia. By the spring of 1811, the strain between Napoleon and Cadore snapped their relations, and on April 16 Cadore retired.

During the period of the Hundred Days, from March to July 1815, between the time when Napoleon escaped from Elba and Louis XVIII arrived in Paris, Cadore avoided Napoleon. As soon as the Restoration commenced, he (like Talleyrand) went over to the Bourbons. Talleyrand personally convinced Tsar Alexander, whom he had met in the famous pavilion on a raft in the Neman River while negotiating the Treaties of Tilsit, to support the return of Louis XVIII. Napoleon must have loathed Talleyrand and, on St. Helena, claimed to have himself dismissed him.

Anne-Jean-Marie-René Savary, Duc de Rovigo (1774–1833)[17]

Invited to the house of the Duc de Rovigo, Burr saw a hundred carriages outside the establishment. This was a rare opportunity to hobnob and see how a First Empire aristocrat entertained. Once inside the duke's the affair was as dull and stilted as it looked imposing from the street: "Now and then one advances and says something commonplace to one of the ladies, then returns to the male side."

Savary has a memorable, if "unsavory," story. From a military family, he was a soldier at age 16 and became Napoleon's aide-de-camp in 1800. When the head of the Paris police, Joseph Fouché, displeased Napoleon, young Savary replaced him; Savary's job included the cloak and daggery of watching over Fouché. In 1803 he personally investigated a royalist conspiracy and, promoted to general, presided over the execution of the Duc d'Enghien— a low mark in Napoleon's rule, as the duke proved innocent. It was a blot on Savary's record as well, as he had opposed another general who wanted to let d'Enghien plead his case directly to Napoleon. Savary's most valiant feat was commanding a French army against a Russian one at the battle of Ostroleka, which won him a huge pension and top braid of the Legion of Honor.

Napoleon encouraged the general to marry a relative of Josephine's and gave him the title of duke in 1808, with a large monetary salary. The general went right off to Spain and strong-armed the switch from the rule of the Spanish Bourbons to the government of Joseph

Bonaparte. As Talleyrand's and Fouché's influence with (and loyalty to) Napoleon were on the blink, Savary became the most intimate confidant of the emperor. In 1809, he was named minister of police. Legality didn't carry with Napoleon and the new Duke de Rovigo imprisoned detractors of the Empire whether royalist or republican.

Parisians detested the new minister of police even more than they had detested the notorious Fouché. In a decree issued during October 1810 Rovigo required all the maids of Paris be counted at the ministry of police and made all the police prefects keep records on all prominent people in their jurisdiction, including their fortunes, political views, and family situations. The prefectures also were instructed to keep tabs on all girls approaching marriageable age so as to prepare a list of prospective brides for the officers of the Grande Armée. By this means, the emperor and the Duke of Rovigo planned to unite the aristocrats of the ancien régime with the imperial one—as the two men had done personally. Another of the duke's nasty missions was tracking down the ever-increasing ranks of army deserters.

In October 1810, in a move instigated by the duke, Napoleon tightened the strings of censure on Parisian newspapers, limiting their number to four. At this time, books were elite and less interfered with in general; it caused a stir of protest when Savary forbade a work of Madame de Staël, *De l'Allemagne*, before the censors even got their hands on it. Savary faulted the book for its omission of France's military successes against Prussia. Copies were destroyed, the presses broken, and the author exiled.

Ever the loyal servant, Savary accompanied Napoleon on the HMS *Bellerophon* to Saint Helena but was not permitted to go into exile with him.

Napoleonic history reveals strange crisscrossing such as the following. Karl Marx made the acquaintance of Friedrich Engels at the Café de la Regence in Paris 46 years after Napoleon played chess there (1798); the marble table where he played would have been pointed out to Marx. Napoleon married Marie-Antoinette's niece in Paris only 16 years after the queen was beheaded there. A third connection relates Savary's methods to the near present. Napoleon, who valued order and control over all other functions of government, had a perfect acolyte in General Savary, Duke of Rovigo. The duke proved a hardliner vis-à-vis the establishment of the Algerian government, fomenting Arab hostilities and championing a most repressive type of colonial rule, with clearly deleterious long-term results.

Emmerich J. Von Dahlberg (1773–1833)[18]

"Versatile" and "versatile" are called *faux amis* when English speakers study French, as to say someone has various talents is "polyvalent" and the French word spelled the same means "inconstant" or "fluctuating." The line between betrayal and a timely switch is often faint. During the postrevolutionary period in France, shifting sides was mandatory for political personages. Even police chief Joseph Fouché, for whatever reason, got understandably fed up with Napoleon. Emmerich Joseph von Dahlberg, the man who helped Burr exit from France, was a model of political versatility. If not rivaling that cat of nine lives, Talleyrand, he had the confidence he could weather any minor repercussions resulting from doing a favor for Aaron Burr.

Von Dahlberg was of old German aristocracy. His family owned properties on the left (not right, and this became important) bank of the Rhine between the towns of Speyer and Worms. His father, Wolfgang Heribert, Baron von Dahlberg, directed the prestigious Mannheim Theater and was the first to present Friedrich Schiller's first play, *Die Rauber*, a Cain and Abel melodrama, in 1783. Emmerich Dahlberg's mother belonged to Hessian nobility. His uncle, the last archbishop of Mainz, known as a reformer, supported Napoleon but lost his dukeship when Napoleon was defeated at the Battle of Leipzig in 1813.

Emmerich grew up in Mainz because his father was chamberlain at the Palatine court and director of the theater there when Mainz was a lively artistic center. The Dahlberg family moved in a circle where French taste and language prevailed. In keeping with the parents' status was the education of their son in artistic subjects as well as academic ones and he showed talent in drawing and watercolors. He studied law in Gottingen, and went to Vienna with the expectation of an imperial post, but the government was shifting from imperial to Austrian and he was turned away. In 1803, Dahlberg was appointed Baden's ambassador to the French imperial court and went to live in Paris, where he took part at the French headquarters in Napoleon's war against Prussia (1806–1807). He entered the service of the French because his patrimony was on the left side of the Rhine, making him a French citizen and his properties part of the empire. Napoleon named him a duke and appointed him to serve on the council of state in 1810.

When Burr met Dahlberg, not only had the latter's star just risen at court but so had his wife's. He had in February 1808 married the 18-year-old Pellina, Marchesa di Brignole-Sale, whose mother was lady-in-waiting to the French empress, and after Emmerich and Pellina returned from their bridal trip of several months in Genoa, her native city, Pellina was made a lady-in-waiting (dame du palais) as well. The court was very international in composition, and the dames du palais were from Belgium and Genoa and Baden. Presumably, she forgot to tell her husband that Aaron Burr, far out of her busy circle, had called. Meanwhile, it is likely that Dahlberg was more interested in Paris's art than its politics. Eventually Dahlberg's historical and contemporary master drawings, purchased mostly in Paris, consisted of about 1400 sheets. The nucleus of the collection of Dahlberg's drawings, sold to pay feudal taxes to Ludewig, Grand Duke of Hesse, in 1812, are in the Hessisches Landesmuseum of Darmstadt.

During the military operations of France against Prussia, Dahlberg forged a relationship with Talleyrand, with whom he later conspired against Napoleon. One contemporary source has Dahlberg communicating with another officer with invisible ink via a note stashed in a peasant's boot. The relationship of Dahlberg and Talleyrand outlasted Napoleon's regime. Both were on the commission at the Congress of Vienna, chosen to draft a new constitution promising freedom of the press and religion and restoration of properties, when Napoleon fell in 1814. Dalhberg lived in France until 1828 and then traveled, mainly in Bavaria and Naples. In 1832 he retired to his castle, Herrnsheim, near Worms, where he died in 1833.

Dahlberg's personal experience with the shifting sands of imperial favor, his cultivation, his secure position at the imperial court and his secret opposition to Napoleon contributed to his accessibility and helpfulness when Burr needed a friend well placed in government.

Maret, Duc de Bassano[19] (1763–1839)

Hugues-Bernard Maret, Duc de Bassano, was instrumental in issuing Burr the passport that made it possible for him to leave France and go home. Napoleon had shifted the focus of his Lebensraum away from Spain and its colonies to Russia, so Burr's idea of independence for Mexico was neither here nor there. Also, Napoleon knew he had nothing to fear from Burr, that he was acting on his own. All the same, the personal experience of the duke may have inclined him to extend assistance to Burr.

Born in Dijon in 1763, Maret was a lawyer in Paris before the revolution. He was a moderate revolutionary whose contribution to the cause was having an outstanding memory and keeping a detailed bulletin of the debates of the National Assembly in 1789. This was officially declared a newspaper the next year and Napoleon controlled it via Maret. The paper was initially called *La Gazette Nationale* and was purely political in content. But Napoleon wanted a bigger name and scope for his pet publication, so it began to run articles on art, literature and science and became *Le Moniteur Universel* on January 1, 1811.

The unusual experience Maret had that may have inclined him to be a bit indulgent to the American yearning to return to his homeland and family were the years Maret spent in a Tyrol prison. The Austrians captured him and another envoy of Napoleon and they remained in captivity for 30 months between 1793 and 1796, until Napoleon obtained their release in exchange for the daughter of Louis XVI, Marie-Thérèse, from the Temple Prison in Paris.

Maret became the chief of Napoleon's cabinet. He wrote another courtier in 1809, "I could only accept a very grand and very honorable position, being in the Emperor's household." In the summer of 1809 during the campaign against Austria, he had charge of the plays put on in Schonbrunn Castle, where Napoleon had residency, and often had a chance to converse with the emperor over meals. Shortly after he became a baron and prefect of the Rhone, a position he used to advance his and his wife's relations' positions, he wrote in October of that year that his family was bound "to all eternity to serve the Emperor and his family." Meanwhile, the duchess's salon was the most influential in Paris, where, according to French historian Philip Mansel, "puppet shows were performed mocking Talleyrand's and Caulaincourt's love of peace. Conversations favored war with Russia. The Empire was now such a courtly, military monarchy that Madame de Noailles remarked: 'At this time we talk about chivalry as much as during the revolution people talked of liberty.'"[20]

An essay on Maret gives an aperçu of the actual job of imperial secretary: "Each week, Maret must become acquainted with the ministers' reports and make an oral account (compte rendu) in a tête-à-tête with the First Consul. He goes to all the meetings, receives the minutes and decrees, signed by Bonaparte, and transmits them to the ministers for execution. All the reports of the high police are addressed to him as well as an account, hour by hour, of both day and night, of what is going on in Paris. After his administrators prepare a succinct analysis, he carries them to the office of the chief of state." Maret's work continued unchanged when Napoleon was proclaimed emperor. He accompanied the emperor everywhere and had so many assignments it was as if he were simply moving around a chessboard, including organizing the government of Poland (1806) and rewriting the constitutions of Portugal, Holland and Westphalia (1808). He even signed a treaty of alliance between Persia and France. He is said to have encouraged Napoleon to seize Spain and to have promoted the emperor's marriage with Marie-Louise.

In 1813, Talleyrand policies and the longtime police chief Fouché accused Maret of being behind the bellicose of the emperor. Maret was not among those who gathered around the restored Bourbons. In 1814, he stayed at Fontainebleau at Napoleon's side, to say goodbye, until the emperor departed for Elba. What's more, he stuck by Bonaparte during the Hundred Days and, exiled by a ruling of 1815 by Louis XVIII, went off to Austria. His short second political life came five years later, when he was briefly the president of the royal council under Louis-Philippe.

How Talleyrand and Napoleon judged Maret makes quite an extraordinary contrast. Talleyrand said of him, "There is but one man stupider than Monsieur Maret and that's the Duke of Bassano." When Napoleon wrote his memoirs he commented, au contraire, that he had "a good memory of his minister, a very able man, of a gentle nature, an uprightness and a delicacy proven over and again."

Napoleon wrote a singular letter to Maret, which has been preserved and came up for auction in 2012.[21] This coded message, written in numbers, translates as, "I will blow up the Kremlin on the 22nd at three am," and is signed "Nap" at the bottom. The letter is addressed to Hugues-Bernard Maret, Duc de Bassano, and is dated October 20, 1812, the day after Napoleon retreated from the center of Moscow. In the letter Napoleon also requests Maret to provide supplies and more horses for his freezing troops. The attack was carried out as planned and destroyed a number of the Kremlin's towers and walls. Meanwhile, Napoleon and his Grande Armée were forced to carry out the Great Retreat.

A Most Illustrious Acquaintance

This must have been an especially fine moment to meet one of the most dazzling scientist adventurers of all times, Alexander von Humboldt. Humboldt, with his irrepressible French expedition companion Aimé Bonpland, made meticulous observations of plants, animals, rocks and the atmosphere, notably in South America. In 1810, Humboldt was living in Paris and publishing the accumulated findings of his travel research in Central and South America. Meeting the active scientific community was part and parcel of meeting Humboldt, as they swarmed about him. (A biographer describes him in the social swim in 1808, despite putting his money into his books and science: "Sometimes, when the Athenaeum had a bal soirée, one could catch a glimpse of the famous Humboldt. By now Parisians had accepted him as one of their stars.")[22] Also, Humboldt judged people on individual merits; he launched into conversations about science and geography with everybody he met. Although he had to cadge certain favors from the rulers of Prussia, France and Spain, he was independent minded and wouldn't have given tuppence for Burr's politics but for his conviviality and brains. Humboldt was the most famous of numerous men of science and technology whom Burr interacted with; generally the scientific men, many connected with the Institut National and the Jardin des Plantes, and the denizens of Parisian bookstores were congenial people for Burr to socialize with in Paris.

At this time, science, economics and philosophy were open to all inquiring minds. For Burr to have entertained business ideas related to technological inventions—a way to purify water, produce a better vinegar and build fireplaces that drew well—was in character. First Benjamin Franklin and then, while Burr was in Paris, Humboldt paved the way for amateur adventurers in science like Charles Darwin. The young Humboldt studied earth sciences and was a mining expert in Prussia in advance of becoming arguably the most multifaceted and indefatigable scientist of the modern age. Early on, he aimed to master the systems of geomagnetic measurements and helped manage the Napoleanic switch to the metric system. Then Napoleon reneged on financing his expedition to Egypt so Humboldt went to Spain and obtained permission from the Spanish government to visit its colonies in Central and South America. No one had acquired such permission previously, the colonies being out of bounds and only viceroys and Catholic priests having access to the vast empire.

Humboldt crossed the ocean to the western hemisphere with Bonpland and spent five years, 1799 to 1804, covering over 6,000 miles on foot, on horseback, and by canoe, in tropical forests, desolate plains and wilderness, braving inanition, mosquitoes and so forth. They ended their travels in Mexico, whereupon the Mexican government offered Humboldt a post he refused. He returned to Europe, but on his way stopped briefly in the U.S., where he expressed a wish to pay his respects to President Thomas Jefferson. He did so in the company of the painter Charles Willson Peale, going to the White House in May 1804. On June 27, 1804, from Philadelphia, the 34-year-old German explorer wrote Burr that he was leaving for Paris straightway and thus the two would not meet but he sent his regards.

From 1807 to 1827, Humboldt stayed in Paris and published his findings on climate, mining, flora and fauna, volcanoes, population and social conditions and the like. In his "Political Essay" on the Kingdom of New Spain, translated quickly into English in 1811, he decried slavery and oppression of the indigenous peoples he saw on his travels. Remarkably, the courtiers of Europe did not back his publications: he paid for them himself in Paris. He also offended Napoleon by not showing up at a party.

Humboldt and his linguist brother, Wilhelm, had mortgaged lands in Poland, which under the Treaty of Tilsit Napoleon bestowed on his ally the king of Saxony. This resulted in the brothers receiving no profits from their Polish property as of 1806, Alexander's only regular income being a modest annual pension from the king of Prussia. Humboldt wrote the Swiss naturalist Marc-Auguste Pictet in March 1808 about having to cut back on living standards: "I work and sleep at the Ecole [Polytechnique], where I consequently spend my nights and mornings. I share the same room with Gay-Lussac. He is my best friend, and I find his company most consoling and stimulating, and the stimulus seems to be mutual. Although I have lost everything, I fancy that I shall be able to enjoy Independence on forty sous a day."[23] He lived in a modest apartment at the top of an old house in the Latin Quarter—13, quai Malaquais near the corner of the Rue de Seine, in the 6th arrondissement. Later, his money invested in Poland was freed and he could afford a manservant and his own carriage, but he stayed in his small set of rooms near the institute, which were like the lodgings of the students who were his neighbors.

Large libraries, governments and private collectors purchased the mammoth publication of Humboldt's work. Through sales he recouped some expenses and kept going for the 30 volumes. This enormous undertaking testifies to Paris publishing at the time. The only publication in France that rivaled Humboldt's works in production costs was the *Description de l'Egypte* (1809–22) by the French army.

While Humboldt's life had privations, he was acclaimed in Paris and warmly welcomed at private salons. He knew that on appointed days he could drop in at the prestigious salons without formal invitation. The pace of his day as a foreigner sheds light on Burr's day as well, as a foreigner at the outskirts of the same world: study and work in the morning, a quick lunch in one of the smaller restaurants au coin, the afternoon conferring over business and more private work; dinner with friends; afterwards attending a soiree (a difference that stands out is that Humboldt rarely went to theatrical entertainment); home at midnight, writing or reading until two AM, four hours sleep enough to refresh unless he was in poor health (rheumatism).

When Burr met Humboldt, he had already published his volume on plants of the monumental Voyage aux regions equinoxiales du Nouveau Continent. This connected with several of Burr's interests expressed in the journal, as well as his dreams regarding Mexico.

Where Was Lafayette?

"Lafayette had only one idea," wrote Chateaubriand, "and happily for him it was the idea of the century." Lafayette and Burr were both veterans of the American Revolution founded on the principle of freedom from tyranny. They would have seen and kept up on any gossip about each other, without seeking each other out.

The outlook had been bleak for liberty in France from the moment Napoleon Bonaparte became First Consul. The marquis de Lafayette was a moderate reformer who was nearly guillotined and had to flee at the brink of the Reign of Terror, in 1792. He would have liked to return to America. However, when he presented his wish to do so to Washington before his death, "stay and help your homeland" had been the American leader's reply.

Under the Directory he remained an exile. At first when Napolean came to power he refused to let Lafayette enter France. Thus Lafayette remained on the list of exiled émigrés. His wife, Adrienne, however, sent him a passport bearing a false name, and back Lafayette came. After a few days of hiding in Paris, he wrote Bonaparte extolling the new republic and expressing gratitude for the coup. The fact that Lafayette took clemency for granted offended Napoleon. Talleyrand and Abbé Sieyes (one of the instigators of Napoleon's coup) advised Lafayette to turn tail for Holland. Instead, Lafayette went to Adrienne's estate. La Grange-Bléneau was located about 40 miles east of Paris and had a farm, chateau and 700 acres. Here Lafayette took up serious farming and lived like a Cincinnatus ready to take a more public role but keeping out of political activity.

Napoleon crossed off the original National Assembly members from the list of émigrés in March 1800. Now Lafayette was legally entitled to live in France and out of danger. Napoleon, using the principle of conciliation, brought former royalists and radical revolutionaries all within his new government. He invited Lafayette to a three-day fete at Joseph Bonaparte's chateau in October 1800 and, Lafayette later recalled, told him that the French had lost their enthusiasm for liberty: "You Parisians, for instance, oh, the shopkeepers, don't want it anymore."

But when the Legion of Honor was created [1802], Lafayette refused to fall in line. He objected to making Napoleon president for life and totally opposed putting him on the throne. People were clamoring for posts in the government but Lafayette decided Napoleon was a hopeless despot. Lafayette refused, when the hour of truth came, to be bought. Explains Olivier Bernier, the doyen French historian, "It was very honorable to turn down an appointment as senator because senators were very well paid—not only a salary but the income from a geographic area. Napoleon would arbitrarily assign a larger or smaller area, either convenient or extremely productive, or a remote next to nothing. Lafayette was offered a lush senatorship and turned it down." Bit by bit all over Europe, Lafayette symbolized David standing up to Goliath.

Lafayette slipped on the ice crossing the Place de la Concorde in February 1803 and got poor medical treatment from a doctor friend who had just invented a machine for bone setting. Lafayette had a stiff leg and a permanent limp, so he would not have been seen much promenading in the capital. Friends who shared Lafayette's disappointment in Napoleon clustered around him. His beloved wife of 34 years, Adrienne, died on Christmas Eve 1807.

According to Olivier Bernier, "In 1811 Lafayette was completely sidelined and also short of cash. Having refused to become a senator, he was watched by the police because Napoleon took the accurate view that he was potentially dangerous. Except for his family and a very few friends, his role was passive. But he maintained his interest in the United States and corresponded with people in the U.S. There is every chance he would have met any American who came to Paris because the United States remained the great interest of his life, until the very end. So he kept out of political activity at La Grange but was seeing every American he could" (personal communication, spring 2013). Writes Henry Levenstein, social historian,

> Practically every American visitor to Paris was invited to Tuesday soirées at his Paris mansion and to La Grange, his country estate. He would show them his collection of American memorabilia—portraits and busts of American political leaders, Benjamin Franklin's cane, George Washington's umbrella, a chair cushion woven by Martha Washington. His own beautiful cane, he would point out, was carved out of wood from the apple tree under which he and George Washington breakfasted on the morning of one of the great battles of the Revolutionary War. He was a regular speaker at American residents' Fourth of July and Washington's birthday dinners, where their hearts would go out to the man who helped bring liberty to their country but could not do so in his own.[24]

It can be supposed that when Colonel Swan waxed enthusiastic about the enterprise of raising merino sheep, he mentioned Lafayette's success with them: by 1811, his *troupeau* numbered 720. The next year, the fate of friends and relations in the Russian campaign saddened Lafayette, but he continued to farm and boasted he had become a good farmer, "without making any great scientific claims."

Burr was likely to have seen General Lafayette at the Paris Opera—the marquis was a big fan of the starring tragedian Talma. Both men would have discussed the grand heroes and would have cared for debate of questions about life, death, honor, betrayal and ruling men that were the stuff of classical French theater.

Five

Money Matters

Letters Burr wrote his daughter indicate that he intended to finance his travels in Europe through $3,000 in notes payable to Burr by one E.W.L. In a letter to Theodosia from London dated April 22, 1809, however, Burr acknowledged that there was no hope of E.W.L. paying up: "The perfidy of the person on whose notes I relied for support; whose ability is known, and whose promises were the most solemn, had nearly produced the effect which, I am persuaded, he meditated. If any friend had been active after the first failure [to pay] in December, payment might have been produced. But do not now enter into any quarrel about it. I feel myself now above dependence, and have hopes of other resources. I go cheerfully on this voyage. It is one I have long desired and meditated."[1]

The voyage referred to was the result of an order expelling him from England. "I was ordered to withdraw. Whither? No place could be mutually agreed on. In short, the government would agree to no place but Heligoland, a barren island about sixty miles from the coast of Denmark, now in the possession of Great Britain This difficulty, however, was yesterday, the day allotted for my embarcation, solved by the Swedish minister, who very courteously, on my application, sent me a passport for Sweden." Burr believed that the British acted "to conciliate the government of the United States." The idea of deporting him to the North Sea foreshadowed the British expulsion of Napoleon to the island of St. Helena seven years later.

Theodosia wrote a moving letter to her father from South Carolina, "stupefied, as if stunned, by the blow" of his deportation and commiserating over his financial setback:

> I have written a second time to the gentleman who promised us the supply of funds; but there is little to be hoped from him. On inquiry, I find that his character does not stand very high as a man of punctilious honour in money dealings. The style of my last letter was open, and my name to it at full length. Perhaps he may be teased into a performance of his engagements. His conduct is a serious addition to all the accumulated difficulties which already pour in upon us, and which would absolutely overwhelm any other being than yourself. Indeed, I witness your extraordinary fortitude with new wonder at every new misfortune. Often, after reflecting on this subject, you appear to me so superior, so elevated above all other men; I contemplate you with such a strange mixture of humility, admiration, reverence, love, and pride, that very little superstition would be necessary to make me worship you as a superior being; such enthusiasm does your character excite in me. When I afterward revert to myself, how insignificant do my best qualities appear. My vanity would be greater if I had not been placed so near you; and yet my pride is our relationship. I had rather not live than not be the daughter of such a man.

As Mark Van Doren stated in his 1929 collection of the letters between Burr and Theodosia, "Few fathers and daughters have stood in a more interesting relation than that which the following correspondence reveals to have existed between Colonel Aaron Burr and his only child. The two of them have never been surpassed, I think, in the quality of their mutual devotion."[2] Theodosia's emotional support sustained Burr through his repeated low points in Europe; so did his habit of ending each day by writing a journal entry addressed to her. Financially, he managed to just get by, largely on hospitality and loans, including a loan from an unexpected quarter, as discussed in a later chapter.

Sometimes, loans came to Burr without his asking. For instance, there was a windfall in Copenhagen the entry for October 26, 1809, describes: "[Friends] brought me a letter from Lüning; a most affectionate letter, but something more; enclosing a draft on his correspondent at Hamburg for 1,000 marks! Did you ever hear of anything to equal this except in novels? I am quite embarrassed what to do. In the evening, to my great surprise, and uninvited, tapped gently at my door Tempe. You know I never disappoint people if I can help it and so T. was not dismissed; 4 rix dollars. With great trepidation I opened [your] picture on Sunday morning. It has suffered no injury. It hangs in my room; but I am quite out of humor that my visitors have expressed only commonplace admiration" (Journal I/254–55). Burr had met Lüning in Sweden, and Lüning's letter to Burr was indeed affectionate: "I cannot tell you how much I am thankful to Providence for having given me the pleasure to get acquainted with a man whom I admired long ago. I esteemed you before; now I love you."

In Paris as elsewhere in Europe, Burr tended to spend the proceeds of larger loans—most of which he seems never to have repaid—on travel, living expenses and prostitutes, also buying many books and presents for Theodosia and his grandson. At the frequent intervals when his cash on hand ran out, he borrowed small sums from friends, whom in general he did repay, also resorting to selling or pawning his valuables, including a collection of rare European coins intended for his grandson. Burr dedicated a large portion of his journal for the latter half of his four years abroad, the two years when he was detained in Paris and London, to the details of his precarious financial affairs.

His journal also contains entries concerning various moneymaking schemes, sometimes self-mocking or fanciful, other times serious but equally fruitless. Burr's detractors called him a schemer, but in Paris and London he was more of a dreamer. At least dreams like the following served to keep Burr's spirits up:

> Am much stared at here [in Yarmouth]. Think of showing Gamp [Burr] for about 2 shillings each person; half price for children. Have this evening changed my last bill, being one of 10 pounds, to pay my host; voilà mes montres déja mangés, et encore je dois à ma hôtesse à Londres [now my watches are gone, and I still owe my London landlady]. But having made more than a million of guineas last night, as you shall know anon, feel quite easy, and give with great liberality to the domestics, &c. When last in New York, the steamboat had just got into vogue. Being in company with a man knowing in such things, I suggested (but very slightly, as becomes an ignoramus) how the thing might be simplified and improved. He thought the hint of no value, and I said no more. My friend D.M.R., and another, whom I met at Graves's, both great projectors, have taken patents for inventions on that subject. I examined their several models, but was not smitten with their value. My old idea ran now and then in my head, but said nothing. Ruminating, after going to bed last night, on the state of the treasury, the thing came up again, and engrossed me for at least three hours. I found it

perfect; applied it to sea-vessels, to ships of war; in short, to everything that floats. Sails and masts and rigging, and the whole science of seamanship, are become useless. My vessels go at the rate of twenty miles an hour, and am in hopes to bring them to thirty. From Charleston [Theodosia's home] to New York will be a certain passage of thirty hours; from New York to London of six days; but to tell half I did would fill a quire of paper. Rose at 9 this morning; the same project in my head, and have thought of nothing else the whole day. The moment of my arrival in London shall sell all my books; your books, poor little Gampillo; and all my clothes, save two shirts, to put the thing in execution; and so soon as I get this million, Lord! what pretty things will buy for thee and Gampillo. Laid out, however, a great deal of money last night. Thought of the faithful in the United States. Bon soir.

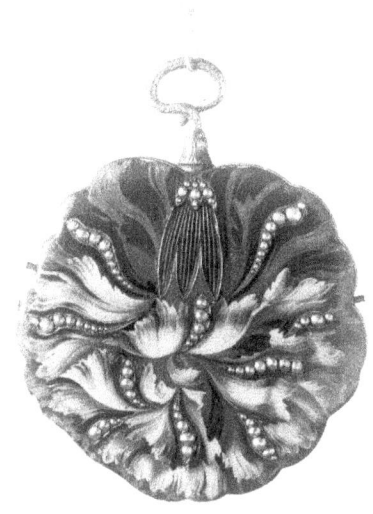

Watch with tulip-shaped case (early 19th century). Elaborate watches in Europe were made for the wealthy and also for an export market to the Middle East and Far East. This Swiss example has a gold cover, green enamel leaves, and pearls outlining the petals (courtesy Walters Art Museum).

Historian Gordon Wood writes that "Burr certainly sought to live the life of an eighteenth century aristocratic gentleman" but relates that Burr and others who "sought to establish their genteel independence by acquiring landed estates could not fulfill their ambitions of emulating the English landed aristocracy since land in the New World was a far riskier investment than it was in England."[3] Nevertheless, nostalgia for this lifestyle—which the 1801–1825 Virginia dynasty of Jefferson, Madison, and Monroe could keep up, thanks to their hundreds of slaves—remained highly appealing to the political elite of Burr's generation. The 18th century study by Basil Willey suggests why:

> The first half of the eighteenth century was a period in which the English aristocracy enjoyed about as near an approach to earthly felicity as has ever been known by man. They had most of the wealth, all the political power and all the social influence in the country. The monkish and superstitious Middle Ages lay far off in the dark backward abysm of time; and the conflicts of the seventeenth century, so uncouth and so theological, which had for long interfered with their full enjoyment of the splendid plunder of the Reformation— all these were over and done with. The Crown had lost its power to strike, and the Church was docile. The vulgar, not yet indoctrinated with nonsense about the Rights of Man, were content with the lot to which an inscrutable Providence had fortunately assigned them; or, if not, they consoled themselves with gin, or (as advised by the clergy and the more conventional moralists) with thoughts of the future life…. At this distance of time we can afford to yield a measure of (not necessarily ironic) admiration to so perfect, if so brief, a phase of civilization.[4]

But even a Virginian whom Burr encountered in London, David Meade Randolph, a few years younger than Burr and a cousin of Thomas Jefferson, could no longer play the part of the landed aristocrat and he, like Burr, turned to dreams of profiting from technology, as the machine age was now upon them. Burr drew an interesting sketch of Randolph, in which Burr could almost be describing himself and his own meager chances of success in his endeavor to hit on some invention to retrieve his fortune:

> But, first, let me make you better acquainted with the said D.M.R. He is about 60 years of age, very healthy and active; has good sound sense, little education, or little acquirement. He came to England about six months before me, with commercial views, having got through his fortune in Virginia. He had very good letters, being universally acknowledged an honest and an honorable man. At the moment that he supposed himself in the high road to success and fortune, came on [Jefferson's] embargo, which put an end to all commerce, and annihilated his proposals. He then got from the United States Bedford's patent for making shoes, and took out a patent for it here; but, for more than a year, he could get no moneyed men to set up the business in that way. At length W. Gilpin, army clothier, agreed to try it, and advanced D.M.R. 500 pounds for the patent rights and half the profits. This was a very seasonable relief, for he was quite run out. He now thought he would invent something himself, and turned his mind to improvements in wheel-carriages. He worked day and night for some months; at length, thinking he had hit it, and for fear some one should steal it from him, he hastened to take out a patent, and then wrote a pamphlet; but no mortal took any notice of either. Being now project mad and one Adams having come from the United States with a new project for impelling boats by steam, D.M.R. associated himself with this man; bought half the invention for 200 pounds, and at this moment Adams dies, and the steamboat and the wheel-carriages sleep quietly together; but D.M.R. had now got rid of his last farthing. His head, however, runs more on wheel-carriages than on all other subjects. At least twenty times since my return to this island he has told me of his having explained "his principles" to Mr. Such-a-one, who was "delighted"; and scarce a week passes but he meets some one who is thus "delighted"; but of all these delighted people not one is disposed to advance a penny to make an experiment of "his principles." Whenever he gets on his "wheel-carriages," away he goes, and the devil can't stop him. He can hardly pass a cart or a carriage in the street without stopping you or calling your attention to the amazing stupidity and obstinacy which prevents people from adopting his improvements. "Only see how those horses labor for nothing; whereas if that axle-tree was so and so, and the height of the wheels so, and the pole fixed so, one horse would draw more than those four; and the thing is so demonstrable," &c., &c. [Journal II/329–31].
>
> [Some weeks later:] I completed the draft of a power of attorney for D.M. Randolph, to be sent off by this packet. I wished to have written you by the same opportunity, but the 4 shillings and 6 pence requisite for postage is a fatal objection. D.M.R. having four three shilling-pieces, lent me two of them; but one proved a counterfeit. He was in good spirits, having met one of his country acquaintance some time ago who was "delighted with his principles on wheel carriages." This is certainly very nearly allied to insanity [Journal II/353–54].

French Dentures and Vinegar from Wood

Burr tried to exploit two supposed innovations, imported by him from Paris to London, hoping to raise money for passage from England back to America. First, he tried to capitalize on the knowledge of denture-making that he had gained in Paris. Held up in Paris while waiting for his passport to be issued, Burr commented, after one of his final visits to his Paris dentist and friend G.A. Fonzi, "To Fonzi's, where nearly finished everything. It is nearly worth the twelve months I have been detained here to have got so well dentified." However, Burr's plan to profit in London from what he learned in Paris about dentures went nowhere at all:

Reading over Fonzi's pamphlet, it occurred to me that my knowledge of his art might be turned to good account here. Went off to see Delmehant, the most celebrated in that line, for the purpose. He had moved and could not discover the address.... I was so much with Fonzi at Paris that I became as good a dentist as himself; and, on coming off, he confided to me an assortment, perhaps one thousand, of teeth of his fabrique. I had intended this for Greenwood; but it occurred to me that something might be made of the dents and my science here. Have called on three of the most celebrated dentists. The first was engaged, and was not seen; the second was engaged, but I saw him, and made an appointment to call Saturday next. The third I had a long talk with; he showed me his own fabrique, which I was constrained to acknowledge was fully equal to Fonzi's; and, indeed, I think, for beauty, superior, but not solid; he, however, held Fonzi's in contempt, so nothing to be done. Tomorrow will make further trial. It is unpleasant and unpromising.

A Fortunate Friend

For an ambitious careerist like Aaron Burr, being away from his American home could seem like lost years. Even John Adams had suffered homesickness while performing his official duties in Paris, whereas Burr was merely biding time and on his own nickel. However, in one way Burr gained years during his self-exile and that was the story of his excellent dental treatment, beginning with a lady tooth-puller in Germany who deftly extracted a tooth, followed by his great good fortune of a friendship with G.A. Fonzi.

Vanderln introduced Burr to the dentist. When Burr was in Altona, a city on the Elbe in Germany, waiting for a passport to France (Louis de Bourrienne, the French minister in Hamburg, disobeyed the emperor's instruction and gave it to him), he didn't get out much because he suffered from a dreadful toothache. The remedy of camphor and opium was of no benefit to the molar. His gum and jaw swelled and the pain, according to his jocular note in the journal, was exacerbated by having been bitten in the lip by a woman in a "paroxysm [i.e., an orgasm] of great good humor." The affliction worsened until the lady dentist extracted the tooth and he recovered.

Burr's problems were not going to end with one extraction; Dr. Fonzi (in the journal referred to as just "Fonzi") was not only Burr's dentist but probably was the closest friend he made in Paris. Early in their acquaintance Burr noted the following: "At 7 to Fonzi's, a visit. He is not only a dentiste, but a man of education, of talents, and considerable acquirements; franc et enjoué [candid and merry]." Burr, Fonzi and Vanderlyn formed a friendship of the "what are you doing tonight?" sort. Burr and his dentist were the same generation, both sophisticated professionals, and with the kind of wanderlust that drives a body to seek something better just over the next hill. Both had lived stirring adventures beyond the ordinary, and at the time they met in Paris, both had bitter enemies for political reasons. In character both were proud, independent and inclined to keep secrets. Their exchanges must have been fascinating; Fonzi's brilliance and resoluteness made him an ideal friend for Burr. Fonzi was as strong a chemist as dentist, and scientific inventions were ever on Burr's mind. Above all, Fonzi's status as an outsider in Paris made him available for companionship. Expatriates are likely to pal with other foreigners, especially true in Burr's case given the standoffishness of the French, a subject of periodic comment in his journal.

Giuseppe Angelo Fonzi was born in 1768 in Orsogna, a small town in the Abruzzo region of Italy where his father was a deputy of the prince. Other brothers were at college and the father could not afford college fees for this son, so Fonzi concluded his formal studies with high marks at 16 and ran away from home, taking a silver spoon, fork and knife to make his way. First, from Naples, he joined the crew of a Spanish warship that cruised the Mediterranean and took him as far as Constantinople. He learned the skills of navigation and wrote home to his father that everything was going smoothly, thanks to having his abilities recognized by the commander of the vessel. However, when that captain was transferred, his successor was horrid and after a year as a sailor Fonzi abandoned his post while the ship was anchored in a Spanish port. He then tried different lines of work in Spain.

As the story goes, one day he watched a tooth-puller extracting teeth in a public square and saw his future. He bought the tools for extraction and became a traveling dentist en plein air. Paris was the center of studies of dentistry and, in 1795, Fonzi arrived there to practice his profession and further his knowledge. He set up a dental office and soon had many clients.

For a time, in 1801, missing his family, Fonzi went back to Italy. He stayed with relatives at Orsogna and then started a practice in Naples. However, Queen Maria Carolina, sister of Marie Antoinette, was in a tizzy and apparently wanted Fonzi, who treated aristocrats and highly placed people, to be her spy. The Queen of Naples was a believer in the Enlightenment until Marie Antoinette met her sorry fate, a result of which Maria Carolina became extremely suspicious and reactionary. Fonzi had left his dental laboratory in the charge of a trustworthy person, and he went back to Paris and resumed his profession and his researches, attending especially to a perfecting of the manufacture of mineral teeth and the mode of their application.

Giussepangelo Fonzi. This drawing is after a miniature of a painting now in a municipal office in Italy, possibly by John Vanderlyn, circa 1813, when Dr. Fonzi was age 45 (courtesy Dr. Francisco Javier Sanz Serrulla).

Burr writes of visiting not only Fonzi but also his affable wife. The letters between the couple back and forth to Italy tell a clouded picture of this union, which fell apart just after Burr's departure for America.[5] Fonzi's companion from 1807 was named Hélène de Clecy, When he wrote his sister Pippa from Paris in a letter marked December 2, 1808, among other things he told her that he had married a good and sensible woman who looked after his interests, and whose love compensated him for the disappointment of not having children (he was 40 and the implication is that she was somewhat close to his age). Perhaps his family was concerned he would be led astray by a pretty Parisienne, as though he protests too much, or his sisters may have simply been inclined to criticize.

Among Fonzi's letters were some that Hélène wrote. One (December 22, 1811) was addressed to his brother Orante and in desperate tones tells him how she is suffering from a terrible illness for which there exists no cure—"une maladie de poitrine," i.e., tuberculosis.

She writes that a mere year earlier she was totally swept up in "love, passion, and the kind of union of souls that purifies all the actions of life, and gives birth to every good idea in the heart," and now she has to renounce all sweet illusions of life. In the fourth of five long paragraphs she says that her husband would write Orante himself but he is too busy and also too upset to overcome his usual laziness about writing letters. In the letter's closing, after wishing Orante, his sister and his amie the best in this life and the next life as well, she signed, "Helene de Clecy, femme Fonzi."

Fast forward a year and a half and Fonzi, who, as he himself confessed, considered letter writing a waste of time, wrote his brother on June 8, 1813, a letter with a passage that paints a scandalous picture of the affectionate and devoted Hélène:

> The woman who up to now you believed to be my wife is no longer in my house. To you and to the public I had given to understand she was my wife, because of the excessive consideration I had for her. That woman is the worst monster that exists on earth. I loved her much, but she has deceived me for the space of three years. I have sent her away and though she merits only contempt, I notwithstanding continue to maintain her; and this because she made me believe for two years that she was going to die from one day to another, announcing an attack of the chest and lungs. The melancholy I suffered in consequence of this caused me eight months of continual illness, and if I had not sent her away I should not now be alive.

Fonzi never married. The year 1809 found him at 1, Place des Italiens (now Place Boieldieu in the 2nd arrondissement), engaged in continual study of science, especially chemistry, as well as treating patients. From 1811 to 1814 he advertised as "*Officier de Santé*" and "*Inventeur des dents incorruptibles, terro-métalliques, approuvé par l'académie de médicine, et couronné par l'athenée des arts.*" His practice was listed in a new residential area of the city at 12 rue Taitbout and his lodging at 19 Rue Taitbout, close to the Cul de Sac Taitbout, where Thomas Jefferson had lived during his first year in Paris.

Fonzi prospered in everything he did; when Burr was in Paris, Fonzi specifically stated he never lacked for funds. He wrote Orante in an earlier letter (May 1, 1811) that he had made "large profits" but was working extremely hard: "You think that I am amusing myself! Know then, that I have remained in the house without ever going out for four years, so assiduous and heavy was my work. I have created a new art, a beautiful and useful art, and my contemporaries heap blessings and gratitude upon me." One has to think that one advantage of Fonzi as a friend for the expatriate Burr in Paris was that he could almost always be found at home or in his laboratory.

A portrait engraving of Fonzi that is reproduced in sources about him was actually created by his biographer, Vincenzo Guerini, from possibly either a self-portrait or a portrait by John Vanderlyn done in 1813.[6] This means that two years after Burr, Vanderlyn and Fonzi were comrades in Paris and visitors at Vanderlyn's studio. Fonzi, who had never been recorded as producing artwork previously, executed a respectable oil painting. He appears affable and relaxed, with one fine hand carefully painted over the other wrist, wearing a white linen shirt and dark suit jacket, with the collars open at the front and high at the back. The painting was preserved by his descendants and acquired by Dr. Guerini and given to the George Eastman Institute in Rome, where it is now displayed. It has been authenticated by Valerio Burello, president of the Italian Society of the History of Odontology.

At the end of the 18th century, dental care was primitive. Colin Jones has described how the flickering smile of the French courtier resulted from not wanting to swallow the poisonous white cake makeup and having to conceal the state of one's teeth. "Opening the mouth in a painting (let alone in a court setting) would reveal a lack of gravitas that one found mainly in representations of the insane, of the overly-passionate and of humble plebeians."[7] For instance, Louis XIV has his mouth firmly closed in the grand classical-style portrait of the king in his coronation costume, by Hyacinthe Rigaud, 1701, because he was toothless from the age of 40, and gaping teeth after a certain age were commonplace. Good looks and articulacy suffered.

"*Mentir comme un aracheur des dents*"—"to lie like a tooth-puller" was a French expression, because the teeth operators were generally in disrepute. However, dentistry was making progress and becoming an art. In the 18th century in France there was a new diploma of "expert pour les dents" (from 1699) made by Louis XIV. And France was the most famous country in the world for dental art. All countries in the world learned dental art from French books (77 in this century). But with the "Révolution" the diploma was not necessary to practice until 1892 when another new diploma was required.[8]

Meanwhile, the alternative prosthetics for lost teeth were both varied and insufficient. Silver, gold, mother of pearl, wood, bone and agate, as well as the teeth of horses and other animals, were tried. The earliest examples at the museum of dentistry at Johns Hopkins University are fabricated with carved ivory tooth sections. George Washington's last dentures were a block of hippo ivory riveted to a sheet of gold. Wire springs and brass screws were part of the apparatus. Burr, who spoke of the spring of his "rat" breaking, probably had teeth of a similar sort before his trip abroad, although since he had a tooth removed in Germany he must have needed only a partial set of dentures when he had tooth trouble in Paris.

The manufacture of porcelain teeth began in about 1774 with Duchateau, a pharmacist in Saint-Germaine. Also, explains Dr. Scott Swank, head of the National Museum of Dentistry in Baltimore, Maryland, "much of the credit goes to one Dubois de Chemant, also a Frenchman. The time period for this experimentation with all porcelain dentures was the last quarter of the 1700s into the 1800s. All porcelain dentures never were very popular due to their cost, plus they were heavy, made noise while speaking and broke easily" (personal communication, January 4 and 6, 2014). Nicholas Dubois de Chemant fabricated total dentures in porcelain but they were not durable and were unwieldy, being a single block. It was Fonzi who developed a porcelain paste, known as terro-metallic, that was durable and could be produced in many shades and shifted from the blocks to an assembly of individual porcelain teeth. Earlier dentures had been made (baked) in blocks, which were uncomfortable and one-size-fits-all. Fonzi developed the single porcelain tooth held in place with gold and, later, platinum pins. He presented his innovation to the Académie des Sciences in 1807, and while the response was that his invention was ingenious and well-made, it also was called trivial and of dubious value. Politics were at the heart of the rejection. One killjoy was Vincent Dubois-Foucou, who had been dentist to the old king and now was dentist to the emperor. Undismayed, Fonzi made a few modifications and asked the Athenée des Arts to study his porcelain teeth and process for making dentures in 1808. There was a reversal—they gave him a medal and a crown, their highest award.

Jealousy of Fonzi simmered for the next several years. It seemed that the award backfired when members of the medical community called him on being… a foreigner. However, he was the talk of the dental world and would go on to treat the tsarina of Russia, Josephine's son Eugene, and Napoleon's brother Lucien.

Prior to Fonzi's improvement in 1808, the teeth were difficult to affix to a denture base successfully. However, even after Fonzi's improvement, the early porcelain teeth did not catch on, dentists preferring teeth carved from ivory blocks (still sold by the Ash company in 1870) or those extracted from the deceased, due to their better color. The use of porcelain teeth in the fabrication of dentures didn't really take off until the S.S. White Company began manufacturing them in a variety of colors in the 1840s. In any case, if Fonzi did, in fact, make Burr dentures one could assume that Fonzi would have used the porcelain teeth with platinum hooks of his invention. The denture base material could have been gold, silver or platinum. The National Museum of Dentistry in Baltimore, Maryland, has early 19th century dentures in its collection with bases of both gold and silver including gold and silver coil springs for holding the upper denture against the palate while the mouth was open.

Technically, Fonzi advanced in more ways than one the structure of dentures and composition of false teeth. He made the teeth of a secret formula of numerous metallic oxides, producing 26 color tones. In the mass of the porcelain teeth were two tiny staples or studs for which he used gold or platinum. These parts served to solder the artificial teeth to a base. He mounted the teeth on a plaque of gold that was modeled after the person's mouth. He then soldered a band of platinum to the studs and affixed rubber to the part of the denture in contact with the gum.

Fonzi would be appointed court dentist to the tsar of Russia and asked to establish a dental school in St. Petersburg, which he refused to do, as well as summoned by the king of Spain. He decided to manufacture porcelain teeth in Naples but that venture failed and he returned to Paris. In 1835 he turned his workshop over to his nephew and finally settled in Barcelona in 1836 (personal communication with Dr. Pierre Baron, November 2, 2013).

Fonzi responded to Dubois-Foucou in 1809 that he was content with paving the way to the future and offered to let his jealous rivals have the terro-metallic teeth and process he used to manufacture so they could try them out. Thus gradually he distributed his teeth through a chain of colleagues and promoted the idea of the industrial fabrication of prosthetic teeth. Gradually the more prominent dentists like Dubois-Foucou and Louis Laforgue recognized that Fonzi had taken "incorruptible" false teeth beyond theory into practical reality. It was in 1819 that a French dentist, A.A. Planteau, brought porcelain teeth to the United States.

Burr's other scheme to raise money in London also came from a process learned of in Paris, a method of making vinegar from wood, invented by Gustave Eiffel's uncle Jean-Baptiste Mollerat. (Eiffel studied chemistry and would have taken a job in his uncle's vinegar works, but a family dispute diverted him to an engineering career, culminating in the Eiffel Tower). Burr's Paris journal refers several times to his reading of a pamphlet by Mollerat on his vinegar-from-wood process. An 1809 report by the Institut de France confirmed that the Mollerat process did result in a product that, "if it be always prepared with the same care with what has been presented to the Institute by M. Mollerat, we may safely employ for all the purposes answered by the vinegar of wine." Of course, vinegar from wood never became a commercial product, despite Burr's pinning his hopes on it. The following scene, where Burr pursued his scheme to profit from Mollerat's invention, typifies Burr's famous ability to charm or "get round" a person in pursuit of his various enterprises. Burr and his inventor friend David Meade Randolph visited a factory outside London:

Were shown into an office where was Mr. Wilkes, the managing partner, dressed very coarsely, and even dirty, with an old, greasy hat on his head. Showed him Reeves's permission. "Who is this man who writes this note?" I told him who was Mr. Reeves. [Reeves was a minor figure in the British Alien Office who obliged Burr on numerous occasions.] "Why, by God, I don't know the man! ... By God, sir, this is the most extraordinary thing I ever heard in my life! A fellow I never saw gives a man permission to come and examine my manufactories!" He was going on, and, doubtless, would have concluded by turning us out of doors; but I interposed; told him that I was, as he saw by the note, an American, and about to leave England in a few days; that I had no desire nor curiosity to see his manufactories, but that I had understood that, in the process, he procured a sort of acid of little value; that, having been lately on the Continent, I had seen that acid employed to important purposes; and, happening to mention it to Mr. Reeves, he thought the discovery of very great value, and that it was totally unknown here; that the sole object of my visit was to get a barrel of that acid; and that, if I could succeed in the process it would render the acid of very great value; that Mr. Reeves had informed me he had understood that Mr. Wilkes was a very polite gentleman, and had no doubt that he (Mr. W.) would take pleasure in gratifying me in a matter so essential to his own interest and to that of the public. "Now, sir, if you are not disposed to do so, I have only to beg your pardon for the trouble and bid you good-morning." The idea of gain softened his muscles; he asked us to sit. Sent a servant to bring some of the acid for my inspection; ordered a bottle to be washed, and filled, and well corked for me; offered to send a servant with it to my lodgings, to save me the trouble of carrying it; gave me the address of his agent in London, and promised to send, by his own wagon, a barrel of the acid to my friend Allen immediately. I asked what would be the expense. "Oh! nothing at all, sir; my teams are going constantly, and it will give me no trouble; you may, if you please, only send an empty barrel to my agent, to replace the one I shall transmit." I came off with my bottle of acid, quite content.... The moment [the barrel of acid] arrives, friend Allen and I shall go to work, and, if I succeed, most certainly I shall have some hundred guineas of it [Journal II/306–308].

Burr did not make a hundred guineas, or any money at all, from his vinegar venture.

"X"

The scheme that Burr often referred to in his Paris journal as "X" followed his 1806–1807 Western adventures that led to his trial for treason in 1807. One explanation of what Burr had in mind at the time of his arrest, while floating down the Mississippi with his band of followers, is that he intended to lead a filibustering expedition to liberate Mexico from Spanish rule upon what he believed would be an imminent declaration of war by the United States against Spain. Project X remained on Burr's mind when he first landed in London in 1808 and met the English philosopher Jeremy Bentham, who befriended Burr and advanced him funds. In his memoirs, Bentham describes how Burr made his acquaintance: "I was brought acquainted with Colonel Aaron Burr thus: He had given a general order to a bookseller to forward whatever works I should publish. I was then very little known. This was good evidence of analogy between his ideas and mine. He came here expecting this government to assist his endeavours in Mexico; but the government had just then made up their quarrel with Spain. We met: he was pregnant with interesting facts.... I lent him my house in Queens Square Place. He meant really to make himself Emperor of Mexico. He told me, I should be the legislator, and he would send a ship of war for me.... He said, the Mexicans would all follow, like a flock of sheep."[9]

Five. Money Matters

After his expulsion from Britain, Burr attempted to revive X with the French government in Paris. He discussed X with an official in the French ministry of foreign affairs, Louis Roux, from March through July 1810. Roux's notes of his conversations with Burr ended up in the French national archives, where Samuel Engle Burr, Jr., a collateral descendant of Burr's, discovered them and published an English translation in 1969. The notes cover many pages, and detail many of Burr's military schemes, one more extravagant than the next. Burr focused on his understanding that the Spanish colonies were ready for independence from Spain, as indeed they were, and that if he had resources from Napoleon to liberate them, these colonies and their riches and trade would fall to the benefit of the French empire, rather than into the orbit of Napoleon's archenemy, Great Britain. Roux's summaries of Burr's ideas give a flavor of Burr's quixotic train of thought: "The approbation that His Majesty [Napoleon] gives to the plans for the independence of the Spanish-American colonies coincides with the feelings and wishes of the inhabitants and makes its execution certain and probably very near at hand…. Is His Majesty not interested in taking part in these great events? Will he abandon these areas to the caprice of chance? [If so,] Great Britain will act in that capacity and avail herself of all the advantages proceeding therefrom. She will have the monopoly of all their trade. Her bank and her treasury will become filled with the precious metals she will draw from them."

In a later conversation with Roux, Burr expanded on his plan:

> Mr. Burr proposes, with 1200 men, to lay hold of Pensacola, the only port on the northern Gulf of Mexico capable of receiving large vessels, and where the Spanish have only 800 men. Once in control of this gateway, along with Mobile, St. Augustine and other cities which would offer no resistance whatsoever, 4,000 men—all robust experienced hunters—could easily be raised in Florida; 4,000 men likewise in New Orleans and to the left of the Mississippi; and the number that would be needed, in the districts of Ohio, Cumberland, and Tennessee. 10 or 15 thousand men would be embarked in the small boats that trade along the coast and would disembark on the eighth day at Vera Cruz, whence they would continue on to Mexico City. As it would not be a question of conquering the colonies, but only of protecting them from Spanish domination, Mr. Burr relies heavily on the good disposition of the inhabitants; otherwise, it would be enough that they remain passive in order to execute the undertaking…. Mr. Burr would desire that your Majesty entrust to him two frigates and a few small ships with the money necessary for the initial arrangements—he could leave by the first of July [1810]. By means of these frigates, he would begin by seizing the Bahama Islands, where he would find boats, ammunition, and men—the Spanish forces in America are non-existent at this time, and they have not a single man of talent.[10]

How the French or Burr himself could have taken this plan seriously is hard to say. Burr's adherents at the time of his arrest on his way down the Mississippi River to New Orleans in 1807 numbered only 50 to 100 men and women, traveling on ten small flatboats, as the French must have known. The idea that Burr, whom many in America still considered a traitor despite his acquittal in the 1807 Richmond trial, could raise thousands of men to liberate Mexico must have struck the French as wildly improbable. Furthermore, Napoleon had already written off the western hemisphere. As Napoleon stated to his ministers of the colonies and treasury at the time of the Louisiana Purchase in 1803, France could not match the British navy: "Our national glory will never come from our marine." War with Great Britain was about to resume, and effective control of Louisiana would be threatened by the British navy: "I must expect to lose it." The British had twenty ships in the Gulf of Mexico, "whilst our affairs in St. Domingue [Haiti] have been growing worse every day since the death of Leclerc [the French general who had failed to put down the Haitian revolt]."[11]

Although the American negotiators had come to Paris in 1803 with a brief only to acquire New Orleans, Napoleon told his ministers, "Irresolution and deliberation are no longer in season. I renounce Louisiana. It is not only New Orleans that I will cede, it is the whole colony [the vast western watershed of the Mississippi River] without any reservation. I know the price of what I abandon…. I renounce it with the greatest regret. To attempt obstinately to retain it would be a folly. I direct you to negotiate this affair with the envoys of the United States. Do not even wait the arrival of Mr. Monroe: have an interview this very day with Mr. Livingston. I want fifty millions and for less than that I will not treat…. I require money to make war on the richest nation of the world."

From 1803 to 1810, when Burr was meeting with undersecretary Roux, British naval superiority over France had increased, and Britain had initiated a campaign to oust Napoleon's army from Spain. A harebrained naval and military adventure in the western hemisphere led by Burr was the last scheme designed to appeal to Napoleon. In addition to the military offensives, a sequence of domestic events was precipitating a very severe economic crisis in France at this time. Historian Colin Jones observes that, "This mixed in an old style subsistence crisis due to harvest failures especially in 1811, with a more commercial and financial one. The industrial and commercial problems were very much the result of the failure of Napoleon's Continental System, the attempt to keep British goods out of Europe. There was growing unemployment and by 1812 the spike of high prices prefigured in 1811" (personal conversation, April 12, 2012).

The Holland Land Company Stock Speculation[12]

While in Paris, Burr pinned his most enduring financial hopes on a plan to speculate in the stock of the Holland Land Company (HLC). This Dutch company acquired several millions of acres, an area larger than Connecticut, in western New York and Pennsylvania from American financier Robert Morris in 1792. But HLC was unable to settle Indian claims to the land until 1797, the year in which the real estate bubble in Western lands burst, also the year in which Robert Morris was clapped into debtors' prison, where he remained for three and a half years. Unable to resell this Western land wholesale, the Holland Land Company proceeded to sell it off in small parcels to settlers from New England and Europe over the next forty years.

Investors (primarily Dutch) in the company held both its bonds and, following a recapitalization in 1796, an issue of stock. The price of the stock, traded on the Amsterdam stock exchange, had fallen drastically, by almost 90 percent, from its 1796 issue price to its all-time low in September 1810, the month in which Burr first mentioned a plan to speculate on what he correctly believed would be an increase in value of the stock. Burr was engrossed in the stock scheme and mentioned it many times in his journal. He never explicated how the scheme was supposed to work, although an explanation pieced together from what he said is possible and follows below. Of equal interest, however, are Burr's mood swings from day to day as his progress in this affair was alternately frustrated and advanced. Two entries four days apart are illustrative. On January 12, 1811, he recorded, "Thinking of other things as I walked, got to the Pantheon without thinking where I was going. I then stood some minutes to discover who I was; in what country I was; what business I had there; for what I came abroad, and where I intended to go."

As usual Burr's despondency was short-lived. In line with his resilient, Micawberish philosophy that "something will turn up," four days later, on January 16, Burr had found several associates willing to advance him money to buy Holland Land Company shares and to split with him the anticipated profits of resale. His spirits soared: "Now, if I can get a passport to Bremen and Amsterdam, I will send you [Theodosia] a million of francs within six months; but one-half of it must be laid out in pretty things. Oh, what beautiful things I will send you! Gampillo, too, shall have a beautiful little watch, and at least fifty trumpets of different sorts and sizes. Home at 10 and have been casting up my millions and spending it. Lord, how many people I have made happy!"

Speculation

The HLC speculation depended on contingencies beyond Burr's control, for example, obtaining a passport to Amsterdam; persuading American friends in Paris to advance him money to buy HLC shares; persuading the Dutch directors of the company to sell previously authorized shares; buying those shares in a timely fashion while the stock price was still low; and then exploiting a hoped-for quick rise in price so he could sell at a profit. It is not surprising that in the midst of extreme uncertainty over the outcome of this speculative venture, Burr acted on many occasions in accordance with his biographer Nancy Isenberg's insight that "sex was one of the few things he could control," including an occasion on January 15, the day before Burr "spent" his imaginary millions of francs:

> It was that pretty Clotilde of whom something was said six months ago. All remonstrance was in vain. I have no money. "No matter, I have." Passed two hours very pleasantly.... I had, indeed, a crown (5 francs) which on parting I offered; but it was refused as an indignity. "I'm not a Parisian woman [i.e., not mercenary?].

Regarding the HLC, Burr wrote that his stock speculation scheme was founded on "things known to me alone." In July 1810, at a Paris library, Burr came across "news, which, I find, is of some consequence to me, if, indeed, anything be of any consequence." It may well be that this news related to the initial funding by the New York legislature in the spring of 1810 of a commission to explore a route for the Erie Canal, connecting the Hudson River to Lake Erie, a canal which would open a vast market for crops and goods produced by future settlers on the HLC properties in western New York. In September 1810, Burr apparently decided that the company's share prices, then being quoted on the Amsterdam stock market at an all-time low, didn't properly reflect the Erie Canal news.

Burr's journal contains enough clues to show his awareness that any major purchases of HLC's thinly traded stock on the Amsterdam market would drive up the share price too quickly. So instead, in the spring of 1811—by which time HLC's share prices had already started to rise—Burr finally secured a passport to travel to Amsterdam, taking along substantial funds he had raised in Paris, with a view to persuading the Dutch directors of the company to issue to him previously authorized shares at the current market price. Burr evidently believed that the share price would continue to rise, and he may well have had in mind actively boosting the value of any shares he ended up buying by hyping the Erie Canal news for all it was worth. But, in line with all his other schemes, his mission to Amsterdam failed—the Dutch directors of the HLC refused to even meet with him. Burr's financial disappointment may have been mitigated somewhat by his amorous success with a Madame D he encountered on his trip to Holland, a lady whom we meet in a later chapter.

The HLC affair was another case of Burr's being vindicated in the long run. Ground was not broken on the Erie Canal until 1817 and the canal was not completed until 1825. The canal did eventually greatly increase the value of HLC's land holdings, and by 1836, the year of Burr's death, HLC share prices reached their all-time high, one hundred times greater than the September 1810 valuation at which Burr spotted a buying opportunity in Paris. So, in sum, a good example of Lord Keynes' dictum that "in the long run, we're all dead." Similarly, on receiving news in 1836 of the liberation of Texas from Mexico, Burr exclaimed, in the last year of his life, "I was only thirty years too soon! What was treason in me thirty years ago is patriotism now."

Six

Lifestyle

The military triumphs of Napoleon were over when Burr arrived in 1810. The violence of revolution had been deflected and now the emperor was consolidating his power by bread and circuses and putting his stamp on his capital. Military historian Michael Broers calls Paris "a favourite, almost pampered city," writing, "Napoleon spoiled his capital, just as he did the Imperial Guard, for they both stood close to the levers of power. During the subsistence crisis of 1810–12, he plundered the grain resources of northern France to satisfy the Parisian working classes as thoroughly and ruthlessly as he plundered the regiments of the line for recruits for the Guard."[1] These years were the period of imperial glory, the cracked golden bowl. Military sorties continued but only England remained at war with France. Even workmen could afford imported tea, coffee and sugar, and bread was at a low fixed price. The new Canal de l'Ourcy, 110 kilometers long, was supplying all of Paris's water (it would until about 1850). In 1812, Napoleon would leave for his ill-fated invasion of Russia, but for now he had it all, even an heir as of 1811.

Exhilarated at being a new nation, the Americans at this time tended to see being in Europe as a fillip to their education or development of their business but not a vastly enviable experience. The man who wanted to conquer Mexico was now in Paris, soon rigidly economizing, huddled at the fire reading *Travels in Florida, Louisiana, and the Mississippi*.

Burr had trouble regulating his sleeping, drinking, and eating. He was never a big drinker but now he and a friend would order two bottles of wine between them, and he was sleeping it off the next morning. He sought order by bringing himself and his personal habits up short in his journal. He couldn't resist buying books for Theodosia but was making ever-new attempts to economize. He claimed he engaged a barber because the barber's arrival got him up and going in his day. Meanwhile, Burr's life was bifurcated between the misery of dependency on the goodwill of near-strangers for money and other assistance and the excitement of the great European capital.

Frequently Burr harked back to descriptions of his lodging. The first room he took was but 14 feet square, with a brick floor, up two flights of narrow stairs. Eventually he moved to the first floor to a superior, larger room. Finding the big fireplace didn't supply adequate heat, he described putting in a new fireplace. Still the heat was inadequate. In France, a two-star hotel is today a typical businessman's hotel, no frills, and this is apparently the sort of establishment in which Burr stayed. The initial address on the rue de Grenelle seemed a lively mix of restaurants, cafés and shops. Later, in the fall of 1810, he moved to a new address, boarding with a Swiss family, the Peloughs, on the rue de Croissant near the Palais Royal. He lived frugally as before. The room was as cramped as the other one, and he wrote that, no problem, he could reach everything without moving.

Burr went about outfitting himself to make his social calls. He broke a spring in his false teeth and went to the dentist for a new set. He forgot his umbrella or didn't take it along. He lost his hat. He took long walks. These are the homely notations of a solitary person getting by alone.

Used to a gentleman's life, Burr tried to establish a state in Paris where he had amenities enough to sustain good cheer. This chapter focuses on his comfort, apparel, and health, all related to his personal lifestyle. In a later chapter, we look at the situation of public lighting as well as water and sanitation, the basic amenities of daily life.

First of all, what level of comfort did Burr expect and what was his concept of comfort? A Canadian historian, John E. Crowley, has studied the concept of comfort in the period around 1800 and is enlightening on Burr's expectations concerning the "mod cons," the modern conveniences of that time.

Small Conveniences
by John E. Crowley[2]

In November 1795, upon returning to his Norfolk home from London, the Reverend James Woodforde noted this: "We drank tea, supped and slept at our comfortable quiet, happy, thatched dwelling." Over the forty-five years he kept his diary, from 1758 to 1802, Woodforde carefully analyzed his physical comforts and discomforts. For example, he assessed, as Aaron Burr would, the quality of his sleep: "Very ill indeed today having had a very indifferent night of rest last night, owing to the night candle filling the room in being so long going out with intolerable smoke and stink." He not only recorded when he was too hot or too cold but also verified his subjective impressions with thermometer readings. He noted whether he used bedwarmers. The minutiae of his reporting on comfort included the use of an umbrella on numerous rainy days. He noted almost daily what type of meat he ate for dinner.[3]

Woodforde's attention to comfort poses a historical problem precisely because its standards seem so similar to those of Anglo-Americans since his time: how natural is the desire for physical comfort? His catalogue of basic physical comforts could confirm the commonsense retort to the claims of relativism, that people over time are basically similar, whereas in fact, anthropologists have found that technology, social structures, and belief systems dictate widely varying designs in domestic environments.

Physical comfort—self-conscious satisfaction with the relationship between one's body and its immediate physical environment—was an innovative aspect of the society of Great Britain and its colonies, one that had to be taught and learned. During the eighteenth century, Anglo-Americans used the word "comfort" with increasing frequency to express their satisfaction and enjoyment with immediate physical circumstances. This usage indicated a disposition to criticize traditional material culture and to improve it. When Thomas Jefferson in 1785 described most Virginians' housing as "impossible to devise things more ugly, uncomfortable, and happily more perishable," he was applying a set of values that his neighbors had apparently ignored or resisted. Similarly, a few years later, Jefferson's former compatriot Benjamin Thompson, Count Rumford, recommended the technical virtues of his design for chimney fireplaces by appealing to "those who have feeling enough to be made miserable by anything careless, slovenly, and wasteful, which happens under their eyes, who know what comfort is."[4] Jefferson's and Rumford's new emphasis on comfort anticipated a new material culture.

For centuries, "comfort" had primarily meant moral, emotional, spiritual, and political support in difficult circumstances. To be "comfortless" had meant being "without anything to allay misfortune," and "discomfort" involved feelings of "sorrow," "melancholy," and "gloom" rather than physical irritability. The word comfort was almost invariably in reference to providential blessings. The eighteenth-century consumer revolution brought a new emphasis on physical comfort. Theories of political economy in the first half of the century made comfort a legitimizing motive for popular consumption patterns. By the middle of the century, the imperatives of physical comfort had focused scientific and technological expertise on more amenable designs of the domestic environment. By the last decades of the eighteenth century, the ideal of physical comfort had sufficient ideological force for humanitarians to incorporate it in their appeals for social justice towards the poor, the incarcerated, and the enslaved. By the turn of the nineteenth century, comfort was asserted as a right of the unprivileged and a humanitarian responsibility of the propertied. The language of comfort gave meaning to a consumer revolution in Anglo-American society, as more people had more money to spend on more goods.

What was previously an oxymoron, David Hume's "innocent luxury," had become a topic for reform-minded analysis by political economists, social commentators, and scientists. Among mid-century philosophes, Benjamin Franklin showed the most explicit interest in the history, anthropology, and science of basic household comforts, and he committed himself to closing the gap between the ideals and the technology of comfort. He promoted spermaceti candles for their steady, clean illumination; he suggested self-experiments to show how increased ventilation improved sleeping; and after his invention of a "Pennsylvanian Fire-place," his name synonymous with smoke-free and draft-free heating. In Pennsylvania, Franklin could consider a range of ethnic alternatives in domestic comfort. He was particularly attentive to the Dutch and German stoves that entirely enclosed the fire and were used only for heating. Such stoves reduced drafts because the only air going up the chimney was that introduced to the firebox from outside the room being heated.

Franklin contrasted the efficient, clean heat of these stoves with that provided by the two fireplace types among English colonists, a traditional design with high, wide, and deep hearths and a "newer-fashion'd" style with "low Breasts, and narrow Hearths" for new and remodeled urban housing. In "the large open Fire-places used in the Days of our Fathers, and still generally in the Country, and in Kitchens," people could warm themselves by sitting within the hearth itself. But such fireplaces had a long list of "inconveniences" by Franklin's standards. The need to provide a draft from an outside door made it impossible for them to heat an entire room. These traditional fireplaces exposed people to the fire with a directness characteristic of the open central hearth of the European peasantry. With their smaller chimney face, the new fireplaces were less smoky, and they did not need an open door to supply air for combustion. But they still drew room air for combustion, through all the small openings in the walls. Franklin argued that these more intense drafts posed greater health risks than the slower entry of large volumes of air to the older fireplaces. Genteel fireplaces were cleaner but not significantly more warming than the traditional fireplaces; their chief advantage was suitability to elegant living, not physical comfort.

Franklin identified himself with participants in an enlightened subculture who criticized fashionable domestic priorities in the name of comfort. For them, the fireplace itself as a source of heat became the object of scientifically sophisticated innovation. Rather than leave such everyday technical problems aside after he established a transatlantic scientific reputation, Franklin went on to become the foremost authority on smoky chimneys. He took no offense when Hume's cousin, Lord Kames, wrote him for advice on such a mundane matter as smoky chimneys in a new house. "I have long been of an opinion similar to that you express," Franklin replied, "and think happiness consists more in small conveniences or pleasures that occur every day, than in great pieces of good fortune that happen but seldom to a man in the course of his life."[5]

By 1800, Anglo-American social thought had naturalized the desire for physical comfort. The mature work of Thomas Malthus represented and synthesized the invention of comfort in material culture and social thought: the indeterminability of distinctions between necessity and luxury, the acceptance of popular consumption patterns, the benevolent impulse to establish minimal entitlements to comfort, and the demonstrability of respectable family life by comfortable domestic environments. Between the first edition of *An Essay on the Principle of Population* in 1793 and the second in 1803, largely as a result of his travels comparing English living conditions with those elsewhere in Europe, Malthus came to the realization that a desire for comfort and convenience was crucial to the "moral restraint" that allowed sufficient control over the principle of population to maintain happiness in a society. Malthus's image of the comforts of English life came straight out of genre representations of happy cottagers: "a good meal, a warm house, and a comfortable fireside in the evening." The desire for such comforts, wrote Malthus, "put in motion the greatest part of that activity, from which spring the multiplied improvements and advantages of civilized life."[6]

Comfort had become a set of expectations, physical designs, and personal imperatives.

His Apparel

Burr wrote Theodosia from Gothenburg, Sweden, on May 5, 1809, that he was detained over the matter of the loss of his baggage, and "my whole wardrobe is gone. Rather awkward for one without money and without an acquaintance." In this era, one's good clothes were part of one's material wealth, and a man's tailoring attested to his breeding. "Ready-made" had begun around the time of Burr's youth, while the clothing of a New York sophisticate like Burr was bespoke.[7] It must have been trying for him to be meeting new people and going new places with just the clothes he had worn on the sea voyage (acceptable by day but lacking for more formal occasions). Characteristically, Burr minimized the adversity to

Theodosia. It is certain that in 1810 and 1811 in Paris he was wearing clothes made on the Continent. Even in the assaults on his character it was never indicated he appeared less than a gentleman. Thus, he invested in decent clothes even when he had so little money and they would have been correct to the last detail. He was also middle-aged and from the democratic country of America, and he joked about having to rent a hat—a chapeau de bras, or the flat version of a cornered hat—and sword for a reception at a French dignitary's. (Benjamin Franklin had called the Latin language the chapeau de bras of high culture, carried by a man of fashion under his arm even though the wig made it superfluous.)

In 1810 Paris, you could tell if a man was fashionable and correct. However, appearing dandified, like the ultra-sheer, classically pure, all-white female style, had vanished: male fashion was finding new footing after the revolution. Now a man's outfit emphasized his shape, not the luxuriousness of the fabric. According to Brenda Rosseau, supervisor of research and design at Colonial Williamsburg, "In 1810 the cut of men's clothes changed significantly. Tails separated from the coat and became two pieces, and a new seam at the waistline meant the waistline was not just shaped but cut and nipped in" (personal communication, January 10, 2014). In February 1805, the novelist Stendhal, 23, described in a letter his attire as "never more brilliant": "I was wearing a black waistcoat, black silk breeches and stockings, with a cinnamon-bronze coat, a very well-tied cravat, a superb shirt-front. Never, I believe, was my ugliness more effaced by my general appearance.... I looked a very handsome man, after the style of Talma [the actor]." Alistair Horne commented that dressed as he was, Stendhal "could also have paraded down St. James's without being taken for a French spy."

Now that a more sober elegance reigned, there would have been nothing flashy about Burr's attire. He wore a swallowtail coat of fine wool (dark green, blue or brown) with tails to the back of the knees and light-colored breeches fastened by steel buckles, or trousers (which were a dominant item by the 1820s) of lighter color. His white linen shirt had an attached collar (saved on laundering), higher in the back, and a nice white neck cloth that he may have called his cravat. The cravat was of a finer fabric than the shirt and up to three yards in length. Both the shirt down the neck opening and the cravat were ruffled and perhaps pleated, the cravat neatly tied and immaculate. Burr probably had several waistcoats, from plain to dressy. The waistcoat was his most decorative apparel; a fine waistcoat was cashmere or silk, with the collar raised spiffily at the back. He doesn't mention gloves as accessories but he probably had kid gloves and his watch chain showed visibly from the little oblong pocket on his waistcoat front. (He mentioned that he had two watches, one big and one small, in Gothenburg, even though the luggage was lost,

Portrait of François Joseph Talma in Paris (1810) by Rembrandt Peale (1778–1860). Burr agreed with popular opinion that the tragedian Talma (1763–1826) was the greatest actor in Paris. Here Talma was about 47 years of age. Peale did the pencil drawing on his second visit to Paris in 1809–1810 (courtesy Walters Art Museum).

which suggests he carried them on his person.) Attached to the watch chain was a key to wind his watch and perhaps a seal bearing his personal mark.

His shoes were black leather with low heels and steel buttons. He wore them when visiting a lady (that was de rigueur), but he was as likely to wear boots. Since he noted repairing, losing, and finding umbrellas and mentions the hatter's only to rent a hat—certainly a chapeau-bras (a big two-cornered hat) or a more formal get-up—it may be he did not wear a hat in general. He was clean-shaven and shaved himself. As the ponytail for men was out of fashion, he wore his now sparse hair short.

The sobriety of Burr's attire as civilian contrasted greatly to the attire of the Hussars in town. While the distinctive feature of a foot soldier's uniform was tasseled boots that curved up towards the knee in front and the rest of it was plain, the cavalry's uniforms were furnished with frogs, braids, cords, velvet trim, and fancy buttons, coupled with the plumes and metal of headgear. These uniforms were to attract not women but more men to the military, as the number for Napoleon's army was continuously short. As for the new courtiers, in official dress they were as sumptuous as ever under the Ancien Régime. That the basic look (which varied for administrators, judges, and professors) was designed by Jean-Baptiste Isabey was like having a uniform designed not by Ralph Lauren but by Yves St. Laurent. For instance, Marshal Berthier, Napoleon's chief of staff, had uniforms in hunter green velvet, blue velvet and purple silk, while Marshal Bertrand, who followed Napoleon to Saint Helena, was gorgeous in an amaranthine (deep red purple) uniform.

The clothing scene of a gentleman was cosmopolitan, Brenda Rosseau, explains:

> Clothing production took off about 1800, especially with the advent of cotton. But England was still making the wool outerwear and Lyons in France was the major industrial center for silk. It was a very complex market economy. Burr, an American abroad, might be having breeches of leather from South Carolina, a French or English silk waistcoat, and a coat from the U.K. made up wherever he had it tailored. Many factors—occupation, locality, age, and personal choice—determined his dress. For example, Thomas Jefferson, who fancied himself everyman, as he considered himself a democratic American, met the British ambassador while in the White House in a wrapping gown not formal attire, and answered the door himself. I think Aaron Burr would have had a business attire of three-piece suit—breeches, long or short, vest and coat, with shirt and cravat, and would have worn shoes for visits and boots for riding. He wanted to make a good impression and dress correctly in a modern look.

An emphasis on a man's form, no wigs, use of long-lasting wool, and the fact that he could dispense with a costly overcoat favored the poor, dignified visitor in Paris. As costume historians Cristina Barreto and Martin Lancaster write, "Attitudes changed in this period.... Men became more virile, practical and democratic and their clothing reflects this. Men's fashions had a standard of dress that made it difficult to tell the difference between the simple inhabitant of a small town and the high-ranking men of London or Paris. For the first time gentlemen were not judged by what they wore but by how they wore it."

The Status Accessory

The time has come to talk of Burr and watches. According to Sabine Kegel, the Swiss expert who heads the international Watches and Wristwatches Department of Christie's, "In the early 19th century they were absolutely unaffordable for the larger public, a pure luxury object and status symbol in Europe, Asia and America, with the wealthier owning the more elaborate, complicated and decorated examples." Sometimes Burr appears to have been a Mad Hatter, going to and fro for watches. They were signally important to him, in the same league as books. In December 1810, he was "haunted all day and all this evening by the watch and ring." And he had this to say: "Restless. Dreaming of the watch. Caught thief; battles. Alas! All dreams; the watch irrevocably gone." He was accustomed to beautiful things and shopped in the upper echelon, at least for Theodosia's watch: "To Bonnet's, from whom I had a note this morning, telling me he was sic. We had consultation about your watch, which I perceive will ruin me; and to enhance the evil, have got another whim in my head which will add several Louis to the cost, i.e., to enamel the other side the picture of F."

As for purchasing a fine watch, this wasn't as simple as going to a shop and choosing one. The journal entries in July 1811 mark several stages of the enameling of a watch for Theodosia: twice taking along Vanderlyn to the enameler's—"He will make a horrid thing, and I fear you will be little pleased, except with my endeavors to please you." Another time he went just to look at progress. In a single day, he made two watch-related trips: "To Badolet's to get the case of your watch to the enamel head. Tired, for this cursed disease weakens me. Took ab. And to the enameller's to give him the watch-case." He also noted when he picked up his "silver repeater" from a watchmaker named Bonnet for seven Louis.

Jean-Antoine Lépine (1720–1814) was 90 when Burr visited him in Paris. Lépine was the maker of the watch he lost and, since it was an expensive watch, Burr was very upset about its loss, but he also had more than one watch. Sabine Kegel notes, "At this time, Paris was one of the centers of pocket watches. Some of the most elaborate watches made in Paris, Switzerland, London and elsewhere in Europe were also for export to China or Turkey. These were highly enameled and sometimes had precious stones and particularly those for China often complex automata."

Burr had a watch made for either Theodosia or his grandson and he wanted John Vanderlyn to paint a miniature of his 1802 Theodosia portrait for it. Burr wrote that he had to sell several items such as coins he had collected for Theodosia and "Gampy" to have the funds to make it home. It seems unlikely he would have parted with any portrait depicting his daughter.

The leading watchmaker of the day, Abraham-Louis Breguet (1747–1823), was in his sixties and also living in Paris. He had his shop on the quai de l'Horloge on the Ile de la Cité, where he employed outstanding watchmakers as opposed to just apprentices. Breguet was from a family of Protestants who had fled to Switzerland after the revocation of the Edict of Nantes in 1675. His stepfather came from a family of watchmakers and had a showroom in Paris. By 15, Abraham showed his talent and was apprenticed to the master watchmaker in Versailles, a center for the craft. Sabine Kegel calls him the Father of Horlogerie: "Breguet invented nearly everything that the pocket watches are and that is still in use in watches today. His firm still exists. He invented the tourbillon, the perpetuelle, or self-winder, and the overcoil. He perfected the level of ruby for the escarpment. His watches were very individualized."

Breguet made a famous watch for Marie Antoinette (not completed until around 1802) and he was marked for the guillotine during the Reign of Terror. Luckily, he was a friend of the radical journalist and revolutionary Jean-Paul Marat. Breguet had been with Marat at the house of a mutual friend when an angry crowd gathered outside shouting, "Down with Marat!" Breguet dressed up Marat like an old woman and they left the house arm in arm, unharmed. The clientele for Breguet watches included Napoleon and Josephine, Tsar Alexander, and the Duke of Wellington.

According to Sabine Kegel:

> The pocket watches were more accurate than the modern wristwatch. They are also fairly robust, not as delicate as one would think.
>
> The repeating mechanism was useful at night and also something to show off when the owner pulled out his watch. It would tell the hour—"Now it's two—ding, ding" or give the hours and quarter-hours as well, so for 2:15, "ding-ding, ding-dong." The very complicated examples even indicated the minutes, so for 2:20 it would be ding-ding (for the two passed hours), ding-dong (for one passed quarter), and ding-ding-ding-ding-ding for the five passed minutes after the quarter. Some of the watches featured also calendars including moon faces, the cases with engravings, enameling, pearl or precious stone setting.
>
> The production of the watch involved specialists in the different stages. There was someone who made the movement, the casemaker or jeweler, the enamellist who made the white enamel then usual for the face, and sometimes an artist who enameled a miniature painting at a final stage. This was done on a plate that fit into the gold case.

A gentleman had his pocket watch on a little chain and it went into a gilet, or waistcoat. It might sit on a stand on his desk as well. The pocket watch was an object of theft and could be damaged by rain, so a person took great care of it. When, in *Les Enfants du Paradis*, Arletty is accused of stealing a watch from a bourgeois bystander of the mime, this was a crime of taking something of great value. (The mime shows how the true thief slipped his fingers into a vest pocket and made off with the pocket watch, the act having nothing to do with the pretty spectator Arletty.)

Umbrellas Lost and Found

Europeans traveling to Persia had brought back the idea of protecting themselves from the sun with a parasol ("against the sun"). Ladies favored dainty parasols to shade their complexions and complement their fashions, and as a result, men in England shied away from umbrellas until nearly 1800. In New York, Burr, as a cosmopolitan person with places to go and people to see, would have used an umbrella before 1810. In Paris, a person above working class walked in the street with an umbrella if rain threatened. Sheltered by his umbrella, Burr could avoid traffic and the muck of the street and hug to the buildings, heedless of the projecting spouts and wooden or metal shop signs that would send a rush of rain and dirty water not onto his person but instead onto the umbrella.

Sometimes Burr went out without an umbrella and the weather changed: "A brilliant morning. Sun shining bright for this hemisphere. Went out without my umbrella. Before I got one hundred yards it began to rain. Went back for the umbrella. At 10 to Fonzi's, and there till 1. Home. At 2 to Vanderlyn's, by appointment. On the way called to leave note in reply to Fenwick, who being at home and alone, sat a few minutes. Found Vanderlyn engaged, and asked me to call in ½ hour; during that half hour amused myself by walking in the rain and a most tempestuous wind." He makes a little self-deprecating joke of his issue with umbrellas—an opportunity to tell his journal and, in his mind, his daughter that he is resilient: "On coming out from the St. Pelasgie it rained very hard. I had no paraplui, and

Umbrella seller, flower seller, mattress carder and bellows seller, an engraving from *Costumes of Paris Through the Centuries*. The four figures are represented plying their trades in the center of the city. The umbrella seller and bellows seller were tradesmen Burr sought out (Bibliothèque des Arts Décoratifs, Paris; photograph credit: Gianni Dagli Orti/Art Archive at Art Resource, New York).

was resolved not to take coach if one had offered. Got home wet to the skin from head to foot. Jul. made me a good fire, for my chimney was reformed a little. Changed clothes. Caf. Blanc, and am quite refreshed."

An umbrella was worth repairing and all too easy to lose, especially in July: "Left my new umbrella at that confounded ventriloquist's and am sure shall never see it again." And the following day, "My umbrella is lost; lost 32 francs. Paid for our ice-creams 3 francs." On the other hand, he found one about two weeks later that wasn't his: "To near Luxembourg to get an umbrella which some one, unknown, left...." When the rain stops, an umbrella can be forgot. Burr's absentmindedness about his umbrella may have stemmed from the fact that the practice of carrying one was not engrained in his youth. And yet, when he had none, someone else's turned up in his room, because he was in Paris, where the rain umbrella had been introduced in Europe and was ubiquitous.

His umbrellas had jointed ribs so as to fold back, were self-opening, and had a slide and catch like present-day ones. A ring joined the ribs at the top and a second ring over that was for carrying or suspending the umbrella. There were probably eight ribs and the umbrella was smaller than today, about 28 inches across, but with a longer handle. It was made of oiled silk, glazed cotton or alpaca, and the ribs were of whalebone or possibly steel.

The ribs tended to crack after continual exposure to rain (tempered steel would become the ubiquitous skeleton of a next generation of umbrellas), and one had to shake out one's umbrella to open it because the fabric stuck together.[8]

George Washington is not visualized walking and holding up an umbrella, yet in March 1794, while living in a rented house in Philadelphia during his second presidential term, he paid for "mending an umbrella to be kept at the door."[9] Umbrellas had been introduced to Paris from Persia, then to England. That the French led in the use of umbrellas is evident from the fact that General (then Lieutenant Colonel) James Wolfe wrote from Paris in 1752 that people there used umbrellas for sun and rain, and he wondered why the practice did not obtain in England. The French manufacturer Jean Marius had developed the first umbrella that folded, marketing it as a "pocket umbrella." When around that time a Doctor Jonas Hanway (1712–86), who had seen similar devices in Persia and Italy, began to tote an umbrella, his habit was mocked as effeminate. Detractors, when they saw him with his umbrella, met him with, "Frenchman, Frenchman! Why don't you call a coach?" English gentlemen were referring to their umbrellas as a "Hanway" but the French with precision called the lady's version a parasol and the men's rainy day version a parapluie.

Benjamin Franklin, who preceded Burr in Paris, gained pop star status in the French scientific community. Jacques Barbeau-Dubourg, a physician who admired Franklin, translated some of his early works and published them in his medical journal. The two men also maintained a correspondence. Following in Franklin's footsteps, Barbeau-Dubourg designed the remarkable "umbrella-lightning" rod, fitted with a tall spike and a chain that trailed to the ground.[10] He also invented a "chronographic machine," now in the Rare Books Division of Princeton University, which unrolled 54 feet of famous historical persons and events (the doctor's handwritten notations included, for instance, Franklin's 1752 kite experiment).

The Portable Lightning Rod, or the Umbrella-Lighting Rod of Barbeu-Dubourg. The spike and trailing chain were supposed to draw away electricity in this invention by Dr. Barbeu-Dubourg, Franklin's translator and admirer (Album/Art Resource, New York).

Boots That Fit and Fit In

An understanding of Burr's boots in Paris come from D.A. Saguto, the shoemaking archaeologist at Colonial Williamsburg, who has written a specialized history of shoemaking in the 18th century that centers on *L'Art du Cordonnier* (Art of the Shoemaker) by M. de Garsault, 1767. This work was the basis for shoemaking treatises well into the 19th century, and shows that the period when Burr was in Paris was a "high-water mark" for traditional methods, before assembly-line mechanization. According to Colonial Williamsburg bootmaker Al Saguto:

> Burr may have started out from New York with one kind of footwear and in Paris worn another—the shorter boots fashion called for. This was a period of upheaval and a big change in fashion ensued. The big change in boots was a shift from the "close" or "top" boot with a stocking-like fit, ending just below the knee and worn with knee breeches, over to the "Hessian" or "Austrian boot" (in the U.S. called the "Suvorov" or Swarrow) with longer pantaloons that came into wear during the Napoleonic Wars. The military image has ever appealed romantically to men and Count Suvorov was the Russian general famed for never losing a battle. That shift started in the 1790s and continued through the teens of the next century until the "top" boots with their contrasting colored "top" (in shades of tan, brown, white or Beau Brummelesque "champagne and peach marmalade"—or even black over black) the style George Washington's in portraits elegantly wore were seen no more....
>
> Burr may have left America and top boots and got to England and France and jumped on the new styles. The cut was completely different. The new boots were shorter ending below the knee, seamed-up each side, often scalloped at the top, and some were decorated with silk tassels at the top. There was an accompanying revolution in men's clothing styles overall, as the knee-breeches ceded to pantaloons and eventually to long trousers [personal communications, November 2013].

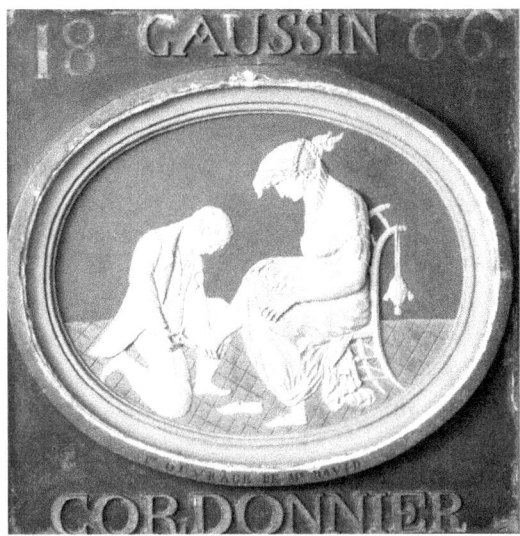

Shop sign of Caussin the cobbler by David d'Angers (Pierre-Jean). Shop signs were one of the most decorative elements of 19th century Paris, this fine one being from Angers, the historical capital of Anjou southwest of Paris (copyright Musees d'Angers, photograph by P. David).

Boots were for riding horses until it became fashionable to wear equestrian style dress while on foot. Walking in tall boots came into fashion shortly after the American Revolution. The Hessian, or Hussar, boots were copied from the flamboyant uniform dress of the Hussar regiments in armies of the day. The style had originated with the 16th-century Polish Winged Hussars, shock troops who wore colorful, soft, mid-calf boots with scalloped tops. According to the Colonial Williamsburg bootmaker,

> "They were seen as foreign and exotic at first. The English were slow to adopt foreigners' ethnic styles. Although there were Hussar units in the British army throughout the 18th century, the civilians had their own national style—the English 'top boot.' When the side-seamed wrinkly little Hessian/Hussar boot was adopted in England, they were at first derided as inelegant and clumsy compared to the close-fitting top boot, and popularized by trendy military officers. The gentleman who wore these new boots didn't care whether he owned a horse or not. They cost almost half as much as a cheap horse in Virginia—up to four or five times the price of a shoe."

This was a good reason why Burr would have taken good care of his pair.

Boots were the most telltale feature of the clothes of a proper gentleman. Burr went from a close boot to the looser-fitting styles. He likely skipped the more extreme version of Hessian boots popular in England—with showy scallops and tassels. In any event, the style of men's boots, as did the practice of making them, varied (sometimes in the smallest details) from one country or region of Europe to another. The French boot would have been recognized as such in England or Germany, for instance, by its leather and the way the heels were sewed on. There was no uniform "Continental style," says Saguto. "Fashion changed by decade and altogether different styles were preferred in Paris, Berlin, or London."

By the time De Garsault wrote his treatise on shoemaking, he had compiled other treatises in the "Descriptions" series on drapery, tailoring, saddle and harness making, wig making, tennis racquet making and court keeping. The only craftsman that Garsault credited by name was "M. Soudé," a master bootmaker who by 1777 had a firm at Rue Dauphine, under the sign of a large gold boot. In 1775, Paris had 1,500 master shoemakers, each of whom had up to a dozen journeymen in their shops, plus apprentices and family members. The shoemaking guild was dissolved by the French Revolution but their number did not decrease. In this period the demand for footwear probably exceeded that of any other single article of apparel. The work for the cordonnier was strenuous and painstaking and to stay in business he and those he employed worked from dawn to nightfall.

The shoemaker was an artist. Becoming one took years of apprenticeship. When a person became a master shoe or boot maker, he didn't require patterns once he took a customer's measurements. The twain did not meet between the shoemaker and the boot maker, or the maker of ladies' shoes and the maker of men's shoes, at least not in the capital. The repairer Burr went to was another craftsperson. For example, the seams might weaken or the bottoms wear thin. The boot maker had dozens of tools to do his craft, and he worked with varieties of leather, thread, and wax. The seams of the boots were most critical to strengthen a pair of boots. Garsault describes waxing a thick thread, tipped with a wild boar bristle for a needle, with a ball of rosin melted with tallow. The spinning of thread for constructing shoes and boots was specialized work for female spinners.

On Boots

by Al Saguto[11]

The urban shoe-scape for men was predominantly boots by 1810. The *incroyables*[12] had worn shiny riding boots, the military wore stiff boots and the fashion was shifting from one style of boot to another at this at this time. A fashionably booted gentleman showed a narrow, long, tight-fitting boot—this was the elegant foot. Enameled leather—now called patent leather—made a debut in Paris in 1800, though patented by Peal in London in the 1790s. The boots were polished; having no servant, Burr polished his own.

In England when Burr had visited was the height of Beau Brummel's social prominence. Born in the middle class the son of an ambitious father, Brummel went to Eton and Cambridge and led the fashion away from dingy neckties and breeches with white cotton stockings to fancy snowy white cravats, long black coats and light-colored tight trousers. Beau

Brummell was lampooned for polishing his black boots with a concoction called "vin de champagne"—champagne and marmalade: "My top-boots, those unerring marks of a blade—With champagne are polished, and peach marmalade."

Napoleon wanted to set the style in dress as in everything else. Boots at this time took their names from military figures or had military association, and they definitely looked the part. In Paris there were the Hessian boot, the guard boot, and the top boot, all from the 18th century; but there were also a number of newer boots, such as the Murat and the hunting boot. Napoleon wore the military guard boot high over the knee and cut out lower in back. The shorter boot was worn under trousers, which were replacing breeches in Paris—the trousers often of light neutral colors and of drill or nankeen.

In Paris, Burr found in vogue, and probably bought, Hessian or Suvorov boots because in wartime people dress more macho. These boots were of calfskin. As they were for urban wear, he wouldn't have wanted too military a look or to wear boots like Napoleon. Some of the French were imitating the English dandies with their black dress coats and shiny riding boots, but as Burr didn't have an overcoat he would have worn the more military-looking Hessians. Lower-cut and looser fitting than top boots, Hessians were lighter in weight and more suited to walking than the firmer style. Style, comfort and durability were all important to Burr, and a good pair of Hessians were nice, light, and low.

He bought boots in Paris and kept them in good shape by having them repaired. He could have easily walked 10,000 miles in Paris, on cobblestoned, or paved, often muddy streets, and boots were his most important item of attire. He might have needed new soles and heels twice a year.

Like boots (and shoes, but not ballet slippers), Burr's boots had a left and right. Until 1600, all shoes were made left and right. When the heel came into fashion they economized with one single, symmetrically-shaped last. After 1790, "crooked" lasts became fashionable again, so the shoes and boots were made with right and left lasts, for "crooked" footwear, fitting the right or left shoe. Garsault stated that shoes changed daily from one foot to the other pinched the toes and wore out faster than if you kept them on one foot. Straight lasts were an economy for shoemakers, so that most 18th-century shoes had straight sole shapes when they were new and unworn. From 1790, matched pairs were more prevalent and were advertised in the Philadelphia newspapers as the latest thing. Soon higher priced shoes had left and right shapes; straight lasts survived mostly for the manufacture of cheaper goods up through the 1920s.

Some people wore leggings or spatterdashes of cloth when they were on foot and leather for riding. Burr took his new boots to the shoemakers for galoshes or claques. He wore claques to protect against muddy streets. Garsault describes claques or galoshes made entirely of leather and how to insert the booted foot and kick it against some hard surface to make sure it has reached the boot toe. The galoshes were made uniquely for that person's pair of boots and were intended to be removed on entering an anteroom of the apartment.

The boots Napoleon wore were named for him after his reign. This makes sense and nonsense. In her memoirs, Madame de Remusat recalled, "From his caprice or awkwardness, the entire renewal of his wardrobe was constantly necessary. Among other destructive habits, he had that of stirring the wood-fires with his foot, thereby scorching his shoes and boots.

This generally happened when he was in a passion; at such times he would violently kick the blazing logs in the nearest fireplace." The boots were tall, cut high to rise over the knee in front and cut lower behind. And like the man, they were stiff, shiny, and, naturally grandiose.

Imperial Fashion Magazines: Reflections or Models?[13]
BY CLAUDETTE JOANNIS

To follow the evolution of fashion during the consulate and empire nothing equals the fashion reviews. Towards 1770, following France's lead, fashion reviews began to spread across Europe—the *Galerie des modes et costumes François* and then the *Cabinet des Modes* started to publish plates in color, a feature that continued long after the ancien régime. Reflections of aristocratic tastes, these plates are no less the witness of changes that proceeded at a rapid pace. Created in 1797, the *Journal des dames et des modes* would be in a certain way the bible of elegance until 1830.

It was due to a priest-become-editor after the Revolution, a man named Pierre de la Mésangère, that credit can be given for the distribution and success of a magazine so important that Napoleon called it "the official monitor of fashion." The plates of the *Mésangère* (thus did one shorten the name of the journal) appeared in the magazine every five days, accompanied by texts and descriptions of the clothes reproduced. They were ordered from excellent artists like Debucourt, Horace and Carle Vernet and later Jean-Francois Bosio. Pierre de la Mésangère assiduously frequented all the public places where he might observe men and women gather: cafés, city streets, and balls (then very much in favor). Accordingly, he had an eye to note the transformations in the elegant outfits according to the seasons, hours of the day, and circumstances. This refined detective was at once an observer and an instigator, because he associated with a range of people—from the textile merchants to the linen maids—with a goal of inciting women to changes and to novelty. The color illustrations show in general one person or, at times, two persons presented frontally or from the back dressed with confident nonchalance. The models wear clothes—for a promenade, for attending a ball, or for their lives in the city—of greater or lesser finery.

The etchings of Jean-Francois Bosio (1761–1827) are particularly significant vis-à-vis the evolution of women's dress. One sees transparent and "with a long tail" clothing during the Consulate, then shorter or rounded into the Empire, while men displayed a cutaway and cloth breeches and a very high-collared shirt. Of these fashion-conscious Parisians, the merveilleuses, who were so often close to being prostitutes, wore provocative garments that caused doctors and writers of memoirs to recoil; thus Sébastien Mercier writes, "It is inconceivable how these poor girls can stay eight days in good health. They have absolutely nothing on their bodies beyond a very flimsy and perfectly clinging white dress. Very likely they don't have a chemise underneath, because if they did there would be at least a tiny fold in evidence, given they all hold up their dresses behind, hugging them against the fannies, in order to let nothing be missed of their form."

Less extravagant was the imperial fashion, which presented women dressed in long dresses with small balloon sleeves adorned with either a *décor en tablier* (embroidered

Six. Lifestyle 71

The Public Viewing David's "Coronation" at the Louvre (1810) by Louis-Léopold Boilly. In painting of the coronation, the women carry their shawls fashionably on their arms; Josephine popularized wearing shawls and Napoleon gave Marie-Louise dozens of them as one of his wedding gifts. A few who have the air of provincial tourists actually look at the painting on the wall. Oil on canvas, 24-¼ in. × 32-½ in. (61.6 × 82.6 cm) (gift of Mrs. Charles Wrightsman, 2012 [2012.156]; image copyright © Metropolitan Museum of Art; image source: Art Resource, New York).

pinafore) or a *volant* (flounce) *en ruche*. *Douillettes* (quilted dressing gowns) and redingotes inspired by the English riding coat supplied warmth to the lightly dressed, while during the Empire one wore little cloches and, for evening, long gloves. The vestimentary precious applied to any woman who wished to be elegant like the princess. In effect, as is generally admitted, Empress Josephine created the fashions, innovating by the sumptuousness of her dresses or more simply by a detail—a style of embroidery or the importance of a shawl. Women who had a more restricted budget followed the precepts of the magazines. Madame Moitte, wife of the academic sculptor Jean-Guillaume Moitte (1746–1810), left a diary for the years 1805 to 1810 that is very instructive, because Madame Moitte altered a redingote, mended her stockings, and bought fabrics, embroidery patterns and fichus from regular *fournisseurs*. Like all women beginning with the empress and ladies of the court, Madame Moitte delighted above all in muslin. This very light type of cotton was made in India and Napoleon forbade its commerce subsequent to the continental blockade in 1806. Nothing, however, stopped the muslin craze, not even the threats of the emperor, who wrote to General Junot, then governor of Paris, "Have your women take care that I am fully aware they wear dresses of English cloth [Indian muslin reached Paris by way of England]. If the wives of the high officers do not provide an example, of whom must I ask it? This is a big question, it's a question of life or death for France and England."

In effect, from the time of the Consulate in 1802, Napoleon had wanted to revitalize the French economy (moribund after the revolution), by giving priority to the Lyonnais textile industry for silk and satin for dressy clothes and linen for more ordinary clothes. He didn't tolerate disobedience and didn't hesitate to crumple and even tear the dress of a woman if he thought it to be muslin.

After the coronation in 1804 appeared in the book *Le Cérémoniel francais* the desire of the emperor in regard to costume was that it correspond to the etiquette of the ancien régime. One reads in the *Courrier des spectacles* of October 18, 1804, "You have our assurance that it is at present obligatory to ladies who present at court to be dressed only in French fabrics—velvets and satins seem both generally adopted. 'Tails' are made of them on court dresses that are a type of trained coat or mantle adapting to the dress beneath, around the hem of which rich embroidery rules. Men's costume is also fixed and to them is assigned colors and embroidery designs after the drawings of Isabey." (The painter Jean-Baptiste Isabey, who was in the service of Napoleon, had the task of making Josephine up for the coronation.)

The costume was, for men, approximately the same as during the reign of Louis XVI: an embroidered suit, white stockings and black pumps. However, in Paris the masculine dress had departed substantially and was considerably different from the outfits worn at court. In 1805, the gastronome Jean-Anthelme Brillat Savarin wrote to a friend: "You won't recognize Paris when you come. The number of coaches has doubled, each day new roads penetrate the city, and, above all, what people are wearing has changed. The fracs (swallow-tail coats) have turned into suits." And an English traveler remarked, "The unkemptness here of men contrasts with the elegance of the pretty women." The informal style, someitmes called undress, allowed for both greater comfort and a new self-expression.

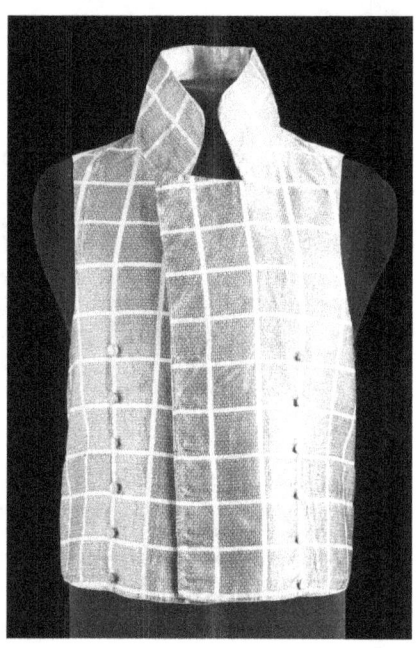

Men's vest (circa 1810). The raised collar at the back of the neck balanced the fullness of the cravat. Such a lined silk waistcoat would have been in Burr's wardrobe and this one would have accented his blue eyes (image and copyright Collection Central Museum, Utrecht).

As it is evident, during the imperial period fashion was constructed of details. For instance, the high-waisted gowns were accompanied by accessories like shawls, fichus, and hairstyles, while men exchanged the habit for the frac and the jabot for the cravat, and adopted various headgears. All these modifications are perceived in the illustrated plates of the *Mésangère*, which were propagated in Holland, England, Germany, and so forth, establishing Parisian fashion as the taste of the day.

Military Presence

In France during the Empire, artist Rembrandt Peale observed, "The whole nation rapidly assumes the appearance of a great military establishment." Peale described how, in a military revue, soldiers broke through the imperial guards to present petitions, which the emperor received "very graciously"; an aide followed him with a large bag expressly to collect them. Napoleon was victorious, but Peale predicted that even one defeat would "cure them of all their delirium."[14]

Napoleon needed hundreds of thousands of soldiers to carry out his ambitions. The conscription during the imperial era was a list of all healthy eligible males aged 18 to 25 who were called up to serve by a lottery. The affluent could purchase a substitute or replacement, as was also true in wars in other countries during that era, including America. Napoleon had captured a British fleet in the harbor of Grand Port on Isle de France (Mauritius), and his Grande Armée had advanced in Spain, conquered Seville and was pushing the British forces out from the Iberian Peninsula. Meanwhile, in Paris, the troops paraded, far from the battlefields, in formation to the war beat of drums and brass bands—spectacles created a rousing mood that drew new recruits.

Burr saw in Paris one military parade after another—elite regiments of war veterans marching in perfect martial formations or riding their mounts briskly to a drum roll. He describes going to a parade on a late afternoon in June 1811 with Fonzi, who was wearing a ribbon and star, which allowed the pair to go through a square where the troops had already passed. They found a room from which to view the parade but the window would not open. It was stuffy and the window obstructed light—which was probably why the cubby was empty in the first place. Burr had the crafty idea to bash through one of the windowpanes; they could pretend it was an accident and pay later. To his surprise, Fonzi "seized a billet of wood and enfonced [Burr's pun on Fonzi] the pane." They watched Napoleon, whom Burr identifies as "H.M.," and his suite appear, and, the journal noted, after the regiments themselves about 32 pieces of artillery each drawn by four horses "and followed by 135 carriages and wagons, with furnaces [fires to ignite the cannons], &cc, entered at one side, passed near the arcade of the Thuilleries where H.M. then stood, and out the other side. The whole exhibition was magnificent and imposing."

The troops wore either tall hats that added a foot to their height or gleaming helmets and polished black boots. The uniforms—a distinctive type for each fighting unit—had sashes, fringed epaulets and braided cord. The cuirassiers, heavily equipped to crash through the enemy's resistance, had shiny breastplates and iron and brass helmets with a visor and red or green plume. Napoleon himself often dressed as a colonel of the imperial guard, either of the *chasseurs à cheval* (green with red collar and cuffs and piping) or the foot grenadiers for dress parades and usually on Sundays (blue coat, white facings, red revers, and gold embroidered epaulettes). With whichever uniform, he wore a bicorn hat, usually black (worn sideways on the battlefields), and his Legion of Honor sash. He didn't care when his attire during a campaign got bedraggled: this signified a token identification with the battle-scarred soldiers, who were often ordered on forced march. The showiest unit of the parade was the Lancers of the Guard, dressed in white pants and long red coats and wearing red tall square hats with black visors and gold ornaments. The uniforms had complete military chic, down to the detail of a V of silver or gold buttons on the tunic. The regimental standards bore the number of the unit written in gold in the middle of a braided laurel, and banners tied to a pole had the eagle, symbol of the empire. Each regiment had its own brass band.

Captain Jean-Roch Coignet, a patriotic warrior of the Napoleonic period, wrote a memoir detailing the thrill of proximity to greatness, like the time the toddling king of Rome tore off his plume, and how Empress Marie-Louise played billiards leaning over the table just like a man. Coignet was decorated with a cross of the Legion of Honor at a ceremony at the Invalides on June 14, 1804, of which his description gives a vivid sense of the glamour in which Napoleon clothed his military revues in Paris: "The Consul arrived at noon, mounted on a horse covered with gold; his stirrups were of solid gold. This elegant horse was a present from the Grand Turk; it was necessary to set a guard over him, so as to prevent anyone from approaching him (the saddle was covered with diamonds). He entered. The most profound silence reigned in the chapel. He passed before the whole corps of officers, and seated himself on the throne, which was opposite in a box to the left."[15] The next day Coignet bought "some nankeen" to make short breeches to go with the long stockings and silver garter-buckles of his summer uniform, described as follows:

> Nothing could be handsomer than that uniform. When we were on dress parade we wore a blue coat with white lapels sloped low down on the breast, a white dimity waistcoat, gaiters of the same, short breeches, silver buckles on the shoes and breeches, a double cravat, white underneath and black on the outside, with a narrow edge of white showing at the top. In undress, we wore a blue coat, white dimity waistcoat, nankeen breeches, and seamless white cotton stockings. In addition to all this we wore our hair brushed out in front like pigeon's wings, and powdered, and a queue six inches long, cut off at the end like a brush and tied with a black worsted ribbon, with ends exactly two inches long. Add to this the bearskin cap and its long plume, and you have the summer uniform of the imperial guard. But one thing of which I can give no real idea is the extreme neatness which was required of us. When we left barracks the orderlies inspected us, and if there was a speck of dust on our shoes or a bit of powder on the collar of our coats we were sent back. We were splendid to look at, but abominably uncomfortable.

For a large display of fireworks, the court assembled on the balcony of the École Militaire and watched the maneuvers in the grand expanse of the Champ de Mars. After the maneuvers, each platoon and battalion in turn fired into the air with gunpowder that created colored "baskets of flowers" that poured down on the soldiers like falling stars.

Napoleon's militarism in full display constituted a whole different experience compared to what Burr had known of soldiering and war. Burr had spent the winter of 1777–1778—at the age of 21 already colonel and commander of a regiment of raggedly dressed American rebels—at Valley Forge. By the end of the winter at Valley Forge, 2,500 out of 12,000 men had died of starvation, exposure and disease, along with 700 horses. The warm spring brought some relief, but conditions were disorganized and unsanitary in the extreme. What a contrast the parading French troops Burr saw in Paris were to his four years in the army, at the end of which he resigned his commission on the ground of ill health and returned to law school.

Compared with New York, Paris had venerable buildings, parks restored after having been ruined during the revolution, and fine new boulevards. In New York, Burr may have crossed paths with a French architect, Pierre Charles L'Enfant, who served with General

Lafayette as a military engineer and who was with George Washington at Valley Forge. The vision L'Enfant had to lay out the new nation's capital on a grid was discredited because it was all too modern. He was never paid proper wages, yet today the streets in Washington, D.C., largely remain as he designed them. However, even in D.C., cows were still grazing on the Mall in 1810 (while L'Enfant practiced architecture in New York), a far cry from the sheer size and grandeur of Paris.

Seven

Exploring the Capital

During 1810 and 1811, the city of Paris was like a femme fatale putting on finery and posing in front of a cheval-glass. Such a frenzy of beautification and monument building was underway that Maurice Druon quipped that Napoleon "leaves behind a Paris that is one immense construction site." It was a fair time for tourism too, although in the winter months having colder cold and rainier rain than Burr anticipated. Burr explored the capital midway between the 1807 Treaties of Tilsit with Russia and Prussia, under which Napoleon was acknowledged as master of Europe, and the 1814 occupation of Paris by the same Tsar Alexander who had capitulated at Tilsit, when Russian Cossacks camped in the Champs Elysées. Imperial rule was on display: the state occasions of Napoleon's wedding and the birth of his son, the emperor's embellishment program to make the capital reflect his self-perceived glory, and a continuing patriotic pageant. Writes Johannes Willms, "Attention was no longer focused on the problems of the Revolution but on the pageantry and festivities celebrating Napoleon's many victories."

Wedding of the Year

Napoleon was free to search for a new wife when his first marriage was dissolved in January 1810. Archduchess Marie-Louise of Austria was the eldest child of the Hapsburg emperor Francis II. Soon the obedient daughter was led to Paris from Vienna to marry her father's archenemy; Austria had been at war with France in 1809 and lost. Custom decreed that Marie-Louise cross into France naked and be dressed ceremonially in her new trousseau, as her aunt, Marie Antoinette, had been.

The proxy marriage took place in Vienna on March 11, 1810, and Marie-Louise met Napoleon at Compiègne on March 27, remarking to him, "You are much more handsome than your portrait." Her dog had been left behind, and Napoleon surprised her with it at Compiègne, the ploy to show his gentle side mimetic of the fact that Josephine's pup had jumped into his first nuptial bed five years before. In a rush to have an heir, the emperor bedded the Austrian princess on the coach en route to Compiègne, or perhaps in the royal hunting lodge, before the ceremony.

Politics halted while Napoleon masterminded the wedding. He directed every detail from the colors of the chamberlains (scarlet), equerries (azure) and master of ceremony (lavender) to the red and blue pens with which the marriage documents were to be signed. The civil wedding was at the Château de Saint-Cloud on Sunday, the first of April. On

Seven. Exploring the Capital 77

The Galeries of the Palais Royal (1809) by Louis-Léopold Boilly (1761–1845). The dogs at the left of the scene betoken sexual sport. Surprisingly, Boilly's painting of prostitutes was intended for the Salon Carre of the Louvre. 50 cm × 63 cm (Musee de la Ville de Paris, Musee Carnavalet, Paris, France; © RMN-Grand Palais/Art Resource, New York).

Monday, under fair skies, the procession started for the capital. Napoleon and Marie-Louise rode to Paris in a gilded coronation coach drawn by eight Andalusian horses harnessed in silk and gold cord. The procession paused for speeches at the head of the Champs-Elysées before driving down past the Place de la Concorde to the gates of the Tuileries Palace. The imperial guard, with sabers drawn, lined the route; and equerries on prancing chargers escorted the 30 or so carriages that led the procession, followed by the herald-at-arms and the carriages of notables.

The wedding occasioned a distribution of chickens, geese and joints of roast to the city, and barrels of wine were set up in the squares. Thousands of spectators lined the route of the imperial cortege. Every great house and public building bore signs with the monograms of the bridal pair. Church steeples had streamers and on the towers of Notre Dame a temple of Hymen had been constructed.[1] Public games, entertainments, and musical and acrobatic performances took place in every large square. At night, fireworks lit up the sky, a time-honored way to mark a royal celebration.

Some spectators might have glimpsed the 19-year-old Austrian princess as the great parade passed; she wore a diamond tiara in her blond hair. At the Tuileries, the crowd below the balcony could see Marie-Louise aglow in a high-waisted, figure-hugging confection of silver tulle sparkling with pearls and gold thread (made by Josephine's favorite dressmaker), beneath a purple velvet mantle. It is said that Marie-Louise winced in pain

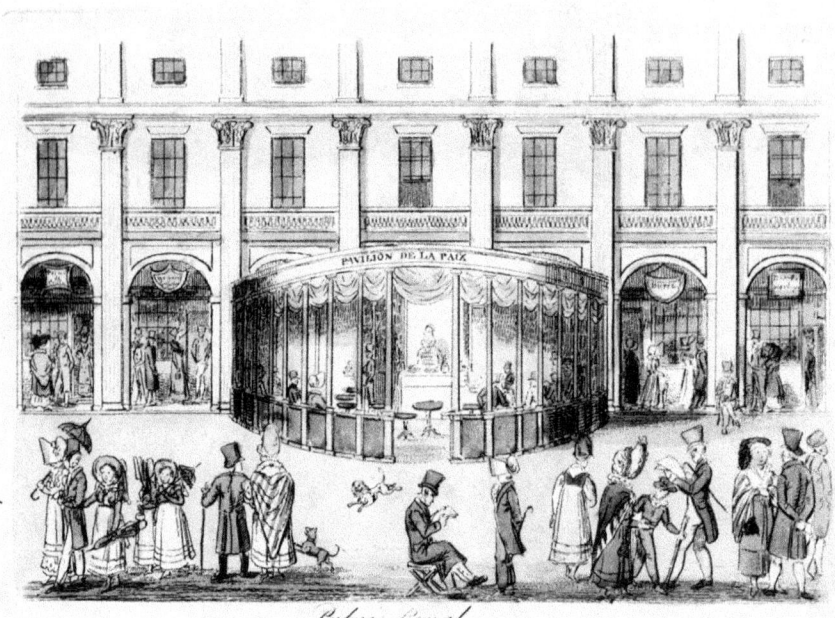

PALAIS ROYAL.

ORIGINALLY designed as a palace for the Duke of Orleans,—the centre of attraction in Paris,—is of an oblong form, with a handsome Arcade, under which are shops, (where dealing is rendered, to say the least, very unpleasant and irksome, from the universal spirit of unconscionable exorbitancy) affording a glittering and gay outward display of temptation in a variety of shapes,—and, when lighted up at night, shining with tenfold lustre, by means of reflectors placed in front of them.

Above, are spacious apartments, some appropriated as gambling, billiard, and coffee rooms; and dancing, music, &c. are carried on in others.

Beneath the shops, are cheap dining-rooms, Cafés, and Caveaux; also, a spacious theatre, where rope dancing, &c. are exhibited,—the tiers and pit being fitted up with chairs and tables, at which the spectators regale themselves with refreshments called for——in return for their *free admission*.

In the centre, is, the *Pavilion of Peace*,—a great resort for its excellent ices, &c.—some persons are seated, reading, others taking a cooling saunter near a fountain which usually plays in the centre, but not seen here;—

      "A friend, a book, the stealing hours secure,
       "And mark them down"
           Pour passer le tems!

Palais Royal (circa 1820), possibly from *Paris and Dover* by Rober Book'em. The café in the center of the picture is called the Pavilion of Peace. Its customers are sitting reading, eating ices, or enjoying the fountain (not visible) that "usually plays in the centre" (courtesy Lewis Walpole Library, Yale University).

Seven. Exploring the Capital

Plan & Elevation of the Arc de Triomphe of the Etoile by Chagrin and Charles Normand. The immense project of building the monument's foundation was underway when Burr was in Paris; he also saw the mock-up of the façade, under which Napoleon passed with his Austrian bride. The wording was rewritten by Napoleon, A Napoleon A Marie Louise, and the next line, La Ville de Paris. This is the prop fashioned to show the arch that was to come (courtesy Napoleon Collection, Rare Books and Special Collections, McGill University).

Louvre and Carrousel (1810) by Belanger. The children doing handstands and making music or noise with their instruments underscore the festive tone of the parade, which passes under the Carousel Arch by the Tuileries Palace (Art Resource, New York).

the whole day due to white satin, silver-embroidered slippers that had been made too small.

The architects Charles Percier and Pierre Fontaine created an intimate, stagey chapel out of the Salon Carré, a room in the Louvre, as Napoleon didn't want to march up the aisle of Notre-Dame de Paris twice. A large cross and six vermeil candlesticks topped the altar and gold-embroidered hangings draped the walls. George Rouget, who had collaborated on Jacques-Louis David's painting *Le Sacré de Napoléon* (The Coronation of Napoleon), depicted the moment of the nuptial blessing pronounced by the cardinal.

Despite the fabulous procession, music, parades and fireworks, the devil was in a number of details. First of all, since the Arc de Triomphe was only at the foundation stage, a full-scale painted paper prototype (*en charpente et en toile peinte*) was erected on a wooden framework. The workmen involved had refused to work for the pay of 18 francs. Six who protested were thrown in jail and the inspector general of the police gave the other carpenters a mere four francs. The emperor had commanded that while it need not be full size it should be of good dimensions for the grand entrance of the bridal pair into Paris. When he saw the maquette, it was already decorated with painting and inscription. He didn't like the conjunction "et" between "a Napoleon et a Marie-Louise" because he said it didn't have a "lapidary style," so he had it expunged and replaced with the distilled inscription "A Napoleon A Marie-Louise, la Ville de Paris."[2]

Burr could see the Arc de Triomphe as he walked up from the Tuileries, as it was visible as far away as Saint-Cloud. This staged version for the wedding turned out not to

Entrance into Paris of the Emperor and Empress the Day of Their Wedding Ceremony, 2 April 1810, by Charles Percier, Pierre Fontaine, and Charles Normand (courtesy Napoleon Collection, Rare Books and Special Collections, McGill University).

be frivolous, as it helped determine the position of the monuments and resulted in a reduction in the number of bas-reliefs. The fake arch stayed up 15 months, until Bastille Day 1811. The Arc de Triomphe itself was supposed to be done in 1814, and Napoleon pushed impatiently for its conclusion. But two factors, the death of the original architect early in 1811, and the decline of empire, delayed its completion until 1836.

During the preparations for the wedding, fur flew between Napoleon and Vivant Denon, director of the Louvre. In the Salon Carré, to increase viewing and provide seating for the guests, loges had to be constructed and a path cleared for the procession to walk to the Salon Carré from the Tuileries Palace. This meant displacing many artworks hung on the walls. When Denon objected to having to remove the very large paintings to make way for the two-level gallery of seats, Napoleon gave him a choice: take them down or I'll burn them.

Also, several cardinals boycotted the ceremony. They objected to the dissolution of Napoleon's marriage to Josephine, and though commanded by the emperor to attend, they didn't show. Furious, Napoleon banished them from court and forbade them to wear their red robes in public until they made amends; for this reason they are known as the "Black Cardinals."

It is reported that, compared with the other biggest shows of Napoleon, there was a mood of apathy in the city regarding Napoleon's wedding. As Consul of France, Napoleon had reigned in peace after the Treat of Amiens, but continual wars had followed. And why were the Austrians the enemy if the emperor married their princess? Napoleon sensed the disaffection in the people of Paris and may have heard the rhymes about his marriage that circulated in the streets, such as the ditty "On rosse le papa," caricaturing how he thrashed the father and slept with the daughter, and the father dared not protest for fear of being whacked again. "I have spoiled the Parisians," Napoleon said in the Tuileries afterwards. "I

Marriage Ceremony of the Emperor Napoleon with Marie-Louise of Austria, Celebrated in the Chapel of the Louvre, 2 April 1810. The ladies-in-waiting bear the train docilely, unlike the fuss Napoleon's sisters made at his first wedding. Behind them stands a sparse attendance of prelates. Napoleon is putting the ring on Marie-Louise's finger and receiving the blessing of Cardinal Fesch. This cardinal had also performed Napoleon's first marriage to Josephine. He was from Ajaccio, Corsica, and, by his half sister, Napoleon's uncle. Little more than a month after the wedding, despite Fesch's attempts to reconcile Napoleon and the pope, Napoleon demanded annexation of the papal territory to the French Empire (courtesy Napoleon Collection, Rare Books and Special Collections, McGill University).

have heaped so many marvels on them that I could not astonish them now if I were to marry the Madonna herself."[3]

Both Napoleon's wives professed love for Napoleon, enjoyed their position, and essentially did as they were told—except neither really stayed in line. Josephine cheated on Napoleon (which stayed a secret for nearly two hundred years until certain letters were made public). Marie-Louise, after four years of marriage, had the independence to abjure his order to go to Elba with him. Knowing that the two wives of the absolute ruler rebelled might be considered heartening.

Window-Shopping

Like any tourist, Burr window-shopped. He generally thought of Theodosia and his grandson—gifts to take them but also oddities and books for himself. On the first of January 1811, he "took a tour round by St. Denis. Bought a pair of andirons for 12 sous. Along the quai from St. Martin to St. Denis is a row of stalls with ironmongery. All sorts of trash; old nails, pieces of hoops, shreds of everything, the [illegible] of kitchen furniture, military weapons, &c. At first I asked the price of chevrettes [andirons], 24 sous; at the next, 40 sous, the next, 16 sous; the next 12 sous, being precisely the same article. If you are taken for a foreigner, double and triple is asked." On one excursion, he had his eye on elegantly

Galleries of the Palais Royal (1800). The scene shows the diversity of those mingling in the colonnades of the Palais Royal. Pen (drawing), wash with India ink, watercolor, 31.5cm × 45.3cm (Bibliothèque Nationale de France [BnF], Paris France; © RMN-Grand Palais/Art Resource, New York).

bound folios (Moreri, Bayle and a dictionary), which were way underpriced: "You will see ruin in such a purchase. Hold a little, Madame! I can buy them at 8 sous a pound. Yes, a pound; but have not bought. Hope to get them for 7."

Palais Royal: The Universal Medley

The Palais Royal, with its cafés, restaurants, gaming houses, and brothels, was viewed as the center of Parisian life from 1780 to 1840, through a tumult of social and governmental changes. Wrote Burr in his journal, February 22, 1810: "Palais Royale, where the eye and ear may always be amused, and the other senses, if you please."

Yet, about 90 years after Burr's sojourn in Paris, the writing of a Chevalier d'Honneur of France evinced the abiding ambivalence commentators had about this Paris landmark: "These gardens and galleries have been the theatre of a great many important events in French history. In it power once dwelt that was long in open rivalry with the ruling sovereign, and in it the great Revolution of 1789 began. Pleasure, vice, dissipation, industry, have all flourished within its limits; and prodigalities, miseries, and curious contrasts have jostled each other under arcades that once were the hell and the paradise of Parisians."[4]

Louis XIII had the Luxembourg Palace constructed to please his mother, Marie de Medici. It recalled the palace of the Medicis in her native Florence. Louis XIII also permitted Richelieu to erect the huge complex of the Palais Cardinal, still under construction at Richelieu's death. The minister bequeathed it and its important theater, where Molière's plays were performed, to the king. Thenceforth called the Palais Royal, it had a parterre and fountains, and arcades and passages that lent themselves to performances, cafes, bookstalls, and assignations.

After his majority, Louis XIV always stayed in it when in Paris, preferring it to the Louvre, his official residence. When Henrietta Maria, wife of Charles I of England, arrived in France after her husband's execution, the Palais Royal was assigned her for residence. She occupied it until 1661, when it became the residence of "Monsieur," Louis XIV's accomplished and openly gay younger brother, Philippe I, duc d'Orléans, to whom it was a present. Upon the Duke's death, the palace became the property of Philippe d'Orléans, who lived there when he became regent of France during Louis XV's minority. The lifestyle of the palace was voluptuous and luxurious, because courtiers who rankled at the severity of court flocked to it. Thus began the identity of the Palais Royal as a pavilion of pleasure.

As real estate, the Palais Royal provided income for the princes, for whom it became a land development enterprise. When Burr went there, the large rectangular park was enclosed by four-story neoclassical buildings hanging over a walkway lined with colonnades. The ground floor comprised shops, with luxury goods, and cafés and restaurants. Over that were apartments—mostly bordellos. Hedonism plus a place where manners could be free became closely associated with the Palais Royal. Women from every level of society strolled in the duc d'Orléans' gardens, attended the spectacles, and sat at the cafés before the revolution, as they would after it.

In 1780, the Duc d'Orléans gave the complex to his son, Louis Philippe Joseph d'Orléans, whose lifestyle required massive revenues. He converted the garden of the palace into an area of mixed use that would generate rental income. The original design of a cut stone arcade was never realized; instead the contractor finished the job early by erecting cheap, hanger-like wooden galleries outfitted with three rows of commercial stalls separated by two alleys. Light entered from windows along the roofline and the floor was bare earth. These temporary structures were the state of the Palais Royal during its wild popularity when Burr was in Paris, and they were demolished by the Duc d'Orléans's son, the future King Louis-Philippe, only in 1828. Policemen had no jurisdiction in the Palais Royal and the uses that evolved caused public opinion to express itself in sarcastic epigrams about princes turning palaces into shops and drinking places. The shops put fixed prices on their wares—an innovation in commercial history—and the galleries offered bustle and a perpetual fair.

The Palais Royal was confiscated when the duc d'Orléans was beheaded. Now gambling houses were opened on its upper floors, and many lower ones were turned into restaurants. After Napoleon's takeover, for a time the law courts held their sessions at the Palais Royal. Then Napoleon decreed the property a part of the crown domain, and the stock exchange used one of its wings. After the fall of the First Empire the property was restored to the future King Louis-Philippe, whose father had perished on the guillotine.

Thomas Jefferson, during his residency in Paris from August 1784 to September 1789, was impressed by the Palais Royal as an "ornament" and "convenience" and wanted to create a similar complex at Shokoe Hill in Richmond, a whole square of arcaded galleries forming a covered promenade around gardens, for businesses, entertainment, and residences. Jefferson dropped the plan but it shows how the Palais Royal stimulated his imagination. At the Palais Royal, he bought ivory-handled knives and a "pendule" at Verrier's, dined at an unnamed restaurant, went to see plays at the theater known as Les Variétés, located in a wooden structure next to the palace, and even played chess above the Café de Foy in the Salon des Échecs. To top it off, on April 22, 1789, he went with Gouverneur Morris, who had arrived in Paris in the winter and was staying at a hotel, to get tickets to have their profiles done at Quenedey's shop, by a mechanical process that used a new invention called the physionotrace. Too late that day, the two men returned the next, when Jefferson got the one ticket; Morris had his profile drawn a month later.

In 1794, Mary Wollstonecraft, similar to other commentators, drew a sordid picture of the Palais Royal as "a very superb square, yet the last in which a person of any delicacy, not to mention decorum, or morality, would choose to reside; because, excepting the people in trade, who found it convenient, it was entirely occupied by the most shameless girls of the town, their hectoring protectors, gamesters, and sharpers of every denomination." The arcade structure of the galleries, writes Michael Marrinan, "incarnated and valorized the privileging of sights that was an essential quality of the flaneur's mythic lifestyle. It also instantiated a precarious social situation."[5] To help a man make the transit to the elegant space there were boot-scrapers (equivalent to shoeshine stands). The early Paris guidebook writer Sébastien Mercier noted the following in 1796 of the galleries of the Palais Royal: "The jewelry boutiques are always numerous and dazzling, as if neither poverty nor misfortune existed. One sees only watch chains—half in pearls, half in diamonds—hanging among watches designed to display the day of the month. Those who have barely enough money to buy a loaf of bread look at these precious jewels, separated

Prostitutes at the Palais Royal from *La Mode du Jour* (early 19th century) by Claude-Louis Desrais (1746–1816), engraving by Fortier. In the imaginary "seraglio shop," in this satiric engraving, the commerce is lively. The man at the left is beseeching a woman, perhaps a madame, for something, possibly a reduced price (Bridgeman Art Library).

from their hands by only a transparent sheet of glass, and yet this fragile barrier is respected religiously."[6] Surely window-shopping for Theodosia's watches and even for jewelry, e.g., a gold chain for Mrs. Fonzi, was part of Burr's pleasure in spending time in the Palais Royal.

Important to reimagining the Palais Royal is understanding that it had its different moods in different hours. In the morning, the financial people were having a quick coffee. During the day, ladies lunched. In the afternoon, the young clerks and soldiers had rendezvous with their working-class mistresses, and then, wrote the author of *Voyage descriptif et historique* (1814), somewhere between five and eight o'clock, "the nuances disappear, everything is confused. You see ... men women of every condition, maids, children, soldiers, lawyers, merchants: it is a universal medley. But finally, at sundown, the nymphs descend from their lodgings and rush to the garden; they number in the hundreds and can be divided into three classes. Those who stroll under the wooden galleries and in the narrow alleys of the garden are called half-beavers, those of the galleries are the beavers, and those of the terrace of the Caveau are the fine beavers."[7]

Burr explored the activities of the Palais Royal, going there to stroll, eat, shop for books, and the like. It seemed to answer his curiosity about humanity, as on July 1, 1811, he "went for five minutes into a famous gambling-house. Many stars and ribands. When the number of the house is transparent, i.e., on a box where is a lamp, it is the signal of a gambling-house. I contemplated with pity the anxious faces." "Stars and ribands" typifies his jocular attitude about the ruling military establishment.

Mass Entertainment: An Urban Fair Ground

Before coming to Paris from Hamburg on December 9, 1809, Burr prevaricated to Joseph Fouché, minister of the Paris police, that his purpose in wishing to go to Paris was purely touristic: "The undersigned, desiring to visit Paris from motives of curiosity and amusement only has the honour to request that a passport for that purpose may be transmitted to the officer of police in Mayence, where he (the undersigned) proposes to be in the course of this month." Rome, Pompeii, Paris—not many places in Europe would have been credible at that time as prime tourist destinations. As it happens, what Burr stated became true, as the 15 months he spent in Paris abounded in curiosities and amusements.

Burr referred to coming upon performances during his excursions time and again: acrobatics, ventriloquism, mimicry, tightrope walking, mime, juggling, camera obscura demonstrations, puppetry, and street singers. Where the gaming tables and ice cream stalls, billiards, and panoramas were stationary and housed in rotundas, the baladins (street performers) and baladeurs (wandering musicians) could be found everywhere. If the Palais Royal was the Big Top, the city of Paris was a fairgrounds. *Les Enfants du Paradis*, hailed by some reviewers as among the top films of all time, produced during the German Occupation, re-creates the 1820s and 1830s scene of popular entertainment that Parisians enjoyed. The movie is about the lives of the poor, echoed by the fact that the citizens of Occupied Paris stole food from the street and market scenes as soon as they were filmed. The man-magnet Garance (played by Arietty) starts working in a carnival show and becomes a theater star. Jean-Louis Barrault played Baptiste, the love-struck mime. At first, pursued by many men, Garance is haughty to the mime, but eventually she sits in a balcony and watches him perform night after night. A wealthy man accuses Garance of stealing his watch while they watch the mime, dressed as a Pierrot, perform on the Boulevard du Temple (nicknamed in the movie and in reality "Le Boulevard des Crimes"). When the police seize Garance, the mime saves her by acting out the scene and showing how the real thief dropped the gold watch in her pocket. *Les Enfants du Paradis* represents Burr's context in Paris to a tee—it's as if he stood in the crowd perfectly at ease, admiring both the clever Pierrot and the beautiful actress.

Robert R. Livingston, whom Thomas Jefferson appointed minister to France in 1801, described the popular entertainment with great excitement in a letter to his mother of December 12 that year (Robert Livingston Papers, New York Historical Society):

> I went in company with Minister & some other gentlemen to see what effect Fantasmagorie would have on us—after having examined many ocular deceptions [to include illuminated likenesses of Franklin, Voltaire and Rousseau] we were astonished by a ventriloquist who also did voice imitations; then various magic tricks and spectres-ghosts & skeletons appeared in different parts of the room they approached very near us & then suddenly vanished from our sight [finally] rose an enormous head—the mouth opened—the eyes rolled about—then

appeared an arm with a dagger in its hand & stabbed it in the cheek the blood gushed out—the head immediately vanished—a violent storm of hail rain lightning & thunder closed the scene. I intend going again so much was I pleased with the wonderful ocular deceptions.[8]

The street performers also came indoors to entertain and some were itinerants. Burr remarked, "At Fonzi's was a garcon who imitated dogs, cats &c., and played very prettily on a little flute flageolet about six inches long."

Burr noted going to the panorama, a Franco-American popular tourist destination in the Passage des Panoramas. In 1799, Robert Fulton, the painter who later invented the steamboat, was awarded a ten-year patent, later extended by five years, by the French government for a tableau circulaire (circular painting or panorama) like the ones in Britain. He and his partner, James Thayer, from Charleston, South Carolina, purchased part of the park of the Grand Hotel de Montmorency on the Boulevard Montmartre and constructed two towers, each 46 feet in diameter, to house the panoramas.[9] A painter of historical scenes, Pierre Prevost, did the "endless paintings" supervised by Fulton: "He painted a total of eighteen panoramas over the years, beginning with the port of Toulon, which the British had evacuated in 1793; the burning of Moscow, a subject which had been popular for over a century in France, and which was reenacted in 1812; and a view of all of Paris as seen from the top of the Tuileries. The venture was an enormous success from the start.... Panoramas remained very popular for twenty years and led to the diorama, and all manner of 'orama' shows, songs about panoramas and, of course, Le Café des Panoramas. The two towers were taken down in 1831."

The panorama signified an invention as well as a painting, something between a 3D-movie theater and a circus tent. In the center of the rotunda was a platform bordered by a balustrade, arranged so that you could not see the last portion of the narrative until you reached it. A giant umbrella over the heads of spectators manipulated the lighting, masking the origin of light and preventing their shadows from falling on the painting.[10]

The money that Fulton made helped subsidize his submarine and steamboat ventures. While living in France, he used the considerable profits from the panorama and income from his rope-making machine to fund his submarine boat invention, the design for which he first submitted to the Directory in 1797, calling it the Nautilus.[11] A trial trip of the little boat took place in the Seine in front of the Hotel des Invalides in the summer of 1800, when he went to a depth of 15 feet and had two people with him and a lit candle and stayed under an hour. Napoleon approved a fund that covered a portion of the expense but not enough, so Fulton turned to the problem of navigating by steam on a commercial scale. When Napoleon declared himself emperor, Fulton realized his objective was domination, not peace, and he returned to America.[12] An art official during the Directory wrote Fulton (September 8, 1799), "We owe you the double advantage of traveling very economically and getting to know the most interesting cities ... a sort of geographic learning as curious as instructive."[13]

Inspired by the panorama in Paris, Burr encouraged Vanderlyn to paint an "endless painting" and exhibit it in America. Home in Kingston, New York, Vanderlyn embarked on an ambitious panorama of the gardens and palaces of Versailles. The panorama, built by Vanderlyn with his own funds and those of his supporters, opened just prior to 1820 in the first art museum in Manhattan—a neoclassical circular building near city hall rented for one peppercorn a year from New York City. The panorama (now at the Metropolitan) occupied the second floor, with Vanderlyn's paintings, which Vanderlyn considered superior to the panorama, on the ground floor. It's conceivable that the smartly dressed flâneur who surveys the scene is Burr himself, while nearby, Vanderlyn is in discussion with a man whose profile resembles his recently deceased friend, Robert Fulton (personal communication with Katherine Woltz).

Other Divertissements

Burr noted the performance art of ventriloquism several times, once in a cellar café at the Palais Royal, where "music and a ventriloquist" proved so interesting that he and the Chevalier "agreed to neglect Madame F." It was a signal diversion at the time.[14] As soon as Charles Brockden Brown completed his pre–Gothic novel *Wieland; or, The Transformation: An American Tale* (1798), pivoting on ventriloquy, he sent it to Thomas Jefferson. In the story, a mysterious stranger with quasi-supernatural powers to throw his voice infiltrates an ideal community on the outskirts of Philadelphia, and with his strange gift he manipulates others to insane deeds. Ventriloquists had been attributed with supernatural power, or the imitation thereof, until the Enlightenment, when the disembodied voice wasn't demonic anymore and began to be described as "thrown." Science offered explanations for voice projection involving vocal cords. Now they had an ambivalent appeal to people of reason. They despised credulity; not wishing to let themselves be duped, they exaggerated the dangers of fraud. On the other hand, they also acknowledged being stupefied by the ventriloquist's phenomenal talent, and Paris was the center for the ventriloquists to perform in Europe.

Masked balls had outshone other court festivities under the Ancien Régime. Lit by candles, the ballrooms were dark enough to make the disguise effective; naturally, flirting with a person of different rank was a gleeful possibility. By 1810, the old hierarchies did not pertain, the lighting was brighter, and the revolution had given the elite that survived a free pass. Consequently, Burr

Miniature on ivory by Jean-Baptiste Isabey (1812). The imperial court painter, Isabey portrayed Napoleon as a young officer in the grenadiers. The frame dates from 1808 and is decorated with imperial symbols, including bees (a reference to ornaments in the form of cicadas mistakenly identified as bees in the tombs of Merovingian rulers) and eagles, associated with Charlemagne, the French king Napoleon emulated (courtesy Walters Art Museum).

was disappointed in the masked ball he attended; it wasn't up to what he'd heard about masked balls: "On Tuesday a minuit au grand bal masque at the Theater Imperial. There were very few characteristic dresses, and about a thousand people. It appeared to me that at least 900 ennuied [bored] themselves. I was without mask. Took seat in the boxes, promenaded a little in the room, and came off at 2 o'clock. A gentleman remarked that the English had no word to express ennui, which he thought the more remarkable as they were so subject to that evil."

Had Burr been invited to the Grand Duchess of Berg's party at the Elysée-Napoleon (now the residence of the president of the French republic, known simply as the Elysée), he would have seen a masquerade in the old style. The Grand Duchesse selected a costume of Tyrolese peasantry for 16 young female guests, and the Duchesse d'Abrantes recalls in her memoir how they were preparing their quadrille dance at her house and were ready to go to the palace when one grotesquely stout lady in a Tyrolean costume appeared, seized her by the waist and attempted to kiss her. "I felt a rough beard in contact with my chin.... I now saw before me the unmasked face of his Royal Highness the Prince Camille Borghese." Napoleon, reported the Duchesse d'Abrante, liked such masquerades, which he called saturnalia: "He loved to disguise himself completely, and allow some individual to assume his character.... In personating Napoleon, Isabey found it most difficult to disguise his hands, which were exceedingly large, while the Emperor's were small and beautifully formed. With the exception, however, of his hands, Isabey personated the Emperor to perfection."[15] (Jean-Baptiste Isabey (1767–1855) was a miniature painting artist employed by Marie Antoinette, a pupil of Jacques-Louis David patronized by Napoleon, and favored during the restoration as well.)

Burr went with Fonzi to his country place, possibly on horseback, and "after dinner played at shuttlecock." One day he played loup et brebis, a game of tag, and had fun. (As our games have become more formal and governed by rulebooks and requiring equipment, the simpler games have become more for children.) He also purchased a set of *dames* to play checkers, a favorite game of both Napoleon and the Duke of Wellington.

No Puritan, Burr liked a bright crowd, a variety of amusements, and fresh air, and that meant above all other locales the Tivoli Gardens. An early afternoon found him "home for ½ hour to smoke segar and repose. Then to—, a sort of gourmand restauranteur, where dined; 4 francs 10 sous each. There we parted for an hour, Vanderlyn to see Florentine and I to M'lle Prevost. Found Vanderlyn at Fonzi's and thence we went to Tivoli. Les danses; les puppet; les ombres Chinois; les tight rope sauts; les grimaces; les feu d'artifice. Home at 11 and at 12 a.m. about to couche."

The Tivoli Gardens were an outdoorsy counterpart to the Palais Royal. Here was music, dancing, spectacles, marionettes, panoramas, and refreshment, but with more decorum, as there was an entrance fee to the gardens. The fireworks commenced at ten at night and were a special draw. The common people, for no admission, could look in and see the "Race of Cars," where a fellow could take his sweetheart on a horseless go-cart that ran down an artificially constructed hill, riding arenas and the sliding rink covered with soap instead of ice. Opened in 1795 on a former park, the Tivoli continued until 1825, when it went out with a flourish, its last gala being for the newly installed Charles X. Ten thousand people might visit the Tivoli on a Sunday afternoon, and thousands of colored lamps illuminated it at night.

Mechanical illusions were high on the list of urban recreation. A French inventor from Grenoble named Jacques de Vaucanson created the acknowledged masterpieces of such wonders in the previous century. His automatons not only imitated the movement of living things but simulated them. In 1738 he exhibited in Paris a drum and fife player, a life-size shepherd who played 12 songs on a flute, and *le comble*, "The Digestive Duck," who flapped its wings, drank, ate grain, and excreted.[16] Burr gave more details than usual about the type of mechanical entertainment, viewed August 9, 1810: "Went ... to see Mr. Pierre's theatre Mechanique, and was much amused. He exhibits, like a scene in a theater, a town, castle, or remarkable place, painted in the manner of a panorama, but you see carriages of all sorts, horses, men, women, children, dogs, cattle, all in motion like real life. Boats rowing and sailing. Sportsmen shoot ducks, and their dogs jump out of the boat, swim to the killed duck, and bring him to board.

"Another evening to the cosmorana, which is pictures (seen through camera obscura) of various antiquities—Balbec, the Coliseum of Rome, and one other were pretty well executed. The rest execrable."

The Eaglet

Once a rank-and-file mistress of Napoleon had a baby boy (Charles, Count Léon, 1806–1881), the emperor resolved to divorce Josephine. Until then, looking at her son and daughter, he figured he was infertile, and given the urgency of having an heir, Napoleon wasn't going to wait and see. In January 1810, he got a nullification of his six-year marriage to Josephine, on the grounds that only a parish priest had done the ceremony. Then Napoleon wed Marie-Louise in a proxy marriage in Vienna on March 1, and had performed a religious ceremony in Paris on April 2. Marie-Louise produced Napoleon Francois, a nine-pound infant, the following year, on March 20, 1811. The birth was very difficult and, to relieve his distress during the last stage of labor, the emperor had to take a hot bath. Then he strode into the delivery room and saw the baby was on the floor. Napoleon exited in despair, only to be told the child was a healthy boy, and that, through an oversight, no one had planned for a simple swaddling table.[17]

The people of Paris were ecstatic when the cannons began to boom. Napoleon, a born Hollywood director, had arranged 21 firings for a female and 100 for a male, so the good citizens cheered madly at the 22nd shot: "*Et bon, bon, bon. C'est un garcon. Vive Napoléon.*" In his journal Stendhal wrote that he was informed how, in the rue Saint-Honoré, people cheered as they would a famous actor coming on stage.

Napoleon Francois's baptism, along the same lines as the spectacular similar events of the Bourbons, was held on June 9 and occasioned a great parade. The child, given the provocative title of "King of Rome," to irritate Pope Pius VII, was placed in a throne-shaped cradle made of 617 pounds of silver and inlaid with mother-of-pearl.[18] It was based on a design by the painter Pierre-Paul Proud'hon and bore a single gilt eagle. The child soon had a governess and four assistant governesses in blue merino uniforms, as well as cradle-rockers and valets, nurses in black silk aprons, physicians, and a lady who supervised the wet nurse, who was allowed to leave the Tuileries only when riding abroad in a carriage with a chaperone.

The child's favorite toys were flags, trumpets, drums, and a hobbyhorse that had to be frequently repaired. When Napoleon had a moment he liked to have the baby brought to him, to hold him to his chest or on his knees, and, when the King of Rome grew to be a toddler, he was permitted to play on the carpet with mahogany blocks bearing military unit markings, which the emperor used to scheme battles. In a crazily intense manner, Napoleon prepared his son to be a sovereign.[19] He ordered from Sèvres a dinner service with plates that represented the chief episodes of Roman history and the history of France. A set of 4,000 volumes was specially printed of the best books in all branches of knowledge to serve the child as he grew.

The boy had a child-sized coach among his other endless toys and books. The coach was equipped with coachmen and equerries and bore the imperial arms. The baby's aunt Caroline provided the two trained sheep that drew the coach. Both the cradle and the coach are now at Schonbrunn Castle in Vienna. Napoleon also took the boy with him on his horse for reviews, to accustom the populace to think of the new line of rulers.

Marie-Louise didn't want her son to be a figurehead in danger when the empire crumbled. She hadn't chosen her husband, although he wooed and won her affections, apparently in the bedroom. But she was still an Austrian girl and for her safety and comfort she had in mind to escape to Austria.

In August 1814, the Count von Neipperg was charged by Talleyrand with escorting Marie-Louise to a spa at Aix-les-Bains, but he had secret orders from Talleyrand to dissuade her from going to Elba to meet Napoleon. This gentleman, who had intrigued against Napoleon—for example, encouraging Bernadotte to enter the coalition in 1813—made love to Marie-Louise and she turned a deaf ear to Napoleon's wish to have her and their son with him. The emperor often had got from no to yes, but abdicating in favor of his son in 1815 failed to resuscitate the empire. Talleyrand welcomed the return of kings. Can one blame him? He was instrumental in giving the Bourbons another chance, by having the guillotined king's brother, Louis XVIII, crowned.

Eventually Marie-Louise and the Count of Neipperg had two "morganatic" children; and in 1821, four months after Napoleon died, they wed. Today known as Franz, Duke of Reichstadt, Napoleon Francois grew up to be a fine young man who impressed everybody with his wit, good looks, and energy. He had grown to six feet. He joined the Austrian army and died of tuberculosis at age 21.

In time, the King of Rome, Duke of Reichstadt, Napoleon II would be remembered as L'Aiglon, the eaglet, especially after the play by Edmund Rostand, which premiered in Paris in 1910, three years after his *Cyrano de Bergerac*, starring Sarah Bernhardt.

More Sightseeing

Paris enchanted and impressed, and like others of its governors, Napoleon aimed to make it more beautiful, to embellish his capital. Honoré de Balzac over and over in his *Comédie Humaine* spun realistic tales of the bewitching effect of the capital, the epicenter of French life that captivated dreamers and foiled parvenus, "a city that swallows up gifted individuals born everywhere in the kingdom, makes them part of its strange population and dries out the intellectual capacities of the nation for its own benefit…. And as soon as a merchant has amassed a fortune, he thinks of taking it to Paris, the city that thus comes to epitomize all of France."

The Grisettes [Working Girls] *Rise, or, Picture of Paris no. 1* (1817), possibly from *Paris and Dover* by Rober Book'em. The three mirrors indicate the prosperity of the four "grisettes," or prostitutes, the cheval glass in which one dons her garters being the latest mode of furnishing. The suggestion is that they rose in time to doll up for the evening, and since grisette is related to "little gray kitty," one of the women is playing with a white cat (courtesy Lewis Walpole Library, Yale University).

There had been a pause in building projects during the 1790s and now the work was continued. What Napoleon didn't do was change the face of Paris. His architects emphasized continuity, viz., the neoclassical style, matching his ideas of Roman stoicism and civic virtue. Writes Anthony Sutcliffe, "The French Revolution was no architectural turning-point. None of the pre–1789 architectural legacy was discredited or even significantly questioned, and classical architecture continued in Paris without interruption."[20]

The interior budget doubled as Napoleon took absolute control, and building was brisk, but various of his grand plans for Paris did not go beyond the drawing board. Most of the building program went on between the Peace of Amiens (1803) and the Treaties of Tilsit (1807). At Tilsit, Napoleon had talks with Tsar Alexander after the French won a crushing defeat against the Russian army. Meanwhile, "a thousand miles away, he would be fretting that the fountains of Paris were not working properly, or that the Ourcq Canal wasn't completed, or he would be decreeing demolition of the old houses on the Saint Michel bridge." He wrote his minister of the interior a warning note from Tilsit: "Monsieur le Ministre, peace has been made with the foreigners; now I am going to make war on your offices."[21]

Burr's sightseeing was far from systematic. His Paris was the locations of the bookstores he liked, his friends' houses, and all his haunts. The Place de la Concorde, once Place Louis-XV, was a most striking and extensive visual witness to imperial achievement. To the north the Church of the Madeleine was begun in 1807 and a surrounding square was laid out. Architect Pierre Vignon took Napoleon's direction to create a rectangular Graeco-Roman temple with a peristyle of Corinthian columns. Vignon placed third in the competition but Napoleon rejected the top and second winning designs as too ecclesiastical. On the Left Bank a large Roman portico had been added to Palais Bourbon (the Chamber of Deputies) in 1806–1808. By now, especially with French military ventures into Italy, there was a great deal of archaeological research available, resulting in the neoclassical holding sway a long time in Paris compared with other European capitals. The Madeleine, as well as the Bourse, designed by A.T. Brongiart and started in 1808, reflected this.

The Arc de Triomphe was begun at the summit of the Champs Elysées at the Etoile in 1806. The designs, by J.A. Raymond and J.F.T. Chalgrin, were for the largest triumphal arch in history—162 feet high and 52 feet wide—with gigantic relief panels and statuary. Napoleon also planned a lake at each side with boats. (Just after the cornerstone was laid in August, Napoleon set off for the Jena campaign.) The engineers predicted the weight would be so great that a foundation eight meters deep had to be dug. That year Napoleon made a brittle comment that the work was futile except as a means of encouraging architecture. It took over two years just to lay the foundation. When Burr was in Paris, hundreds, if not thousands, of laborers would have been working there every day beginning to build the colossal monument. Huge blocks of uncut stone were at the site and the masonry was beginning to appear over the foundation. If Napoleon didn't get to see its completion in 1836, after numerous modifications, he got to take his bride past a wood and painted canvas mock-up of the arch. The mock-up made for purely ceremonial reasons allowed Chalgrin to make some last-minute changes in the design.

The same year the Arc de Triomphe was commenced, work was begun on the small triumphal arch of the Carrousel, to mark the main entrance to the Tuileries Palace, Napoleon's chief residence, which took its name from an ancient tile factory. It would also commemorate his victory at Marengo in northern Italy. (The Tuileries burned down during the Commune in 1871 but the gardens of André Le Nôtre remain.) The Carrousel was a design of Charles Percier and P.F.L. Fontaine, major exponents of the neoclassical imperial style. Napoleon had the bronze horses he pilfered from above the portal of St. Mark's placed at the top of the Carrousel as the main feature of the arch. The sculptor added a chariot that was initially to carry a statue of Mars, then Napoleon.

The Carrousel was clad in scaffolding for two years after the work was inaugurated. Napoleon fulminated to his intendant-general, asking when the scaffolding would finally be removed. They were waiting only for the statue of his majesty, he was informed. Napoleon flew into a rage: "What statue are we talking about? I never asked for one; nor did I order that my statue should be the principal subject of a monument raised by me, and at my expense, for the glory of the army which I had the honour to command." He insisted that the chariot remain empty. This much more modest design was completed the following year. The emperor did not like to see himself as a charioteer, so the chariot was left empty until the Restoration, when a goddess was placed in it. When Burr saw the Carrousel it had metal gates on either side, framed by booths.

While Burr was in Paris, on August 15, 1810, the Vendôme Column was inaugurated in the Place Vendôme. Unveiled with solemn ceremony, it would mark the end of Napoleon's military successes. This 148-foot column commemorated Napoleon's victory at Austerlitz

Colonne de la Grande Armée
Érigée en Bronze sur la Place Vendôme à Paris

Column of the Grande Armée Erected in Bronze on the Place Vendôme. This triumphal column was designed to emulate Trajan's Column in Rome, only instead of being formed of drums of Carrara marble, bronze plaques surround a stone core. To make the plaques, 1200 cannons taken from the Russians and Austrians were melted down, and the column was finished in August 1810 (courtesy Napoleon Collection, Rare Books and Special Collections, McGill University).

on the model of Trajan's column in Rome. It was constructed of very hard stone and covered with bronze plates made by melting down hundreds of cannons captured from the Austrians and Russians. A ribbon of bas-reliefs around the column depicted Napoleon's victories. Originally intended to have Charlemagne at the top, instead Napoleon's statue was placed there in 1810 (removed during the Restoration but Napoleon III put his great-uncle back atop dressed as a Roman emperor, which is how the column appears today). Construction had setbacks: The grand marshals of the emperor were not happy over the small place they were allotted on the design, and the bronze plates attached with difficulty to the stone.

A bomb blast that came close to assassinating the emperor on Christmas Eve 1800 gave a rationale for clearing away medieval sections of the center city—which were narrow and poorly lit. There was already an axis from the Tuileries to the Champs-Elysées and Napoleon wanted another to leave Paris to the east. He decided to create a thoroughfare from the Place de la Concorde along the Tuileries and the Louvre. The result, the Rue de Rivoli, Rue Saint-Honoré and Rue de Castiglione were for fancy new shops and dwellings. Napoleon decreed that any trade that used "an oven or a hammer" be banished and gave investors a generous tax exemption as an incentive to create businesses and apartments. Percier and Fontaine designed the continuous street architecture (façade) of the Rue de Rivoli, where the massive arcade incorporated an entresol set back from the street, with three full floors above and continuous balconies on the first and third floors. The government built the arches and vaults of the arcades but the houses above were not completed until 1814. Napoleon wanted the most fabulous of all the streets of Paris to bear his name; it was called Rue Napoleon until the Restoration, when it was renamed Rue de la Paix.

Austerlitz Bridge. This bridge, of stone masonry, completed in 1805, linked the Faubourg Saint-Antoine on the Right Bank with the Jardin des Plantes on the Left Bank. In the mid–19th century it was widened to accommodate traffic (courtesy Napoleon Collection, Rare Books and Special Collections, McGill University).

Utility was on the agenda as well as monuments. Now Paris would have a Halle des Vins, or trading center for wines. The firemen were organized into brigades of firefighters who manned casernes 24 hours a day. Despite a police ruling in the spring of 1800 that the streetlamps be illuminated continuously at night, even when the moon shone, the shops and dwellings at street level often didn't comply and this made journeying at night difficult. For example, outside theaters, porte-falots wanted to guide people home for a fee. Under the empire, new lights were installed in the center of the city on the Right Bank, whence it was reported in the *Journal de l'Empire* of January 16, 1812, "*La nuit à Paris est plus belle que le jour*" (Paris at night is more beautiful than in the day).

Two new major bridges were built across the Seine. The Pont d'Iéna, which leads down from Trocadéro, was begun in 1808, under construction when Burr saw it, and completed in 1814. Its name, taken from the German city of Jena, where Napoleon defeated the Prussian army in 1806, nearly got it blown up when General Blucher entered Paris with his army in 1815 and viewed the bridge as an insult to the Prussians. The Pont d'Iéna with its five arches and four intermediate piers, was a huge construction project. Statues were added in 1853. Named the Pont d'Austerlitz, after the Battle where Napoleon defeated Austrian and Russian troops in 1805, Paris's first iron bridge had five cast-iron arches on stone piers. A masonry arch bridge replaced it when cracks began to appear in 1854. Napoleon also had cannons installed on the Pont Royal, which he renamed, first, Pont National and then Pont des Tuileries.

After one of Paris's periodic floods in 1801, Napoleon set about reconstructing the quays. He extended the Quai d'Orsay to the Ecole Militaire. He replaced the 40 old slaughterhouses with four buildings at the extremities of Paris and erected granaries (*greniers d'abondance*) near the Place de la Bastille. Cemeteries were put outside the city.

Tourists at this time raved about the splendor of the palaces of Versailles (Burr admired the gardens) and Chantilly but they also sought out the sights of the near-present, i.e., the revolution. For example, Gouverneur Morris acquired a special passport from Lafayette, then a commander of the national guard, to visit the ruins of the Bastille a week after the prison was stormed on July 14, 1789. Americans in Paris also sought out the site of the guillotine; the lamp-iron at the Place de Grève, site of revolutionary lynching; the Invalides, stormed after the Bastille; the Tuileries, where the king was arrested; the Place Vendôme, a rallying place for violent crowds during the legislative assemblies; and the Abbey of Saint-Germain, site of the September massacre. The revolution was still very recent. The September massacre, during which thousands of prisoners were murdered, occurred in the late summer of 1802, not quite eight years before Burr arrived in the city.

Given that many American tourists were business people, they visited the factories of Sèvres and Gobelins. At the Sèvres factory, Burr would have seen being made or described the "Service des Maréchaux," a set of hand-painted porcelain, 1810, featuring Napoleon and 13 of his marshals. Thomas Jefferson had not been interested in "mechanical arts" and "manufactories" because he said America was not going to be a manufacturing power during any contemporaries' lifetime. However, Jefferson's view was atypical: "He [Jefferson] was the exception among American travelers, many of whom did in fact express a heightened interest for French manufactories, their output, labor force, wages and prices, and technological processes employed…. Commentary on 'internal improvements' as well, i.e., roads, bridges

Fountain at the Place de la Bastille (circa 1813) by Jean-Antoine Alavoine (1778–1834). This is the mock-up of the elephant, which was never cast in bronze as had been Napoleon's intention, and was taken down in 1846. Victor Hugo housed Gavrotte in the prototype's decayed plaster belly in the novel *Les Miserables* (courtesy Napoleon Collection, Rare Books and Special Collections, McGill University).

and canals is abundant indeed, because here the interests of the businessman converged with those of the general traveler."[22]

At the Place de la Bastille, where the prison had been, the Fountain of Regeneration had been built in 1793, with a sculpture of a woman with water pouring from her breasts. That was torn down, while or just before Burr was in Paris, and construction was begun on Napoleon's 78-foot bronze elephant. It was to be made of melted cannons of defeated Spanish troops until Napoleon switched the source to Russian cannons taken during his Friedland campaign. The colossal elephant featured an interior staircase and observation deck and water spurting from its trunk. Napoleon wanted to remind people of the war elephants used by the Persians in ancient times, and by Hannibal crossing the Alps. (Another association between elephants and empire was made in Jacques-Louis David's *Napoleon Crossing the Alps*.)

Napoleon had been tempted for a time to make the elephant his symbol. On the eve of empire, opinions ranged from the bee and the lion to the oak tree and the fleur de lis. When Napoleon brought the matter to his henchmen they voted for the cock, which had been incarnated for several past regimes and was still at the top of most flagstaffs in 1810. However, under Denon's influence, Napoleon issued an imperial decree on July 10, 1804, proclaiming the eagle as his symbol. The elephant would make a magnificent fountain instead!

Denon took charge of the project and his artists submitted drawing after drawing, fantasies right out of the *Thousand and One Nights*, with motifs such as a camel, a warrior ready to throw a javelin, a crenelated tower on the elephant's back, and the beast covered with a carpaison and pompoms. No one could persuade Napoleon that a fountain ought to focus on the leaping waters, not just water from the trunk of a great elephant. Meanwhile, the engineers contemplated that the water for the fountain would come from the canal of the Ourcq River, where it passed underground at the Bastille on the way to the Seine. In 1810, the underground work was under way. A model was made at the Jardin des Plantes, finished in February 1811 and Denon had two bronzes made, one with ornaments and one without, that were placed under the scaffolding to show what the 40-foot elephant would look like. A full-scale plaster cast of the elephant was mounted and unveiled in the summer of 1813, and then was left to crumble, although a guard continued for years to live inside one of the feet.

Between diplomatic appointments, John Quincy Adams met his wife and son in Paris. He was at leisure, passing time as he wrote in his diary "as agreeably as any part of my life."[23] By happenstance, the visit of Adams coincided with the return of Napoleon from Elba, called the Hundred Days, which ended with his defeat at Waterloo. In his diary entry of March 28, 1815, Adams mentions a chat with the doorkeeper of the elephant, who told him that 200 men once worked on the job, but now, under Louis XVIII (the restored Bourbon monarch), only 7 or 8. With Napoleon's return, said the doorkeeper, work on the fountain would resume "because that one doesn't sleep" (*car celui-là ne dort pas*). The artist was unable to persuade the government, when the monarchy returned, that the elephant had naught to do with Bonaparte. It figures in Victor Hugo's masterpiece *Les Misérables* when a ruthless crook occupies it and, showing a loving heart, shelters a street urchin. The basin remains today.

Cleaner Water

Napoleon's fountains gave drinking water to the population, that is, children drank water, not beer. The water was free, not purchased. And the apartment would have had a separate water closet equipped with squat toilets (adopted from the Turks) and a bucket to wash it after use. Some restaurants and cafes had W.C.s, even one for ladies and one for gents. These were hooked into the sewer system that branched under each important street.

Some men swam in the Seine, which was appealing on hot days—a long tradition, dating from the Middle Ages—except people also dumped refuse into it. Under the Restoration there would be the worst cholera epidemic in Paris in its history. Napoleon merits points for delivering fresh water to Paris. If serving Paris with water from the d'Ourcq River by canals was not be a consummate success, Paris gained 40 new fountains, and the emperor commanded that fountains run all day (instead of a few limited hours) and that the water be free of charge.

It is possible that some of Burr's coffee tasted sour not from the quality of coffee but the water. Remarkably for someone who was very aware of his health, he never complained of the water. He did, however, take an interest in an invention to make it easier to dig a well. When the inventor of a process to make vinegar from the sap of any tree was not in his shop, Burr and a friend, "Crede," went to see another invention: "We went then to see Mons. Cagniard, and his new invention of raising water and performing any mechanical operation. His apparatus is a screw of Archimedes turned the reverse, air, water, and quicksilver. Cagniard was abroad; but we saw a model, and worked it, and got the report of a committee of the Institute on the subject. If the thing performs what is said I will apply it to give water to Charleston."

Perhaps the most laudable of Napoleon's policies were utilitarian city works, especially bringing clean water and sanitation to Paris. The improvements to infrastructure included new quays to prevent floods, new gutters and pavement, new aqueducts and fountains, and relocating cemeteries and slaughterhouses to the outskirts of the city. This was also a way of keeping up employment. An Austrian aristocrat in town during Napoleon's wedding to Marie-Louise wrote his mother, in Vienna: "Nothing can give an idea of the immense projects undertaken simultaneously in Paris. The incoherence of it is incredible; one cannot imagine that the life of a single man would be enough to finish them."[24]

It was a tall order. Previous rulers had been aware of the problems and one big engineering initiative, a failed marvel, had been the waterworks at Marly, located on the banks of the Seine about seven miles from Paris. Louis XIV had it constructed to pump water from the river to his chateaux of Versailles and Marly. This was the machine marvel of its age, with 250 pumps that forced river water up a 500-foot rise to an aqueduct, and it was a sight Burr mentions going to see. By 1817 the "Marly machine" had deteriorated because it was made of wood, and the waterworks were abandoned.

Charles-Augustin Sainte-Beuve, the prominent 19th century literary critic, wrote that there had been "ten years of anarchy, sedition and laxity, during which no useful work had been undertaken, not a street had been cleaned, not a residence repaired nothing improved or cleansed." Postrevolutionary Paris was at a nadir in terms of both the inadequate, disease-ridden water supply and the filthy streets, which were basically open sewers, deep with black mud and refuse.

"Napoleon," writes Alistair Horne, "was obsessed by the water of Paris, and everything to do with it."[25] Like other tyrants, he distracted the populace with public works and monuments to his glory. Napoleon himself wrote his minister of the interior, Montalivet, that the four most important contributions to Paris under his reign were the canal, the market at Les Halles, the wine market and the slaughterhouses, the first and last being directly related to making Paris clean and the water sweet. His plans to improve and extend the quays crystallized after serious floods in 1801 and 1802, which went all the way to the Champs-Elysées, when boats were required to travel on streets near the Seine. The Pont d'Iéna and the Pont d'Austerlitz were completed as well, all except for his decree of January 1810 to place colossal statues of eight dead generals across each bridge. All were to be toll bridges. On foot Burr paid five centimes, and with a coach and two horses paid 20 centimes, as these were toll bridges.

Parisians had mostly been getting their water directly from the Seine or lining up at the scant pay fountains. In 1806, nineteen new wells for fountains were dug that flowed day and night and were free. Napoleon had a canal built 60 miles from the River Ourcq, ordering 500 men to dig it, while still a consul in 1801. It brought water to the Bassin de la Villette, opening in 1808. Some doubted the wisdom of having such an abundance of water—an oriental luxury that might incur moral decay. Now the supply of water for firefighting was also much improved. The canal had light boats, as Napoleon tried to make back some of the huge expenditure by licensing navigation, and a circular aqueduct from which underground conduits went to the central city. In 1810, there were still many water porters wheeling barrels through the city.

Now Napoleon attacked the problem of the Seine as a catchall for pollution. Parisians were so used to it that men swam naked in the river and a contemporary guidebook advised merely that the water of the Seine had no ill effects on foreigners so long as they drank it mixed with wine or a drop of vinegar.[26] Thus houses on bridges were demolished and an immense push began to clean and modernize the city sewers.

Sanitation

With the capital's population explosion, something had to be done to improve sanitation standards. Plans and initiatives were launched during the empire although the sewer system did not undergo major improvements until the 1830s. The septic system was filthy and there was no proper sewage drainage. Residents emptied chamber pots into the street, and each day hundreds of tons of waste was shoveled into wagons and dumped into the Seine. The situation was similar to what Burr knew from New York City, which had a population of 60,000 and lacked basic sanitary measures—trash left to decompose on the street and street cleaning left to scavengers collecting manure to sell. In 1798, New York had a yellow fever epidemic that claimed hundreds of lives.[27]

Meanwhile, a great advance was going on right under Burr's boots. Napoleon began in 1805 to build a modern vaulted underground sewer system in Paris, following the topography of the streets. Practical changes for the better were already in place when Burr was in Paris. Sewer floors were lowered and new lines were created everywhere between 1805 and 1812, while at the same time the existing sewers were disinfected and the flow of water purified.[28]

During the Enlightenment there was a movement for improved hygiene in France, and investigations of public health. Napoleon was a forerunner of hygiene for his armies and for Paris. In the first place he paved streets and did away with the flowing gutters in the middle of the road. Second, he wanted to give Parisians clean water. In 1802, he commissioned Pierre-Emmanuel Bruneseau as his inspector of works for the City of Paris to chart the sewer system and also keep them clean. Under Napoleon, the existing network was extended, 19 new miles of sewers were added. By 1812, vast improvements had been made. Bruneseau died in 1819, but Baron Haussman studied Bruneseau's maps in the mid-century, rebuilding, constructing new gas-lit and vented sewers. The sanitation models of Paris were adopted by other cities in France and around the world.

A survey of 50 kilometers took seven years. It was dangerous as well as putrid work. While Bruneseau was hailed as an intrepid adventurer, he had difficulty all along with hiring assistants to keep up with him. Victor Hugo was Bruneseau's friend and hailed him as an adventurer. The engineer inspired Hugo to write the portion of *Les Misérables* in which

Jean Valjean carries Marius, wounded at the Barricades in 1832, through the sewers to safety. Hugo called the sewers "the conscience of the city" and created a whole metaphor around the sewer system: "A sewer is a cynic. It tells everything."[29] It wouldn't have been possible for Jean Valjean to make his way carrying Marius through the sewers before the curage methods introduced by Bruneseau. The rushing water when gates are opened to clean the sewers with great hydraulic force, as well as the manholes and dripping pipes, are well described in the novel.

Eight

Cultural Diversions

Not only was there a kaleidoscopic array of shows, inside new theaters and in empty spaces and parks, in the decades after the revolution but an energy came from the unprecedented social mix that patronized these diversions. The world of entertainment manifested a republican fraternité presumably less fulfilled in the real world.

Burr was avid in his pursuit of good performances in the city. He went to shows big and small, popular and elite, and had a royal good time. He enjoyed a show of rope tricks, farces and a fandango at the Vaudeville. He saw performances at more established theaters built or refurbished by Napoleon—the Théâtre Français at the Palais Royal (having been "squeezed to death" in the crowd, he heard Napoleon's favorite "tragedian," Frederic Talma, perform Manlius). He also attended the Théâtre Imperial and the Théâtre Comique, as well as the Opéra for music and ballets. He must have accumulated a trunkful of librettos and scripts, and he liked to note what impressed him. This chapter will draw back the curtains on the performances Burr saw.

Theaters of the Elite

Overall, theater was Burr's favorite cultural diversion. It was Paris's liveliest art form then. Tickets were inexpensive, plays changed often, and it was customary for people, from tradesmen to parvenus, to go once or twice each week. If Burr didn't see as many plays as John Quincy Adams, who likewise spoke French and went to the theater each night (33 nights in a row)[1] when in Paris during a hiatus between diplomatic assignments in 1815, Burr couldn't equally afford the admission and the transportation. Like Adams, Burr went to theater high and low and also partook of numerous other cultivated amusements, including looking at art and fine books.

Theatergoing

Vacationing foreigners today are known to register sights and views rather than the performing arts (theater in London and opera in Italy being exceptions). There is something thrilling about a Founding Father who is sensitive enough to culture to gauge the pulse of a country he visited by its arts. Burr described his reason for going to the theater and buying copies of plays on July 12, 1811, after having been in Paris for several seasons: "I have had a great desire to know how the political changes of this country for the last twenty years have affected their théatres and dramatic works."

He composed "a list of the best tragedies and comedies during that period, amounting to thirty-five," which he went about buying, filling out his original six obtained cheaply by going to a "bookselleress au P.R. [Palais Royal]," ready to bring them home as an enthusiast might concert programs and playbills in contemporary America. Sometimes he bought plays he had not seen as well: "Home again. On the way bought three plays, at 8 sous each. Have read two of them." It is conceivable that Burr brought along a copy of the play to follow the speeches by the light of the Argand lamps, five to ten times as bright as a candle, a factor in the new profusion of theaters. Going to an elite theater like the Française was, as Oliver Wendell Holmes averred a quarter-century later, enlightening on French manners and correct language.[2]

Burr saw plays in two theater districts. The elite playhouses with their impressive porticos were located in the main theater district on the Right Bank. The other, smaller, district consisted of popular theaters clustered on the Boulevard du Temple, which Anthony Sutcliffe describes as being built in the 1790s "in a more relaxed classical style using round arches and Serlian windows (with three lights, the central one arched). The influence of Italian theater persisted here rather longer than in the new, royal théatres, but the effect was nevertheless one of elegance, even where the buildings were quite small."[3]

Napoleon, in the fifteen years he was consul and emperor, saw 374 plays.[4] He attended theater nearly once a week, a total of 682 times, and had favorites such as the heroic dramas by Pierre Corneille, commenting in 1803, "There is nothing which compares to Corneille, or to Racine. There is no way of reading [Shakespeare's] plays, they make me sorry for him." Napoleon had a theater built at Malmaison that was inaugurated with Beaumarchais' *Barber of Seville*, performed by a dilettante cast including his stepdaughter Hortense in the lead female role of Rosina. At the Comédie Française, his family and all dignitaries were required to keep boxes.

Through the end of the Directory, the theater had functioned as an outlet of public opinion. Halls and dilapidated churches were adapted for stages and more or less anybody could put on a play. Because Napoleon was suspicious of the power of spectacle to sway the citizenry, beginning in 1799 he tightened controls. Motivated first by a wish to destroy factionalism, within a month after coming to power, on November 16, 1799, he banned propaganda plays whether they were for or against the new government. The Odéon, the Comédie Française, and the Opéra now were the trio of royal theaters that dominated all genres of neoclassical-style drama. For example, one saw Corneille at the Française, which was granted the privilege to put on tragedies, and at the Odéon, select comedies such as Molière's. The neoclassical in theater, art, furniture and even clothing was encouraged by the new court, with more of a Roman orientation than in the neoclassical movement of the 18th century. For instance, Talma, the lead actor at the Comédie Française, wore a short Roman haircut to perform in Voltaire's *Brutus*, and by 1810 most gentlemen wore their hair cut over their ears in the same neoclassical style.

The moment Napoleon arrived at a theater unanimous applause ensued. It gave him an opportunity to make contact with his public. But almost immediately the irrepressible parterre would resume its liberty to demonstrate for or against the play, and on at least one occasion its hostility prevented the conclusion of a play even with the emperor still in attendance. Once in the royal box, Napoleon could be seen lying full length on a sofa of velvet, arms and legs crossed. Standing behind him would be his grand chamberlain, in full uniform. Only seven weeks after Austerlitz, in January 1806, Napoleon's late arrival at the theater caused the first scene to be played again.[5] Once the play was in full swing, actors would insert clever remarks and thus foil the censors and entertain the masses outside the theater later who heard the remarks repeated. Skill at making a *calembour* (pun) and being a good dancer were the great assets for a courtier in the previous century, and now the public waited for a witticism embedded in the script or improvised by an actor. An example comes from a letter of William Lee to his wife on February 10, 1810: "Critically annotating Napoleon's policy of occupying the throne of every European vassal-state with a relative, whom he then elevated to the rank of grand duke or king, popular hearsay spread the witty pun of a famous actor. Requesting more light on stage, the mime was brought candles. 'Give me bougies [candles], he quipped. 'Il y a assez de Sire à Paris.' Here, the pun plays with the homophony of 'Sire' and 'cire' ('wax'): There is enough 'wax' (or 'Sire') in Paris."[6]

The emperor financially supported the theaters and regulated their organization. When he was in Paris, he attended performances there several times a month and the Comédie was called to wherever he was, such as the little wooden theater built at Malmaison or specially built stages outside France's borders, to amuse the sovereign. In 1808, a command performance was held at Erfurt where Napoleon and Tsar Alexander were meeting. A company from the Comédie, including Talma and Madame Duchesnois, performed classics of the French stage for 16 consecutive evenings. The Erfurt productions became known as the "parterre of kings" because of the many German and Russian princes in the audience.

Burr loved the scenery. J.B. Isabey, the same gifted designer who did uniforms for the army, employed a galaxy of fine scene painters. At 19, Isabey had worked for Marie Antoinette doing miniatures at Versailles, and he continued painting for royal patrons through the First Empire and the Restoration. Isabey not only did the work for the royal theaters but also did the drawings and models for the imperial coronations.

Burr probably sacrificed on other extras to be such a major theatergoer. On February 12, 1810, he noted, "This is coronation day, and, of course, a fete, which means that there is illumination and the principal theaters gratis." He liked the gamut of offerings, which included Paris's "boulevard theaters." Then again, Burr simply loved excitement. When he went to the Francaise one summer night and it was "complete" (he adopted the French for "sold out") he persevered for a night of theater and a whisper of intrigue:

> At 6 au Théatre Francoise. It was full, and no admission could be had. Told my valet to take me to the nearest théatre. Paid 3 livres for a place. It was a rope-dancer. The first performer, a boy of about 7 years; the second, a girl of 5 or 6; the third, a lad of 12, the fourth a pretty girl of 16. Then successively three men who did wonders. You would think these fellows were made, like Bentham's tongs, of air and steel. Made a very pleasant acquaintance, who was in the adjoining box. We walked ½ hour. "Vous parroissez plein de genie; la quelle de toutes vos talents vos fier vous le plus?" "Je n'ai cultive que celle de plaire." She gave me her address and invited me to sup, which I declined. How wonderfully discreet! But then I engaged to call on her to-morrow. How wonderfully silly! Home at 9.

Burr felt that seeing Talma was a great cultural experience and alludes to seeing him several times in performance (January 31 and July 15, 1811). In the winter of 1810 he went to the Comédie Française to see Talma and recounted, "Obliged to wait forty minutes in the crowd, nearly squeezed to death. Heard the tragedy of 'Manlius.' Did not wait to see the after-piece. For the characters, see the gazette ci joint. M'lle—- is very unjustly condemned. She had more of truth, of nature and feeling, but less of vehement action, which is the taste of the day."

One summer day he noted, "At ½ p. 6 au Francois. 'Hamlet initie de l'Anglois,' and 'Le Coutin.' Both pieces were extremely well supported. Talma is really something great, and M'lle Duchesnois has much merit. But we will read the pieces together. I laughed a great deal at the comedy, and cried a little at the tragedy."

Burr also saw the "tragedy of *Manlius*," which was a story of rivalrous brothers that may have hit close to the bone given the duel with Hamilton (which Burr mentioned in letters as a misfortune but which does not come up, nor do any events related to past misfortunes, in his zesty, present-oriented journal).

Francois-Joseph Talma (1763–1826)
BY MARVIN CARLSON[7]

With his demands for court presentations, his devotion to a sterile classicism, and his support of a rigid and frequently arbitrary censorship, Napoleon often worked in opposition to the theater he so clearly wished to support. A similar paradox can be noted in the company of this period, for though the Comédie rarely possessed a more talented group of actors than those of the Empire, their effectiveness was steadily undermined by a series of the most bitter artistic rivalries of the century.

Much of this conflict grew out of the major changes that took place in the Comédie's company between 1800 and 1810. Many important actors left the house during these years—almost all of those careers stretched back to prerevolutionary days. Since the revolutionary years had caused a break in the development of young actors, Talma and Mlle Mars were left almost alone as the established talents of the theater, and a whole group of younger actors had to be integrated rather rapidly into the company without clear guidelines as to what parts would fall to each. Friction was therefore inevitable.

The first major conflict involved Talma. There were those both inside and outside the Comédie who felt that Talma's superiority had gone too long unchallenged. They saw in the young tragedian Pierre Lafon a talent which could be developed to Talma's discredit. Chief among these opponents of the older actor was Julien-Louis Geoffroy, dramatic critic of the influential *Journal des Debats*. One of the first dramatic critics in the modern sense, Geoffroy published articles twice weekly from 1800 until his death in 1814. Though his power was not absolute, it was enormous, due in part to the artistic instability of the times. In his columns there was information for everyone: summaries of the plays, informed comparisons with similar earlier works, critical judgments, anecdotes of author, play and actors, and regular news of happenings backstage. Unfortunately for Talma, his orientation was distinctly conservative; he upheld the classic and neoclassic style, and viewed Shakespeare, the Germans, and early hints of Romanticism with considerable suspicion.

In certain parts there seems to have been justice for this apparently exaggerated claim. Lafon had a youthfulness and dash, what the French call panache, which was far removed from Talma's passion and fury and which gave the young actor a distinct advantage in part of the repertoire. This was clearly demonstrated in 1804 when Talma was at last goaded into accepting a series of productions in which he and Lafon could be seen on alternate nights in roles where Lafon's supporters claimed he was superior. The older actor soon had cause to regret allowing his wounded pride to prevail over his prudence. Lafon's best roles, such as Achille and Orosmane, were precisely those which Talma had always found most difficult, both physically and temperamentally. Moreover, members of the company who resented Talma's preeminence organized a cabal which hissed him throughout each performance. When the dramatic duel was over, Lafon seemed to have carried the day. He began almost contemptuously referring to Talma as "the other."

Talma finally realized the folly of fighting his battle on the enemy's home ground and turned his abilities to works more suited to him. The first of these was a revival in 1804 of Ducis' version of *Hamlet*, the same production Aaron Burr would have seen six years later. As in all of Ducis' Shakespearian adaptations, great care had been taken to adjust or weed out English irregularities. Ophelia is made the daughter of Claudius to give Hamlet a Corneillian choice between love and duty. Gertrude deserts the king to aid Hamlet, who is not killed but crowned at the end. Even so, the work remained sufficiently distinct from traditional French tragedy to encourage Talma to attempt some experiments in production and interpretation. He didn't want the standard costume of tragic heroes, such as that of the chevalier—plumed helmet, velvet-lined tunic, great knotted sash, white tights, and yellow boots—so he set the designer Garnerey to work studying lithographs of productions of *Hamlet* in Denmark and Germany. Garnerey found actors playing the role, in Hamburg and Copenhagen, dressed in the black costume of a sixteenth century Spanish captain. He designed a similar costume for Talma, in the name of historical exactitude.

Contemporary critics were less struck by Talma's costume, however, than by the emotional quality of his interpretation. Geoffroy took a predictably dim view of both play and actor. As the play had "no character but a lunatic and a visionary" it had to be Talma's frenzied acting that drew audiences—"his distorted features, his wild eyes, his quivering voice, his somber, lugubrious tone, his taut muscles, his trembling, his convulsions."

The 1806 revival of Antoine de Lafosse's *Manlius Capitolinus*, on the other hand, drew praise even from the classicists and the cabal of Talma's enemies. The ambiguous feelings experienced by Manlius upon discovering that he has been betrayed by Servilius, his passionately loved friend, allowed Talma to develop a character of such subtlety and power that even Geoffroy was moved to praise. After this triumph, Talma revived *Manlius Capitolinus* regularly, and even in these generally unprofitable years, it could always bring large crowds to the Comédie. In a single blow, the rivalry with Lafon was over. The defeated challenger made a rather unsuccessful foray into comedy, then returned to serious roles, but he remained ever after a respectful second to Talma.

Mademoiselle Mars (1779–1841)
by Marvin Carlson

The notorious controversy between Talma and Lafon was scarcely under way when other rivalries developed, this time among female members of the company. The rivalry of two young actresses who debuted in 1802, Catherine-Josephine Duchesnois and Marguerite-Joséphine George, sharply divided the theater world of Paris. Mlle. Duchesnois, who appeared first, was not a physically attractive woman, but she gained the adulation of many with her lovely voice and her natural and spontaneous delivery. Mlle. George provided an almost perfect contrast. She was as beautiful as Duchesnois was plain, and the classic delivery she had learned was in direct opposition to Duchesnois' spontaneity. Indeed, a dispute between proponents of classic acting and natural acting was to some extent involved in most of the apparently more personal conflicts of the period. Opponents of Talma's realistic innovations gathered behind Mlle. George. Geoffroy, of course, lent his support to this party. His first reviews of Mlle. Duchesnois were mildly favorable, but when Mlle. George appeared, he was enraptured, writing how, surrounded by her nymphs in *Iphigénie en Aulide,* "her entire person would be a perfect model for the brush of Guerin."

The director of the Comédie, le comte de Remusat, was forced to promote both actresses to sociétaires on the same day, March 17, 1804, to avoid disputes over seniority. Paris was sharply divided between the Georgiens and the Carcassiens, who gained their rather inelegant name due to their heroine's slenderness, and both sides wore tokens on hats or lapels to indicate their preferences. Critics, journalists, and cartoonists fanned the flames. Even the imperial family became involved. Mlle. George was for a time the mistress of Napoleon, while Josephine discreetly supported Duchesnois. Each side hired audience members to applaud its favorite and to hiss the other, thus developing the claque, which within a few years became an accepted theatrical institution. The feud continued until 1808, when Mlle. George abruptly disappeared from the Comédie after a grand success in Delrieu's *Artaxerce.* Eventually, word arrived in Paris that she had gone to Austria to escape her creditors. This defection scandalized the capital. From Austria, the delinquent actress went on to St. Petersburg, tempted, it was said, by the prospect of an aristocratic marriage.

The field of tragedy was thus left open to Duchesnois, but other conflicts kept the Comédie in turmoil. Mlles. Dupont and Merson fought over the soubrette roles left by the retirement of Emilie Contat until Mlle. Merson's ill health forced her to retire. The public was the ultimate loser in this contest, for Mlle Dupont's talent was slight, but her victory over Mlle. Merson left her in a position sufficiently strong to prevent the development of any subsequent rivals. The roles left by the retirement of Louise Contat, Emilie's sister, inspired an even more bitter contest between the well-established Mlle. Mars, who had made her debut in 1795, and Jeanne-Emile Levard, who had come to the Comédie in 1808, only a year before Louise Contat's retirement.

The stir over division of these parts was so great that in 1812 Napoleon wrote back from Moscow to attempt to resolve it. He instructed Remusat, now general superintendent of the Comédie, the Feydeau, and the Odeon, that Mlle. Mars, already playing leading roles, should not be given any of the grandes coquettes—a second major employ. The ruling, however, was never enforced. Remusat's director of the Comédie, the rather weak Maherault, was edged out of this position by his assistant Bernard in 1813, but neither Bernard nor Remusat was a match for Mlle Mars. She was generally acknowledged the superior talent and had, moreover, the argument of her longer service. Remusat eventually yielded to her demands, granting her a special dispensation to play "first roles, first loves, and grand coquettes. Poor Mlle Levard spent the rest of her career obscurely understudying these parts. Like Mlle Dupont, Mlle Mars emerged from this struggle determined to brook no more rivals. She refused to train young actresses and held on to her wide range of parts, including young lovers, until her retirement in 1841 at the age of 62.

Theater for the Populace

During the ancien régime, government authority had held the distribution and repertoire of theaters under a clamp. The theater people at the Comédie Française and the Opéra made a living and guarded their monopoly of traditional genres; the actors at the popular theaters lived insecure lives, with their sails continually trimmed. Not only did the law forbid a word of dialogue, but traditional stage actors even moved to limit the popular theaters to tightrope walking—no marionettes! However, the lines became muddied while the formal restrictions grew tighter and the theater scene changed in the twinkling of an eye with the revolution. Meanwhile, the corps de ballet at the Paris Opéra traded in their ancient régime high heels for slippers worn by the "rope dancers," who wore soft shoes. Once the melodrama had emerged, it influenced not only what occurred on stage but also how people thought about themselves and their society. It is as though the servants of *Downton Abbey*, instead of getting a break from serving to have a glass of Christmas cheer, took the opportunity to write and rehearse a play about their world.

Richelieu had set down the rules for French theater in the 17th century, not only unities and verisimilitude but also—at which the popular theater thumbed its nose beginning in the first decade of the 19th century—to never blend tragedy and comedy. Romanticism would soon bring a total mixing of the genres, and in the boulevard theaters the melodrama was experimenting with the mix—corresponding to that of real life. An instance follows, recorded in Burr's journal, related to a minor house founded in 1792, the Vaudeville, that excelled in sketches of contemporary life: "At 6 to the little Vaudeville Théatre, where were performed 'Le Mar. de—, Le—, et le fandango, each about an hour long. Home ½ p. 10. The theater is small and very plain. No scenery but a change of rooms. Paterre [sic] orchestra, and five rows of boxes. For the first and second row of boxes and orchestra you pay un ecu de 6 francs. All the parts extremely well acted."

The dozen-plus "boulevard theaters" that gained great popularity during the Napoleonic era had evolved from traveling fair theaters, which were limited to pantomime, dancing, acrobatics, puppetry and fireworks. When Burr referred to "the Boulevard," he meant a string of streets in northeastern Paris. When Louis XIV had a wall built around the perimeter of Paris, the inner medieval fortifications were transformed into wide avenues with double rows of trees. These boulevards were paved with cobblestones and had grand houses. Here carriages paraded that could hardly wedge into the narrow streets of the center city. In the Boulevard du Temple, also known as the Boulevard du Crime during the Empire, many theaters offered inexpensive or even free shows, and were patronized by the upper classes as well as the common people in the postrevolutionary period.

Along with the Parisian populace, Burr was able to attend the boulevard theaters frequently, given that the seats at the Ambigu-Comique and Gaîté theaters, for instance, cost as little as 60 centimes. He saw plays with themes of love intrigues, the lower class rising to heroism, relations between masters and servants, and dastardly crimes. They stayed clear of politics and turned on the peripeties of real life. The special effects and costumes accentuated the action, often in exotic settings. What made them middlebrow was that they were not subtle and were performed in prose, not poetry. Burr took keen pleasure in this genre of theater and in the cafes and assemblages of people that were a chief attraction of "the Boulevard." In mid–November 1810, he was going out on the town in Volney's coach: "After dinner V. proposed to take us to see the Chat Merveilleux. We then went in his carriage, but there was no seat to be had."

Recounting theater to Theodosia would intensify his own amusement: "After dinner to the Theater Port St. Martin, where saw a great pantomime, La Ruine de Persepolis. You will have it and then I'll tell you more." For Burr personally, theatrical performance not only informed on the world of Paris at the margins of imperial control but must have caused him to relive and reflect on the enormous change in his own country's governing.

On March 9, 1810, Burr was at the Théatre Ambigu, known for outstanding melodramas (a genre the emperor disliked). With a stage only 12 by 17 yards, the Ambigu had beautiful scenic art.[8] The Ambigu's designer, Daguerre, dreamed of "putting every phenomenon of nature" on the stage. A contemporary spectator described a set for a play called *Le Sage* performed around 1810: "The summit of a high mountain amid the ruins of a gothic chapel. In the moonlight appeared an immense vista broken by a wandering river, reflecting repeatedly the brilliant stars. Passing clouds at times cast heavy shadows and at times thinned to mere wisps, disclosing the luminous disc which brought the scene into new clarity."

At the Ambigu, Burr saw a double bill of the *Musico-Manie* and *Les Highlanders*. He watched the plays from the parterre and someone he had known back home passed him a friendly note. The popular theaters on the Boulevard du Temple had evolved from the earlier traveling fair theaters and took off after the revolution when the little theaters could at last contain plays with spoken dialogue. The new form of theater, the melodrama, combined music with spoken dialogue, stock characters and real-life conflicts and aspirations. Calling the melodrama "the period's most popular and innovative theatrical genre," Davidson writes:

> Having emerged by 1810 as a recognized theatrical genre, melodrama would have international and long-standing influences on popular culture and mentalities. The melodramas incorporated traditional plot structures and characters into stories that expressed the lingo of the people. Thus melodramas portrayed as constant the hierarchy of birth, male superiority, and masters dominating servants, but they also broadcast new democratic messages, as the heroes were often of lowly birth, while many villains were aristocrats. Women and men from virtually every level of society—from the newly returned aristocracy to artisans and shopkeepers and even laborers and servants—attended melodramatic plays and enjoyed their entertaining scenery, music, and dances.[9]

Sometimes the spectacles had a clear lineage from street performances. Burr went to an unnamed theater on February 19, 1810, and saw a rope-dancing performance. Virtues of the small theaters were buying a cheap ticket on the spot and scalpers. Burr and his friends seemed to wander into spectacle entertainments *à l'improviste*.

In mid–November 1810, Burr noted, "We then went to Franconi's to see 'Angelica,' &c., in which a horse is the principal actor; but Franconi's is not open to-night." This was the Cirque Olympique, often known simply as Franconi's, established by an Italian, Antonio Franconi, in 1783. By 1810 it was under the direction of his two sons and featured animals such as monkeys and dogs that did tricks and pantomimes with elaborate sets. Franconi trained the animals himself and by 1810 the equestrian-type acts were probably also performed by trained deer. An account of 1816 has a drawing of Coco the deer, who leapt from rock to rock and stayed immobile when shots were fired, and Azor, who walked unbidden into the nacelle of a balloon that was then raised so the deer "flew" in the air.

Burr was entertained by pantomime, a rich French tradition stemming from the spectacle hierarchy dating from the eighteenth century, by which only elite theatrical performances had a license for "talkies." *Children of Paradise* (Marcel Carné's film) is set ten or twenty years after Burr was patronizing Parisian theaters, and the depiction of diversions is faithful to what Burr saw. In fact, Burr's note that "they always ennui me when they speak" could constitute a hilarious bon mot for the pantomime genre as it began to fold into melodrama. When Burr was in Paris, the Théâtre des Funambules was an informal theater space on the Boulevard du Temple, which in 1816 moved to an indoor performance space in Montmartre. The Funambules had famous pantomimists Carné memorializes in the character Baptiste, played by Jean-Louis Barrault. In the story, the actors perform pantomime melodramas so close to real life that Baptiste creates an exquisite skit in which his passion for a statue drives him to near suicide. The set is moving and boasts mechanical devices and pyrotechnical display. The rich occupy the boxes while the poorest are a voluble crowd up in the *paradis*. Outside the theater are tightrope artists, a strongman, a con man, a religious article seller, a pamphlet seller and carnival games. Inside the theater are the performers—jugglers, acrobats, lady dancers—who are fined if they speak onstage and fined a little less for making noise backstage. One bops another and it starts a stage brawl. Here is the memory of the Terror that has been hushed up elsewhere: there's talk of the guillotine and an executioner-murderer who harps on death. Garance, the opaque and elegant slut played by Arletty, is a star attraction at the Funambules, and the fact she first appears in a supposed and actually modest nude show attests to the proletarian character of the pantomime theater.

Burr recorded going to several pantomimes. He writes for example, on February 1, 1811: "After dinner to the theater, Port St. Martin, where saw a great pantomime, 'La Ruine de Persepolis.' The only distinction between the good and the evil genii was in the colour. Of course, the devils were black. It would be a most diverting comedy to have a hundred or two of your Oaks blacks in the parterre to witness the exhibition. There were fifteen or twenty little black devils, apparently eight to ten years old, who danced very much a la negre." Burr, as it is seen here, was no more sensitized about racism than his peers. His humor is offensive today but commonplace for the time; "Oaks" refers to Theodosia's husband's property in South Carolina.

February 4, 1811, proved to be a busy day. Burr went to Denon, who advised him to write to the Duc de Rovigo about his passport application. Then he stopped by Madame Robertson's, who unburdened her issues: "Toujours le meme. Asked to dine, which declined. To Fonzi's an hour, and then home. Din. chez moi; bouillon gras, beef and potatoes. At 6 came in Vanderlyn, and I took him again to see 'La Ruine de Persepolis.' Was amused, and shall go again. 'Bas les schawl. Sortez la femme. Basse le coulisse' (au francois), which interrupted for five minutes an interesting scene. The little negroes amuse me most. The new danceuse did not appear to-night. It was my principal motive in going to see her." Just as in the present, 19th century men liked to see a pretty actress, and the audience must have called for the dancer of a shawl dance to remove her clothes. Clearly, Burr thought it a fine thing to go to the same show twice.

A week later (February 8) he went to a pantomime of the bestselling tragic novel of young lovers Paul et Virginie, and on February 14 he saw another pantomime, *Le Jugement Supreme*, again at the theater at Port St. Martin. A description by historian Michele Root-Bernstein of a typical melodrama shows the fashionable kind of show Burr saw:

> The Black and White Prince revealed in its structure a subtle alteration of the formulas and dramatic action typical of more traditional boulevard plays. Since The Black and White Prince had not abandoned the subject of frustrated love, certain of the love intrigue formulas—parent obstacle and revolt of the young—were to be found in the pantomime. The decrees of an oracle stood between Zulica and the young girl he loved, Rosine, but in spite of any and all fairy-obstacles, he awakened Rosine to the feelings of his heart. Unlike the traditional love intrigue, with its emphasis upon the inappropriate marriage schemes of the old parent or the mischievous shenanigans of the servants and masks, Audinto's sentimental pantomime concentrated upon the nature and development of emotional ties between the young. And it was this sentimental emotion, rather than any attempts to hoodwink parental authority, that overcame parental obstacles and resolved dramatic tension. Rosine unwittingly transformed Zulica into a monster.... Touched by the young girl's sentiment, the fairy restored Zulica to his former self and the oracle was forgotten.[10]

The plays Burr saw on the boulevard were bound to have been new because the new law was that after five years the copyright was up. In plays written at this time, sentimental love was apparently grafted onto the traditional love intrigues and the exotic settings were exploited in scenery and costume. These plays drew artisans, workers and ordinary people as well as bourgeoisie and aristocrats. The wealthier people came, often in large parties, and looked down at and watched the behavior of the more humble spectators as well as the theater, and vice versa. Professor Davidson delves into the nature of the plays and the total experience of the mixed audiences:

> Melodramatic theater spoke to and soothed anxieties about reading social markers, as most plays revolved around people's true identities always becoming visible. Plots often involved cases of mistaken identity in which an innocent young woman would find herself in a terrible situation through no fault of her own. By the end of the play, however, people's true natures won over all other complexities. Characters were always perfectly evil or good, and several theorists of the genre see that 'visibility' as a key component to melodrama's appeal. Encouraging intense emotional responses to frightening situations portrayed on stage, the biggest hits often caused their audiences to shriek and even to faint.

The Paris Opéra

At the Paris Opéra, the city's largest theater, Burr saw ballets and operas performed before over 2,000 spectators. The Opéra, then as later in the century, was the ultimate venue to see and be seen. To attend opera, Burr invested in (bargained for) opera glasses and was amenable to standing in the pit if he wasn't someone's guest and could not get another ticket from the scalpers who hung outside the building, then the Théatre des Arts, long before the beautiful iconic Palais Garnier was built by Napoleon's nephew, Napoleon III, and inaugurated in 1875.

Nowhere else in the world could one see gorgeous spectacles like those in Paris. To see them was life-changing. In the spring and summer of 1784, when Abigail Adams went to performances, she admired the movement and gauzy dresses of the dancers and wrote her sister that, even if initially taken aback, her shock wore off and she watched the dances with pleasure. Olivier Bernier comments that "her life in France, that strange, sophisticated, and rather frightening country, had called up new resources."[11]

Napoleon visited the Paris Opéra only 13 times between 1810 and 1815. He preferred Italian music to French. Also, perhaps an alleged assassination attempt on October 10, 1800, as he exited the opera house affected him. All the same, he took the Opéra very seriously, as a jewel in his crown. Opera, which combined drama, music, words, décor, dance and costumes, was the ultimate setting for his heroic cult. He wrote his minister Champagny in January 1807, "In general, the best way to praise me is to do things which inspire heroic sentiments in the nation, in our youth, and in the army." At a performance in March 1807, a set had collapsed, throwing a singer over her throne so that she suffered a broken leg and a concussion. From a military campaign Napoleon wrote, "I see that the Madame Aubery affair occupies the Parisians more than all the losses that my army have suffered."[12] The next year, he sketched out details of a new opera house that he wanted his architect Fontaine to design.

The emperor exerted control of all aspects of the Paris Opéra—the choice of spectacles as well as the 40 persons employed at the Academy of Music, which created the ballets and operas. Napoleon was shaping his authoritarian dynasty rather than holding the skeins of culture in a tight fist, so the spectacles weren't propaganda but they were rather severely vetted. Opera was his favorite art form because it exhibited heroic sentiments, whereas ballet had the preternatural silence.[13] Two men were key. The Comte de Remusat, superintendent of spectacles from 1807, acted as the first chamberlain of court as well. He approved the repertory of the Academy of Music, over which the emperor had final say. Remusat was the *sublime porte*, who transmitted the emperor's will to Louis-Benoît, artistic and administrative director of the Opéra from 1807–1815 and Remusat's close friend.

Contemporary authors wrote most of the works. Half of the productions given from 1810 to 1815 were recent works by modern composers, predominantly French and Italian, who were also salaried in the Opéra's employ. They participated in the selection juries, which from the time of the revolution also had outside members. These committees scrutinized every production and were very cliquey, so their criteria were political before artistic. On average it took five years from composition to approval and performance. Occasionally Napoleon contravened them, notably permitting the mounting of operas by an outstanding composer of the period, Jean-Francois Le Sueur, whose *Télémaque dans l'Ile de Calypso* was one of six operas Burr mentions seeing by name. The Opéra had kicked out Le Sueur in 1802 because of his scathing pamphlet about its methods, but Napoleon plucked him from impoverishment, had him compose the march for his coronation, and named him a Chevalier d'Honneur.

Antiquity was the privileged source of inspiration, with the figures of Alexander the Great and Mars furnishing flattering points of comparison with Napoleon. Judith Chazin-Bennahum, dance historian, connects the classical education of the revolutionaries (including Napoleon) with the perdurant mythological and classical themes.

Reality was transformed by remarkable feats of scenic engineering, both in ballet and in opera. These were learned from the Italians Jacomo Tortelli and Carlo Vigarini, and under the veil of illusion princely flattery was perpetuated. One might wonder why French politicians of the revolution seated themselves so comfortably before the altar of these gods who had been used as aristocratic playthings. The answer may lie partially in their rejection of Christian allegory and their detestation of the clergy.[14]

One inclement evening, February 16, 1811, Burr, now an old hand in Paris, arrived at the opera and figured he would see the performance from the pit, "but finding it crowded, and seeing a place in the amphithéatre back of the pit and just below the front boxes, I paid the additional sum, 3 francs 18 sous." He records his dismay that *Anacreon chez Policrates* (1797), was "dull beyond expression and not relieved either by scenery or dancing or any merit." Fatigued, he missed *Persée et Andromède*, another mythological opera in the repertory that followed that same evening, staged by the eminent Pierre Gardel, who had introduced the pirouette into dance history in 1800. Exoticism was the other dominant theme, and on February 16, 1811, the operas that celebrated the national past were absent since Napoleon had consigned the kings of France—excepting the remote Charlemagne—to oblivion. Operas were also subject to censorship, but by 1810 self-censorship did the job of assuring that each and every production praised the emperor.

The intention to share with Theodosia the cultural highlights of Paris was very marked in Burr's notes about attending the Paris Opéra:

> Home from the opera at 12. Was in the box two hours alone; but in the adjoining was again Madame de Lille, who was very civil in answering all my inquiries. She is also pleasant in conversation. At ¼ past 9 came in F., with three gentlemen and one of his Majesty's pages. The pieces performed were Iphigen en Aulide and Le Dansomanie, a pantomime. The grand opera, particularly the chanting in dialogue, fatigues me mortally. I have no taste for French music. To relieve it, we had three fine scenes and some dancing. The Dansomanie amused me much. I bought both pieces. You observe that I buy all the pieces which I see performed. Sometimes make scratches or notes in them to assist our memories when we shall talk them over.

The Louvre

Everyone who came from America after the French Revolution visited the Louvre museum. It was very often the first thing tourists went to see (attested to in numerous published diaries). A journalist from Philadelphia, Mordecai M. Noah, traveling in 1815, wrote that he was so well versed in the Louvre that he knew the position of the rooms and their contents before entering the museum's doors. Another popular museum was the Museum of French Monuments. Those who were very interested in art sometimes tried visiting the studio of Jacques-Louis David, then the most famous painter in Europe and court artist to Napoleon.

Aaron Burr would have wanted to see David's *Coronation of Napoleon*, displayed at the Louvre in 1810—a scene captured in a painting, by Louis-Leopold Boilly, now at the Metropolitan Museum in New York. David himself dedicated his genius to restoring monarchical traditions. Napoleon systematically looted art from churches and palaces in other lands wherever he had military campaigns. He also understood the value of the fine arts as an ornament to his empire. Touring the museum, he stood in front of the coronation painting, lifted his hat, bowed his head slightly and said, "David, I salute you." The painter received the salute "in the name of all the artists, happy to be the one to whom you design to address it." Napoleon had the *Mona Lisa* in his bedroom at the Tuileries until 1804, when he allowed it to be installed in the Grand Gallery of the Louvre. Yet the great chameleon David expressed to a pupil how he disapproved of building up the Louvre by stealing art: "The site of a work of art, the distance one must travel to see it contribute singularly to our notion of its worth. This is particularly true of the paintings which once hung in churches. They will lose much of their beauty and effect when they are no longer seen in the places for which they were made. The sight of these masterpieces will perhaps produce scholars, men like Winckelmann, but artists—no!"[15]

The three works of art Burr mentions by name were all secular in subject matter— *Venus de Medici, Apollo de Belvedere,* and *Laocoön,* all of which were taken captive during the largest seizure of Italian art from 1795 to 1797. The gallery, like the works, was very large; Burr admired the gallery and noted its length in both meters and feet. Like his fellow tourists, Burr must have been proud to be at the Louvre, hoping to learn and doing what was comme il faut and for appearance's sake. He would have seen many artists copying the works.

Foreign visitors were allowed in any time. For most of the week, artists and foreigners had exclusive access to the Louvre. On weekends, the general public was allowed in and it was crowded. Burr visited frequently with John Vanderlyn, who would have been copying old masterpieces.

A Painting at a Feminist Shore
by David M. Lubin[16]

Habituated to Old World attitudes toward art, John Vanderlyn was (or claimed to be) perplexed. When a customs agent prevented him from exhibiting *Ariadne Asleep on the Island of Naxos* in Havana in 1828, the artist responded, "Who would ever have dream't of such a thing in a place where the negroes go stark naked?" He missed the point. Ariadne was not a debased African slave toiling in a hot clime, and that is why she was not permitted to go stark naked. The larger point is that "war was made upon" paintings such as Vanderlyn's for deeper reasons than simply "on account of their nudity"—reasons having to do with America's various social classes jockeying for positions of dominance, embracing or rejecting one another's racial, sexual, and moral ideologies along the way.

Depending on who the viewing (or defiantly nonviewing) audience was, the nudity of the figure elicited widely diverging responses. Those who desired American cultural parity with the Old World were likely to approve of *Ariadne* for its proficient variation and recapitulation of European high-art subject and technique and to consider their personal appreciation of such work evidence of their own "refined and cultivated taste." In the period after the Civil War, cognoscenti might have admired *Ariadne* as a harbinger of the fashionable and in Europe substantially accredited salon nudes of Cabanel, Bouguereau, and others, which began entering American collections at this time.

Try to imagine how the painting could have been regarded as a sentimental parable in which a male fantasy of using and abusing women is morally condemned (even while, at a different level, that fantasy is entertained) inasmuch as the young woman depicted has been left helpless and bereft by a seducer who tires of her as soon as he has had his way. In contrast, Ingres's *Jupiter and Thetis* (1811) is unadulterated sex fantasy with no pathos or sentiment to disturb its exaltation of supermasculinity. Although Ingres has depicted an allegedly nonsexual incident—the Nereid Thetis imploring Jupiter's intercession in the Trojan War on behalf of her son Achilles—what we have here is not exactly a sentimental depiction of maternal love. Thetis's pliant submission to one hypermale figure for the sake of another reinforces at the level of theme the work's emphatic depiction of femininity submitting to virility.

While I would hardly claim that Vanderlyn's painting is less erotically charged than Ingres's or that Ariadne is any less a sex object than Thetis, a significant difference between the works is that Vanderlyn literally foregrounds the woman's subjectivity while treating that of the male as peripheral. True, the narrative of abandonment is merely a pretext for presenting viewers with a highly sexualized rhetoric of abandonment, but still that narrative of a woman's emotional pain (or pain-to-be) occupies center stage and cannot or should not be so easily dismissed.

Vanderlyn may even have been signaling ambivalence about his personal treatment of women as objects of desire. *Ariadne* could reasonably be taken as a treatise—romantic in its concerns, classical in its analytic form—on erotic relations, a male artist's self-criticism of sexual philandering while also, intentionally or otherwise, validly or not, an advertisement of his sexual prowess.

In 1796, the year Vanderlyn first went to Paris, Mary Wollstonecraft was abruptly deserted in that city by her lover, Gilbert Imlay, a dashing American adventurer and careerist—a Theseus, so to speak—shortly after the birth of their daughter, Fanny. Wollstonecraft attempted suicide, and Imlay, exiled from the American expatriate community for his notorious behavior, pushed on to the Isle of Jersey. There is no reason to think of *Ariadne* as a *peinture à clef* concerned with these events, and yet not to look at the painting in terms of the gender inequalities that Wollstonecraft thematized in her life as well as in books such as *A Vindication of the Rights of Woman* (1792) is to be perversely unfaithful to the historical context from which the painting emerged.

The Wollstonecraft-Imlay scandal preceded *Ariadne* by more than a dozen years, but the radical disparity of genders it bespoke was by no means a dead letter. Aaron Burr was one American who did not hold Wollstonecraft in general abhorrence. He called *Vindication* "a work of genius" and wrote to his wife, "I had heard it spoken of with a coldness little calculated to excite attention; but as I read with avidity and prepossession every thing written by a lady, I made haste to procure it, and spent the last night, almost the whole of it, in reading it." He then wondered why "I have not yet met a single person who had discovered or would allow the merit" of Wollstonecraft's book.

Burr's feminist sympathies in no way dissuaded him from an avid commitment to amorous intrigue and libertinage. Those who vilified Wollstonecraft for her unorthodox opinions about female sexuality would not have been surprised by the licentiousness of her disciple Burr. And had they looked at the Ariadne painted by his protégé, they probably would have regarded it as the unfortunate but predictable saga of an innocent turned voluptuary, a maiden who, upon abandoning the patriarchal homestead, is herself abandoned—and deservedly so.

Reformers of the early nineteenth century, refusing to recognize that young women abandoned the patriarchal homestead primarily out of economic necessity, assumed that it was the failure of public morality, particularly among the poor, that was causing the sharp increase in seductions, desertions, and illegitimacies that appeared to threaten the republic's very foundation: the family. Middle-class common sense blamed the profligacy of poor women on what was taken to be working-class laziness, ignorance, and lack of self-control. When the victims of sexual seduction were of the middle class the blame was placed not on any intrinsic failings of that class but on excesses of sentimental fiction and French atheism. It was much easier, that is, to decry factors such as these than to attribute the problem to the onset of industrial capitalism in the case of the one class and, in that of the other, to the yearning of bourgeois females for social freedom and sexual parity with men.

Art at the Louvre

The royal art collection had been open under the Bourbons but the Louvre was then a palace. It was within days of the fall of the monarchy in 1792 that the revolutionary government carried out an old project of transferring the royal collections to the Louvre—a testament to the legitimacy of the new government. The National Assembly declared on August 19, ten days after Louis XVI's arrest, that it was an urgent matter to bring the collection to a national museum, and the new Louvre became a symbol of popular sovereignty.

The precedent was also nearly immediate to remove art from conquered lands, beginning with a huge addition of spoils from the Belgian campaign of 1794. Bonaparte's trophies of conquest spoke more loudly and enduringly of his success in war than reports of victorious battles ever could. Moreover, as a result of his Italian campaign, tricolors were hung everywhere in the Louvre and plaques were mounted declaring the glory of imperial majesty. One of the convoys of art was the cause of a giant celebration on July 27, 1798. Barges came up the Seine, where the booty was then transferred to huge carts. Since the art was itself crated, the attraction for spectators was the festooning of the carts (bouquets, wreaths and laurel branches) and the lions, panthers, tigers, camels, and exotic plants. The song composed for the occasion ended with the refrain, "Rome is no more Rome/It is all in Paris." Actors chanted while scholars marched alongside the treasures respective of their fields. The looting of foreign art continued until the end of the empire. "Let your Majesty at least leave something in Italy!" the neoclassical sculptor Antonio Canova said to Napoleon.[17] The final consignment, dated December 1813, never left Italy.

It was during the Napoleonic era that the Louvre became a must-see tourist attraction. Under the direction, from 1802, of Dominique Vivant-Denon, and as a result of further military conquests in Prussia and neighboring German states, Vienna, and again Italy, the Louvre expanded significantly between 1804 and 1814. In 1811, Denon, a polished courtier and former diplomat who had done the elephantine engravings during the Egyptian campaign was, Paul Johnson suggests in his biography of Napoleon, "a fig leaf on Bonaparte's naked dictatorship." Denon went to Italy in search of "primitive" pictures, beginning with Cimabue. A grand new staircase was constructed and the Grand Gallery modified with columned arches into nine sections and long-awaited skylights between 1805 and 1810. Also, paintings were hung to cover every inch of the way of the Grand Gallery, changing the earlier restrained installations to an overcharged tapestry effect, reminiscent of princely cabinets of the past. Alistair Horne notes that the museum guards were paid only a pittance, and that Napoleon, when he visited the museum in September 1806, was horrified to see stoves burning to keep them warm. He had the stoves removed, and "it was hardly surprising that in 1810 thieves broke in to make off with some priceless tapestries."[18]

The Duke of Wellington would insist on the restitution of hundreds of works of art following Bonaparte's defeat at Waterloo. The Louvre, however, rebounded and quickly regained its status as the world's premier museum. Some travelers experienced the Grand Gallery as a wilderness of frames, but the gaps on the walls were soon filled with works originally intended for the Louvre prior to the revolution, whereupon a national emphasis of the collection naturally emerged.

Besides being dazzled by the Louvre, Burr would have taken in its military air. The Louvre of Napoleon is suggestive of Walter Benjamin's famous essay "On the Concept of History" (1940): "There has never been a document of culture which is not simultaneously one of barbarism."[19] Tourists like Burr, however, educated during the Enlightenment, entered into the receptive mood that the museum encouraged. Late-eighteenth-century museums initiated the practice of isolating works of art from each other, through hanging and framing, and from the social roles and physical contexts that they originally enjoyed, in the service of direct or transparent viewing. Andrew McClellan, professor of art at Tufts University, explains that the paintings were hung at an appropriate distance for viewing and not piled up as they had been in princely collections: "The desire for transparency entailed erasure of the life of a picture, its purpose and critical fortunes, between leaving the artist's studio and entering the museum, at the same time that newly developed restoration techniques sought to insulate it from the ravages of time…. Transparency in the museum encouraged (and still encourages) the illusory sensation of direct contact with the act of creation, the fiction of a canvas as fresh and as present as the day it was painted."[20] A contemporary British visitor to the Louvre reflected on how the collection had been amassed: "Others have gone to the seats of these sacred monuments to admire and venerate—but they went to pack and transport. Their armies advanced, burning houses and violating women; and in their rear came the members of the Institute to worship fine art and commit sacrilege in its temples…. Let the student be led in a painful pilgrimage to the honour of his divinity, from Paris to Germany, from Germany to Rome, from Rome to Florence. The sacred flame will be fanned by the motion, and his mind be informed and corrected by observation."[21]

Denon was a person close to the emperor whom Burr called on often, yet by the time Denon met Burr, Burr was no longer jockeying to get to Bonaparte to promote his political ends. Rembrandt Peale, in Paris with his family from August 1809 to October 1810, painted Denon's portrait and later claimed the Louvre's director "was especially kind and serviceable to me, allowing me privileges in the Louvre that he extended to no one else; and when I was preparing to return to America, pressed me to remain saying that … he would give me all the Imperial portraits to paint."[22]

In July 1811, Denon not only figured in Burr's acquiring a passport but also made him a present of his *Carnets de Voyage en Egypte*. Burr went alone to the Louvre. He also went there on a date with a "beautiful German" and with Vanderlyn. He bought a catalogue for 20 sous. One can imagine that Burr relished the art but raised an eyebrow at the plaques that boasted of the art as the emperor's booty, rather than equating the magnificence with ideal government.

According to Andrew McClellan, the greatest masterpiece that would have been pointed out to Burr was Raphael's *Transfiguration*. Burr probably went when the other tourists did. He would have seen many artists copying (personal communication with Professor Andrew McClellan, Tufts University, November 6, 2013). The reason James Fenimore Cooper was inclined to watch Samuel Morse copy (miniaturizing) paintings day after day was that painting was considered to educate the senses in a serious "religious" way.

Paintings possessed transcendent value as vehicles of noble ideas, formative historical events, and aesthetic principle, but marble tables, clocks and porcelain were irredeemably marked as private commodities whose presence undermined the museum's identity as a public and pedagogical institution. As David declared in 1794, "The museum is not supposed to be a vain assemblage of luxury goods that serve only to satisfy idle curiosity. What it must be is an imposing school." And a school it was. Following the dissolution in 1793 of the Royal Academy of Painting and Sculpture, which had provided the framework for formal instruction in the arts since the mid-seventeenth century, the Louvre became the official training ground for aspiring artists. When Burr watched Vanderlyn paint, and when he went to the Louvre, he was participating in this transformative spell. Interestingly, although the Louvre had been renamed the Musée Napoléon in 1803, in Burr's journal it is still "the Louvre."

Book and Map Hunting

For a learned gentleman from the new nation of the United States, the bounty of the European book trade was alluring and boggling, as getting the volumes home was a challenge and a chore. Burr had to deal with all his property being examined by authorities at ports on both sides of the Atlantic, and on at least one occasion the detention of boxes of books until further payment was made. That Burr, despite his privations, took home 300 books purchased abroad confirms he loved to read and wanted good books at hand, that buying books was an affordable recreation, and that having a library was something that vouched for his status as a gentleman.

First of all, books had a monopoly on knowledge; Benjamin Franklin even learned to swim from a book. In March 1810 Burr described "running all this week to booksellers to hunt something, particularly dictionaries for you." The balance of available titles was reedited classics, used books and new titles.

In France, the government, publishing, and bookselling were in symbiotic relations. By a series of trade regulations, Napoleon limited the printers in Paris in 1810 and made all the booksellers and publishers take out licenses and go through procedural registering of every tome; but this also protected copyright and thereby stimulated the book trade. Carla Hesse, writing on publishing in revolutionary Paris, explains, "It was a new regime based on surveillance rather than censorship as the chief preventative mechanism of cultural control. The 1810 regulation significantly reduced the number of prints, but really it was more of a consolidation than a reduction in numbers of presses running (i.e., small printers sold out to larger ones). Meanwhile the re-imposition of censorship and reduction of periodicals meant that there were fewer legal pamphlets."[23]

Second, a well-appointed library has always been a sign of taste and wealth. Antiquarian booksellers at the time could appeal to customers' sense of personal prestige, books being a major brake on the fluidity of social classes. Kristian Jensen, head of Arts and Humanities at the British Library, has delved into the symbiosis between marketing and collector. He points to an English bookseller, Thomas Frognall Dibdin, as the figure who read the minds of the elite and influenced the European scene with his *Bibliographical Decameron*.

Dibdin presented to the public the competitive collecting of books as an activity which was essentially social, as against reading, which was essentially private. He focused on conversations between men of a desirable class whose lives centered on old books, not least on their acquisition, and whose status made real association with them unattainable for most. He associated book collecting with medieval aristocratic values, an early sign of the medieval revival. In the middle of the century when Brunet, the French book dealer, looked back at the early years of the century and examined what had happened in the market for rare books, one of the greatest changes was the reappraisal of the past of the aristocracy: "Never was there such a demand for books on the art of heraldry and the history of noble families after the nobility of France, spoiled of its ancient privileges, preserved of its past only memories, titles, and blazons." The change can be illustrated by Francis Douce's contrasting view, from before 1812: "Heraldry, the pursuit of vain and empty minds, is altogether contemptible and unworthy of the name of science."[24]

These objects, removed from the public, became symbols of the immense distance between the rich collectors and those who might buy books for reading, but the strategy of exclusion sought to make the reader desire to belong. Dibdin cited prices incessantly and gushed over the luxurious aspects of individual objects; he showed no restraint, least of all with his name-dropping anecdotes, which gave the objects extra social meaning. Sometimes the books sound like celebrities of our time, famous in a circular way for having been owned by famous people who then gained fame from having owned them, exactly the attitude which had been denounced by the Abbé Rive on the eve of the French Revolution.

The glamorous life around the collections of rare books and the trade is presented to the public for admiration and also for emulation. Any man with money could create something for himself which was, if not similar, at least analogous. This was important for the trade, and also for the social function of the books to persist.... His enthusiastic phrases of the admired objects conjure up an impression of a cultured and prosperous world, the books being an essential tool for the public display of wealth and accomplishment.

When considering Burr's hobby of hunting for books, it is important to realize that he was quite accustomed to seeing books in modern foreign languages in America, especially French. Already in colonial times a thriving market for French literature from the Enlightenment and also the Classical period existed in cities like New York and Philadelphia. The Americans had fought side by side with the French to liberate their country, and it has been pointed out that because of the domestic censorship in France, Americans arriving in Paris might have been better informed about current events of Napoleon's regime than the French citizens themselves.[25]

Burr bought books as souvenirs and also to have good reading material at hand. When the American ship *Vigilant* was captured and sailed into Yarmouth and Burr went to Yarmouth (December 1811) to claim his baggage, he informed the customs official that the two large trunks contained principally books and pamphlets and the smaller case dictionaries "and nothing else," and further, that these books had been "all in common use among the passengers during the fifteen or twenty days they were on board." Thus Burr saw his books as objects to be handled, not merely to sit on the shelf.

Burr seems to have spent more time reading than anything else, and second to that was walking. The two went together as he browsed in the bookstalls on the quays and also went to bookshops, some of which were along the quays, and others around the university, the Palais Royal and elsewhere. Many books of this period were sold "broche," or uncut and unopened in plain or marbled wrappers. The purchaser could take the book to a binder to have it bound, as Burr mentioned doing. There was a profusion of binders in Paris and some had their own shops, which, especially in the smarter streets, offered popular books already bound up in the front of the bindery. Certainly some of the older books came from the libraries of nobility that had fled.

The stall-keepers on the quays of the Seine have belonged to the Parisian scene for centuries. In medieval times, on the Pont Neuf were sold patent medicines, broadsides, caricatures and sheet music of topical interest, and religious paraphernalia. Small dealers of secondhand books appeared in the 16th century and competed with bookshops. The humbler dealers displayed their wares from raised boxes or trestle tables or laid out on a cloth on the pavement. Some hawked their books in the street with a wicker or wooden basket strapped around their necks. Despite laws to discourage them, they remained and multiplied around the Pont Neuf. By 1796 the count was up to 300.[26]

Ehrlich Blake limns the mysterious world of the *bouquinistes* (booksellers) in the mid–20th century:

> After a few years, some of the pamphlet sellers added real books to their stocks, and very soon the established booksellers on the "mainland" began protesting about the cut-rate competition. They brought suit before the Parlement, the city's highest legal body, charging that the bouquinistes on the bridge were purveyors of dangerous literature, and they won. The Parlement ordered them banished from the bridge in 1649. They then took root on the quais, where they still flourish. Today they are wards of the Prefecture de Police, which limits their number to 230. If the bouquiniste dies or quits, his privilege of operating a bookstall is automatically voided.... The size, shape, construction, color (bureaucrat green) of the stalls are all prescribed by police regulation. The bouquinistes have their own trade association, whose president lately observed, "I have been in this business all my life, and during this time business has always been terrible."[27]

The Pont Neuf by William Henry Lake Price (1810–1891). Lights are strung over the bridge at two points, and one carriage driver avoids the bridge traffic or toll by going into the Seine to reach the other side (Yale Center for British Art, Paul Mellon Collection).

As the sellers were the bouquinistes, the browsers were known as bouquineurs, from the word "little book" in Dutch due to the lively book trade with Flanders and Holland. There were over a hundred bouquinistes, each with as many as a dozen boxes, when Burr was in Paris. Some were public intellectuals, some antiquarians, and others had no care for the contents of what they sold. In pouring rain, Parisians and tourists alike today go to the quays and take shelter under the awnings that sheltered a good number of the green boxes. In medieval times, stalls of dealers in books, china, jewelry, and glass lined the Pont Neuf, and the passage was known as well for pickpockets and street singers. According to the author of a monograph on the bridge, it was the largest of reading-rooms, not only by reason of the gazettes and lampoons that were sold there, but also on account of the books that were there found in multitudes and lay on the two long parapets that stretched across the river like rows of shelves in some immense library.[28] Of importance, there were a great many books of moderate price.

(Burr mentioned going to the Café Anglais [on the corner of the Rue Dauphine and the Quai Conti], which served as a club for men of letters, lawyers and foreigners. They went to drink lemonade or coffee, and to read the British newspapers, spending their leisure hours there.)

When someone died, the books were not sold at auction as in some other European cities but to dealers, sometimes by the yard. Burr noted that in July 1811 he could buy Bayle at stalls for 8 sous per pound.

Secondhand books from the rare to the quotidian were a Parisian specialty by the 18th century and collectors and readers had colossal opportunities after the revolution.

Superb editions, wide-margined volumes in red morocco, and folios were all in the stalls. Thomas Jefferson was a regular customer of the bouquinistes. He amassed many used books that were used to relaunch the Library of Congress after the invading British burned it in the War of 1812. Madame de Genlis, in her memoirs, wrote about the book scene after the revolution: "I stopped on the quays before the little stalls wherein the bound books bore the arms of a number of people I knew, and in other stalls I noticed their portraits exposed for sale."[29]

The very early writer of guidebooks, Mercier, in chapter 221 of his *Paris pendant la Révolution* wrote, "The borders of the quays are covered with books; there are even more bookstalls than cake-stalls. People must be reading prodigiously, for everywhere there is nothing but books. There are libraries on wheels, which are run off when it rains, and return when the sun reappears. On every side you turn you see the permanent fair of France.... The secret has been discovered of cramming the greatest number of stalls into the least possible space." A scholar named Achaintre did double duty as a book dealer on the low wall of the Seine facing the imposing Institute of France across from the Louvre. The learned but tattered man often troubled to note the books he sold. A story from 1811 is that a student on the quays asked him, without knowing who he was, for information about an edition of Juvenal by the admirable Latinist. "But I am Achaintre," the seller beamed.[30]

Burr also shopped for maps. He was sorry when a geographer rescinded an offer to lend him a map—maps were prized and more expensive than the ordinary book. When in Altona, Germany, he had commented in a letter to a Professor Ebeling about the superiority of the engraving "to anything which had theretofore appeared in the United States."[31] Maps were no longer created under royal patronage and the title "geographe du roi" (Royal Geographer) had disappeared. With the empire, the demand for maps of foreign realms increased, while the methods of printing were slow and expensive—until lithography was perfected in Germany in the 1820s and allowed French map publishers to meet the market demand.[32] A good map was crucial and not bought lightly. The modern map didn't fill terra incognita with invented flora and fauna; thus there was more science and less art to mapmaking, but it would be 1825 before lithography superseded engraving. Craftsmen combined the skills of cartographer and copperplate engraving, and Paris became the center of the European map trade.

Booksellers and geographers congregated along certain streets like the Rue Saint Jacques around the Sorbonne and certain quays. Engravers and cartographers customarily were located on the Quai de l'Horloge on the Ile de la Cité, also the traditional location of opticians, whose products such as compasses and rulers were required for mapmaking. But once booksellers were free from restrictions of location after the revolution, many of them removed to the Right Bank, and the geographers and engravers scattered throughout the Left Bank instead of clustering on the two quays. The business of mapmaking passed through generations and a mapmaker did not have to set foot out of Paris to make a detailed map of a distant land, because the maps were made from "all resources ancient and modern, verbal or graphic, published and unpublished."

Nine

Dining In and Out

At His Lodging

Burr wanted to have a variety of good food and drink. In the journal he recorded entries about ordering, tipping, and being a foreigner at restaurants; rustling up a meal for himself; different ways of preparing coffee; his sleep pattern and coping with insomnia related to his diet. For instance, when he couldn't sleep he said that it couldn't be the fault of the café blanc, because he had prepared it to remove the acid.

The price of grain doubled in 1811 and 1812. In early 1812 riots broke out across France in areas most dependent on agriculture, and groups of up to a 1000 unemployed men moved across open country, vagabonding to survive in the face of food shortages. However, since Napoleon imposed price controls and opened up vast quantities of grain he had stored for just such lean years, the crisis wasn't affecting Burr's consumption—he was simply poor.

Burr was self-aware about food and also curious and inventive. For example, he bought some *sirop de raisin* (grape syrup) in lieu of pricier sugar, "as an experiment" to sweeten his coffee, and noted that it was "something like very dirty molasses diluted exceedingly with dirty water" and "the taste corresponds with the appearance." Moreover, looking at his comestibles with inventiveness and an eye to restoring his fortune, he even had a scheme to make vinegar from wood (sap).

On the whole, Burr expressed contentment with his frugal meals *chez lui*: "[I] had by my fire an excellent bouillon gras, a bottle of cider on my table, and I boiled some potatoes, which with bread, butter, and cheese, I dined better than His Majesty." He said he liked his breakfast at home before he went to breakfast, meaning lunch, elsewhere as someone's guest. On rare occasions when he was in funds, he splurged on wine, expressing the "opinion that though a man may be a little the poorer for drinking good wine, yet he is, under its influence, much more able to bear poverty." Burr's favorite French wine was Roussillon. Roussillon, a stony strip of land along the East Pyrenees, produces "vins doux naturels," which are fortified by adding alcohol, like port. His preference evinced his sweet tooth.[1]

His Drink of Choice

Thomas Jefferson had complimented the French for never drinking to an inebriated state. Burr liked wine but craved his coffee, the supply of which was not taken for granted. The journal exhibits a constant tension between his economies and an inclination to have his pleasures. He noted that brewing his own café blanc would save him money, yet he was continually at cafes with his friends.

Café culture had taken off in Paris after the revolution. The young Grimod de la Reynière, the first French food journalist, hosted lingering philosophic breakfasts at his elegant neoclassical hotel where the American Embassy now stands. No guest clouded his mind with alcohol; instead the beverage quaffed was coffee. Historian Giles MacDonogh says that the number of cups of coffee drunk was 17—possibly a Masonic number or a magical number to the young Grimod. Moreover, "the man who put away 35 was instantly made Perpetual President." Someone who had gone to Grimod's coffee salons would recall that one could drink all the coffee one wished, as the brew was weak.[2]

It had been the French fashion to drink milky coffee only at the start of the day. Around this time a Parisian epicure and friend of Grimod's named Dr. Gastaldy invented filter coffee, black. Burr usually preferred at all times his cafe blanc, or white coffee. He focused on preparing the beans and probably did not use the filter method. "Couche 12. Rose 6. The white coffee maintains its reputation, and I became more reconciled to its flavor. In a little while I shall like it. The disadvantage is, that it takes double the quantity. Don't imagine that I use it perfectly raw. Not so, Madame. The roasting took me two hours, so afraid was I that it would be spoiled. I succeeded to dry it in an iron machine made for the purpose of 'burning coffee,' till the whole was nearly a cream color, more nearly approaching very pale cinnamon, or something between both."

Methodical and sparing about whatever simple repast he prepared at home, Burr noted one October day making a point of getting fresh milk. But milk could sour quickly: "Read two hours in my Sp. Grammar. Made caf. blanc. Having no sug. Took of that infernal sirop de raisin, which with sour milk made a mess fit for the devil's feast, but swallowed it, and am still alive as you see at ½ p. 12."

He tested how to make his coffee nonacidic, so as not to jiggle his nerves, and to roast the beans at home a long time. "Vanderlyn came in and sat two hours. Had coffee blanc. I am making an experiment of coffee not burnt, having somewhere read that the burning made the oil acid, which was the cause of the nervous effect. I have drank two large cups. You will know to-morrow how I sleep. Vanderlyn found it detestable, and I confess it was somewhat mawkish." He really preferred coffee with sugar and felt deprived when he had to sweeten it with a concoction of grape juice. Sugar at that time was bought at the apothecary's shop and an observer said that the Parisians put so much sugar in the coffee that "it was nothing but a syrup of blackened water."

Clearly Burr had enjoyed his dish of coffee in America. The English were a tea-drinking nation and tea had been the most prevalent drink in the colonies until the patriots boycotted it along with clothes of British manufacture. Thus the American predilection for coffee drinking began; however, New York in Burr's day had taverns, not cafés.

The French began drinking coffee by picking up the custom from travels to the Middle East in the seventeenth century.[3] The vogue began as a classy pastime in 1669 when Suleiman Aga, the Turkish ambassador of Mohammad IV to the court of Louis XIV, arrived in Paris with a considerable quantity of coffee to serve the needs of his entourage and himself during his stay. The ambassador did so much entertaining that the fashion for drinking coffee took hold. He stayed a year and dazzled the upper class with sumptuous coffee functions replete with fancy cups on gold-fringed silk doilies. Exotically dressed slaves served the beverage, brewed Turkish style. The beans were pulverized in a tiny mill or a mortar and pestle, and an ounce of ground coffee was measured for a pint of water and boiled ten times over to reduce the bitterness. Women especially liked to add sugar. The first café au lait appeared in about 1685; by 1690, Madame de Sevigné was referring to a mixture of "coffeed milk" in a letter.

Two years later, Pascal Harouthioun, an Armenian who may have come with Suleiman Aga, opened a coffee-drinking booth at the Saint-Germain fair, which took place every year during the first two months of spring near the Saint-Germain-des-Près Abbey. This is where the public consumption of coffee began. After the fair closed, the sale of the beverage continued in the streets of Paris: Pascal sent out Turkish waiters bearing trays with lamps and cauldrons of coffee to hawk to presumably elite customers. Pascal next opened a coffee shop on the Quai de l'Ecole near the Pont Neuf. Meanwhile, at several other fairs, coffee booths opened up, accentuating the Middle Eastern origin of the beverage with their décor of tapestries, candelabra, and mirrors; those owners like Pascal had side businesses in Paris. When Pascal gave up his business in Paris to go to London, where coffee had more currency, other street vendors from the Middle East took his place. As cabarets "a caffe" opened in Paris and other French cities, their distinguishing characteristic was an atmospheric presentation, demitasse porcelain cups and fancy saucers brought around on trays being de rigueur. The steaming cups were called "petit noir."

Originally all the coffee in France was Arabian. Coffee from the Caribbean through Santa Domingo was popular during the empire except that the English blockade prevented nearly all coffee, chocolate, rum, and sugar from coming in from the French West Indies. Purportedly, Parisians took to hanging a piece of sugar from the ceiling, with each family member dipping it swiftly into his or her cup of coffee (or chocolate).

Coffee might have earned an aristocratic identity and fallen out of favor after the revolution. After all, Madame du Barry was an ardent coffee drinker. However, from the advent of the public sale of coffee in the fairs, where all classes mixed, coffee managed to be slightly sybaritic if also free of class or gender associations.

Cafés

Street vendors in Paris had since the 1670s had used portable coffee makers, circulating with trays, braziers, spoons and cups.[4] A coffee maker of a new type appeared in French cafés after 1800, based on the percolation system invented by the Archbishop of Paris, Jean-Baptiste de Belloy. "La Debelloire" had two stacked containers separated by a compartment containing the coffee. Boiling water was poured in at the top, and the coffee gradually infused and trickled to the bottom—a common method today. By roasting the beans intensely, Burr was anticipating the process of making espresso, which would be invented in 1820. He probably ground or pounded the beans to a powder, added water and boiled the mixture, since he doesn't mention a Debelloire, although he probably saw one.

Nor does Burr mention a struggle to understand the waiters. He evidenced a working knowledge of French, which, as anyone knows who has lived abroad, will, as opposed to book knowledge, take one everywhere. Burr went "au Coffee house," "au Coff'e," and "au caff'e" with utter abandon and with a heedlessness of standardized spelling common in his time.

Compounding his indifference to French orthography, he was a person of action, not a poet. He didn't belabor verbal expression concerning the amenities he savored.

While the Paris cafés had sizzled with political activity before and during the revolution, now customers came in to grab a cup of coffee and get on with their day or to muse and relax among a few people involved in a similar pastime. Cafés were multiplying, in part because apartments were small, and became a symbol of Parisian life during this period. Estimates of their number range from one thousand to four thousand. Many cafés had distinguishing features. For example, the Café des Aveugles had a blind orchestra, and the Café des Milles Colonnades was run by a beautiful woman who took money and gave orders in a vast colonnade room of mirrors.

Burr had his home, his buddies to visit, and cafés to go to. Jean-Paul Sartre said that for he himself cafés were synonymous with a feeling of plentitude. According to Sartre's existential philosophy, man is the being through which nothingness enters the world; he acts and chooses whereas the café is "condemned" to stasis. Sartre juxtaposed people with things so as to reveal the reaches and limits of the human mind.... If, for example, he went to a café hoping to see Pierre but Pierre was not at the café, Sartre saw his friend's absence, the nothing where Pierre should be. This lack was not a condition of the café. In itself, the café was what it seemed, a plentitude: with its patrons, tables, booths, mirrors, light, smoky atmosphere, and commotion of rattling saucers and footsteps which filled it, the café was a fullness of being. But for Sartre, missing his friend, the café signified a lack: "This figure which slips constantly between my look and the solid, real objects of the café is precisely a perpetual disappearance; it is Pierre raising himself as nothingness on the ground of the nihilation of the café."

Sartre, a Parisian, chose a café to show the human attempt to impose meaning on experience. Similarly, making his own time in Paris count was very much on Burr's mind. The acquaintances Burr seeks out often are not home or where he expected to find them, and as Sartre says, "Pierre absent haunts the café and is the condition of its self-nihilating organization as ground."[5]

This is the experience of anyone but it is acutely that of a foreigner. So it was for Burr, with his tight, barely furnished quarters where he rarely entertained, and friends who, like him, bobbed on the surface of the city. Thrown from the context of home, Burr threw himself into a life in Paris. He belonged in the sense that he accepted the world of Paris and didn't balk at new customs (*moeurs*) or fume at inconveniences. His pattern of going to the café with friends is part of building comfort with his social surroundings. Like Sartre, he patronized a café expecting to possibly see friends, or with friends, or to keep up with goings-on he would otherwise miss out on as a stranger. Thus cafés epitomized his situation—both the uncertainty and the need to act and take shelter. "Man is a social being," wrote Ben Franklin, "and it is for aught I know one of the worst of punishments to be excluded from society."[6] Cafés as an aspect of Parisian culture were proliferating from the platform of famous and successful cafés during the First Empire, and the café culture provided Burr with a social milieu, a neutral zone expanding beyond his lodging and the homes of his acquaintances, as follows:

- He was casual about going into this or that café, not a regular customer at one establishment.

- He went to Paris cafés where they were most concentrated, the Palais Royal, and liked to promenade there under the arches after a "dish of coffee."
- He sometimes ordered a meal at a café; he mentions a price for four courses, which indicates an upscale bourgeois café.
- He liked cafés with entertainment, such as music and dramatic performance, and didn't note political or philosophical conversation.
- He was sensitive to atmosphere and remarked on it in his journal, noting the stunning effect of the piers sheathed in mirrors at the Milles Colonnes and the cavernous, plushy feeling of the Café des Aveugles.
- He mentioned meeting an acquaintance by happenstance; thus, the café functioned as a bit of a clubhouse.
- Going to the café could be a diversion for him at almost any hour.
- Burr sometimes identified a café by location, not name, e.g., a café at the corner of Rue de Lille and Rue de Bac, on the Left Bank, across the Seine from the Louvre.

Whereas restaurants were not for ladies, cafés were, ever since a "limonadier" named Francesco Procopio from Palermo opened the Café de Procope in 1675 or 1676, aimed at a high-class clientele: "In contrast to what one might assume, women, even upper-class ladies, could go to cafés without causing a scandal."[7] Women, along with men, sat outdoors watching and contributing to the parade of people.

When the Comédie Francaise moved to today's Rue de l'Ancienne Comédie, the Café Procope moved to number 13 across the way, where it still can be found today. The café had marble tables, was dark inside and became a gathering place for the intelligentsia and artists—Voltaire preferred a mix of coffee and chocolate and had his favorite chair. When Ben Franklin died, in 1790, the walls of the Procope were draped in black.

The most popular promenades were in cafés along the grand boulevards that spilled over into the outdoors, the most famous of these being Frascati, on the Rue de Richelieu. An 1811 guidebook, *Le Ciceronne*, describes the café Burr goes to as "the most famous of the cafés of the Boulevard…. Its unique form, the beauty of its garden and terraces, the immense crowd that fills it, everything adds up to a spectacle of infinite variety."

During the French Revolution, the common man spoke his piece at the café. Napoleon as a young artillery officer liked to go to the Procope, as well as the movers and shakers of revolution like Marat, Robespierre and Danton. Napoleon would play chess and once Monsieur Procope made him leave his hat "*en gage*" for an outstanding coffee tab.

On Sunday, July 11, 1789, Louis XVI dismissed the very popular finance minister, Jacques Necker. The next day, hearing the news at the Café du Foy in the garden of the Palais Royal, a friend of Danton's and political journalist named Camille Desmoulins leapt onto a table outside the café and gave a speech urging the citizens to "take up arms and adopt cockades by which we may know each other," whereupon riots quickly spread throughout the city. Two days later the Bastille fell. Once, at the Café de la Regence in the Palais Royal, Robespierre played chess with a young woman disguised as a man to protect the life of her lover.

The English guidebook *A Paris Sojourn of 1718* reported that "almost everyone" went for coffee after lunch and Paris had an "endless number of cafés." According to Joan DeJean, there were fixed times of day, "women's hours," when women were particularly likely to frequent cafés. On their behalf, the food introduced was light fare, "nibbles," and garcons served wearing long white aprons and black vests. Already during the Old Regime the fashionable set took their coffee alfresco: "They began to have tables, chairs and all the café accouterments set up under trees or on outdoor colonnades, creating in effect the original sidewalk cafés."[8]

Cafés were subject to many regulations for a time, and then next to none with successive regimes. Writes W. Scott Haines, "Despite his authoritarianism and mania for regulation, Napoleon subjected cafés to few restrictions until the end of his reign."[9] Around the time of the revolution, working-class cafés were where the people had their voice; afterwards they were going about their business, and the political nature of their cafés went into eclipse. By contrast, among the middle class, in the more upscale cafés of the Palais Royal, Burr heard dissenting ideas. Cafés were understood to be a rallying place for foment, and after 1808, growing political discussion and agitation in Paris, coupled with political and military setbacks, prompted the prefect of police to watch cafés more closely. The tradition of informers, spies and agents provocateurs went back to the Old Regime, when one police prefect said that when three people were chatting in the street, one of them surely was his man. An estimate in the mid–19th century put the number of these agents at 2,000.[10] According to Haines, political discussion in upper-class cafés reemerged after 1805 but had little impact on the working class: "Aside from a few enragés, virtually all the 'café orators' who came to the attention of the authorities in the latter part of the First Empire were middle class—professionals and former government officials, called exclusifs."[11]

Between six and nine in the evening, Parisian bachelors would enjoy themselves in this epoch in these locales. The Boulevard des Italiens had many cafés and Burr refers to going to the boulevard, possibly meaning there. The most famous of them was the Café Tortoni, called simply Tortoni, founded under the Directory. Situated at the corner the boulevard formed with the Rue Taitbout, the Tortoni gave a view of people strolling superior to any except in the arcades of the Palais Royal, because few streets in Paris had sidewalks. Furthermore, this was before Baron Haussmann oversaw the widening of streets in the 1860s. Tortoni, close to the Bourse, the Opéra, and G.A. Fonzi's, was a place to see and be seen. Established by a Venetian ice-cream maker and next owned by a Roman ice-cream maker and his son, the Tortoni symbolized modern life. Among its scattered chairs and tables one could run into people from all walks of life. The improvements when Francois Xavier Tortoni became sole owner in 1804 give a picture of the café of Napoleon I's era. Tortoni put in small salons at ground level and on the second floor a big billiard room, where the billiard champion that Talleyrand liked to watch was playing by 1809. On the boulevard, Tortoni installed six tables and straw chairs, where carriages (calèches) stopped and people chatted while eating ice cream. As it was so near the Bourse, bankers, speculators and officials, especially, came in the morning, with the fashionable people arriving for a lunch at two and being served all evening. In Stendhal's *The Red and the Black* (1830), he mentions the billiard room: "How arrogantly he stared at me last night in the Café Tortoni, pretending not to know me!"[12] Honoré de Balzac, a patron of the Tortoni, wove it many times into *The Human Comedy* as being where the exclusive people hobnobbed and went for dessert. Joseph Conrad used the Tortoni as a setting in his story "The Duel" about two legendary officers in the Grande Armée. One afternoon, sitting on the terrace of the Tortoni,

The Billiard Room (1808) by Nicolas Antoine Taunay (1755–1830). The competition seems serious and the appurtenances, like the velvet banquette at the right, are classy. Oil on wood 6-⅜ in. × 8-⅝ in. (16.2 cm × 21.9 cm) (The Jack and Belle Linsky Collection, 1982 [1982.60.49]; image copyright © Metropolitan Museum of Art; image source: Art Resource, New York).

General D'Hubert learns critical information about his antagonist by accident, "from the conversation of two strangers occupying a table near his own."

July of 1811 found Burr at ease reading the newspapers in a café. He would have looked for papers from home, even if they were two months old. The French papers had been heavily censored since the Directorate, and Americans visiting Paris were "universally dismayed at the state of the French press under Napoleon."[13] The government named the censor and editor-in-chief for each Parisian newspaper, and by imperial decree of February 4, 1811, all but four newspapers were suppressed. Washington Irving, in France during his Grand Tour of 1804–1805, remarked, "The French gazettes contain nothing but fulsome adulation of Bonaparte and details of his Equipages his levées and his robes imperial."[14] In another letter, to Elias Hicks, July 25, 1804, Irving inveighed against censorship: "The papers are miserable tools of government.... They dare not say any thing of themselves, and their paltry paragraphs always commence with 'on dit' (they say) which answers to the mode in which some of our American gazettes launch out—'a correspondent informs.' One of these unfortunate papers having been rather free with his 'on dit's,' was laid hold of by the official paper at Paris entitled the '*Moniteur*' and poor 'on dit' got such hetcheling." The newspaper that discussed Napoleon's plans risked having its presses stopped and its editor replaced.

The prime place for news and gossip to be circulated was at cafés. Here one not only could get hold of a foreign newspaper, but also tune in on letters from friends and family sent to compatriots that had escaped interception by the police or hear the news relayed by a traveler. Burr wrote Theodosia in code, which he sometimes changed. Once, the letter reached her before the key to the new code. "For God's sake," she wrote back, "resume the old cipher. The new one, to which no key has reached me, is a severe addition to my anxieties and disappointments.... Not one word can be made out. I needed not this new mortification."[15]

The Best Cafés
by Giles MacDonogh[16]

The Palais Royal still took pride of place among the centers of Parisian gastronomy. It was a warren of cafés and restaurants. One of the best of the cafés was the Café de Foy, occupying seven arcades of the Palais; in 1806 Horace Vernet had decorated the ceiling with a swallow in the course of an animated dinner. Another was the Café du Caveau, which had been patronized by musicians before the revolution. During the empire it had an extremely important patron in Archichancellier Cambaceres, who came daily at eleven for his cup of chocolate. The patronage of the second power in the land allowed the proprietors to build a rotunda in the garden, which remained there till the end of the last century. Nearby was the Corrazu, which had been favored by Barras and the man to whom he referred as that "sly little Corsican"—Napoleon. There was a dance hall upstairs with the evocative name of *pince-cul* (literally pinch-bottom). The Café Anglais still existed for those "who liked to lunch in the English manner" (beef and bread). The Café Egyptian was decorated in that modish style which commemorated Napoleon's Egyptian campaign. Meanwhile the Café des Aveugles would seem to be an exercise in poor taste: an orchestra composed entirely of blind people from the Quinze-Vingts (eye hospital) serenaded a group of *louche habitués* [shady regulars].

Dining Out

Of lunch Burr said, "You observe that, before I go to these breakfasts, I always breakfast at home."

Napoleon's nouveaux riche entertained a great deal. They had reputations to make as they clambered to the top imperial posts, and fancy foods made a comeback. Such dinners began late compared with the habits of the ancien régime—at seven or so (which led to the second breakfast, or *déjeuner*)—and were characterized by service *a la française*, consisting of platters or tureens each containing a separate dish, placed in a pattern on the table, from which the guests partook. The dishes and sauces were made with separate bouillons, which encouraged new recipes, and the new nobility often had fine chefs.

A well-read American gentleman had read Cicero's condemnation of luxurious foodstuffs and praise of vegetable dishes and porridge, associating them with the plain virtues of the Roman republic.

Being convinced he should eat moderately and simply and see what effects foods had on him in order to balance his diet, Burr did not think this an easy matter. First of all, he was too indigent to have staples on hand and what he ate was hand to mouth—rice someone gave him, noodles from the grocer's, sometimes take-out from a cook shop, whatever the landlady provided, and so on. He patronized the neighborhood purveyors when he ate in and went further afield to restaurants with friends. Sometimes he invited a friend in to share his repast, as when, one fall day in 1810, he served his friend Crede potatoes.

He had digestive complaints. Sometimes what he ate increased feelings of malaise. He suffered wakefulness from coffee (which, by the way, Jean-Jacques Rousseau loved) and tea. Burr once complained the sole and turbot "had been kept at least eight days" at "Conchal, famous for excellence in every sort of fish." Moreover, his outings with friends to restaurants (or someone's house for a meal) seem more improvised than planned.

Eating Establishments

Burr learned quickly that at some restaurants there was no tipping and service was included. Often his meal was a progressive one, as being out is where a man alone often would like to be. He might have beer and biscuits one place and then sangaree (an 18th century punch of red wine, sugar and nutmeg) at a fashionable café, and other fare at yet another establishment. At Le Conchale, Burr praises the fish (perhaps named after the word for conch shell). He dined at Le Café des Aveugles and Le Café des Variétés.

Gastronomy during this period witnessed the genesis of the restaurant, which offered a place to eat in the evening, catering to new bureaucrats and out-of-towners. A maid where Burr was staying made him "restaurants," or thick bouillons, when he caught a chill. But "restaurants," in the sense of eateries with printed menus, flexible hours and private tables, were just opening up in Paris, especially in the Palais Royal area.

In the eighteenth century, the restaurant began as a place to have restorative bouillons of medicinal purpose. Voltaire, a passionate gardener, had written that a good cook was a fine doctor too. Rousseau was all for eating simply, little meat, and cooking with ingredients of local origin. But the vogue for restorative, or haute, cuisine had passed and the nomenclature changed. By 1810 the signs of a variety of eating-houses said "restaurateur." A lively atmosphere prevailed, as well as gentility relative to, say, New York City's taverns. Here people could converse over champagne or a full meal. One might not lunch with a lady in a café but it was permissible to dine with her in a restaurant, sometimes in a separate room. In the future, the restaurant itself would become a tourist attraction equal to Versailles or the Louvre. But from 1805 to 1810, due to war and blockades, there were not so many foreigners in Paris, and the world of the restaurant centered in the Palais Royal along with shopping, gambling, and prostitution.

The revolution had accelerated the trend of dining out, and the heyday of Napoleon's empire was a period of great excitement and dramatic change in French gastronomy and the pattern of Parisian public dining—in a word, there was more of it. Tasty ingredients and lengthy preparation, as well as individual, refined flavors were the "in" thing. By 1810, there were already cookbooks with recipes for sauces; the age of Carême was launched. As Priscilla Ferguson, food historian and professor at Columbia, says, "It was the beginning of the golden age—well, a golden age, of the restaurant, the beginnings of gastronomic criticism, and the advent of gastronomy as a recognized social practice—the word appeared in 1801" (personal communication with Priscilla Ferguson, November 15, 2013).

Most of the former cooks of the nobility either went abroad or established their own restaurants. The restaurant was a Parisian phenomenon. Paris had no guilds or system that limited the proprietors of cook-shops and "restaurants" (where a restorative or bouillon was served) to certain fare. Paris had 2,000 restaurants in 1804, while there were next to none in the provinces and only a scattering in other French cities. Writes Rebecca L. Spang in her study, *The Invention of the Restaurant*, "Both a strange and confusing world, wrapped opaquely in gastronomy's rules and vocabulary, and a publicly open and available space, a bit of daily French life to which travelers had easy access, restaurants were the perfect mixture of the familiar and the exotic, the intimate and the extraneous."[17]

The word "menu" is French in origin, deriving from the Latin minutus, something made small. At Le Procope, now Paris's oldest restaurant, Burr might have looked at a printed menu. But more restaurants would have had a chalkboard (a *carte*, thus à la carte), or the server announced the dishes, or the fare was standard, chosen by the proprietor or chef and simply delivered to the table. The fare might be table d'hôte or à la carte. Wines were not paired exactly with food; both red and white wine would probably appear on the table and each guest would choose his preference. At the restaurants Burr found a variety of oysters, fresh and saltwater fish, all kinds of fowl, veal, mutton and beef in pastry, and so forth. The French began to think of their country in terms of what Grimod de la Reynière called "alimentary topography."[18]

The Expansion of the Restaurant World

BY PRISCILLA FERGUSON[19]

There were restaurants in the late 18th century, but urbanization made their fortune. They were notable for their number, their variety and their culinary, as well as social, stratification. Second, the beginning of gastronomic journalism was with the work primarily of A.B.L Grimod de la Reynière and his *Almanach des Gourmands* (1803–1812) and *Manuel des Amphytrions* (1808).

One found foreign visitors in Paris restaurants, including women, though there were more after the beginning of the restoration (1815). Generally, respectable French women of the middle and, especially, upper bourgeoisie did not frequent restaurants, even later in the century. But ladies of lesser distinction certainly did. It has been argued that restaurants served as something of a safety valve for the constraints of bourgeois life.

The printed menu was one of the great innovations of the modern restaurant, which set it against the table d'hôte, where there was no choice. The contemporary menu first appeared in France during the second half of the eighteenth century, the Romantic Age.

Prior to this time customers ate what the house was serving that day and sat at a common table. The establishment of restaurants and restaurant menus allowed customers to choose from a list of unseen dishes, which were produced to order according to the customer's selection. A table d'hôte establishment charged its customers a fixed price; the menu allowed customers to spend as much or as little money as they chose. The more elegant restaurants such as Véry or the Rocher de Cancale had printed (or hand-lettered) menus. The further the restaurant was down the line, the less likely it was there would be a printed menu. Menus were often posted outside so that passers-by would know what they were getting into.

Some restaurants were bawdy, though there were often private dining rooms for select

The Ice Cream, plate No. 4 from *Le Bon Genre* (1827). This colored engraving of three women in an elegant café comes a little later in the 19th century than when Burr was in Paris, so it cannot be certainly known what sort of women in 1810 would have sat alone at a café. The artist shows them licking with sensual display from serving dishes that look like cones, but French waffle cookies did not morph into cones until the St. Louis World's Fair in 1904. Still, the ladies prefer to hold up the dishes and leave the little dessert spatula spoons on the table. The tasseled seat at the right is Turkish and the reticule hanging from the chair and poodle indicate some means. The waiter offers "seconds" from a menu of seven flavors—peach, apricot, "crème" (vanilla), pistachio, "panaché," lemon, orange, or sorbet. Jeri Quinzio explains the mystery flavor: "Panaché, also spelled panachee, means mixed or layered. It's often used to describe jellies layered with different flavors/colors and here would mean mixed, as in two different flavor ice creams in one serving. There's also a French drink by that name that's lemonade and beer poured into a glass so they form layers" (Bibliothèque des Arts Décoratifs, Paris/Archives Charmet/Bridgeman Art Library).

debauchery. Entertainment was not a draw in the upper reaches of the restaurant world. As already mentioned, the restaurant scene was notable for its diversity and its stratification, both culinary and social. As with restaurants in big cities today, different social groups/classes frequented different kinds of establishments, the choice being dictated by taste, by culture and, of course, by disposable income.

The range of eateries was well beyond what an American would have found at home, even in New York (Delmonico's dates from the 1820s and was the primary "fancy" restaurant in the city for a long time. It was run by Swiss, but the cooking was French.) The upper end—fine dining in our parlance—was fancier and finer than in the U.S. There was more variety, and with the influx of temporary residents (politicians, administrators), there was a need for places to eat and to stay. This was also the beginning of the *hôtel garni*, that is, the furnished hotel, more or less as we know it today.

Interestingly, in choosing between staying home for a meal and going out it seems Burr probably preferred to stay home, rustle up his meal or have a good bouillon prepared by a servant or a cookshop, and read a book. He passed the time with good wine, sparse food, "segars" and the quiet where he could reflect and engender plans. He had inhabited other places where he lived more simply than his estate at Richmond Hill—in the army, exploring the West, and most recently the city taverns in Philadelphia before deciding to self-exile. Even when, at five in the evening on January 30, 1811, a note comes from Mr. Fenwick that he must prepare post haste a letter related to procuring his passport, Burr says, "It was then 5, and I had not written a line. Took my dinner and bottle of wine at leisure, and then went to work."

Ice Cream Treats

Burr was in a cheerful mood when he noted "taking" ice cream (borrowing the verb from the French "*prendre une glace*"). He had certainly sampled ice cream in America. In a New York newspaper in the spring of 1777, a confectioner had announced he had ice cream for sale nearly every day. In the summer of 1790, George Washington is said to have spent an exorbitant 200 dollars for ice cream at Mount Vernon, where he owned ice cream pots of tin and pewter. Thomas Jefferson's icehouses held not only many wagonfuls of ice but ice cream as well, and he redacted a recipe for ice cream in his own hand. Meanwhile, in Paris, ice cream stalls were doing a great business a whisper of time after the revolution. By 1800, insulated icehouses in Europe and America made ice cream a commodity that the less wealthy could enjoy, and books on confectionery gave recipes for how to make it. Jeri Quinzio details the nature and popularity of ice cream in Paris in 1810.

Ice Cream in Aaron Burr's Paris
by Jeri Quinzio[20]

When Aaron Burr arrived in Paris, it was the world's ice cream capital, and the city professional confectioners from England and other countries visited to learn the secrets

La Belle Liminaudiere au Caffee de Mille Collone (1814) by Thomas Rowlandson (1756–1827). The middle-aged men look up from their coffees, enthralled by the famed beauty (here lampooned) that worked the cashier (courtesy Rosenwald Collection, National Gallery of Art, Washington, D.C.).

of ice cream making. Only Italy rivaled France in terms of ice cream. America lagged far behind.

Parisians ate their ice cream in style in the chic cafés scattered about the city. There were hundreds of these cafés, with at least half a dozen in the Palais Royal, from the Café de Foy to the Café des Mille Colonnes. At the latter Burr marveled at the many mirrors and the proprietor's glamorous wife, La Belle Limonadière, the server who was mentioned by many contemporary guidebooks as a sight herself. She was pictured by Thomas Rowlandson reading insouciantly at her raised table, dropping cash into an urn, keeping an eye out that customers were satisfied, and adding to the panache of the restaurant as Elaine Kaufman did to Elaine's.

Cafés had begun life as crowded shops where customers might buy medicines as well as coffee and hot chocolate. By the time Burr arrived, they had been transformed into bright airy spaces with gleaming mirrors and sparkling chandeliers where fashionable patrons sipped coffee, chocolate, or absinthe and indulged in all manner of frozen delicacies. The cafés were as famous for ices and ice creams as for coffee and liqueurs. In fact, some were called cafés glaciers, or ice cream cafés. Everyone who was anyone, from actors to diplomats, frequented them. Throughout the nineteenth century, artists including Manet and Guérard immortalized cafés in their paintings. Writers set stories in cafés and wrote about the latest ices. Author Jules Janin called Tortoni's Café "a saloon for sherbet and ices." In his novel,

Splendeurs et misères des courtisanes, published in 1839, Honoré de Balzac described the ice cream called *plombière*. He wrote, "As everyone knows, this sort of ice contains delicate preserved fruits, placed on the surface without affecting the ice's pyramid form, and is served in a small glass." Later, an edition of the book in English translated *plombière* as a sundae. When the translation was published, of course, there was no such thing in America and no such word previously in English.

Earlier, in the latter half of the eighteenth century, French confectioners had published books for other professionals explaining the techniques of ice cream making and offering dozens of recipes. A confectioner known only as M. Emy wrote the first book solely dedicated to the subject and one of the finest, *L'art de bien faire les glaces d'office*, loosely translated as The Art of Making Ices for Professional Confectioners. Another writer, Joseph Gilliers, included a large section on ice cream in his 1751 book, *Le Cannameliste français* (cannameliste refers to sugar work, i.e., confectionery), as did François Menon in his 1767 book, *Les soupers de la cour*. Its English edition was titled *The Art of Modern Cookery Displayed*.

Writers had not quite settled on what to call these iced delights. Glace, glace à la crème, glace de crème, mousse à la crème, biscuit de glace, fromage glacé, neige, eau glacé, sorbet— all were among the names they used. Biscuit de glace was so called because crumbled biscuits, or cookies, were blended into the ice cream. Sometimes they were left in, but more often they were strained out before the ice cream was frozen. Nuts, too, were customarily steeped in the mixture to add their flavor then strained out to preserve the ice cream's smooth texture. Popular preference favored a creamy consistency over a chunky or crunchy one. As one confectioner put it, smooth ice cream was "infinitely more agreeable to the mouth."

Fromage glacé was not iced cheese as the name implies, but an ice cream that was molded. The molds came in many shapes, and some did take the form of a wedge of cheese. In that case, the ice cream would be topped with burnt sugar to imitate the cheese's brown rind. Confectioners occasionally flavored an ice cream mixture with cheese. Gilliers made a Parmesan ice cream, and many others copied his recipe.

Green tea ice cream became trendy in the U.S. at the turn of the twenty-first century, but it was already being made in Europe by the late eighteenth century. Orange flower water ice cream is rare today, but it was a more popular flavor than vanilla until the mid-nineteenth century when the commercial cultivation of vanilla was developed.

Many typical late eighteenth and early nineteenth century flavors—strawberry, chocolate, lemon, pineapple, coconut, coffee, peach, pistachio—are just as familiar now.

However some early flavors strike people today as unusual or odd. These include artichoke, asparagus, saffron, tarragon, and violet, to name just a few. Emy made an ice cream with truffles—the fungi, not the chocolate. An Italian confectioner, Vincenzo Corrado, wrote that there was no vegetable confectioners could not turn into an ice cream, and some seemed eager to prove him right.

Confectioners delighted in molding and coloring ice cream to resemble anything from peaches to fish heads, from pickles to pomegranates. It was so skillfully done that occasionally they were served to intentionally trick the diner. When diners tasted what they thought was going to be a peach or a pickle and it turned out to be ice cream, they were startled. Sometimes they were amused and pleased; occasionally, someone was upset and angered by the deception.

Ice creams served in chic cafés were usually presented in small, stemmed glass cups called *tasses à glaces*, or ice glasses. When the glass was filled, the ice cream was swirled up into a peak. To modern eyes, it looks as if it came from a soft-serve machine. The confectioners created all these flavors and fashioned all of the elaborate molded ice creams in an era without mechanical refrigeration. It was a time when making ice cream was a labor-intensive and rather tedious proposition, since it had to be mixed and cranked by hand. Ingredients like sugar were costly, as was ice, which was difficult to obtain and store. All of these factors meant that ice cream was an expensive luxury. Visiting a stylish café and enjoying a dish of orange flower ice cream while watching tout le monde pass by was a leisurely upper-class pastime.

In years to come, ice cream would become commonplace, and street vendors would sell it to children for pennies, but in Aaron Burr's Paris, it was a refined pleasure.

Sugarplums

On New Year's Day 1811, having gone to bed at one the night before, Burr was up early, at 7:30 a.m., and had a day of social calls. First he stopped at Fonzi's, "busy and indisposed to be more so, being holiday." Then he paid a visit to his friend Valkenaer, who asked him to join him and "Alb." [Albertina] at their New Year's dinner that evening. Burr left a card at the Duc d'Alberg's, spent a half-hour at Dr. Swediaur's and, continuing on, encountered a scene that amused him:

> Then a tour round by Rue St. Denis. Saw near St. Denis in Rue Lombard a great crowd, and soldiers with bayonets keeping order. Joined the mass to see what was going on. It is a famous manufactory of sugar-plumbs and the like; and for fear people, in their zeal to buy, should squeeze each other to death, soldiers were sent by the police. They let in only four or five at a time. When my turn came in I got in. The variety of whims, ornaments, &c., is really curious. I bought a box in imitation of a pear, filled with sugar-plumbs, for 20 sous, and a little cornucopia of painted paper, covered with silk and tied with ribbon, full also of sugar-plumbs, for 15 sous. Note: The sugar-plums are a little sugared on the surface; the rest is flour. Home. Changed my dress and off to Valkenaer's.

The sugarplums seem likely to be a gift to a lady, or a hostess gift, perhaps to "Alb." Sugarplums, some version of which Burr saw in the window, were confections of caraway seeds, nuts or particles of spices like cinnamon coated in sugar. If the sugar was dense the candy was "ragged" but if it was thin, the candy was smooth. The confectioner drizzled many layers of the sugary syrup via a pearling funnel onto the confits. Sugarplums could be colored with spinach for green, mulberry for red, saffron for yellow, and so on. Dressing up the sugarplums in fancy boxes was one manner of selling them, and in drawings of the time usually they are in cornucopias. That Burr waited in line at the confectioner's and joined in the fanfare speaks of his frame of mind, one of curiosity and acceptance of French culture.

Parisians were consuming much sugar, especially in their coffee and their sweets. Before

Antoinin Carême (1783–1833) virtually created the science of gastronomy he was a pâtissier. He learned the craft as an apprentice on the Rue Vivienne just behind the Palais Royal and eventually had a shop on the Rue de la Paix from 1803, possibly until 1813.

Carême began his stellar career as a kitchen boy in a restaurant in exchange for room and board. At 15 he was apprenticed to Sylvain Bailly, a renowned pâtissier with a shop near the Palais Royal. Carême began to make elaborate confections for Bailly, centerpieces entirely out of sugar, marzipan, pastry, and so forth. Pictures circulating from Napoleon's exploits in Egypt inspired him, and Carême modeled the showpiece sweets after Napoleon's so-called conquest of Egypt and architectural drawings of temples, pyramids and ancient ruins, which Carême examined at the nearby Bibliothèque Nationale. Bailly agreed to let his apprentice leave his employ early. Carême, at his own Pâtisserie de la rue de la Paix must have influenced other pâtissiers to excel; it was an elite craft but everyone, including the working people, liked to window-shop for the fine products.

Carême went from Bailly's fashionable confectionery to a job for twelve years as pâtissier to Talleyrand under his chef Boucher. For a ball for the new emperor at the Salle de l'Opéra in 1804, given by Napoleon's generals, Carême created 30 suédois, towers of fruit in syrup molded with aspic and jelly. Napoleon, who raced through his meals, at least noticed and Carême moved on to the next level by passing an extraordinary test. With Napoleon's financial support, Tallyrand employed Carême as chef de cuisine at the palace to entertain diplomats. Famously, Talleyrand assigned Carême the creation of a whole year's worth of menus that didn't repeat and used only seasonal produce.

Talleyrand, of course, did not actually come in person to the pâtisserie on the rue Vivienne. He might well have noted Carême's window displays from his sedan-chair window— the mountains of nougat, meringue, beignets and flanets. But it was Boucher, Talleyrand's maître d', who alerted his sweet-toothed master to the young pâtissier.[21] After the First Empire, Carême became chef to the Prince Regent, later George IV, in London, creating spectacular confections such as a several-foot-high Royal Pavilion in sugar.

Viewed in the popular mind as an American aristocrat, Burr was probably as accustomed to fine dining as any Founding Father, despite some barren patches of late. He had entertained at Richmond Hill, an ornate mansion formerly the home of Vice President Adams when the U.S. capital was in New York, and according to one biographer, "proceeded to entertain visiting celebrities in princely style. No distinguished Frenchman, exile or traveler from his native land, but spent hospitable weeks as his guest."[22] A lingering meal followed by more conversation with the scents of coffee and tobacco filling the room was a natural prelude to spending time with friends in Parisian restaurants, even if the less ritzy and more "du coin."

The Center of Gastronomy
by Giles Macdonogh

Restaurants were still booming under the empire and a less marked division of wealth allowed for a wider cross section of the population to eat in them, even simple laborers who had spent a profitable day "putting aside their cabbage and bacon to eat a pullet with cress" in a restaurant. In 1805 the Palais Royal contained fifteen restaurants, twenty cafés and eighteen gaming tables. Apart from those mentioned above, the best restaurants were both Provençal, being the Trois Frères Provençaux and the Boeuf à la Mode. The three brothers (trois frères) were in fact three brothers-in-law from Marseille called Maneille, Barthélemy or Trouin, and Simon. The restaurant established the vogue for Meridonal cooking in Paris, and sold brandades, a casserole of potatoes and salt cod, and the "various ragouts of their region." It was one of the most fashionable restaurants in the city. It was very difficult to get a seat. The Boeuf à la Mode commemorated that famous dish "that will be a la mode for as long as the Pont Neuf remains neuf." It was founded by another pair of Marseillais in 1792 who were famed for their salt cod, bouillabaisse, green olives and nougat. The sign hung outside the restaurant continued to give offense; it depicted an ox dressed as a belle of the Directory, an Incroyable, according to Balzac's dictionary of Paris street signs, wearing a shawl and a fantastic hat.

Ten

Perambulation

Aaron Burr's New York stride was full of purpose if, as it is today, New Yorkers in 1810 felt a slight stress when their feet punched the pavement. In Paris, Burr settled into a different promenade, an unstressed, flowing motion like the rhythmic quality of the French language. Indeed, if there were no ambient talkers the two promenade styles probably would not have diverged, as the stresses on words affect how people walk where a language is spoken. Walking in Paris is always evocative, but Paris of 1810 exerted a special fascination as the cultural capital of Europe at the beginning of a new century. Civic improvements were being conducted with gusto and the city drew ambitious young people from all over the world. Burr saw it all, as he was compelled to walk a great deal in Paris. One day, 27 July 1810, he noted, "My different walks to-day amount to fourteen miles, and all for nothing." But he seems to have mostly walked to see friends and to destinations in order to have fun.

The quays had a mix of activities and were nice places to walk but walking on streets meant dodging all kinds of traffic. Sidewalks would not be commonplace until the middle 1820s; meanwhile, gutters were the centerline type that poured out into the streets. (Lateral gutters were tested on the rue Saint-Honoré in 1811 but were not in force until mid-century.) The narrow streets with no pavement or drainage quickly made a river of mud in a downpour. It was impossible for Burr to walk on streets in the many rainy days during his stay, which is corroborated by what a young French medical student wrote home in 1810: "Only a very small number of sewers existed. After heavy storms there were quarters that became impossible to traverse. There were torrents, truly impassable rivers. All communications were interrupted, even for carriages. The neighborhood messengers were equipped with planks of wood—a kind of mobile bridge—that they threw over these rivers when it was possible to do so, and one paid a toll to cross."

Contrasting with the narrow, messy inner city streets were the spacious new boulevards, much remarked upon by tourists. The boulevards constituted a festive strolling procession, in which the well-to-do mixed with the working class to enjoy music, dancing, and the scene. The colorful public life of Paris brought men and women and children into urban spaces such as theaters and cafés or just out for fresh air. As they interacted they tacitly worked out new modes of dress and manners.

Many of the public walks and gardens that had formerly been private or royal domain became open to the public. Abigail Adams had noted in a letter to a friend in 1785 that the Tuileries gardens were open to the populace only one day a year, the fête day of Saint Louis. In Burr's time everyone enjoyed the recreation of most of Paris's beautiful parks and walks.

The Tuileries became much more popular to walk in during the First Empire, lively on the outside, if, due to the militarization of the court, as Talleyrand said, triste inside, with few courtiers choosing to reside there.

Denise Z. Davidson writes that people learned to read "new markers of social status taking shape" largely from observing others in public spaces: "the new post-revolutionary social order emerged in part through men's and women's participating in the everyday activities of strolling, sitting in cafes and watching entertainments. Whether this meant the upper classes 'slumming' with the masses on the Boulevard, or workers hobnobbing with the rich and mighty in a public park on a Sunday afternoon, Parisian public life gave ample opportunities for heterogeneous groups to mingle."[1]

People were unclear about how to behave and wanted to see and to be seen to sort out how the society around them was organized. Beginning in the 1820s, people watching, suggests Professor Davidson, waned as Parisians grew less fascinated with diversity and the city had more specific spaces for specific groups. As a foreigner, the great bazaar of Parisian life in 1810 surely helped Burr to acclimate. Only rarely, as when he mentions wearing lace when the other men at a party didn't, did he express feeling out of place. As Burr walked he noted mental pictures to store away, but the company of his friends and carrying out his plans were his primary goals.

Sometimes a prostitute approached and distracted his focus from his round of errands and visits. The presence of women was central to the social positioning after the French Revolution. Women displayed themselves as never before. A paragraph in an 1809 guidebook published in Paris and London criticized the woman of Paris for demonstrating her taste and fashion sense publicly: "Coquettishness, this inborn sentiment among women, the only one perhaps that has entered the heart of every Parisienne, is a vague desire to please and to attract the attention of all men without settling on any of them; it brings a woman, even when she loves sincerely, to desire numerous hommages; she resists, and puffs herself up with the power of her charms in the eyes of he whom her heart has chosen."[2] Davidson suggests, "With confusion about whether birth, wealth, or merit would determine one's status, gender distinctions became more salient, because they seemed more reliable than these other categories. In particular, women's dress, morals, education, and comportment all became matters of great interest as symbols of proper upbringing and thus of a right to hold a certain social position."[3]

Female Apparel

Women's and men's dress was becoming more and more dissimilar. The actress on stage or lady promenading was ultra-feminine, whereas men were beginning to dress more alike across classes and their dress was becoming more stable across classes—of definite benefit to a stranger of exiguous fortune. In a word, the Parisienne was eye-catching in very symbolic clothes. "Fashion plates" were strolling on the streets in filmy, low-cut dresses with tiny sleeves and gathered bodices, limpid fabric that swirled around their legs, and only an artful wrap for outerwear. To appear classically pure, devoid of seditious thoughts, sometimes women in the decade after the revolution oiled their bodies and wet down their dresses to make them cling. Fundamentally what was "in" was to look as if one was poured into one's skimpy white dress.

Evening slippers (1805–1815). Silk slippers were not created for walking in muddy streets. These are of cream silk satin with cream silk grosgrain ribbon (Metropolitan Museum of Art, Brooklyn Museum Costume Collection at the Metropolitan Museum of Art, gift of the Brooklyn Museum, 2009; gift of Herman Delman, 1954 [2009.300.1470a, b]; image copyright © Metropolitan Museum of Art; image source: Art Resource, New York).

Any woman who attended to her hair, dress and slippers could look as glamorous as a queen, as dress of both genders proclaimed the principles of freedom and social equality.

The colored and black-and-white engravings of the period suggest lightness and animation. The woman of fashion wore dainty slippers or bottines (mini-boots) with her simple gown, and around her body she draped and redraped a cashmere shawl. Napoleon and his officers brought Kashmiri shawls back from the French Egyptian campaign, Josephine inaugurated the fashion of wearing them in Paris and Napoleon gave Marie-Louse 17 among his wedding gifts.[4] In pictures of that wedding women wear them folded fastidiously over one arm. Even in portraits, women are posed with languid ease and informality. For example, *The Portrait of a Woman* by Henri-François Mulard, 1810, a student of David, evidences the informal and youthful imperial style favored by women Burr saw promenading in Paris. The portrait's subject has a silk Scottish plaid scarf knotted at her breast and around her hips, and peacock-eye embroidery on the neckline draws attention to a casual décolletage.

Burr must have known that one reliable way to tell a respectable lady from a prostitute was her perfume. It was said that when Marie Antoinette was fleeing to Varennes in disguise, her Houbigant perfume gave her away, as only an aristocrat could afford it. From perfumer François Rance, Napoleon, who kept a bottle of eau de cologne in one of his boots, commissioned two exclusive fragrances, for Josephine and himself. When they were in a room together, her perfume dominated, but when they came together the two perfumes merged to create a unique new fragrance. In 2004, the house of Rance relaunched both perfumes, which Napoleon had forbidden to be released for sale until two hundred years after the 1804 coronation.

Fresh Air

People took walks and drives to get fresh air outside of their rarely commodious apartments. In March of 1803, this note appeared in the *Journal des dames et des modes*:"Parisians

CHAMPS ELYSÉS.

Champs Elysees (circa 1820), possibly from *Paris and Dover, or, To and Fro: A Picturesque Excursion,* by Rober Book'em. The amusements illustrated in the throng include a showman with a troupe of dancing dogs, a fiddler, and, in the background, an aerial children's ride (courtesy Lewis Walpole Library, Yale University).

are strollers by nature; as soon as the weather barely permits it, the boulevards, the Champs-Elysées, all the public gardens are filled with pedestrians who come to liberate themselves from the bad air of their homes and the mud of the city; and the most pleasant sight to see, when one is a stranger to the capital, is the concourse of these good people, flocking in crowds to stroll as soon as the first beautiful days of spring begin."[5]

Lest one picture an Impressionist painting, it must be taken into account that Paris was preindustrial and, despite the street-cleaning Napoleon instituted, the street conditions were poor. A vignette from Burr's journal describes the art of walking safely "the pleasures of Paris" as follows: "No sidewalk. The carts, cabrioles, and carriages of all sort run up to the very houses. You must save yourself by bracing flat against the wall, there being, in most places, stones set up against the houses to keep the carts from injuring them. Most of the streets are paved as Albany and New York were before the revolution with an open gutter in the middle. Some arched in the middle, and a like gutter to each side.... It is fine sport for the hack driver to run a wheel in one of these gutters, always full of filth, and bespatter fifty pedestrians ... braced against the walls."

Since, like the majority of Parisians, Burr had neither carriage nor horse (although sometimes he traveled on horseback), he didn't promenade in the popular upper-class location, the Bois de Boulogne. He did go to the Tuileries. He also strolled the boulevards, using the phrase "the Boulevard" to refer to the string of boulevards in northeast Paris, where, in the period after the revolution, upper class mingled with those who came for the inexpensive dance halls, theaters with pantomime, puppet shows, and melodramas, as well as the free entertainment of street musicians, curiosities, and performers and merchants hawking their wares. As an American Burr must have felt the privilege of seeing the Old World. Paris itself felt large, and Burr was compelled to walk a great deal in Paris. One day, 27 July 1810, he noted, "My different walks to-day amount to fourteen miles, and all for nothing."

To make his mark on Paris presented Napoleon with many challenges, as it was a ravaged city in 1800. For example, it had been a city of churches—by one count, 150 as well as over 200 religious houses and seminaries. Almost all the monasteries and all but 15 churches were demolished or sold during the revolutionary period, most of the statues of Notre Dame were mutilated, the Invalides was dilapidated, and the royal tombs at Saint-Denis desecrated.

The scene during Burr's residency had a shadow reality that Alistair Horne limns, which coexists with the monuments shown on the map (see Appendix C), and that was the catastrophic recent past. Prefacing his remark that Sainte-Chappelle was used as a flour warehouse and bore a for sale sign, Horne writes:

> But a great many churches had been totally destroyed. In the center of squares, pedestals stood bereft of their statues; almost the only monument left was that of the somber Place de la Révolution (renamed Concorde only a few months after Robespierre's execution there). The façade of the Tuileries, which had once housed Robespierre and the dreaded Committee of Public Safety, was still marked with bullet holes, while the Church of Saint-Roch bore the more recent scare of General Bonaparte's own "whiff of grapeshot" from 1795. The great houses of the nobility and the bourgeois had been pillaged, with barely a courtyard gate still left on its hinges. Walls had been brought down, and shacks built upon the girdle of market gardens. On both banks of the Seine Paris resembled one immense housebreakers' yard, combined with a no less enormous junk shop.

When Napoleon commenced to put in sidewalks on a few streets, they were raised too high and seemed to bury the houses and boutiques they passed by. The hydraulic sewers took precedence, so that it was not until 1812 that many sidewalks were built and it became more pleasant to stroll. Accidents were rife. On October 24, 1776, the driver of an ornate nobleman's carriage tearing through the streets knocked down a 64-year-old man, Jean-Jacques Rousseau. The philosopher was walking along a narrow street on his way home when the carriage hurtled at him. A Great Dane that ran either in front of or alongside it seems to have collided with Rousseau. The carriage never slowed down. When the accident was made known later, the nobleman offered to compensate the victim, but Rousseau refused and forgave the dog. Rousseau claimed that being run over made him think more in the moment. Certainly he was seeing the glass half full, as he probably suffered neurological damage. He died two years later.

Burr must have walked his neighborhood, and then much of Paris and the outskirts; *flâner*, to stroll without purpose, was coined at this period. He often saw spectacles by accident, such as a carnival on Pont Neuf, where the revelers were arrayed head to toe in slips of colored paper and harlequin costumes. He wrote in his journal on February 16, 1811, "to tell Theo. of the pleasures of walking in Paris" and launched into the description of the hazards noted earlier—no sidewalks and inconsiderate vehicles. He then described a further discomfort: "The gutters or conduits for the water from the eaves of the houses are carried out a few feet from the roofs, and thus discharge the rain-water over your head. In most places there are no such pipes, and then you have the benefit of the water from the eaves. This was a great ridicule against the city of Albany about twenty years ago; but Albany has reformed the evil."

However, he could stay near lodgings and find everything he required. He wasn't staying on the big boulevards but the typically narrow streets. The rue du Croissant, where he lived, newly paved with stone and drained, was such a street—favored by the press and lively with cafes that Balzac, whose family moved to Paris in 1814 when he was 15, would frequent.

Crisscrossing the City

Sometimes he hired a "cabriolet man" for a few hours. Ordinarily, having no funds to take a carriage compounded his reluctance to spend money on a toll (not all old bridges had tolls, new ones all did). He crisscrossed Paris the day he met the painter David at Denon's, the Louvre museum director, saw Colonel Swan at the prison, visited a lady friend, met a business acquaintance, and came home to pay his tailor—all in the first half of a day. One hears his exasperation, not at having to go thither and yon, which he embarked on with alacrity and did with vigor, but with having to detour to avoid the toll bridge! With so much visiting, no wonder people used *cartes de visite* in this period. "When at Denon's, thought, as it was well on towards St. Pelasgie, I might as well go thither, and set off; but recollected that I owed the woman who sits in the passage 2 sous for a segar; so turned about to pursue my way by the Pont des Arts, which was within fifty paces of me; recollected that I had not wherewith to pay the toll, being 1 sous. Had to go all the way round by the Pont Royal, more than ½ mile out of my way, and this occasioned my meeting G." Unexpected meetings with an acquaintance may have happened in the Rooms at Bath in a Jane Austen novel, but frequently they happened on a bridge in Paris. Meanwhile, just getting the bare necessities and the occasional "segar" kept Burr roaming the city.

Burr was no romantic plunged in his thoughts or surrealist looking for meaning to leap out at him. He was a man of the Enlightenment who liked to apply science and reason to his disrupted personal life. Yet the city that had gone through a cataclysm and the ancient capital before him was in Walter Benjamin's words a laboratory of social change, swept up into an instant empire, and being given a new face. It was the flâneur who, in literature from Balzac to Flaubert to André Breton's *Nadja*, would become emblematic. As Priscilla Ferguson writes, the flâneur could be born anywhere but lived most emblematically in Paris:

> It was not by chance that the flaneur appeared on the streets and in the narratives of early nineteenth-century Paris. The post-revolutionary city both invited and required new urban practices. The disarray engendered by continually shifting political and social bases, like the incertitude fostered by a constantly fluctuating population, undermined the sense of the city as a whole. As David McCullough writes in *The Greater Journey*, much of Paris in the 1830s was still a medieval city. He quotes one weary traveler in Restoration Paris, John Sanderson,

"The streets run zig-zag and abut against each other as if they did not know which way to run. As for the noise of the streets, I need not attempt to describe it."[6]

Honoré de Balzac's "A Double Family," an early story set before 1820, opens upon a serpentine Parisian street encrusted with a permanent layer of mud.[7] The street is so narrow that any rainfall floods it and washes household waste against the base of the houses. "When the sun shone on the capital, a saber blade of golden light illuminated the obscurity of this street for a moment, without being enough to dry the permanent humidity that reigned from the ground to the first floor of those black and silent houses. The inhabitants, who in June lit their lamps at five o'clock, never extinguished them in winter."

CABRIOLETS.

These are very numerous,—and great acquisitions,—plying at regularly appointed stands, to be enjoyed at reasonable fares, and tho' allowing but a confined view of what passes,—afford a refuge from rain and mud, and great relief to those the back sinews of whose legs have not served an apprenticeship, or, a few campaigns, on the *pavé* of Paris.—The drivers being civil and intelligent, whenever a moment can be spared from their vociferous notices of, Garde! Hay-ho! Garde!

Cabriolets (circa 1820), possibly from *Paris & Dover, or, To and Fro: A Picturesque Excursion*, by Rober Book'em. The cabriolets were hailed at stands throughout the city. They allowed a confined view of what passed and, as the guidance to tourists says under the drawing, "afford a refuge from rain and mud, and great relief to those the back sinews of whose legs have not served an apprenticeship, or, a few campaigns, on the pavé of Paris" (courtesy Lewis Walpole Library, Yale University).

The "famous allure and vitality of the great city won them over soon enough," writes McCullough, and so it was with Burr, who embraced the excitement of Paris even under his difficult circumstances. Rather than taking promenades for pleasure, it seems as though Burr took "destination walks." However, he also once says he "ran" with Vanderlyn and another time that he "roved two hours"—so there were different moods of promenades, as one would expect.

A Typical Itinerary

As far as Burr's routes to visit the two gentlemen he passed a great deal of time with, John Vanderlyn and G.A. Fonzi, they were within a not-too-large range (see Appendix C). While Burr moved from the Right Bank to near the Boulevard Saint-German on the Left Bank, he was still only a few streets from the Seine, which provided a feature sensed, if not always seen, from his path. Most of the Paris he circulated in was the densely populated inner core, bounded by the "old" or "inner" boulevards, on both sides of the Seine that had been built by Louis XIV along the lines of the medieval fortifications. The approximate timing follows:

From his first lodging, 7 rue de Grenelle-Saint-Honoré (today the Rue Jean-Jacques Rousseau) in the 1st arrondissement, it would have been a half-hour walk to Vanderlyn's at 72, rue de Vaugirard, which hasn't changed its name and is now Paris 6th or 7th arrondissement; about 20 minutes to Fonzi's at 1 Place des Italiens (now Place Boieldieu (Paris 2nd) or 12, Rue Taitbout (Paris 9th). From his next lodging at 7, Rue de Croissant, it took about 40 minutes to walk to Vanderlyn's, 12 to Fonzi's Taitbout address and 8 to his other place at 1 Place des Italiens.

Burr must have asked for directions. He admitted in a couple of places in the journal that his written French is poor, but he also notes a compliment a Swedish officer gave him on his spoken French. It's likely that Burr mostly spoke French rather than English to communicate in Sweden and Germany with those he met who had a second language, so he would have had practice before arriving in Paris.

From a remark in the journal on "Ciceroni Parisien" containing, among other items, a description of the average weather conditions in Paris, it appears that Burr used a guidebook. This gave him coordinates as he became acquainted with the city. With new thoroughfares such as the Rues de Rivoli and Castiglione, and the Pont de la Cité and Pont des Arts, guidebooks were constantly revised during the imperial period. Writes Priscilla Ferguson, "As Paris expanded and built (Napoleon I started significant building projects virtually as the century began), guidebooks proliferated. Typical of what we now immediately recognize as an example of this most conventional of genres was *Le Nouveau Conducteur parisien ou plan de Paris* (1817) with maps, listings of hotels, means of transportation, sometimes statistics of one kind or another, and useful information ranging from hours and locations of restaurants, museums, and libraries; numbers of houses, streets, and inhabitants; locations of translators; the street numbering system; and so on."[8]

The population of Paris in 1810 had grown to about 600,000 and most of it was concentrated in the inner boulevards on the Right Bank and across the Seine in the Latin Quarter. There were few open green spaces, except for the Tuileries and the area from the Louvre to the Place de l'Alma. The housing shortage was hardest on the poor. Burr, like other Americans with more means, wanted to be centrally located. When he returned from his side trip to Holland on June 22, 1811, he stayed at the Hotel de Normandie (a second choice), which was on the Rue des Boucheries, which has since been absorbed into the Boulevard Saint-Germain. It would have been approximately at the point in the boulevard where the Rue de Buci is now. It may have been a pension situation like many such hotels. It was situated farther from the center of Paris bustle, his friends and activities, and he stayed there but a few weeks.

Nights Abroad

Strolling was a daytime occupation due to dark streets at night. Honoré de Balzac, glancing back at the Paris of the Restoration, wrote of the old streets bordering the bright Palais Royal and Rue de Rivoli:

> These narrow streets, dark and muddy, where such industries are carried on as care little for appearances, wear at night an aspect of mystery full of contrasts. On coming from the well-lighted regions of the Rue Saint-Honoré, the Rue Neuve-des-Petits-Champs, and the Rue de Richelieu, where the crowd is constantly pushing, where glitter the masterpieces of industry, fashion and art, every man to whom Paris by night is unknown would feel a sense of dread and melancholy, on finding himself in the labyrinth of little streets which lie round that blaze of light reflected even from the sky. Dense blackness is here, instead of floods of gaslight; a dim oil-lamp here and there sheds its doubtful and smoky gleam, and many blind alleys are not lighted at all. Foot passengers are few, and walk fast.[9]

In early times, it was expected that houses facing the street should set candles in their windows, and anyone out on the streets after dark was required to carry a light. Public lighting, per se, began in the seventeenth century, with the city's first police chief, Nicholas

Overshoes (1790–1810). These leather toe protectors had a heel strap made of a small metal spring covered in white kid. They became obsolete when heelless shoes became dominant in the late 1810s (Metropolitan Museum of Art, Brooklyn Museum Costume Collection at the Metropolitan Museum of Art, gift of the Brooklyn Museum, 2009; gift of Herman Delman, 1955 [2009.300.1493a, b]; image copyright © Metropolitan Museum of Art; image source: Art Resource, New York).

de La Reynie, who convinced Louis XIV of the merits of street-lighting (by oil and candle lamps). The king commanded that lamps be lit even on moonlit nights, and taxed Parisians for the costs, which involved employing not only lamplighters but metalworkers, ropemakers, glassmakers, and tallow chandlers. The new lights, the flames encased in iron-framed lanterns with glass doors, were hung from cables (ropes) stretched about 15 feet over the street at intervals of 60 feet (a fashion of suspending lamps unique to Paris). Yet, regarding the mid-seventeenth century, A. Roger Ekirch writes, "At that late date, most persons at night still remained on their own, confronting crime and other dangers with, at best, the aid of family and close neighbors.... In Paris, observed a lawyer in 1742, 'no one was out past 10 P.M.'"[10] Not all the lamps hung on the ingenious cables. Some were suspended from pylons, a means many other cities used, for instance, to illuminate a square. Either type tended to obstruct traffic when being trimmed. A silvered reflector is an example of the modifications made on the oil lamps.

Wolfgang Schivelbusch points out in *Disenchanted Night: The Industrialization of Light in the Nineteenth Century* that when these several-times-brighter lamps were introduced to Paris streets late in the 18th century, they didn't make the night-time city brighter. The 6,000 to 8,000 old lanterns in Paris were replaced by 1,200 reverberes and the distance between them was increased from 20 to 60 meters. In other words, the light intensity gained by technical improvements was lost again by spreading the lanterns more thinly on the ground. Reverberes stood out like islands of light in the darkness.[11]

Burr gave some indication of staying up late and sleeping in, due to factors including nerves, restlessness, and anomie: one sees him literally burning the midnight oil as he sips his Roussillon wine, reads Godwin or geographies, and writes, using a quill pen, in his journal. Burr didn't present his insomnia and lucubrations as bizarre, and only sometimes questioned their effect on his health. Moreover, he often was out late: late hours had become fashionable during the royal regime. First, aristocrats had stayed up gambling at Versailles and had their "collation" or breakfast by candlelight well after midnight. Then, as many of them had their "hotels" in Paris, breaking away from the court they turned night to day and day to night in the capital. Craig Koslofsky, having made a profound study of the nocturnalization of early modern daily life, comments, "It was in coffee houses that many burghers first encountered billiards ... as well as chocolate, tea, and fine porcelain. But coffeehouses taught the aristocratic consumption of time as well, leading respectable men into late hours."[12]

A satiric letter from an anonymous subscriber appeared as "An Economical Project" in the *Journal de Paris*, April 26, 1784. Ben Franklin had been the U.S. ambassador to France for eight years, and people quickly realized him to be the letter's author. The anonymous letter writer said he was accustomed to stay up well past midnight and sleep until noon; however, after a very stimulating presentation on the Argand lamp, he found himself awake early, whereupon he discovered that "the sun gives light as soon as it rises." He therefore proposed the economy of rising at dawn and receiving "much pure light of the sun for nothing." It would be after World War I that Franklin's idea was adopted in the United States.

The end of the 18th century marked the first significant advance in oil lamps, which was that very Argand lamp of keen interest to Franklin named after a Swiss physicist and chemist, François-Pierre Argand (1750–1803), who had studied with Antoine Lavoisier, the celebrated discoverer of the fact that materials combust when combined with oxygen.

The Argand lamp had a flat ribbon wick, a glass chimney, and an efficient mechanism that ensured fuel was fully burnt in the flame. However, the Argand lamp gobbled oil; and usually a heavy oil, like a kitchen oil, fueled it, so that the flame could not be adequately supplied by simply placing the wick into the oil (capillary action). The Argand lamps used a larger amount of oil than the old style, so they were not practical to have in the thousands on the streets.

Various solutions were tried to raise oil from the reservoir at the base of the lamp. In 1800 a Parisian, Bernard Guillaume Carcel, created the Carcel lamp.[13] He was a clockmaker, which is interesting as testimony to how advanced the science of horology was. Carcel used a clock-driven pump to feed oil to the wick automatically. Brian Bowers writes that the Carcel lamp was popular in France and, because its output was steady, it was often used as a standard for light measurement. It was never much used in England, partly because it was expensive and partly because the taxation made the colza oil (also known as rape-seed oil) used in Carcel lamps dearer than the whale oil used extensively in the UK and America from the later part of the 18th century. Presumably, having little means, Burr didn't have the Carcel lamp, but he would have seen them in use by his friends, since Fonzi and Vanderlyn both relied much on light for their metiers.

Despite a ruling in the spring of 1800 by the prefect of police that streetlamps be illuminated continuously at night, the public lighting in the city of Paris remained spotty, even on the major streets. People were now flocking in the evening to the theaters of Paris, which by now had not only chandeliers with candles but the chimney "lampes d'Argand" (with their adjustable wicks) ten or twelve times as strong as candles. However, when the audience left the theater they confronted the dark street, and *porte-falots* (lantern bearers) waited there to be hired.

Paris under Louis XIV was described by one writer as "not the City of Light but the city of candle ends." Napoleon wrote from Poland in 1807 to Joseph Fouché, head of police, "I understand the city of Paris is dark at night. The fact that Paris has not been illuminated constitutes a condition of ruin and decay. The contractors for the city's lights are idiots. This abuse, of which the public is starting to complain, must be eliminated!"[14]

Burr would have walked on the major boulevards as much as possible at night but would have ended up on the dark streets as he approached his lodging. Under the empire new lights were installed in the center of the city on the Right Bank. In January 16, 1812, the *Journal de l'Empire* reported, "The night in Paris is more beautiful than the day." The public received such improvements with enthusiasm while in fact the city was mostly still shrouded in darkness at night. The inventor of one of the first gas lights, Philippe Lebon, was stabbed and killed, at only 37 years of age, in the Champs Elysées on the eve of Napoleon's coronation. It is suggested that this tragedy retarded the introduction of gas illumination until the 1840s. All in all, street lighting under the empire continued to be hazardous for pedestrians despite Napoleon's occasional strong complaints. More so than efforts at illuminating the streets, the professional police and firefighting forces made the city safely traversable by night.

Eleven

Female Companions

In this first of two chapters on Aaron Burr's social and sexual relations with women during his Paris stay, Burr will speak mostly for himself. If not an apologia pro vita sua, his journal is far and away his longest work in his own voice, and his entries offer a good deal of insight into his lifelong fascination with women.

Burr's interest in women's intellect was unusual for the times. In an 1807 Portrait of Burr, a Federalist writer described him as the "epitome" of "Lord Chesterfield and the graces." This was to imply that Burr was all surface, without principle, a follower of the Chesterfieldian maxim that "polished brass will pass upon more people than rough gold." It is true that Burr, like Chesterfield, esteemed the social graces, politeness, and good breeding, and like Chesterfield he admired the French for their tone, refinement, and polish. However, from the start of Burr's Paris journal it is clear he would have rejected Chesterfield's advice to his son Philip that "female sovereigns of the beau monde ... are but children of a larger growth. A man of sense only trifles with them, humours and flatters them. They have in general but one object, which is their beauty, upon which scarce any flattery is too gross for them to follow." Chesterfield also told his son, "I would not recommend you go into women's company in search of solid knowledge or judgment."[1]

Fifty years after Chesterfield outlined manly conduct to his son, even the English romantic poets—contemporaries of Burr, but a generation younger—had scarcely a higher opinion of female capabilities. Byron took exception to his wife's interest in mathematics, mocking her as the "princess of parallelograms," and wrote in *Don Juan* (in an unusual rhyme), "But oh! ye lords of ladies intellectual, Come tell us truly, have they not henpecked you all?" Shelley, theoretically a feminist, consistently exploited all of the women to whom he was closest—his mother, sisters, and both his wives, his female servants, and followers like his soulmate, Elizabeth Hitchener.

Even the non-misogynistic Keats wrote an 1817 couplet, "Woman!," epitomizing the prevailing view of women as the weaker vessels: "God! she is like a milk-white lamb that bleats/For man's protection," a sentiment directly contrary to Mary Wollstonecraft's sarcastic observation a generation earlier in *A Vindication of the Rights of Women*: "[Woman's] natural protector extends his arm, or lifts up his voice, to guard the lovely trembler—from what? Perhaps the frown of an old cow, or the jump of a mouse; a rat would be a serious danger."

Burr read the *Vindication* when it first appeared in 1792 and praised it as "a work of genius." He noted to his wife the following year that he alone championed her work among his acquaintances. And here is Burr's assessment re Wollstonecraft's *Vindication*, from a February 16, 1793, letter to his wife:

> You have heard me speak of a Miss Wollstonecraft, who has written something on the French revolution; she has also written a book entitled "Vindication of the Rights of Woman." I had heard it spoken of with a coldness little calculated to excite attention; but as I read with avidity and prepossession everything written by a lady, I made haste to procure it, and spent the last night, almost the whole of it, in reading it. Be assured that your sex has in her an able advocate.... I promise myself much pleasure in reading it to you. Is it owing to ignorance or prejudice that I have not yet met a single person who had discovered or would allow the merit of this work?

Mary Wollstonecraft believed that society conditioned women to frivolity, arguing that,

> The human character has ever been formed by the employments the individual or class pursues [and for women,] seldom occupied by serious business, the pursuit of pleasure gives that insignificancy to their character which renders the society of the great so insipid. [They] fly from themselves to noisy pleasures, and artificial passions, till vanity takes the place of every social affection, and the characteristics of humanity can scarcely be discerned.

Burr supervised a rigorous academic curriculum for his only child, Theodosia, to keep her from the very fate Wollstonecraft wished women to avoid. Channeling Wollstonecraft, Burr wrote to his wife Theodosia Prevost Burr his little regard for pampering: "If I could foresee that Theo would become a mere fashionable woman with all the attendant frivolity and vacuity of mind, adorned with whatever grace and allurements, I would earnestly pray God to take her forthwith hence."

While in Paris, Burr categorized women and their comportment. First came women of an elevated social class, with whom he spent much of his time in Paris while waiting out his passport impasse and with whom he probably did not sleep; he refers to all of these women by their last names. Next, French women of the same class whom he indicates he may have slept with at some point and refers to by the initial of their last names only. Next, women in Paris whom he refers to by name or trade (e.g., Prevost, Edwards, Fleury, Caroline, Clotilde, Albertina, Virginie, Miranda, Marian, Flora, the beautiful laundress, the beautiful lady shoemaker, the painter's model, the dancer), with almost all of whom he seems to have had paid sex on various occasions. And last, many streetwalkers with whom he had paid sex, probably never with the same one twice, and whom he generally referred to by their physical characteristics or how much he paid them.

As the subject of Burr and women, considering just his fifteen months in France, is involved, this chapter relates to the more important individual women in his Paris life, the topic of his dealings with prostitutes being reserved for the following chapter.

Madame D

To get an idea of the type of woman Burr found very attractive, consider Madame D. Burr met her in a coach on a side trip from Paris traveling through Antwerp and Rotterdam on the way to Amsterdam, where he intended to buy stock to further one of his schemes. Due to this lady's social class and married state, Burr observed what seems to be a consistent code of not revealing her last name or whether he ended up sleeping with her—actually, he did sleep in the same bedroom with her on successive nights, but that's as much as he will say:

> But before noticing the events in Rotterdam, let us go back to Anvers [Antwerp]. The places in the diligence [stagecoach] are numbered, and on paying your passage you receive a certificate specifying the number of your seat. I had No. 2; Madame D, also for Amsterdam, had No. 1. At the moment of leaving Anvers, a fat, well-dressed, ill-looking Flemman [Burr's made-up word for a Flemish man] took possession of my seat in the diligence, and I was thrown out into the curricle [an open horse-drawn cart which followed the stagecoach]. The morning chilly and my overcoat not come-at-able. At the first stop, Madame D asked me if I were not the person who had ataken a seat for Amsterdam. Yes. "But come in, please, take your seat." "But I don't like altercations." "Nonsense! Turn this pig out." Nevertheless, I was so charmed with my companions [three young children] that I continued in the curricle. At the second stop Madame renewed her remonstrances. I agreed to assert my rights. I took the seat in the diligence by the side of Madame D. The Flemman came to claim his place. "Sir, if you have more right to it than I, I shall yield to you. If not, no." The coachman was called and desired me to go to the curricle. I refused, and asked him to look at his register. The Flemman, seeing that I was not very docile, retired to the curricle. Madame D and I were tête-à-tête and she appeared coy and difficult. Madame D is about 25, the wife of a former [i.e., before the French Revolution] noble who enjoys a place of some consequence under the present government. She may be described in one line—the very image of Caroline Senat [a French aristocrat who took refuge in New York during the French Revolution and who lived in Burr's household as Theodosia's tutor]—the hair, the eyes, the form, the physiognomy, the wit.

On arriving in Rotterdam, Madame D and Burr found an inn and were shown into "a very large, elegant room, with two beds, one at each end. "I, like a booby, said: 'We need another room.' There was no other. Looked at Madame to see what was to be done. 'This will do.' Supper in our room. Hiatus valde deflendus." This Latin expression, from the Roman poet Virgil, translates as "a gap exceedingly to be lamented." In other words, Burr, according to his code again, drew a curtain over what ensued following their supper (quite possibly nothing amatory). Whatever the case, the two of them were on the road again the next day and shared another room in Amsterdam the following night, after which Madame D continued on her further travels. Burr also recorded this vignette on the morning between their two nights together: "Had breakfast at 6. Was sitting in the parlor below reading a newspaper. Received a smart click on the head. It was Madame. 'But you are quite at your ease there. You left all your clothes lying pell mell. You're not thinking of anything. You're like a child. The stagecoach is going to leave and you're doing nothing.'"

Burr last mentioned the assertive Madame D three weeks later, when he decided he couldn't make a side trip to visit her. At the time he was unwell, suffering from a condition later revealed to be merely piles, or hemorrhoids: "My complaint increases and becomes very painful. Have therefore decided to give up Emden and Madame D, and hasten to Amsterdam [en route back to Paris] where medical aid can be had."

Madame Robertson

Of the many women mentioned in Burr's Paris journal, one Madame Robertson appears more often than the others, probably because she was so persistent in seeking out

Burr's company. Burr had met her some years before in New York. In March 1810, a month after his arrival in Paris, he renewed their acquaintance: "Yesterday called on Mrs. Robertson, the widow of Dr. Robertson, who has here a very elegant establishment. She is amazingly well preserved." "Well preserved" in Burr's terminology did not necessarily mean older than him, since earlier in the journal he praised the looks of a Mme. Sieveken in Hamburg, calling her "about 50, but exceedingly well preserved."

In his next entry, Burr intimated there had been a falling out of some kind: "In the A.M. went to make peace with Mrs. Robertson. She is too good to harbor malice and received me very kindly. Staid two hours, reading over papers of business and talking of matrimony, on which head we have grave quarrels, for I am dead against it. 'What!' says she, with temper and astonishment, 'would you advise me to,' &c. 'Madame, be independent' &c. Took soup there and parted friends.... Note: It is an hour's walk from my quarters to Madam Robertson's, being about one league.... Mrs. Robertson will certainly marry that young Adamson very soon."

Burr frequently exhausted his cash, living hand to mouth for days or weeks, but he could always count on Paris friends such as Madame Robertson for a good meal: "Went on to Mrs. Robinson's [*sic*], where an hour. Wine and water, bread, butter, and ham. Gamp [Burr] was hungry. She urged me so much to come back and dine, that I consented.... To Madame Robertson's to dine at ½ p. 5. After dinner Madame reproached me in terms which did not please me with machinations against her intended match, which is not true. Her expressions were so unkind that I left the room without replying and came off and think I shall not go there again. Home at 8 and did not go out again.... [The next day] A note from Madame R. Very amiable; must make up. So wrote a very amiable answer, q.v. Poor good soul, she is grievously tormented by her lovers and will probably finish by marrying one of them."

Burr's "amiable answer" was as follows, showing that he knew well how to be conciliatory. The letter is included in the 1838 edition of Burr's journal published by his literary executor and former political acolyte, Matthew Davis:

> To Madame _____
>
> It is impossible, my dear friend, that I can ever be seriously angry with you, because I know the invariable and inexhaustible goodness of your heart; but it is true that I was very much hurt by the unmerited impeachment of my candor. As I had not put myself in competition with your suitors, though always your very great admirer and friend, I thought myself exempt from the suspicion of insincerity and I therefore felt your reproach with perhaps too much poignancy.... I must acknowledge that I had not got many steps from your house before I reflected that you had told me that your mind was agitated; that, under such circumstances, we have a claim on the indulgence of our friends; that the sally at me, au fond, meant nothing; that I ought to have parried with good humor, and that I had been too abrupt, and I should actually have returned to have made peace with you if you had been alone. The thing has hung like a weight upon my spirits all day.
>
> A. Burr

Thus, Burr's visits continued as before:

> On to Mrs. Robertson's. She was with her mantua maker, in deep consultation over half a dozen new and very rich robes. I was taken into council, which lasted an hour. Mr. Adamson came in and I came out. Suspect she is going to marry him, though she denies it stoutly.... Note this evening from Madame R. requesting me to make her a law paper, in a great hurry,

as all women are, except you who understand better than even I do how to festina lente [make haste slowly].... Am in a great distress about Madame R.'s paper, for I had promised it to her tomorrow morning, and it will not be done till night. You women are always in such a hurry. In a debate today about women, Gamp [Burr], as always, defending.

At 11, a note came from Madame R. with a bottle of opodeldoc [for Burr's injured foot, this was a liniment prepared by dissolving Castile soap and camphor in alcohol and adding oils of thyme and rosemary], in which I had happened to express faith. She had very often intimated a wish that I should know more of Mr. Adamson. In my reply to her note, I asked her to tell me candidly whether he would be pleased with a visit from me. At 4 received another messenger from her, saying that he would be greatly flattered, and proposed to call on me tomorrow evening. Agreed to receive him at 2. You see into what trouble this will bring me.

This cabriole fare will ruin me [Burr needed to hire a cab due to his injured foot].... Thence to Madame R.'s to get the address of Mr. A., and thence to Mr. A's, where a ½ hour. He has the appearance of a well-bred, amiable man; not deficient in intelligence or education. Thence back to Madame R.'s. She kept me more than two hours. Dismissed my cab. and ordered her carriage for me. To go to England or not; to marry or not; these are the two interesting questions which disturb the peace of mind of my charming friend. Having hitherto preserved a neutrality on the subject of matrimony, she has, at length, extracted from me a promise that I will on Monday give her a decided opinion on both points.

To Madame R.'s, whom found expecting me. She urged again for my advice and I gave it. First, that she should not go to England, and, second, that she should marry A. if she must at all marry, which she avows; says she has not independence and force of character to go on à la française [as a man's mistress]. For six months I have been reasoning against marriage, and in favor of a voyage to England. Now that I have taken t'other side of these questions, she also has changed her language, and reasons against this marriage and in favor of going to England. Took soup and staid an hour. Engaged to dine with her tomorrow, and begged her to ask A. We shall see whether she does so.

Some time ago, Madame R., showing me her jewels, seemed particularly pleased with a [illegible] and earring of Italian sculpture out of conch shell. Of course I admired them. Today she made them a present to you. I declined as long as I could, for though they are pretty curiosities, they are things not for you to wear. Still, they are very pretty to stare at and so you shall have them.

At 4 set out on foot to dine with Madame Robertson. I had desired that Mr. Adamson might be there and Madame Menutzi not. It was so arranged. Jane Evans joined us and the day went very well. Mrs. R. still balancing about going.... Madame urged me so to come tomorrow that engaged to breakfast with her.

My foot is still swollen and troublesome. I walk with pain and limping. For the last two days I have quit opedeldoc and tried cold water, but without any sensible benefit. On Sunday Madame sent her carriage for me, and I took breakfast with her. She has got her passport renewed, and talks of going, but I think she will not. She urged me to dine, which I refused.

On Wednesday received a note from Madame R. entreating me to come either to dine or in the evening, as she must see me.... Then to Madame R.'s. Found there Mr. A. and Madame Menutzi. On entering, "Well," says R., " I have given up the journey and have promised to marry him." So I wished them joy.

I had intended to breakfast that day with Fenwick [another of Burr's lady friends, discussed below], but at 9, just as I was dressed, came Madame R.'s servant, with a note and a gig (her carriage being at repairs), to bring me to breakfast. Submitted and went. She had begun to repent, and thought she ought to go to England to arrange her affairs before her marriage. I rather confirmed this disposition. Mr. A. came in and there were scenes. I made several attempts to go, but she would not let me stir. At length got off on promising to come back to dine. Home for an hour.... At 5 to Madame R.'s and to my surprise there was A. to dine with us. Seemed all peace and calm—and she is to go to England.

> The domestique of Madame R. came in to solicit my aid auprez de Madame to get her off to England and get her rid of A. It seems that the journey is talked of in the same undecided way, but A. is constantly there.
>
> Monday breakfasted with Madame Robertson at 10. She gave me honey, but vile gunpowder tea. She is still "going," but not gone. The probability is that she will be going till worse weather sets in, and then, "Lord, who could think of going in such weather?" Urged me to dine, which refused.
>
> That tea of Madame R.'s does not agree with me. To Madame R.'s at 11. Kept me ½ hour making her toilette. Still going.
>
> A note from Madame R., very friendly and confidential. She proposes to go tomorrow morning. Wrote her that I would call at 5, and if she should not be gone, would dine with her.
>
> Madame R.'s servant called at 8, before I was out of bed this morning, with a verbal message, begging I would call on her today without fail. Agreed to call at 1.... At 1 to Madame R.'s. It was only the old story, wanting me to advise her to things her own judgment condemns.
>
> Forgot to tell you that at 8 this morning, scarcely daylight, Madame R.'s servant with a kind note, begging me to dine today, with some special reasons. Got out of bed, answered the note, saying I was engaged, which was a lie. Then to bed, and slept another hour. [Some days later] Set out at 4 for Madame R.'s, it being an hour's walk, to dine.... At dinner Madame and I had a little difference, in which I thought she was wanting in courtesy. Off at 8. Home. Exceedingly stupid, and a headache from bad wine, of which I drank a few glasses.

Before long Burr realized the reason for the quarrel they had:

> For some days past, and more particularly today, I have been in a state of irritability very unusual. Answer brusque and rapid. Say things almost rude.... Can you imagine from what this arises? The want of muse [Burr's term for sex]. I have found nothing of that kind to my taste here for reasons which shall be detailed at leisure, and now see [from looking at his journal?] for ten days; really I suffer and am scarcely fit for society. The same cause must have occasioned my quarrel with Madame R. on Thursday, for now I think on't, it would have been easy with a little more gentleness and gallantry to have put both her and myself more at ease.

Burr's confession about needing a certain frequency of sex is similar to John F. Kennedy's confiding to Prime Minister Harold MacMillan that he became irritable if he was celibate for three days.

> At 10 came the servant of Madame R. with a note of compliments dated yesterday, and an invitation dated yesterday, and an invitation to dine yesterday or today.... I sent a reply by a messenger (15 sous) that I was engaged today. I think I will not dine any more with her. Voilà, six weeks she has been pouting about that trifling incident at dinner.
>
> [And finally] Thence to Madame R. à la fin! Found her very elegantly dressed, and said some civil things thereon; and all went very smooth. Asked me to stay and dine. Said I was engaged; which was a lie. Asked me for tomorrow, and proposed to send her carriage. Said I was engaged, which was another. Finally, seeing there was no way but to quarrel or to dine, and as we had been in great good humor, I agreed for Tuesday.... At 4 the carriage of Madame R. called and I went thither, taking up Madame Menutzi on the way. We and Adamson were, as usual, the party. Off at 9. Her carriage set me down. Madame R. still doubting, and her lover received as usual.... To Madame Robertson's. Toujours la même. Asked to dine, which declined.... In the Palais Royal met the domestique of Madame Robertson with a note asking me tomorrow, to which assented verbally.

This last entry, dated February 18, 1811, is the final one in Burr's journal concerning his many visits with Madame Robertson. William Bixby, the editor of the 1903 version of the journal noted: "From the 18th of February till the middle of May 1811, the journal is entirely missing."

Madame Paschaud

In the same period he was paying frequent visits to the widowed Madame Robertson, Burr spent much time visiting two other female friends whose husbands were on long absences from Paris. The first of these was Madame Paschaud, wife of a Swiss bookseller. Burr had met her through a letter of introduction from Baron Strick in Germany to a Dr. Swediaur in Paris, who was a friend of Madame Paschaud. Burr professed to "have a very great aversion to letters of introduction, having everywhere found acquaintances, made accidentally, the most agreeable and permanent, obviously because they are made from sympathy." In fact, Dr. Swediaur did seem to break off with Burr later, after Burr accidentally broke the doctor's electrical apparatus. Until that incident, Swediaur treated Burr, not for his medical specialty, syphilis, on which he had written a treatise, but for a sore throat, and Swediaur introduced Burr to Madame Paschaud: "At 1 to Swediaur's, and gave him a louis professionally, the first cent spent this way [i.e., for medical treatment] in ten years. He tells me nothing new, but with the ordinary remedies ["vinegar and water sweetened with honey," we later learn] thinks I will be able to speak and swallow in three or four days.... The doctor gave me the name of another bookseller, Madame Paschaud, a Genevese lady. I was very agreeably surprised to find a beautiful, sensible, well-bred woman. Sat ½ hour, and engaged to call yet again as visitor, though I am as yet incognito."

The preceding entry is dated March 12, 1810, and Burr, who hardly misses a day writing to Theodosia in his journal, lets sixteen days go by without another entry:

> Looking over my scraps, I cannot find that I have written you a line since the 12th inst., nor have I any sort of apology to offer for the negligence. Not want of leisure, for of that I have too much. It was on the day that I saw Madame Paschaud, and I have been there regularly twice a day. Have passed every evening with her save one. Have walked with her; have been to the opera; dined there two or three times en famille.... My principal rival is Monsieur Cha_____, who comes very often with a very elegant equipage. Madame is about the size of Dolley [Madison, whom Burr had introduced to James Madison, the future president], though some ten years younger [making Mme. P about 30 years old], still larger. Very black hair and eyes. A fine, clear, fair brunette, with the complexion of full health. Her husband is at Geneva. I rather think that she must be the cause that I have not written you.

"Eight more days without a line!" wrote Burr shortly after. "Paschaud takes up all my time." However, after Burr left Paschaud for two weekend excursions, the first on his Rousseau pilgrimage to Montmorency and the second to Saint-Germain-en-Laye, their relationship, platonic or not, begins to sour. After returning from Montmorency, as Burr told it: "Arrived at ½ past 10. After embracing my beloved friend Madame Pelough [Burr's landlady, also Swiss and a friend of Mme. Paschaud], off to Paschaud's. The diablesse [she-devil] has gone to the country, too! Pure vengeance. Four times have I walked there (½ league) [a little over a mile] today and at 9 this evening she had not arrived."

Over the next several days, there was strain between them, and then, on Burr's returning to Paris from his second overnight excursion, he "posted over to ma belle amie, about one mile. Gods, how cold, chilling! Not having said that I would be out all night, there was much inquiry and alarm. Finally it was discovered that I had been assassinated, and the maid had got all the particulars; she was at work to get my soul out of purgatory, which she feared would be a long and hard job. But what devil can have got into Madame P.'s head? Called at Fonzi's [Burr's dentist and good friend] on my way home from P.'s. His warmth and kindness recovered me a little from the shock of P.'s coldness."

A few days later he noted, "To Swediaur's, where met Madame P., being the first time I have seen her since my miraculous reception on Monday. We were very civil but no more." And finally Burr registered a permanent parting of the ways:

> But the most important event of this month is the Hegira of Madame Paschaud, who has actually gone to join her husband at Geneva. We had been sulking, as you know, ever since my return from St. Germain. On Tuesday last, received message to dine with her that day, as she should leave town next morning. Dined there, but was grave, silent, appetiteless, and without affectation. Some engagement, forget what, called me away early; but at 10 returned. She was out. Went at 6 next morning. She had gone to the bath. Followed there and waited till she came out. Walked a few minutes in the garden, and had explanations, which on both sides declared satisfactory, and we kissed and made friends; but we are not such friends as we were two months ago. Went with her to the diligence office and saw her off. Adieu, ma belle amie. Vraiment, son absence m'attriste [Goodbye, my handsome friend. Truly, her absence makes me sad].

Adieu rather than au revoir signifies Burr's understanding that they would never see each other again. Similarly, both Burr and Hamilton, on the eve of their duel, ended their letters to Theodosia and to Mrs. Hamilton with adieu and not au revoir, signifying that they might not live to see their loved ones again.

Madame Fenwick

One day in November of 1810, "At 1 came Mr. Fenwick, formerly consul. I did not recollect him, though he is not much altered in ten years. It was a mere visit of civility and to tender services." Burr returned the visit and, as often, the wife and not the husband attracted his attention: "To Mr. Fenwick's, whom saw and eke his wife; belle femme. The marks of superior intelligence, much grace and animation. We said some civil things to each other, and she engaged me to call and see her, which, be assured, I shall not fail. Mr. Fenwick goes tomorrow to Bordeaux, and offered to take letters for me." (Burr, concerned that the French police would intercept his letters, relied on Americans such as Mr. Fenwick, and American sea captains, to smuggle his correspondence back to Theo and to his contacts in America.)

Joseph Fenwick was an American wine exporter based in Bordeaux, where he was the American consul from 1790 to 1801. Madame Fenwick, who married him in 1792, was French, née Catherine Eléonore Ménoire. She was 38 years old when Burr met her in Paris. Burr became Madame Fenwick's admirer and regular visitor, but not her suitor, as appears from numerous journal entries, e.g.: "Took cabriolet to Madame Fenwick's. She had given me a general invitation to breakfast with her any day at 11. At least ½ dozen persons came in, had an audience, and went out. At length the celebrated Barère [the architect of the Terror during the French Revolution] and another came in, had audience, and went out. Barère appears to be worthy of his reputation. I greatly admire Madame Fenwick."

He noted, soon afterward, "To Madame F.'s, whom found alone. Staid an hour with her; am always amused and interested. She engaged me to take tea with her at 9 <u>this afternoon</u>." The meanings of Burr's underlinings sometimes make for interesting speculation; in this case, Burr may have wanted to recollect, as he reread his journal later in life, how long the "tea" continued, given that Mme. F. chose to call 9 p.m. the "afternoon." He continues:

> Thence to Madame Fenwick's as by appointment mentioned yesterday. We entered at the same minute, and had a tête-à-tête ½ hour. Then came in the most gentleman-like man I have seen here, ornamented with some orders. She called him Colonel. The conversation was very gay for ½ hour, and then I rose to take leave; but Madame insisted on my staying; obeyed, and, after a few minutes, the Colonel went out. Then Madame engaged me to dine t. à. t.; agreed. Dined, and staid till 7.... To Madame Fenwick's.... Madame was in bed, ill with a cold. Staid after the rest went out for an hour. Have always new occasion to admire her intelligence and her candor.... At 5 to Madame Fenwick's to dine; tête-à-tête as usual. Came off at 8. Your picture was there, and you were the principal topic. She thinks it worth a voyage to America to see you, and I told her I had written you that it was worth a voyage to France to see her.... Oh, I forgot to tell you that Madame Fenwick made me yesterday present of a barrel of the most delicious honey.... Home at 8 and have been till now reading, by command of Madame Fenwick, a pamphlet on the movement of waves.

The warm and respectful relationship between Burr and Madame Fenwick was a good deal less charged than that he had with Mme. Paschaud. Burr assuaged Mme. Fenwick's loneliness for her absent husband in Bordeaux, she his for Theodosia in America. Burr and Fenwick took an affectionate leave of each other when it finally came time for Burr to depart for America. Confirming the impression that Burr's relations with Mme. Robertson and Mme. Fenwick were not romantic are his notes that, within the space of two days, each tried to set him up with a female friend; "Fenwick asked me to stay and breakfast with a pretty woman, but declined"; "Found on my arrival a note from Madame Robertson, asking me to dine, and meet a beautiful young lady on Sunday. On that day am engaged to Fenwick's, where I shall be more amused, even without a beautiful young lady." The following day, Burr was amusing himself with Clotilde, the "good little Picard" about whom more will be said in the chapter on Burr's paid sex.

Enlightened Anglo-Saxon opinion of Burr's era was highly critical of Gallic lasciviousness, urging men "to act as true knights by curbing licentiousness and eschewing 'loose women' in favor of those 'who join good breeding, and liberal sentiments, to purity of mind and manners.'"[2] In Paris, Burr understood he could have it both ways, conversing in the salons of the likes of Mesdames Robertson and Fenwick by day and being received into the embraces of Clotilde and others by night.

Madame L

The last woman to be mentioned in this chapter shall be called Madame L_____. Who exactly she was, is not clear. Too many women with the initial L are mentioned in Burr's Paris journal in the spring of 1810—Langworthy, Lelande and Loigerot, as well as a Madame L_____—and there is too much mystery or discretion on Burr's part. Our guess would be that she is a Miss Langworthy whom Burr knew in New York, living in 1810 in Rouen with the married name of Madame Lelande. At any rate, Burr did eventually obtain a passport to Rouen to see her, and the following letter from Burr, replying to a letter of hers, was preserved by Burr's literary executor, Matthew Davis:

> To Madame—:
> Paris, May 9, 1810
> It was very kind of you to answer me so soon. I think to leave Paris in the diligence on Friday morning, and to have the honour of kissing your hand the same day or evening; but, not having obtained a seat nor obtained a passport, it is possible there may be further delay. "A little room looking into the garden," and under the same roof with you—nothing could be more alluring. Nevertheless, my dear friend, you must pardon me if I should prefer a bed at an inn, for which I will give you twenty good reasons when we meet. Anything but sleep with you. In the meantime, and at all times,
> A. Burr.

In context, this letter has the ring of studied gallantry to a former, not a prospective, lover rather than a demurral on Burr's part to the lady's offer "to make him a kept man," as Burr biographer Nancy Isenberg would have it.[3] And we note our surprise that Matthew Davis saw fit not to burn this letter despite his boast that on Burr's death, "I alone have possessed the private and important papers of Colonel Burr, and I pledge my honour that every one of them, so far as I know and believe, that could have injured the feelings of a female or those of her friends, is destroyed."

Twelve

Sex and Sanguinity

Whereas the Founding Fathers often seem to wear masks, Burr had no masks. Two currents run through the journal, as well as his life before and after the journal. Burr as a proto-feminist and Burr as a lusty man. And if no society woman offered herself in a way he considered safe to accept, he paid for sex and sometimes recorded it in his journal.

The diary of an upstanding Enlightenment man might venture into stock details from his sex life. A dash and a dot in the diary of Burr's friend William Godwin during a nine-month period beginning August 1796 signified each time Godwin and Mary Wollstonecraft had intercourse. Intimate letters support this, indicating that a plain dash implied something less than full intercourse. For example the day after only a dash and no dot, Mary praised William for his tender "self-government" (they were practicing a rhythm method of birth control) the night before.[1] The famous pair's works around the time they met at a dinner party, her *Vindication of the Rights of Women* and his *Political Justice*, emphasized procreation as the natural objective of sex. However, by the time Godwin was keeping the secret record, they seem to have been hot and heavy into sex for pleasure. Writes their biographer, "By the time Godwin and Wollstonecraft became friends in early 1796 neither believed that the only purpose of sex was to have children nor that desire could be easily controlled. Sex is the 'overflowing of the soul' which intensifies sensibility."[2] The pregnancy that resulted in their only child, Mary, who married Percy Shelley and wrote *Frankenstein*, was an accident.

Burr not only admired Wollstonecraft but was a very frequent visitor of Godwin's household during his two stays in London. For his part, when Burr recorded an assignation in his private journal he often entered "Muse," which appears to have been his own witty conceit.

Muse

Burr frequently used this code word. Thus "muse mauv." meant the trollop wasn't good in bed. After "too much muse" he liked a hot bath. "There can be no doubt that it refers to illicit relations with women," stated William Bixby, editor and publisher of the journal, who identified the word's most likely origin as the venery term for a rutting animal (converging with Burr's own hunts for the enticing ladies of the night).

Yet this portmanteau (from suitcase) or mashup (from shoving together) term may have derived from any one of various sources. It could be from venery, the language of the hunt, or a Swedish word, *mus*, literally "mouse," with a Swedish slang meaning equivalent to our English terms "pussy" and "beaver," with Burr tacking on an extra E. Contrarily, his lingo may have an origin in the Greek muses or be an old English or French word for solicitation. In an endnote entitled "Foreign Element in the Journal" Bixby declared, "What a confusion of tongues is found! It is a veritable Babel! Swedish, French, German, and Latin words are joined together to express one's thought." The note continued: "It is amusing to see how he clung to certain foreign words. For instance, the Swedish words for bread and milk, brod and mjolk, which we find him using, although badly misspelled, long after leaving Sweden."

As shorthand for a paid sexual encounter, the term did appear for the first time in Sweden. He described a first tryst on May 20, 1809, as "amus. av. jungf. deux heur. Tres b." (Had fun with the maid for two hours. Very good). The second sexual encounter of the day with the maid he recorded as muse. So Bixby may be correct in the alternative theory presented in the glossary that muse might be a shortening of the verb *amuser*, to amuse or divert. So Burr may have Gallicized the term he picked up in Sweden or even known it all along in America. The OED has an entry for "muss," meaning "a girl or young woman. Chiefly as a term of endearment or affectionate form of address." Adding to the conflation, Ben Johnson used "hart," or deer, in association with a female beloved in his comic drama *Every Man in His Humor*, first performed in 1598: "Nay kisse me sweet musse," and later, "Sweet hart will you come in to breakfast…. I pray thee (good Musse) we stay for you."

Once in Paris, Burr would have run into the word muse literally out and about, in Le Marais, where it named a very narrow street.[3] Prostitutes solicited at this location, today the rue du Petit-Muse, but having had two other names, the first recorded in the 14th century and each originating from the word muse with the idea of prostitutes "prowling"— the rue du Petit-Muse and rue Pute-y-Musse.

In any event he chose cheerful slang comparable to "a cute trick" as opposed to something repellent. He may even have felt the word was a complimentary choice, given his awareness of the nine Greek muses. The specialized venery term is perhaps the least convincing as a source—except insofar as it was the ancient etymology for a French word for solicitation (as exhibited in the street names). As Professor Forster, author of *Sex and the Founding Fathers*, comments, "If Burr's anything like Gouverneur Morris, he would be using 'muse' as in a sense of wonder or marvel" (personal communication, April 8, 2014).

What Was Customary

Burr was not discovering sexual prerogatives that were unavailable at home. According to Clare A. Lyons' highly documented history of extramarital sex in Philadelphia for a hundred years up to 1830, "Casual sexual encounters became more common after the Revolution. Married men visited brothels, picked up women in taverns and on the streets, solicited and coerced sex from their servants, and turned to other women when their wives were unavailable. Men, like women, also used the toleration of non-marital sexual practices within the sexual culture to establish fulfilling relationships outside marriage. Both men and women established extramarital affairs."

By his friendships of the mind, his flirtations, and his backstairs encounters, Aaron Burr fell in with the life of a Parisian gentleman. Not that Paris corrupted him. After the death of his wife, Theodosia, in 1794, Burr had numerous affairs, so much so that he merited his own chapter in an early tome—alongside chapters on Antony and Cleopatra, Abelard and Heloise, King Charles II and Nell Gwynn et al.—Lyndon Orr's, *Famous Affinities of History* (1914). Burr's electoral defeat in 1804—in the New York gubernatorial race, just a few months before the Hamilton duel—may have had a causal connection with an article published on the day of the polling in a New York City newspaper listing twenty prostitutes who said Aaron Burr was their favorite customer.[4]

Burr arrived in Paris in a mood of exhilaration. In 1794, sixteen years earlier, he had hoped for the ambassadorship to France when France asked Washington to recall Gouverneur Morris. Madison and Monroe recommended Burr to President Washington, but in the end Monroe was named to succeed Morris in Paris.

A wish to scheme with Napoleon attracted Burr magnetically to the French capital. However, curiosity over the reputedly relaxed sexual mores of France may have played a part in his ambition to set foot there. Thomas Jefferson, in 1785, while serving as U.S. ambassador to France, had warned his nephew Peter Carr, who was thinking of joining his uncle in Paris, of the perils of French seductresses. Jefferson wrote Carr that American male visitors found themselves at risk from "beauty begging in every street," from "a passion for whores," and from "female intrigues," in short, from succumbing to "the strongest of all human passions" to the point of considering "fidelity to the marriage bed as an ungentlemanly practice." Other Americans in Paris experienced similar culture shock, and Paris presented all of the above to the widower Burr in 1810 at age 55. We see him, at times almost penniless, engaged in a continual debate with himself as to how best balance his spending on food and on trysts with prostitutes.

On John Adams' second night in France, a Frenchwoman, punning on his name, asked him how Adam and Eve "found out the art of lying together." Adams blurted out something about magnetic attraction and later recorded in his diary: "To me, whose acquaintance with women had been confined to America, this question was surprising and shocking." Gouverneur Morris had a similar reaction when he was sitting in a café with a friend sipping lemonade and two Parisian gentlewomen joined him and engaged him in "a good deal of light, trivial conversation, in which these ladies intimate to me that their nuptial bonds do not at all straiten their conduct, and it would seem that either would be content to form an intrigue." Morris commented in his diary, "What would have induced one of my countrywomen to place herself in such a position?"

Morris did end up falling into a passionate affair, with Madame de Flahaut, who was also the mistress of Talleyrand; but, unlike Burr, he did not acquire a taste for French prostitutes. After drunkenly picking up a prostitute in Palais Royal, Morris recorded in his diary that the encounter made him feel "the object of my own contempt and aversion." Contrastingly, perhaps because of his lack of official portfolio, Burr took to Parisian prostitutes like a duck to water, and his only expressed regrets are comments about perhaps spending too much of his limited funds on paid sex.

Obviously, on both sides of the pond, poverty drove most of the women he slept with to offer themselves. Certainly Burr did not question this, being no William Gladstone on a mission to rescue streetwalkers. Burr was conventional in this regard, even traditional.

He was a feminist in viewing women of his caste as being equals; however, he viewed the prostitutes as degraded already and who had therefore chosen their lot. Nancy Isenberg shows in her biography that historians have often fallen into the trap of confusing Burr's real sexual behavior with the attacks by his enemies. His opponents used sexual satire against him; aspersions on his character can be read as "just politics" and exceedingly ugly politics at that. Professor Isenberg[5] writes, "Burr's sex life was easily used to tar him as a libertine at just that time when certain people were whispering that he might be in a position to succeed Jefferson." She cites various laudable reasons why Burr was the "odd man out," among them that "he was odd because he was the only founder to embrace feminism." Regarding his sexual sprees, Isenberg writes of Americans at home and abroad: "Prominent people drew attention, but rarely moral censure, when they indulged their sexual appetites." Moreover, being a mature bachelor/widower met social approval, with no one expecting celibacy of such a person.

What was Burr's attitude? A *New York* magazine reporter and actress in the present day (2012) ridiculed a waitress at the Four Seasons Hotel: "Suddenly, a waitress named Wendy appears beside our table. I know her name is Wendy because it says so on the tag pinned to her uniform.... At one point, when she asks if we would like something from the bar—'May I inquire whether you will be enjoying a drink this evening?'—our eyes widen as we stiffen from stifled laughter."[6] Their sneering disdain contrasts with the blithe tone of Burr's journal notes on his assignations, the undercurrent of which is that he was appreciative—and considered his conduct a gentleman's. His "sin" was tunnel vision: he emphasized in the journal generally the here and now, an attitude reflected in his sexual behavior.

Also, as distinct from a libertine, Burr was in suspension from monogamy. His sexual reputation as a rake would have been harmless except his enemies portrayed him as dissolute. These were caricatures typical of the day. Burr did not take pleasure in romping with other men's mistresses (as Morris did with Talleyrand's mistress, for example). Nor did he express the disgust Morris did after succumbing to his libido and hiring sex.[7] Accusers besmirched Burr's name with foul rumors such as incest with his daughter, yet he likely was faithful to both his wives. He was also broadminded. His second wife, Eliza Jumel, the intriguing and wealthy widow he would marry in 1833, had an improper past. As a child she was a cleaning girl in a brothel where her mother worked. Burr, if for no other reason than that fathering a daughter sensitized him, would not have excused a lapse from monogamy as Stendhal did when he wrote (in *On Love*, 1822), "There is a great gulf between unfaithfulness in men and in you. With you, it is partly a direct action, partly a sign. Thanks to our military education, it signifies nothing in men. However, thanks to your modesty, in women it is the most unmistakable sign of devotion."[8]

The Male Prerogative

There seems to be an aspect to Burr's paying for sex that he was keeping up his cheer, benefiting and balancing his temperament, probably knowing that satisfying lust was endorsed by the medical community as a healthy means of keeping one's fluids in proportion. In fact he specified early on in his journal how he sought sexual relief, and seems to have been slow ejaculating, becoming calm and contented with release: "Went out to see Dougan but consoled self with the mistress of the house. It still not being satisfactory, roved an hour. That move pleased Gamp fully, two pretty maids. Home at 9 quite tranquil. 'Tis the sole remedy in such cases." This was implicit in a gentleman's education at the time. Some books even related the theory of satisfying male sexual hunger to keeping the four humors adjusted. And so he seems to justify his need for sex but self-criticizes that he goes overboard sometimes. Primarily he means he shouldn't make expenditures for so many of his "follies." But Burr also was ever aiming at a condition of physical balance—moderation in sex, eating, drinking stimulants, and so forth.

When Burr had sexual relations with prostitutes in Paris he was in the same decade of life, his fifties, as Thomas Jefferson was when he made Sally Hemings his slave mistress. Both Jefferson and Burr chose women they could bed without emotional complications, in situations where they had complete control of their degree of involvement. Dr. Jon Kukla, in *Mr. Jefferson's Women*, illuminates Thomas Jefferson's real relations with women from his first love on. Dr. Kukla argues that an elite man of the Enlightenment viewed sexual dalliance in terms we cannot judge by contemporary values. From the commentary by Dr. Kukla that follows, based on a passage in Dr. Kukla's book, it seems very likely Burr rather than being loutish in regularly paying for sex in Paris was simply attempting to stave off old age and gain control over his expat life, as he did with diet and exercise.

The Theory of Humors[9]
BY JOHN KUKLA

Among the medical compendiums of the time, which were part classical lore and part biology, works in many gentlemen's libraries in the late 18th century were the writings of the Swiss medical theorist Samuel Auguste David Tissot.

First translated into English in the 1760s, Tissot's books of advice about health and medicine went through many editions in both languages. While his ideas about human biology were primitive by modern standards, he advocated the benefits of sleep, exercise, fresh air, and moderation in food and drink. Good health was often attributed at this time to the proper balance of humors (blood, phlegm, yellow bile, and black bile) described long ago by Aristotle and Galen. Illness, according to these venerable theories, came as the result of imbalances that could be remedied by bloodletting, purging, blistering, and other "heroic" procedures.

In the Galen tradition, semen was regarded as an important bodily fluid, a humor similar to blood, to be kept in balance for good health. The elimination of excess or pent-up semen was a therapeutic measure analogous to bloodletting. Some writers contended, as did the theologian John Duns Scotus, that retained semen eventually became poisonous. Diderot and other Enlightenment philosophers held similar views.

Human reproduction, the mind, and the nervous system were realms of mystery and misinformation. Dutch scientists first examined human sperm under their microscopes in the 1670s, but the cutting edge of medical knowledge towards the end of the 18th century still regarded "seminal fluid" as a "vivifying liquor" that somehow connected the functions of the brain, the nervous system, and the testicles. Human sperm, according to a physician whom Tissot quoted with approbation, "is the most perfect and important of all the animal liquors, and ... like them derives its origin from the most perfect humors."

By emphasizing the proper balance of bodily humors and fluids as the basis of health and sanity, Tissot's *Onanism: A Treatise Upon the Disorders Produced by Masturbation* precipitated the Victorian-era hysteria about masturbation and madness. Among young men, masturbation was thought to be ruinous because it threatened "the Essential Oil of the animal liquors" with a "dissipation [that] leaves the other humours weak." For workaholic intellectuals of the Enlightenment, however, maintaining the body's proper balance of fluids and humors had converse implications. The perceived dangers of seminal dissipation went back to Galen's time, but so did perceptions (voiced in medical debates about the celibacy of monks and priests) about the dangers of seminal retention. "M. Tissot relates as many examples of illness due to retention as due to emission," Voltaire observed. "There is no stronger argument against the bold vows of chastity."

The French thinkers Diderot and Rousseau went so far as to endorse masturbation. Tissot and other experts recommended sexual intercourse with a healthy woman. Since his advice was aimed at elite men, is it any surprise that Tissot believed that "correspondence with a handsome woman does not exhaust so much as with an ugly woman."

Potency then as now was an indicator of health, and at that period a middle-aged man was "older" than today. Burr was boasting prowess, as Morris did many times over in his diary, that he was *suaviter in modo, fortiter in re*—gentle in manner, resolute in the deed.[10]

It often sounds as if Burr and a prostitute had sex on the spot. That was certainly possible in the arcades of the Palais Royal or along the bridges that crossed the Seine. The Palais Royal remained the center for prostitution during Napoleon's reign. The alcoves must have lent a certain privacy and protection from the elements. The brothels of the Palais Royal were organized into different ranks and the *Almanach des adresses des demoiselles de Paris de tout genre et de toutes les classes, ou Calendrier du Plaisir*, 1800 et seq. (Almanac of Unmarried Girls of Paris of Every Type and Class, or Calendar of Pleasure) gave a full roster—from the sophisticated prostitutes who lived in apartments over the street and offered appurtenances like suppers and piano recitals to sex shows, brothels, and taverns host to the more expensive foreign girls. Some of the whores dressed up like famous stars of opera or theater of the day.

Other times Burr went to the prostitute's lodging. The act was a quick slaking of appetite and if he became enthralled with one woman he doesn't note it, keeping the content of sex entries in his journal terse and lighthearted. He had little concern for dire health consequences from the encounters. He mentions having a drink to cleanse his body, and being a bit reckless, no more. When Benjamin Franklin went to London at 18, he said later he was lucky he didn't catch any disease. Either Burr believed he could cope with the health risks or he would rather have contracted a disease than forgo sex—carpe diem. Only once, the winter of 1811, is he overcome with worry in this regard: "Went to bed last night full of penitence and contrition and promising you any number of times that I would never do so again. Full of apprehension, too, of some physical consequences. Rose at 6 and to my great surprise in perfectly good order. It manifests, at least, the good state of my health."

The Lightness of Being Neoclassical

Burr loved intrigue of all types and Napoleon's capital was the place to devise it. The women of Paris during this period were feeling free and were eye-catching as never before. Fashion had once been a standard at Versailles but now fashion plates were strolling on the streets in their filmy, low-cut dresses with tiny sleeves and gathered bodices made of fabric that swirled around their legs. They were often bare-headed and with only a type of shawl as outerwear. Women's clothes were very symbolic. For a time after the revolution, women wore little red cords around their necks to celebrate those who lost their heads to the guillotine; those gruesome cords evolved into the neoclassic choker. Some wore guillotine-motif earrings too. Fundamentally, though, what was "in" was looking poured into one's unembellished little dress. With a little attention to her hair, dress and slippers, any woman could look like a queen, as there was no aristocratic pretension in the imperial court. The privileged classes had collapsed and society was re-forming. The emotion of a whole people was still the intoxication (if no longer euphoria) of social equality. The principles of freedom were proclaimed in the matter of dress. Public opinion after 1815 would begin to go against the ribaldry and debauchery but the ethos of the First Empire was libertinage. A few yards of muslin and a bit of lace could make a gown and a rich woman still look dressed down because of disaffection with the Bourbons.

Suddenly in Paris there were pictures printed of anecdotal city scenes and elegant ladies, resulting in a new consensus about fashion. For instance, whether people had seen her or not they knew how Madame Récamier, who epitomized beauty, dressed and bore herself. Madame Récamier had a supple but not heavy figure, a curly updo, and a smooth complexion described as being like white jade. She dressed in almost colorless transparent natural muslin or cotton, accented by artful wraps. In the colored or black and white engravings of the period the women all have a lightness about their movements, with their dainty slippers or bottines, and the draping of their cashmere shawls Josephine had made more fashionable. The poses women took in portraits suggested languid ease and informality.

The Scene

Burr was in Paris during the last free-for-all for prostitution. This was at the cusp of the establishment under the empire of an administrative edifice for regulating prostitution that would stay in place for the rest of the 19th century. From 1804, the onus fell on the police to supervise the *maisons closes* or *maisons de tolérance*, a system where prostitutes could conduct their illegal trade discreetly and had to submit to regular medical examinations and agree where and when they could solicit.[11] The so-called French system spread across Europe. By 1810, Paris had 180 officially approved brothels, mostly run by former prostitutes. In 1810, the streetwalkers were at risk for being arrested, yet prostitutes roamed the boulevards and stood on street corners in this period.

From the bouquinistes around the Palais Royal a man who loved books and women could while away time reading by candlelight and get directions from the books about brothels and locations of ladies of the night. Bourgeois society was libertine during the First Empire, yet prostitution was booming. The monthly average number of prostitutes registered in Paris between 1812 and 1815 was about 1,600; and this included only the legal ones at bordellos. (Times were harder for freelancers, as whores during the First Empire were fined, inspected, and imprisoned or sent back to their native provinces.) Sex was for sale on a large scale in certain neighborhoods. Burr patronized these luckless women for zipless encounters that assuaged his appetite if not his loneliness.

That Burr frequented the Palais Royal neighborhood means he was surrounded by all types of Parisiennes—society women shopping, accompanied by male chaperones, probably their relations; clumps of unmarried girls "fronting"; whores mixing with potential customers, dandies, and sexual adventurers. The ladies and filles de joie strolled in arcades just off the street, wore dainty footwear and silk ribbon necklaces and ties, transparent dresses, vegetable rouge, floral-based perfumes and perfumed lace handkerchiefs in violet, hyacinth, and other single scents.

Perfume was one of the ways to tell a lady from a whore, as the lady had a more complex perfume. Seventeen-year-old Marie-Louise, coming by coach to be Napoleon's empress, quipped to her father that she already felt like a French lady because of the perfume of the ladies accompanying her. As has already been discussed, it's said that when Marie Antoinette was fleeing to Varennes in disguise, her Houbigant perfume gave her away because only an aristocrat could afford it; and from Francois Rance, the emperor Napoleon—who kept a bottle of eau de cologne in one of his boots—commissioned two exclusive fragrances, for Josephine and himself.

Burr would have in some measure known the sexual mores before he arrived in Paris, from the accounts of men like Morris and from published guides of where to find streetwalkers and specialty cathouses. Even a teenage girl from Nantes who was a tourist in Paris in 1821 wrote her cousin back home that as an amusement at the Palais Royal she enjoyed seeing, besides lights, ice cream, cafes and theater, the *grandes poupées* (big dolls) who circulated in the galleries.[12] Burr would have been continuing the sex life that was permissible to an urbane, secularized widower in New York City, only the opportunities were greater in Paris.

Kiss and Tell Whom?

This brings up what is very distant to our present understanding, that Burr was writing his journals as a basic set of notes to tell his daughter when he returned. This is the most easily explained ramification of Burr's notes about prostitutes, as he fully expected Theodosia to chuckle over Daddy's exploits. According to Clare Lyons,

> Perhaps the most telling feature of the male sexual histories of the early national period was male boasting about extramarital sexual encounters. We know about the actuals of these men because they talked about them with other men. Unlike the adulterous wives, whose behavior was seen by others, the adulterous husbands' actions were usually recounted for the court by their male peers who learned of their sexual exploits through conversation.... In the male culture of sexual storytelling, their sexual encounters took on a life beyond the sexual experience itself. They took pleasure in telling of their intrigues and shared their satisfaction in getting away with expanding their sexual lives. By telling one another of their sexual conquests, they asserted their manhood.[13]

As taboo as that kind of father-daughter rapport is now, it was in line with the Burrs' forward-thinking and anti–Puritanical attitude towards sex. Burr and Theodosia admired Mary Wollstonecraft and believed that sex should be (theoretically) spoken of as matter-of-factly as the weather. His noting his sexual sprees to tell his daughter would be peculiar in any era yet quite explicable as a demonstration of his masculine authority and proof that despite his misadventures he was hale and fit—"Don't worry about me." He believed that having sex when he wanted was the recipe to maintaining his vital spark.

Keeping Accounts

Burr wrote in his journal that the best women came dear and that ladies at the coffee house would talk, sit, eat and drink but not go forward "unless you make an overture." One day he records that he had two "rencontres," one good and one poor and later a third—thirteen francs total. "Voila de l'economie," he commented jocularly. Burr said that a prostitute whom he had paid previously now was going to give him a session for free, and that when he offered to pay the little money he had, she said, "What do you think? That I'm a parisienne?" If Burr had more money would he have kept a mistress in Paris instead of going with the streetwalkers? Actually, the street vending of sex suited him fine and he said assignations helped him unwind. Then again, self-indulgence is rarely simple and Burr wrestled with himself continually over how the follies cut into his scant budget. Once he indicated that he reined in from a second expenditure. He had been dining at Madame Robertson's. Going home at half-past ten he had a "Renc." (sexual encounter) "but got safe home," the only cost beer at seven sous a bottle, and he then read an hour of a book of recent history. (This was the memoir of a prominent shady character who had been president of the Council of Five Hundred during the French Revolution, but who seems to have plotted with the Royalists and so ended up being deported to Guiana, was eventually arrested and then was found strangled in his cell in Paris in 1804—exciting reading matter for a man who fell from grace due to political machinations.)

To prowl during some of his long promenades—day or night sorties—added purpose as going to have his boots repaired or finding sugar at a good price might. For example, "Find coffee good after muse." Sometimes he made a point of his satisfaction, as on July 16, 1811: "Major Thomas, took me to a coffee-house to dine. The expense with two bottles of wine was 60 sous each. Thence to a coffee-house au Palais Royal. A dish of coffee, 10 sous. Walked an hour under the arches, which is the evening promenade. Saw not one beautiful or very fine woman. The best, you know, is always good. M'aime; 2 Crowns. Home at 9."

If Burr had money in his pocket, he admitted going wild, as on October 9, 1810: "An excellent dinner in a very poor-looking house; 4 francs 10 sous. On my way home renc., near the Pont Neuf, got badly wounded in the foot by one of those infernal hacks; the story is too long to write. The ½ hour I was with Louise (the second renc.), forgot it [his foot], and the half hour I have been writing to you idem [the same], but now that I am writing about it, 'tis impossible." Or, the next entry on October 10: "Sorti at 10 to go to G.'s about certain law subjects. On the way a certain biped took me out of the way, kept me an hour and cost 8 francs."

He showed concern with physical and financial immoderation, not moral turpitude.

For example, two days later he wrote, "How one folly begets another and so on like the holy bread in the New Testament." He would have spent more on prostitutes had his purse been larger is the impression from the journal. Similarly Washington Irving commented, "Above all perhaps a frugal purse is the best guardian I have."[14]

Occasionally in his journal, as on January 17, 1811, Burr provided further comment: "Thence home, but alas! on my way a p. of dem. [a pair of demoiselles], and so 8 francs. How many curses I heaped on poor Gam. [i.e., Gamp—Burr's name for his weaker self], and yet he is rather to be pitied; only see how for the last fifteen days he has been so good and considering his habits, and considering, &c, &c.. And so we will try to forget it till next time. On the way, met an acquaintance who pretended to have something beautiful to show me. It was true; 6 francs."

Artist's Model

As a painter in Paris, and as a painter of nude subjects, John Vanderlyn had access to female models, and of course Burr was impressed: "Walked over to Vanderlyn, who was busy with his beautiful models.... Made arrangement with la modele to call and poser (this is the phrase) at my room. Folie [sex]"; "To Vanderlyn's, where the beautiful de Castro, who has deigned to pose for the head, neck, and arms, all of which, and I suspect a great deal more, are very fine. If de Castro don't pose for the whole, John's a booby"; "To Fleury's [sexual partner], whom took to see Vanderlyn's Ariadne." De Castro was Vanderlyn's paramour, evidently too modest to pose for the whole painting.

The model of Vanderlyn's with whom Burr sometimes had sex may well have been one of the models for Vanderlyn's most famous painting, "the first formal nude in American art," *Ariadne Abandoned by Theseus on the Island of Naxos*, portraying a recumbent nude Ariadne, just after her tryst with Theseus. The 19th century history of this nude painting mirrors censorious attitudes toward Burr as a supposed seducer of women—which by all accounts he wasn't—and as a sensualist, which he certainly was. *Ariadne* returned with Vanderlyn to America in late 1815, parenthetically bringing Theodosia's original portrait with him, as Burr left it with him in Paris.

After exhibiting *Ariadne* at the academy's 1816 show, Vanderlyn set up his own rooms, at his own expense, in the New York Academy of Fine Arts. But soon he was asked to leave on the questionable pretext that the rooms were needed for other purposes. In fact, a nude *Ariadne* was thought to offend public decency. Vanderlyn thereafter exhibited the painting in major eastern cities, sometimes with separate viewings for men and women.

Until after the Victorian era there was a prejudice, at least in Anglo-Saxon countries, against painting from nude female models. In England in 1860, Lord Haddon moved in the House of Lords that government grants be withdrawn from any state-funded school of art employing the living female model. In 1878, the official American delegation to the Paris exposition of that year complained of the display of French art: "Naked women abound—standing, sitting, reclining ... pictures of a debauched imagination, filled with innuendo and suggestion, corrupt in sentiment ... the eternal nude model that the painter has painted from mere emptiness of mind, or for a worse reason, and which he tries to make poetic by the title of his canvas, but who only wakens in us the wish that she would put on her dress and go home."

In the same year, 1878, Vanderlyn's *Ariadne* was donated to the Pennsylvania Academy of Arts—where it resides today—by a respectable society matron. However, controversy surrounding the painting continued as late as 1891, when a handbill representing "over 500 Christian women of Philadelphia" was directed to the academy's management in "protest against the flagrant indelicacy of many of the pictures now on exhibition," and specifically *Ariadne* (David M. Lubin, *Picturing a Nation*, 1994).

Male Bonding

One afternoon he shared a prostitute (the "pretty, good and voluptuous" Flora) with John Vanderlyn. Burr advised his friend that he would like her. This ménage à trois seems to imply a particular intimacy of the males and a bohemian moment, like one offering another a glass of good brandy or a cigar. In the winter of 1810, "At 6 came in Vanderlyn. Walked with him to show him Flora as he was in want of muse; 3 francs; y 2 h. Home at 9 and rather disposed to go early to bed, having been kept awake till 2 this morning by the songs, etc. (a party below) and being obliged to be up at 6 tomorrow, and the labor of the day requires repose. So God bless and reform thee!"

In *The History of Private Life*, friendship is described as "part of a man's sentimental and sexual education, because it provided an opportunity to comment on experience.... Friendships were sealed by long walks in the country or, even more, by joint visits to brothels." Jean-Paul Sartre called it "bachelor freemasonry." Speaking of the place of prostitutes in French society, he observed of the 19th century that prostitutes were "common property. Men shared them and told each other crude stories about their frolics."[15] Burr kept his notational record, but he was not crude.

A parallel type of male bonding from around 1800 is documented by Clare Lyons regarding cases of citizens in Philadelphia seeking wenches together: "For some, sexual storytelling was grounded in their common sexual experience. Men often went out on the town together seeking sexually available women. The case of David Pemble demonstrates the ways these two aspects of male sexual culture, storytelling and sexual practices, reinforced each other. Pemble not only told the tales of his sexual adventures to his friend and fellow tailor Thomas Lyons, but the two frequently accompanied each other to Philadelphia's bawdyhouses."[16]

The shoe fits: Burr was a conventional man of his time and being sexually fit and active was a topic permissible to share with other men. Thomas A. Foster, who has studied views on the sexual identity of elite American men of Burr's period, observes:

> The "Founding Fathers" are constructions of cultural memory. The "Founders," the political leaders of the Revolution and nation's creation, were individuals, flesh and blood, and as such led lives that would not reflect later ideals of manly sexual behaviors and desires. It is, of course, quite ironic that the political leaders of the American Revolution would come to serve as role models of personal life for American masculinity in the Victorian era—and today. Although a segment of our contemporary culture continues to hold the Founding Fathers aloft as more moral and virtuous than today's generation, doing so requires ignoring what the Founders themselves told us about their lives. What is less often acknowledged is that the men associated with an era of supposed morality and Christian values of monogamy and marriage have nearly all been linked to infidelity and sex out of wedlock.[17]

The double standard excused extramarital forays, and Burr was alone and attractive. Where he has jotted "muse" the reader feels he was having a bit of fun. He didn't rape, seduce, or deceive; he romped. He evinced no condescension but rather gallantry regarding the sexual encounters. This was a matter of health and masculinity. He was within the limits of acceptable behavior in 1810. Burr was sad in Paris and he took the view that sexual pleasure, unrelated to marriage and not bound up with enforcing sexual hierarchies, could relieve his sadness and was therefore as advisable as food and drink. His journal offers a rare glimpse of male sexual attitudes and practices of the period, a perspective that there was a middle ground between the duality of the marital model and libertinism. This macho comfort zone lay outside of sentiment and was part and parcel of the sexual pattern of American men in Paris while "*gai Paris*" was a reigning concept for the next 150 years.

Clotide *et les Autres*

While the journal is filled with these brief entries concerning monies spent on anonymous sex with streetwalkers, sometimes Burr wrote of an encounter and mentioned a woman's name. It is apparent from other entries that he was attractive not only to society women but as well to women of the lower classes. For example, he came upon Clotilde, an old acquaintance:

> Strolled gently homeward contemplating the stars which I had not seen for months, when I was stopped by a pretty, well-dressed woman. "Quoi! Vous etes ici?" It was that pretty Clotilde of whom something was said six months ago. All remonstrance was in vain. I have no money. "No matter, I have." Passed two hours very pleasantly and engaged to call sometimes and breakfast and play aux dames (checkers). I had, indeed, a crown (5 francs) which on parting I offered; but it was refused as an indignity. "Je ne suis pas parisienne, je suis picarde (from Picardy)." Home at ½ p. 9. This folly was certainly unnecessary. Voila, for three days past now how much to repent, that is the money [i.e., the 14 francs Burr paid to three streetwalkers on the two days before his free sex with Clotilde]. As follies give me a great appetite, have been eating an hour voraciously. Hot wine, water, and sugar; bread, butter, and honey. Warm rain, mist, wind.

Clotilde reappears in the journal a few days later: "Then, having no engagement, I deliberated whether I should go and do some folly with my remaining 10 francs, or go home and assort my papers, &c. Contrary to all rule and experience, went directly home, where, instead of assorting papers, I spent two hours in reading two law memoirs. Two more in smoking segars and cooking my dinner, and, seeing that nothing would be done, sallied out after dinner and went deliberately and intentionally to take coffee with Clotilde, a good little Picard. Staid two hours; for the coffee 20 sous and no other expense."

Another few days later, Burr begins the day setting out for the promised breakfast and game of checkers with this prostitute. By the end of this day, Burr had exhausted all of his cash: "Had engaged to breakfast with Clotilde. On the way bought a damier [checkers set], 20 sous. At ½ past 9 called. Clotilde had gone out to take bath…. [H]aving left exactly 16 sous, I bought with them two plays for my present amusement and then for yours. Came home at 1 with my two plays and not a single sou. Have been ransacking everywhere to see if no little 10-sous piece could be found. Not one! … In this state of finance have not been abroad since." Money management was clearly not Burr's forte and, in his opinion, food and sex were both pressing needs:

> Deliberating on the state of my finances, found that this sans sous state was not only inconvenient, but dangerous; for instance, this morning I hit a glass window with my umbrella, and had nearly forced it through one of three large panes. In such a case you only have to pay, and there's an end of it; but had I broken the pane and not been able to pay for it, I must infallibly have been taken before a commissionaire de police to abide his judgment. Casting about for ways and means, no one occurred to me but that of robbing poor little Gampy [Burr's grandson]. I opened his little treasure of coins and medals to see what could be spared, and finally seized one Danish dollar (thaler) of Charles VII, and two Swedish thalers of Gustavus IV. With these I went off to a changeur [money changer], who gave me 5 francs 5 sous each, making in the whole 15 francs 15 sous. With this treasure my first resolution was to go and amuse myself with some folly, mus. [sex], &c. It then occurred to me that there were certain other wants which required consideration. I have been three days out of sugar, and more than ten out of coffee, having lately drank tea, and I had not a single segar. After some debating and efforts and struggle, I desperately sallied out once more in the rain, bought one pound of coffee, [one pound of brown sugar, and seventy cigars]. This act of desperation having put it out of my power to go a folly-hunting, I very gravely determined not to go abroad again.

Three weeks earlier, Burr had got himself down to a solitary sou in his pocket and recoups his finances by changing two English guineas for 52 francs. He decided that the first use of these proceeds should be for a sexual threesome: "Then began to calculate how I should dispose of so much money. Having on Monday evening engaged with two [dancers] of good demeanor to take coffee with them this evening, thought I would devote a crown [5 francs] to that. Took in my pocket 7 francs 10 sous, lest the devil might induce me to spend more. It all went, and ran in debt 6 francs more, having been [debited] by one—that one which liked least.... [The next day] called on Madame Fleury to pay my 6 francs, though it was due to the other, whose demeure [dwelling] I did not ask. Madame Fleury asked me to stay and dine on soup and pot au feu, which agreed; 5 francs to make some addition to dinner. Staid till 7 and spent 5 francs more."

Within two days, with other expenditures, Burr had an empty pocket again—not enough left for another tryst with Madame Fleury, but enough to buy her some flowers: "Returning home, 14 sous for a bouquet for Fleury, where called for five minutes only. How very sage I can be when I have but half a crown!" That Burr was on friendly terms with prostitutes—women whom in our view he exploited—comes up again and again. Similarly, the journal mentions a few women who, like Clotilde, offered him free sex.

Touring the Landmark of Sentiment

Merging his feminism and lustiness was the romantic nature of Burr. On February 14 he was wistful that it wasn't the custom in Paris to exchange "those love-messages to which the day is sacred with us among the youth [who observe Valentine's Day in the U.S.]."

When Burr described a lovely woman he said she had looks and sensibility. The French admired *la sensibilité*, thanks in large measure to Jean-Jacques Rousseau, and Burr embodied the emotion: tender-hearted to individuals and upset if he thought he had caused anyone grief (especially a woman) but self-serving and calculating and not particularly moved by the human condition at large. Bertrand Russell defined sensibility as "a proneness to emotion, and more particularly to the emotion of sympathy. To be thoroughly satisfactory, the emotion must be direct and violent and quite uninformed by thought." Russell continued: "Rousseau appealed to the already existing cult of sensibility, and gave it a breadth and scope that it might not otherwise have possessed.... By the time of Rousseau, many people had grown tired of safety, and had begun to desire excitement.[18] The French Revolution and Napoleon gave them their fill of it." And indeed, Napoleon himself claimed, "Had there been no Rousseau, there would have been no Revolution; had there been no Revolution, I should have been impossible."[19]

Montmorency was a destination where Burr experienced his most emotional connection to any of the sites he visited while in France. In his journal he writes of visiting a shrine to the great thinker he hallowed. While he does not mention his deceased wife the elder Theodosia, she must have been in his mind, as the Burrs had admired Rousseau greatly, especially his views of childhood. Nancy Isenberg writes that "Burr and his wife shared a philosophy of education: learning required self-knowledge and constant introspection."[20] Sophie in *Emile* was a portrait of chaste, virtuous, and unassertive womanhood (the opposite of actresses, insisted Rousseau to the women of Geneva). Regarding the role of women, Burr believed, like Mary Wollstonecraft, that women could be educated rationally and their character thus improved, no longer, as under the Old Regime, coquettish in dress or frivolous in manners. Counter to Wollstonecraft's daring in her personal life, she believed that women should influence by indirection.[21] While men's equals, they should wait for their natural dignity to be restored. She like Rousseau counsels a moral makeover. Writes Joan B. Landis, "She envisions woman's change as primarily a residual effect of a larger revolution or turning in society."[22]

The journal entry on May 6, 1810, reads as follows: "Rain in the morning. Cold northerly wind three days past. Mr. and Madame La Harpe part. To Paris. This is the neighborhood in which Rousseau lived and died. The trees where was given le baiser fatal; the house of Eloise; the walks they frequented. Every spot hereabout is consecrated by his memory." Burr thought that this was Rousseau's major dwelling place, when in fact Rousseau lived at Montmorency for only six years, from 1756 to 1762; but it was during his most productive literary period and it was here he wrote three major works, the *Social Contract*, explaining his political philosophy, *Julie, ou La Nouvelle Heloise*, a novel presenting his belief that the self is realized through union with a beloved, and, finally, *Emile, ou l'Education*.

Rousseau fled Paris to stay in the woods in a hut at the country estate of his friend Madame d'Epinay, but when they quarreled he rented a dilapidated rustic house called Mont-Louis, where he chose to reside in a little windswept pavilion at the end of a solitary garden path. Here he hid away and wrote, all the while imploring the owner, the Marechal de Luxembourg, to make the pavilion more livable, until the latter offered him the Maison des Commeres, a small chateau of the park, for the duration of the repairs on Mont-Louis. The chateau is where the marechal sent Rousseau a carriage in which to escape when his ideas on education scandalized the Parlements who ordered Emile burned and Rousseau arrested.

The "baiser fatal" refers to the famous boscal scene of Rousseau's epistolary novel. Julie is the baron's daughter and Saint-Preux is her tutor. Their feelings for each other quicken into impossible love (like Abelard and the original Heloise). Julie and her cousin Claire are outdoors when Claire firsts asks her tutor, Saint-Preux, to kiss her, and then Julie kisses him. Both of them swoon with emotion but Julie's mind gives way and she actually swoons. This unsettles Saint-Preux, who spends the rest of the novel figuring his own ardor out. In contrast to the Enlightenment philosophy that truth is perceived through exteriority, for Rousseau introspection reveals universal truths and romantic passion can open our faculty of reason, through intense mental activity, to greater fineness of character. For a Romantic, the quest was vigorous and passionate individuality. Saint-Preux pens the turmoil the kiss caused in him: "I'm intoxicated, or rather, I'm mad. My brains are turned, all my senses are disordered by the fatal kiss."

Like Burr, Jean-Jacques Rousseau identified with sensual drive and had a fraught and morally ambivalent love life. Sophie d'Houdetot (1730–1813), a countess living in the valley of Montmorency, was the one who got away. She and the poet Marquis de Saint-Lambert had a liaison, tolerated by her husband the count, that lasted the rest of their lives (Saint-Lambert already had a famous liaison and child by Voltaire's mistress, Emilie). Being faithful to Saint-Lambert, Sophie rejected Rousseau's attempts to seduce her. Later she took an interest in the American colonies, hosted Ben Franklin in her home and corresponded with Thomas Jefferson. When the 75-year-old Franklin visited her at Sannois, her seven effusive quatrains praising him as the "father of all" were performed at the table for him by her and her other guests, with toasts between the poetry. A copy of a painting, 1802, shows Sophie, her tall aristocratic husband, and the more portly, shorter Saint-Lambert playing cards.

With a touch of naiveté and self-centeredness he recorded that Parisian prostitutes, while plentiful on the promenades, were rather heartless and "have such passion as they have not in the heart but only in the head." Twice a day, yes, but three times in one day was unusual for Burr to pay for sex: he was poor and also in his mid-fifties. On two occasions, one in Sweden and one in Paris, however, he recorded such very randy days. In Sweden he described an hour of sex with a German woman with whom he had no language in common—"being unable to communicate anything by the ear, we tried, successfully, all the other senses," followed by sex with the maid after breakfast. "I would have preferred that her visit had been deferred till tomorrow. Mais elle est si jolie [but she is so pretty]" and "at 2 came in Caroline." He mentioned paying for the second and third encounters of the day. Here is the occasion in Paris where he did likewise:

> Rose this morning at 6 and with very pious intentions to write a number of letters, &c. You shall see how faithfully executed…. At 11 recollected a rendezvous foolishly made to Violette. You know how religious I am in the performance of all sorts of engagements, so went. Found Mademoiselle in a state of expectation and disposed to be amiable. There an hour; 6 francs; never better pleased with red [hair], which it is my abhorrence in theory…. On my way home the devil put in my way Flora, whom I had often before met and promised to call on; went to sa chambre. Jolie bonne voluptueuse; there 2 hours; 7 francs. Home at 3 and at 4 made myself coffee. At 6 came in Vanderlyn. Walked with him to show him Flora as he was in want of [sex]; 3 francs; there 2 hours.
>
> [The next day] Went to bed last night full of penitence and contrition and promising you any number of times that I would never do so again. Full of apprehension, too, of some physical consequences. Rose at 6 and to my great surprise in perfectly good order. It manifests, at least the good state of my health. [Burr goes on to detail everywhere he goes after rising and notes] I have walked nearly twenty miles today and am not the least fatigued.

A Virtuous Cycle

At a distance of two hundred years, we may see here evidence of a virtuous cycle: lots of exercise—pounding the pavements, in Burr's case—leading to sexual vigor. Today's science confirms the connection: Harvard health guru Harvey Simon can be seen in a video extolling the benefits of exercise while wearing a sweatshirt with the legend "Marathoners Keep It Up Longer." But Burr's frenetic sexual activity should probably also be seen as compensating for his political impotence, frustrated as he was time and again in his main object of securing a passport to leave France. For example, soon after his threesome with Vanderlyn and Flora, Burr was forced to wait in an antechamber for three hours before making another fruitless passport request to the police commissioner, the Duc de Rovigo. It took many months of repeated attempts, having to mark time all the while, before Burr was at last allowed to exit France. So in the meantime, he enjoyed the company of his painter protégé, John Vanderlyn, and a huge network of friends and acquaintances, including many prostitutes and many women of more genteel character.

Today, attitudes toward Burr may divide in large part upon how one views his rampant sexuality, most fully on display in his Paris journal. The answer may well predict one's view of whether Burr's character was on balance good or bad. The most recent of Burr's biographers, Nancy Isenberg, in *Fallen Founder: The Life of Aaron Burr* (2007), inclines toward giving Burr a pass on his sexuality: "Burr's life was not only about sex; and yet sexuality was the stuff of politics.... The sexualization of Aaron Burr was a means for his opponents to increase their political capital.... Burr was in fact 'the odd man out,' but not because he lacked character. He was odd because he was the only founder to embrace feminism."

The details of sexual forays in the journal reveal the writer's personal "unmasked" self. But no matter how they are read on the scale from shocking and lamentable to colorful and candid, they have to be seen in the intellectual context of their times. Sexual gratification was approved as an irreverent (anti–Christian) topic in certain writings of the Enlightenment, which the more sophisticated Founding Fathers like Jefferson and Burr read. In particular, Diderot identified lust as a positive enthusiasm of the human species. In the opening of *Rameau's Nephew*, "Myself" describes how during his habitual daily walks around the Palais Royal he allows his mind to stray to sex fantasies—in a fashion that no proper Christian, no matter his healthy sex drive, would approve. "My thoughts are my strumpets," Diderot had his alter ego say. "The man who despises the pleasures of the senses is either a lying hypocrite or a crippled creature." He also observed, while writing in the same 1758 letter, that our ethical selves and not a "voluptuous sensation" ought to lead us.

Thirteen

Julie

Julie was one of two servants in the boardinghouse at 7 rue du Croissant where Burr rented two rooms from a Swiss couple, the Peloughs. This young woman appears to have been Julie Huguenin, Swiss and about age 25 in 1810, some thirty years younger than Burr. On New Year's Day 1811, Burr gave Julie a small present, noting, "Certainly no person in Paris deserves from me as much as does Julie." Burr's journal is replete with references to Julie's attentiveness—making Burr's fires, offering him gifts of food, even lending him small sums:

> Got into a delicious sleep, when in comes Julie and called several times to know if I was asleep. Replied yes, and sick. [Next morning] Julie, faithful to her system and seriously alarmed for my health, came in at daylight. I was so sound asleep that she was obliged to shake me before I woke. Opened my eyes, and lo! Julie with a bowl of bouillon gras in her hand.
> Lay till 9, though Julie made me a fire of her own good feeling and with her own money. She said it was too cold and that I was not well, &c.
> Waked at ½ p. 8. Was astonished to see a fire and all the materials for breakfast all prepared. Julie had done all this, and I had heard nothing, so sound did I sleep.
> Home and dine; pom. de t. [potatoes]. Julie added the wing of a duck.
> Home. Julie had provided me a fish, a sole, to which I added potatoes and made a sumptuous dinner.
> Home and cooked my potatoes. Julie added a bit of a sort of pudding.
> Home. Took a bouillon for supper, for which had no occasion, to please Julie.
> Dinner chez moi. Julie had prepared a bouillon and fish. I added potatoes and Jerusalem artichokes, and drank a whole bottle of wine—15 sous wine.
> Paid Julie 25 francs, which can't be half of what is due to her.

On one occasion only, it appears that Burr may have had sex with Julie. Just after New Year's Day, Burr notes "Julie has been an hour, and mus., &c." That January night seems to have been a one-night stand for Burr and Julie: the next morning "Julie called me at 8. Told her I had a headache, and must repose. In half an hour she came back with a hot bouillon gras. Under the torment of the pain, I had to contest this bouillon gras for ¼ hour before I could get rid of it and her." In subsequent days and months, relations between the two appear to resume as before, but in the summer of 1811, another servant, Miranda, appears on the scene, and we gather that Julie has not forgotten the January night of muse:

> Had another folie [another of Burr's terms for sex]. Miranda came in at 7 and staid an hour. This was at least unnecessary.
> At 7 this morning came in Miranda. These frequent visits seem to have no motive of inter-

Thirteen. Julie

est, but merely for the love of God. Note: Madame Gardell, the celebrated opera dancer, is very devout. After dancing and showing her _____ [Bixby's, not Burr's, prudish ellipsis] for half an hour, she immediately says her prayers. Then another turn on the stage, and thus the account is kept and balanced.

Slept perfectly sound till ½ p. 8, and then waked by the entrance of Miranda, whom for this time, I wished to the devil. Went through the forms, however.

One day after this last encounter with Miranda, Julie appears in Burr's room first thing in the morning, perhaps to head Miranda off:

A dish of strong coffee kept me awake till 5. At 6 came in Julie. Notwithstanding my drowsiness, I was really glad to see her, and received her most cordially. But alas! little did I imagine the object of the visit. The good and gentle Julie let forth a volley of invective and with a voice that made the whole hotel ring. It was impossible to interrupt this harangue or to reply to it. It lasted a full half hour and was received with silent resignation. Julie departed in a rage. All this on account of the visits of Miranda. I did not before know we were on such terms. It was in vain to try to sleep. The declamation had really disturbed me. I regret exceedingly the folly of Julie and that so good a creature should be unhappy.

Given Burr's use of the word "folly" to describe sex, the "folly of Julie" which he now regretted seems likely to be the one such folly he committed with her in January, six months earlier. Indeed, the above passage is strongly reminiscent of English diarist Samuel Pepys' similar "folly"—groping a servant girl—and its domestic aftermath in 1668:

[M]y wife did towards bedtime begin to be in a mighty rage ... and did most part of the night in bed rant at me in most high terms of threats of publishing my shame, and when I offered to rise would have rose too, and caused a candle to be lit to burn by her all night in the chimney while she ranted, while the knowing myself to have given some grounds for it, did make it my business to appease her all I could possibly, and by good words and fair promises did make her very quiet, and so rested all night, and rose with perfect good peace, being heartily afflicted for this folly of mine that did occasion it, but was forced to be silent about the girle, which I have no mind to part with, but much less that the poor girle should be undone by my folly.

Unlike Mrs. Pepys—who kept her husband up for the next twenty nights—on the evening of Julie's tirade Burr notes in his journal, "Julie is very calm." And she stayed calm. Julie appears to have accompanied Burr to London after his Paris sojourn, the two spending much time together in England during the months Burr was detained there before finally sailing home to America. Nor was their relation all one-sided, as Burr was supportive of Julie in small ways, and continually solicitous of her well-being:

A long visit from Julie to talk about her business, and to get me to write some more letters. Poor soul, she repeats over her instructions 200 times, for fear I should forget them.

Home. Julie talks me to death; but she is so good that I bear it with the patience of a jackass.

Julie has kept me writing letters of business; so two hours last night.

This evening to Mr. G.'s to get his secretary to copy some of Julie's letters.

[Some months later, in London] Julie is, perhaps the only creature in London who does exclusively love Gamp. On my way, passed through Covent Garden, and bought her 1 shilling and 6 pence worth of apples and pears.

Upon obtaining a passport allowing his departure from France, Burr embarked on a ship which he believed would deliver him to the United States and his daughter, Theo. Burr described in great detail how his cabin was fitted up for his Atlantic crossing, concluding, "My little room was the envy and admiration of the whole. It was a great privilege for any lady or gentleman to be permitted to enter. My good little Julie had always that privilege.... La V. spelt hard for an invitation to my cabin; but J. had possession, and she shall maintain her privilege whoever else may pretend."

Unfortunately for Burr, his ship was intercepted by the English fleet and impounded in an English port for many months. After traveling with Burr to London, Julie found work there with a Swiss relation. On two occasions, Burr notes his worries about her, and makes a point of following up: "Greatly surprised to find that Julie had called. Got my dinner, rice boiled, and went off to see what was the matter, being greatly apprehensive that there was trouble. I was right. There lives in the same house a fellow of the name of Voché or Vaché, a Swiss engraver, who has taken upon him to talk about my visits. Staid but a minute, and appointed J. to call on me at 4 tomorrow. I am much concerned with this circumstance. The idea of causing the least inconvenience to so good a soul would distress me."

On the second occasion, Julie's brother-in-law, who was also her employer, gets into a rage at Burr, and Burr writes of his "great fear that it will be vented on J.; and I can't tell you how unhappy this reflection has made me.... [Later that evening, out at dinner] I was engrossed by the concern of poor J., and, of course, bad company.... The position of poor J. occupies me, and unfits me for everything. Not being able to speak a sentence of English, having no friend or acquaintance but this brutal brother-in-law, she will be robbed of all the avails of her industry, for she is confiding and unsuspicious as an infant, and will otherwise be made as unhappy as authority and malevolence can make her. On such occasions I feel the sorrows of poverty."

As it happens, Julie was also the title character in a 1761 novel written by Jean-Jacques Rousseau, a novel which Burr admired greatly, and—odd as it may seem—there may be a link between the novel and the relationship between Burr and the servant girl Julie. Following is a very brief synopsis of an argument supporting that possible connection, taken from historian Lynn Hunt's recent work, *Inventing Human Rights*. Professor Hunt starts with the question of how it became "self-evident" to Americans in 1776 that all men are created equal and endowed with inalienable rights. She then notes that Rousseau was the first person in history to use the phrase "the rights of man," in his 1762 work, *The Social Contract*, published one year after his novel *Julie*. Both works were written in the town of Montmorency north of Paris, to which Burr made his Rousseau pilgrimage.

Professor Hunt then suggests that three epistolary novels of the eighteenth century, namely Samuel Richardson's *Pamela* and *Clarissa* and Rousseau's wildly popular *Julie*—which is based on letters between the aristocratic Julie and her lower class tutor and lover, St. Preux—taught readers for the first time "to extend their purview of empathy across traditional social boundaries between nobles and commoners, masters and servants, men and women.... Human rights could only flourish when people learned to think of others as their equals, as like them in some fundamental fashion. They learned this equality, at least in part, by experiencing identification with ordinary characters who seemed dramatically present and familiar, even if ultimately fictional." Men as well as women responded to these characters. A retired military officer, as Burr himself was, wrote to Rousseau: "You have driven me crazy about Julie. Imagine the tears that her death must have wrung from me....

That reading created such a powerful effect on me that I believe I would have gladly died during that supreme moment."

The central figures in these novels were the three young female title characters, each possessed of strong personality and will. "In each novel, everything comes back to the heroine's desire for independence.... Readers empathizing with the heroines learned that all people—even women—aspired to greater autonomy." Burr's strongly expressed fellow feeling for his own Julie was unusual for its day, quite possibly conditioned by his admiration for Rousseau's *Julie* as well as for the *Vindication of the Rights of Women*.

Fourteen

Saga of a Passport

Dominating all the other threads in the journal is Burr's saga of his continuing attempts to procure official permission to travel out of France so that he could return to the United States and to Theodosia. His frustration increased as the months passed. Jerome Bonaparte, Napoleon's brother and the king of Westphalia, had been Burr's guest at Richmond Hill and was gracious to Burr in Paris but rode off to Compiègne to hunt before helping him with the passport.

After Napoleon became consul, France was placed under elaborate administrative centralization. Gone were the days when you could bribe your way to gain the papers you required. There was only one party, the party of the people; even the mildest dissent was viewed as scheming against the new order. Napoleon feared conspiracies, not military coups so much as intellectuals who would oppose his authority. Enter Aaron Burr, in Paris for vague and clandestine reasons and needing a passport! Burr's weariness by September 1, 1810, is revealed in a typical account of the day:

> Rose at 5, having slept enough, though it was 12 when I couched. At 1 to Duke Rovigo's. I was the first, and placed in the antechamber. The huissier told me that the audience would not begin till 2. "Why, then, sir did you bid me come at 1?" "That you might be ready at 2." There came in to the number of forty-seven; a majority women. Two English women sat next to me. At ½ p. 2 the doors were thrown open, and a huissier cried out, "Mesdames et messieurs, entrez." I was quite surprised, expecting we were to be called in one by one, as I had seen practiced by Fauchet and Champigny. We all went in. The Duc, in full dress, was at the farther end of the room, and we stood, forming a sort of horseshoe, of which the two ends approached him. He began on his right, and so on, hearing and answering, generally, in about one minute. Some of the women kept him three or four minutes, and some talking on after he had given his answer till he turned his back and addressed the next. His first question was, "Qui etes vous?"

The dates missing from the journal, February 18 to May 14, 1811, are the time span when Burr did acquire a passport to leave France. The passport story, so far as it is known, will follow. It is certainly both Kafkaesque and familiar to many who have tried to get working permits and visas in the present day.

Burr's journal records how his desire to please a new female acquaintance, Madame St. Claire, gave rise to a complicated chain of events culminating in an unexpected breakthrough in his passport impasse, permitting his hurried leave-taking of Paris in the summer of 1811: "Before going out received note from Swan requesting me to dine today. At 2 went and with great exertion walked it in forty-five minutes. Found there Madame St. Claire, belle femme, petite et 32. Engaged to call on Madame St. Claire, which shall do on Sunday."

Ticket #1 to the Louvre

To Duc d'Alberg's; lent me his ticket for visiting the museum. To Madame St. Claire's. Very civil; very prettily lodged. Engaged to escort her Friday to the museum, to see the exhibition. On other days the doors are open to all. On Fridays to those only who have tickets.

Home to dress for the Louvre. Took hack and called on Madame St. Claire. Found her dressed and ready. She is really ladylike and handsome; but of all the rest I do not know. She still more ignorant of me, not knowing even my name, having only learnt from her friend that I am a strange animal from the antipodes. Vanderlyn met us at the Louvre, and we passed there three hours. An immense crowd. Several hundred carriages. This, I told you, is the ticket day. Saw Madame chez elle; took a very modest leave.

Mme St. Claire is one possible candidate for the "foreign lady of distinction" referred to by Burr's biographer James Parton in 1858—when St. Claire would have been 80 years old—who told Parton that Burr could hand a lady to her carriage better than any man in the world, and who said, "I feel still the soft touch of his little hand in mine, as he glided across the pavement."

Ticket #2 to the Louvre

Thence to Duc d'Alberg's. The Duchess had promised me a ticket for the Louvre. As she had neglected it, the Duc gave me a note to Mons. Denon (author of the "Travels in Egypt"), who is director-general of the pictures and statues, and of all of the arts of painting and sculpture. Not that such is exactly his title, nor can I tell you now "exactly" what it is. Before proceeding farther, however, I must tell you whence arose my solicitude to have a ticket.... The case is this. The day I was with Madame St. Claire she expressed a very great desire to have a ticket for a friend, and I, having a very great desire to oblige Madame St. C. for reasons which may already be conjectured, took the measures aforesaid. From the Duc's went immediately to Denon's; was admitted, and presented my credentials. Found there the celebrated painter David and another. Denon received me graciously, and I paid him a compliment on his book, and then he was more gracious. He gave me the ticket for "deux personnes." Off set I for Madame St. Claire, assured of a very kind reception.

On the way met Mr. G [Edward Griswold, a New York lawyer who lent money to Burr in Paris]. "Sir," says he, "I am in the most distressing dilemma. A lady, whom I wish very much to oblige, asked me to procure a ticket for the Louvre, and I promised to do it, but have been totally disappointed, and dare not see the lady's face; can you put me in the way to extricate myself?" "Voilà," said I, and gave him my ticket. You may well presume that I altered my course, and did not go to Madame St. C.'s, but Mr. Griswold, knowing that I wished to go to St. Pelasgie [the Paris debtors' prison where Colonel Swan was housed] on business, offered to escort me in a carriage. Thither we went. I saw Swan for a few minutes. We (G. and I) returned and I came home to reflect on the state of things. Thence to Madame St. C.'s; out; of which I was very glad. Home. Rather tired of all this fatigue of body and mind, though I have not told you half.... For instance, ... when at Denon's, thought, as it was well on towards St. Pelasgie, I might as well go thither, and set off; but recollected that I owed the woman who sits in the passage 2 sous for a segar; so turned about to pursue my way by the Pont des

Arts, which was within fifty paces of me; recollected that I had not wherewith to pay the toll, being 1 sou. Had to go all the way round by the Pont Royal, more than ½ mile out of my way, and this occasioned my meeting G.

Ticket #3 to the Louvre (Two Days Later)

Ticket #2 would have been delivered to Mme St. Claire, and that would have been that, but for the fact that Burr had—not for the first or last time—completely exhausted his cash on hand, having not even the 1 sou (the equivalent of 1 U.S. cent) to pay the toll on the Pont des Arts. So, he took a detour to the toll-free Pont Royal to cross the Seine, and there, by happenstance, ran into his friend Griswold, whom Burr obliged by surrendering ticket #2 to him. So another trip to Monsieur Denon was required in order for Burr to obtain ticket #3 to fulfill his promise to Mme. St. Claire. And it was this visit to Denon which led to Burr's finding a way to get round Jonathan Russell's impediments to the passport Burr so desperately needed to return home. For want of a nail, a battle was lost—in Burr's case, for want of a sou, a passport was had.

> At ½ past 10 to Mons. Denon's to get a ticket for St. Claire. There were at least a dozen persons in his hall of audience. Mr. Denon had not yet appeared. Sent in my name. Begged me to wait a few minutes. After a few minutes he came. I doubted whether he would recollect my name or person. On entering, he passed the rest, sought me out, took me by the hand, and led me into his cabinet, and asked me to excuse him a few minutes till he should dismiss the persons waiting. Gamp was justly surprised at a reception so unusual. On his return he took my hand again with both his, assured me of the pleasure he had in meeting me, and his desire to be useful to me. I took him at his word; told him the business which had brought me to France; the memoir [re "X," Burr's Mexican liberation scheme] I had presented, and the ill success; that is, the silence; and that my wishes were now confined to a passport. He offered to speak to Mr. Maret (le Duc de Bassano), supposed to be the most intimate counselor of the Emperor.... Got my ticket and came off in triumph, that I could now fulfill the engagement to St. Claire.

Denon, following through on "his desire to be useful" to Burr, invited Burr to a sumptuous breakfast, just after Christmas 1810:

> My invitation to breakfast was for 1. Was at Denon's a little before that hour. [A]fter 2 Mr. Denon looked often out of the window, and appeared impatient. Just before 3 came in le Duc de Bassano, secretary of state.... At ½ p. 3 we set down to breakfast. The Duc asked me to sit next him. La Duchesse, who is handsome, was opposite.... The Duc engaged me often in conversation. The first course was oysters in the shell, raw, very small; much less than your Pelham oysters, and like all I have tasted on this side of the Atlantic, a copperish taste. Then came in a roast turkey, and roasted snipe; then a large fish, and other things boiled and stewed. Then a sort of cold pastry. The fruits, pears, apples, grapes, and oranges were always on table, and were now served. Wine for ordinary drinking was also always on table, and with the dessert were sent round in glasses various kinds of delicate wines.... Just before 5 we left the breakfast-table and retired to the adjoining room. The Duc took me by the arm. Here coffee was served, all standing, and then liqueurs. The Duc retired first, saying, "It will be an honor for me to see you again," and I soon followed. I had a good deal of conversation with the Duc before breakfast. Told him my story; the vexations I had experienced about a passport; the injustice of detaining me, &c.

It was not until April of 1811, however, that the Duc de Bassano became the minister of foreign affairs, with jurisdiction over the bureau of foreign passports. In early May of that year, Burr did succeed in getting a passport to leave France via Bordeaux, approved not only by Bassano but also, surprisingly, by Burr's nemesis, Jonathan Russell, the American chargé d'affaires. However, this passport got lost in the office of the Duc de Rovigo, the minister of police, who told Burr to start the whole long process all over again.

On May 14, Burr set out on a five-week trip to Amsterdam, in pursuit of his scheme to speculate in shares of the Holland Company, to raise money for his passage home. While in Amsterdam (at this time part of the French empire's Kingdom of Batavia, ruled by Napoleon's brother Louis), Burr found an American ship, the *Vigilant*, readying to return to America. Back in Paris in June, Burr sought a new passport authorizing his departure from Amsterdam, rather than Bordeaux, and he found to his dismay that the obstacle to its issuance was again Jonathan Russell. With the *Vigilant*'s sailing from Amsterdam scheduled for July 23, Burr's frantic attempts to get Russell to yield were unavailing until the Duke of Bassano intervened, as revealed in a series of letters, from Bassano to Denon to Burr, all dated July 18, 1811, and published in translation in Matthew Davis' 1838 edition of Burr's journal, as follows[1]:

> FROM MONS. DENON: Enclosed, my dear colonel, is the letter from the duke; you will perceive by it that your business is in train. If you call on me tomorrow, we will consider what is to be done at the police. A thousand times your friend, DENON
>
> THE DUKE OF BASSANO TO MONS. DENON: The person through whom I could have communicated to Mr. Russell, that he should not have refused a new passport to Mr. Burr, was in the countryside. I wrote to HER yesterday to return. SHE arrived at the moment that your note was received. I shall have the passport [from Russell] in the course of the day, and shall forward it immediately to the duke [Rovigo], and I am convinced that you will receive it tomorrow, to transmit to Mr. Burr. THE DUKE OF BASSANO
>
> FROM MONS. DENON: My dear colonel, enclosed is a second note. Use dispatch in reference to it. You have a friend in the police; make him act. I hope to have the honor of your company tomorrow. A thousand times your friend, DENON
>
> THE DUKE OF BASSANO TO MONS. DENON: My dear Denon, I have received the passport from Mr. Russell for Mr. Burr, and have sent it to the Duke of Rovigo, requesting an immediate return of it. It ought to reach me this evening. Thus there is nothing to prevent the departure of the colonel tomorrow, unless the police should throw obstacles in the way, which I think I have prevented. THE DUKE OF BASSANO

Burr's literary executor Matthew Davis, who did not know French, may have included these letters as translated by Burr himself. But what are we to make of the capitalization of "HER" and "SHE" in the translation of Bassano's first letter? Doesn't it seem as if Burr was enjoying taking a bit of revenge on Jonathan Russell? Because, speculating a bit further, it is certainly conceivable that Bassano himself intervened to help Burr by setting a classic "honey trap" for Jonathan Russell—a time-honored scheme in which a victim such as Russell is lured into a compromising sexual situation so as to provide an opportunity for blackmail. One thing we do know is that Bassano advanced Burr the funds "to discharge all his debts, and to leave the country with credit," as confirmed by an 1835 codicil to Burr's will, which provided a specific bequest to Bassano—still living in 1835—in repayment of that loan.

In his final Paris journal entry, for July 18, 1811, the day on which he received these letters, Burr breathlessly detailed his preparations to leave Paris the following day, never to return:

> Went to Fenwick's to tell my unexpected progress and hopes, and then home, and have written you all this, and now I go to dine. Vanderlyn has just come in, which is lucky, as I want him to do fifty errands, though I shall not feel great confidence till I have the [passport] in hand.... Another note from Denon, enclosing another from Duc Bassano. He has got the passport from Russell; has given his sanction, and has already passed it through the bureau of Rovigo. That bureau of delay and dismay! Now, indeed, I may hope. Now I feel as if I was embracing you and Gamp [here, Burr's grandson]. Shall run over to Fenwick's and do a dozen errands tonight.... Have been running since 5 this morning. Have got my passport. Shall go tomorrow. Have your watch. Have bought you nothing, nor for my poor, dear little Gamp. Shall bring you nothing but myself.

Epilogue

Following a series of delays and setbacks and false starts in London which continued through the spring of 1812, Burr finally did find a ship to take him back to America and money to pay for his passage. It is not established whether he traveled steerage or first class. Paul O'Pecko of Mystic Seaport suggests that he either had a cabin that was a curtained top or bottom bunk, or the more sophisticated single berth with steps to enter it and fitted drawers below. "Passengers socialized and ate their meals in a common area and a steward on board saw to their needs. Most likely Burr would have been traveling in first class accommodations, as the steerage class experience generally would be moldy bread, rancid water and lack of food compared with the upper class experience. The packet ships would change the travel experience from 1815 to 1850" (personal communication, June 2014). Mr. O'Pecko explains that Burr's return sea voyage probably took days longer than going: "Sailing from Liverpool to New York a vessel traveled nearly 500 miles further than New York to Liverpool, which took about 38 days. The eastbound vessels could run a straight course with the winds mostly astern whereas going against the prevailing winds across the Atlantic took longer."

After a harrowing sea voyage, Burr arrived in Boston in May 1812 using the assumed name of Arnot to dodge his creditors and the danger of landing in debtors' prison. He made an amusing story of evading detection by the Boston customs collector:

> Dearborn, the collector, knows me as well as you do, having seen me hundreds of times in public and private; for me to go direct to him to take an oath and demand a permit in the name of Arnot seemed to be an experiment that promised little success, and, in case of discovery, might expose me to serious inconvenience, as the family of Dearborn have been extremely vindictive against me, and no doubt would, under pretense of searching for goods, have possessed themselves of my papers…. Took with me a young man to show me the way to the custom-house, and entered with all possible composure; passed under the nose of Mr. Dearborn into the adjoining room, where the first part of the business was to be done. The officer to whom it was directed asked me to enumerate my effects…. I repeated them off as fast as he could write, though they consisted of eighteen different articles; trunks, boxes, portmanteaus, bundles, rolls, &c. He then bade me sign my name to it, which I did thus: A. Arnot; I think that is very like it [Burr's journal was handwritten, of course]. Then he directed me to take it to the collector, who would sign it; here was the rub. I told the young man, my conductor, to take the list and get it signed for me, for that I was obliged to run as fast as possible to see after my things, the ship being just about to haul out. He took it, and I got out as fast as I could, passing again under the nose of Dearborn. I do assure thee that I felt something lighter when I got down to the street.

Burr's next move in Boston was to write to his loyal lieutenant in New York, Sam Swartout, to ask how the land lay there for his return. Sam answered with a letter "containing a pretty full answer to my queries, with assurance that I have very many and warm friends and no enemies [in New York]":

> The letter is stamped with that enthusiasm which marks his character. As regards business, however, things are not propitious. The two creditors who have judgments against me are inexorable. Nothing will satisfy them but money or approved security, neither of which are in my power. The alternative is to be taken on execution and go to the limits. [The New York City debtors' prison housed debtors who were completely indigent, but for a nominal fee and upon posting bail debtors such as Burr were allowed to arrange their own confinement in private housing within the "limits," an area of 160 acres surrounding the prison.] To this I should have no great repugnance in point of pride or feeling, but there are two objections pretty cogent; first, and principally, you. I fear your little heart would sink to hear that Gamp was on the limits. To be sure, if you could come here and see how gay he was, be supported by the light of his countenance, and catch inspiration from his lips, you would forget that he was not in paradise. The second is, that I have a project of entering into the holy state of matrimony. The charming object is already designated, and love, almighty love! The fair object is a worthy lady some few years older than myself, with fortune enough, and, I think, good-nature enough to make that appropriation of it. Now, this fine sentimental project would be utterly defeated by the limits-establishment.
>
> [The next day:] Have ruminated beaucoup on that limits arrangement. It has even its advantages. I should then be more at my ease; should have nothing to apprehend; could pay my debts in the order I pleased; could live better, be exempt from the trouble of paying visits. On the other hand, there are the weighty objections before stated. I am sure your pride would suffer to have Gamp in jail for debt, for it would be called being in jail. You have already suffered too much on my account, and I come now to sacrifice myself in any way and every way; that of marriage is one, and no hope of that while a prisoner; and as to payment of my debts, if I am confined to the mere practice of the law, debarred from all those speculations in which I might engage if at large, it will be the work of many years, and in all that time I could do you little or no good.

A few pages later, Burr's thousand-page journal of his 1808–1812 self-imposed exile concludes with this entry: "And here I am, in possession of Sam's room in Stone street, in the city of New York, on this 8th day of June, anno dom. 1812, just four years since we parted at this very place" [and just ten days prior to President Monroe's declaration commencing the War of 1812 against Great Britain].

Marrying a wealthy woman! Compared with this latest prospect for riches, "the mere practice of law," at which Burr excelled, seemed less appealing, but it kept him going for the remainder of his life. Burr did achieve his goal of avoiding debtors' prison, and he also managed, late in life, to wed a rich woman, Eliza Jumel, reputedly the richest woman in the United States. However, Burr's marriage to Madame Jumel was short-lived, foundering on a combination of his being too free in spending her money and her claim that Burr had cheated on her, when he was 77, with a woman fifty years his junior. The cheating may have been delusional on Mme. Jumel's part, as was the following story of hers, recounted by a young visitor to her estate in Harlem (which, with its Aaron Burr bedroom, is now a museum, the Morris-Jumel Mansion):

> She [Jumel] says Joseph Bonaparte [king of Spain at the time of Burr's stay in Paris] came to this country to marry her—he knew of her wealth from her European reputation, and she has regretted ever since his death, when she found out he had left three millions of dollars,

that she had snubbed him. He lived at Manhattanville so as to be near her and drove up to see her every day, and, in fact, bored her so much that she had the gate locked, and to her surprise he climbed over one day and went into her kitchen, and she thought it was a great shame for the ex–King of Spain to be in her kitchen and that she would give him a grand dinner to wipe out her bad treatment. Colonel Burr and many distinguished guests were present, and Joseph Bonaparte praised the table so much that she has kept it standing to this day. There in the dining room on the left was the table—china, glass, still there, and gold ornaments and pyramids of confections still standing on this greasy, dusty table, crumbled and moulded. It is à la Havisham in *Great Expectations*.[1]

In 1815, three years after his return to America, Burr wrote to Theodosia's husband, Joseph Alston:

> I have found it so difficult to answer that part of your letter which regards myself and my concerns, that it has been deferred, though often in my mind. At some other time I may give you, in detail, a sketch of the sad period which has elapsed since my return. For the present, it will suffice to say that my business affords me a decent support. If I had not been interrupted in the career which I began, I should before this have paid all my debts and been at ease. My old creditors (principally the holders of the Mexican debt) came upon me with vindictive fury. I was held to bail in large sums, and saw no probability of keeping out of prison for six months. This danger is still menacing, but not quite so imminent. I shall neither borrow nor receive from any one, not even from you. I have determined not to begin to pay unless I see a prospect of paying all.

Alston already knew of the saddest parts of Burr's "sad period" after returning to America: the death of Alston's wife and Burr's child, Theodosia—lost at sea on her voyage from Charleston to New York to reunite with Burr—as well as the death of Alston's only child and Burr's only grandchild, "Gampillo," so often mentioned by Burr in his journal.

Burr's "had I not been interrupted in the career which I began" is poignant as well. How different Burr's life would have been had he not won the United States presidential election of 1800 for Jefferson by gathering up the swing electoral college votes in New York Jefferson needed to defeat John Adams! Following his 1815 letter to Alston, Burr lived for 21 more years, to the age of 80, supporting himself through "the mere practice of law" while also offering comfort for young men and women he raised as his adopted children, providing them the affection he would have lavished on Theodosia and Gampillo. And he left his European journal for us to make what we will of it as we consider the life and character of this controversial American figure.

Appendix A

Reading Burr

Aaron Burr's abundant press has improved over time. The first two major twentieth century works of scholarship: Milton Lomask's two-volume *Aaron Burr: The Years from Princeton to Vice President, 1756–1805* (Farrar Straus Giroux, 1979) and *Aaron Burr: The Years of Conspiracy and Exile, 1805–36* (Farrar Straus Giroux, 1982); and Samuel Wandell and Meade Minnigerode's *Aaron Burr* (G.P. Putnam's Sons, 1925) Goth cast Burr in a favorable light. The fascinating recent biography of Burr, Nancy Isenberg's *Fallen Founder: The Life of Aaron Burr* (Viking, 2007) portrays Burr as a feminist and resides decidedly in his camp.

However, as historian Jill Lepore wrote in her review of *Fallen Founder*, nineteenth century popular historians of Burr missed the mark because they dramatized their accounts of Burr, often using fictionalized versions of him as a foil or cautionary example (Jill Lepore, "Vice," New York Times, May 27, 2007).

Burr's early sketchy reputation derives largely from his own political ally and literary executor, Matthew Davis. A year after Burr's death, Davis published the *Memoirs of Aaron Burr* (Harper, 1837) with this odd epigraph: "I come to bury Caesar, not to praise him." In the early pages of this work, Davis attacks Burr's alleged practice of taking advantage of weak, credulous females, whom Davis calls "deluded victims": "For a long period of time, he seemed to be gathering, and carefully preserving, every line written to him by any female.... Among these manuscripts were ... testimonials of the weakness of the weaker sex, even where genius and learning would seem to be towering above the arts of the seducer.... They were all committed to the flames immediately after the decease of Colonel Burr."

That Davis was himself the person who incinerated the love letters to Burr calls his judgment of Burr's romantic life into question. Thus James Parton, Burr's 1858 biographer, took a totally contrary position and hotly contested Davis's characterization of Burr's intimate correspondence: "Before Mr. Davis received any of Burr's letters or papers, they were carefully examined by two persons, one of them a lady who had an especial and honorable motive for examining every one of them—particularly those addressed to and received from women. Her positive and circumstantial testimony ... enables me to assert, which I now do assert, that Mr. Davis was utterly mistaken as to the character of the letters to which he alludes. He received no letters necessarily criminating ladies!"[1] (James Parton, *The Life and Times of Aaron Burr* [Houghton, 1858]).

Parton also throws out the window Matthew Davis's claim that Burr had seduced the young daughter of a British army officer, Margaret Moncrieffe, in 1776. Indeed, in a memoir many years later, Margaret Moncrieffe described Burr in glowing terms: "Oh, may these pages one day meet the eye of him [Burr] who subdued my virgin heart, whom the immutable, unerring laws of nature had pointed out for my husband, but whose sacred decree the barbarous customs of society fatally violated!" As a later Burr biographer noted, the lady herself had no complaint to make of Burr's conduct toward her (H.C. Merwin, *Aaron Burr* [New Library Press, 1899]).

Nevertheless, during the 19th century Burr's reputation for plundering the virtue of women was kept alive. To take a primary example, Harriet Beecher Stowe did not pull punches in an early portrait of him as a dangerous figure: "He [Burr] whose eye had measured her for his victim verified, if ever man did, the proverbial expression of the iron hand under the velvet glove. Under all his gentle suavities there was a fixed, inflexible will ... that fitted him to bear despotic rule over an impulsive, unguarded nature.... It is said that he once asserted that he never beguiled a woman who did not come half way to meet him, an observation much the same as the serpent might make in regard to his birds" (*The Minister's Wooing* [Derby and Jackson, 1859]). Roger Kennedy, in his recent study, comments that Burr's claim of limiting his attentions to women who met him "half way" must have horrified Stowe, in implying "active sexual engagement by a woman" (*Burr, Hamilton, and Jefferson: A Study in Character* [Oxford University Press, 1999]).

When portrait artist Mimi Van Olsen was looking for a studio and home in Lower Manhattan some years back, she was told a certain building had a shady past because of a tunnel concealed within it that Aaron Burr had dug allowing him to make illicit visits to a woman. This urban legend hung around for 130 years after Burr's death when the city of New York had changed so as to be virtually unrecognizable. As late as 1917, a female novelist depicted Burr as seducer of the wife of Harman Blennerhassett, Burr's codefendant in their 1807 treason trial: "Few women could resist the persuasions, blandishments and personal magnetism of Aaron Burr ... and his constantly expressed admiration of her charm and beauty made the fascinating, vain wife of Blennerhassett his.... However evil the reputation of the rake tempting her, a woman tempted ... soon comes to believe the love and fidelity of the rake ... and, unhesitatingly, she gives all. Piff! Puff! After an hour of dalliance he wings his flight, like an inconstant, painted butterfly, to a newer, more attractive rose" (Elisabeth Brandon Stanton, "*Fata Morgana*": *A Vision of Empire; The Burr Conspiracy in Mississippi Territory and the Great Southwest-Natchez Love Story of Ex-Vice President Aaron Burr: A Historical Novel* (Signal, 1917).

Margaret Blennerhassett and Margaret Moncrieffe figure as the only women named among the supposed legions of Burr's female victims. With regard to Mrs. Blennerhassett, another principal basis for Burr's enduring reputation as a "seducer"—both of innocent females like her and of Burr's fellow political intriguers—traces to Burr's 1807 trial for treason. At that trial, prosecutor William Wirt accused Burr of employing his "seductive power" to enlist the Blennerhassett couple in support of Burr's alleged scheme to separate the Western states from the Union:

> A stranger [Burr] presents himself [on the Blennerhassetts' idyllic island in the Ohio River]. Introduced to their civilization by the high rank which he had lately held in his country, he soon finds his way to their hearts, by the dignity and elegance of his demeanor, the light and beauty of his conversation, and the seductive and fascinating power of his address. The conquest was not difficult. Innocence is very simple and credulous. Conscious of no design itself, it suspects none in others. It wears no guard before its breast. Every door and portal and avenue of the heart is thrown open, and all who choose enter it. Such was the state of Eden when the serpent [Burr] entered its bowers.

Appendix A: Reading Burr

According to historian Joseph Wheelan, Wirt's speech "became an instant classic" and "single-handedly did more than anything else to fix Burr's villainy in the public memory" (despite Burr's acquittal). During the trial, Burr and his defense team "adopted the habit of launching into mock recitations of Wirt's speech as a standing joke, [and] Burr amused his friends for the rest of his life by reciting passages from Wirt's speech ... then sometimes describing Blennerhassett as he really was" (Joseph Wheeland, *Jefferson's Vendetta* [Carroll & Graf, 2005]).

The prosecutor's "serpent in the garden of Eden" speech did lasting damage. Robert Ferguson writes that the speech fixed Aaron Burr in the American psyche as a counter-example to "the pantheon of founders," casting him in the role of a harbinger of the horrors of secession, "as the risk of a divided nation grew more likely across the antebellum period" (Robert A. Ferguson, *The Trial in American Life* [University of Chicago Press, 2007]). For the next century, American schoolchildren would memorize William Wirt's famous speech.

Ferguson also reads in the speech the "spice of [a] sexual connotation" of Margaret Blennerhassett succumbing physically to Burr ("The conquest was not difficult.... Every door and portal and avenue of the heart is thrown open...."). As little basis as this insinuation had, it played neatly into Wirt's dominant theme of Burr as a dangerous intriguer.

In 1903, the same year William Bixby published his definitive edition of Burr's European journal, a group of Burr partisans made an attempt to restore his reputation and exonerate him from the charge of having seduced Margaret Blennerhassett. A newly formed Aaron Burr Legion held a meeting that July in the town of Burr's birth—Newark, New Jersey—and later in the same year published a "Memorial" of the meeting, including speeches and panegyrics relating to Burr. Charles Felton Pidgin, founder of the Legion, set forth in his opening speech at the Newark gathering, as one objective of the Legion, the taking "all proper and legal measures to secure the expunging from all reading books, or other text books used in the public schools of America, of that portion of the speech of William Wirt during the trial of Aaron Burr at Richmond, Virginia, which refers to the alleged intimacy of Colonel Burr and Mrs. Blennerhassett" (*Grand Camp of the Aaron Burr Legion* [The Aaron Burr Memorial, Mount Vernon Book & Music Co., 1903]). Following the meeting, Pidgin issued a challenge to a reference in a Pennsylvania newspaper concerning this "alleged intimacy":

> Dear Sir:
> In your issue of July 29, 1903, I find the following paragraph: "For women, he [Burr] apparently had little or no respect, and in at least one instance returned the hospitality of his host by becoming the despoiler of his home." ... I have no doubt you will agree with me that such things should not be said about any man, living or dead, unless the assertion can be proved. You will greatly oblige me by sending, in the self-addressed, stamped envelope enclosed, the proof of your assertion, or the name and address of some person from whom I can secure such proof.

This letter to the editor appears in the Aaron Burr Memorial under the heading, "An Unproved Assertion: No Answer Yet."

While the Aaron Burr Legion headed by Charles Pidgin had a short life, the Aaron Burr Association, founded in 1946 for similar purposes—namely, "to secure for Burr the honor and respect which are due him as one of the leading figures of his age"—held a recent annual meeting in the restored Blennerhassett mansion on Blennerhassett Island, with a Margaret Blennerhassett reenacter welcoming the Burr group to her island, perhaps further putting to rest this one—of many—charges lodged against the memory of Burr.

Appendix B

Aaron Burr and His Protégé John Vanderlyn in Paris, 1810–1811

KATHERINE WOLTZ

> Katherine Woltz offers additional insight into Burr's state of mind abroad with her study of his close friend and boon companion in Paris, John Vanderlyn. Woltz is a scholar of American art and history and director of the Vanderlyn Catalogue Raisonné. She is writing a book on the relationship between Vanderlyn and Burr, which shines new light on the alleged Burr conspiracy.

It is no small irony that the death in 1836 of Revolutionary War hero and U.S. statesman Aaron Burr—neglected for nearly three decades by contemporaries following allegations of treason—ushered in a revitalized era of intense interest in, and scrutiny of, the man and his complex legacy. Although admittedly a personality that inspired devotion or its opposite—dread—in his more dour contemporaries, Burr nonetheless was belatedly—if grudgingly—elevated by both parties into the mythical halls of the Pantheon of American Revolutionary founders. There he was figuratively positioned onto his respective pedestal, where his looming, statuesque figure continued to taunt the mere mortals below. They continued to debate, parsing as it were, his merits and demerits. Above all, they asked one another, just who was Aaron Burr, this larger-than-life man whose reputation assumed ever-widening, mythological dimensions as time progressed? Today, the question remains moot or rhetorical, depending on one's perspective.[1]

Before he was twenty years old, Aaron Burr (1756–1836) attracted notice as the hero of the patriots' siege of Quebec in 1775; he reached the height of his career by his mid-forties as Vice President during President Thomas Jefferson's first term (1801–1805).[2] His autobiographical trajectory can be likened to a shooting star, or to put a finer point on it, his career path careened rather than plummeted upon reaching its highest arc, public fascination buoying his reputation and preventing any devastating crashing or burning. The reason is simple: Burr left unanswered many questions that persistently dogged the clouds hovering over his reputation, refusing to disperse them and give contemporaries the clarity and closure they craved. Burr's defense was characteristically peevish if to the point: he resolutely denied the accusation made, during and after his trial for treason in 1807, that his plans for revolutionizing the west included dismembering the Union.

The gravity of this and other alleged misdeeds, however, did not ruffle the faith, esteem, and trust of the small group of men assembled around Burr's deathbed that day. This trusted

Appendix B: Aaron Burr and John Vanderlyn (by Katherine Woltz)

circle included stars within America's legal profession and emerging capitalist titans such as Judge Ogden Edwards and Cornelius Vanderbilt, according to an eyewitness. And if they pressed Burr for answers, they also honored his collateral request for privacy. Burr the lawyer knew well the maxim that when injured parties found themselves thrown into the brier patch typically the less said the better. Thus vital keys for resolving the most tangled, misunderstood incidents that profoundly impacted Burr's life and that of America's fragile formative period were kept from public consumption.

Missing from the illustrious assemblage that day were two people that Burr most cherished. They were his devoted protégés, his daughter, Theodosia (who died at age 29 in a shipwreck on New Year's Day 1813), and the now-famous artist John Vanderlyn (1775–1852). Burr befriended the latter in 1795, when the precocious youth faced the prospect of giving up his dream of becoming a fashionable portrait painter. Tipped off to Vanderlyn's plight by a mutual friend, Burr vowed to "rescue genius from obscurity" and subsequently went about preparing Vanderlyn for a brighter future. Vanderlyn became the first American to study professionally at the Ecole-des-Beaux-Arts in Paris, receiving the rank of academician in 1798, thanks to Burr's careful grooming and largesse.

Unfortunately, in 1836, the same year Burr was forced to acknowledge his increasingly deteriorating health condition and accept lodgings in a staffed hotel on Staten Island, New York, Vanderlyn was hundreds of miles away in Charleston, South Carolina. However, Vanderlyn had visited Burr just prior to his death after receiving a letter written "in a shaky hand," requesting that he come to Staten Island. What they discussed is not recorded.

In his hotel room that fateful day, Burr was surely comforted by the next best thing to having his protégés by his side, for he owned Vanderlyn's portrait of his daughter, Theodosia, painted in 1802, and Vanderlyn's self-portrait.[3] Exhibited in Paris at the Louvre's Salon of 1800, the *autoportrait* was later presented by Vanderlyn to his erstwhile patron as an expression of gratitude. Following Theodosia's death, contemporaries correctly surmised that now Vanderlyn alone bore the burden of Burr's most intimate secrets. Their relationship did not fit the conventional patron-artist mold, rather it more closely resembled a strong friendship, even a familial bond. They recognized, therefore, Vanderlyn's unique, privileged position and perch for studying Burr—perhaps early America's most misunderstood personality. More than anyone else, Vanderlyn could envision Burr's most ambitious aspirations and formulate appropriate or suggestive responses to the pressing queries of critics and the low slings of political pundits. Best of all, he could do it by taking the high ground of art—renowned within influential circles of the literati in the preelectronics era for its wide spectrum of expressive possibilities and political potential.

When Burr's fortunes were reversed, Vanderlyn acted during the height of the controversy by taking up his brush, deploying it much like a cultural weapon. He quietly resolved to restore a measure of the public's trust in his friend, his aim being to allude to the much less publicized but equally compelling Burrite point of view, with which, of course, he was intimately acquainted. Vanderlyn framed his multifaceted response with characteristic discretion, but above all as a thought-provoking, visual lure, situating it within the cultural cognoscenti's "court of debate"; that is, he endowed his most intriguing and famous paintings of that period with unique, early nineteenth-century "Da Vinci codes." Armed with the artist's toolbox, Vanderlyn laced his paintings with paired ciphers and guideposts, each uniquely forged to point to a contemporary geopolitical or topical subject of debate.

In accordance with the lofty strictures of history painting, such devices were designed to work in tandem and aimed to remind the viewer of a fable or other traditional moral teaching. In essence, the artist's ruse was a gambit; it baited viewers into resolving problematic issues by teasing them with emblematic riddles or allegories. Following Renaissance precedent, the artists subtly wove these pictorial devices into the fabric of the nominal biblical, classical, or mythological narratives pictured upon their canvases.

Conventional scholarship continues to vigorously debate Burr, his movements, and his motives. Curiously however, the telltale footprints left by his artist-protégé Vanderlyn are overlooked or at best sidelined. This chapter, a partial précis of my ongoing research, writing, and presentations, marks the first study to advance the conversation in new and important ways by utilizing the lens provided to us by Vanderlyn. Rejuvenating the debate by offering new dimensions for consideration, it includes analyses of thematic paintings by Vanderlyn which strongly suggest artist-patron collaborative efforts; it also discusses two caches of letters discovered in Kingston-on-the-Hudson, New York (Vanderlyn's hometown) around the turn of the nineteenth century. More pertinent discoveries and notices of related letters also deserve mention. As a group, these previously unexamined letters suggest, among other things, that the political ties uniting the Burr and Vanderlyn families may have preceded 1795—the year traditionally cited as the starting point of the Burr-Vanderlyn alliance.[4]

Although the old Dutch-American town of Kingston provides the locale and opening for conventional histories detailing Burr's official patronage of Vanderlyn, this chapter will temporarily reorient this setting, for the most panoramic vista for understanding Burr and his artist-spokesman Vanderlyn begins with the metropolis of Paris and continues with the time they spent there together between 1810 and 1811. To that locale and point in time our narrative now turns.

Paris Calling

Updating his journal in Göttingen, Germany (at that time within the Napoleonic Kingdom of Westphalia), in December 1809, Burr excitedly reported the development that Napoleon now planned to support movements for liberating royalist Spain's possessions in South America and Mexico. Burr musing about the possibilities that intelligence now opened for "X," the code symbol he used to denote his own similar liberation projects, he continued writing: "Now, why the devil didn't he tell me this two years ago?"

Unrolling Vanderlyn's portrait of Theodosia, Burr updated her on the good news, his joy only somewhat muted by the semi-blue cloud which had dogged him since the days of his trial in Richmond. In the portrait, Theodosia's eyes looked into his, as if she was right there in the room with him. Looking into her eyes, he promised his daughter that he would stay out of mischief; gratefully he acknowledged that as his secret confidante she remained among that select, shrinking circle that knew his designs were, and had always been, honorable and altruistic. He drew in a deep breath and felt oddly comforted: it was time for him to secure a prized passport that would gain him entry into First Empire, Napoleonic Paris. His sadly wounded reputation and legacy would receive a much-needed boost if things went as planned.

Burr also entertained the possibility that Vanderlyn might soon return to Paris from Rome. He was so proud of his protégé. He had shown Theodosia's portrait to many people during his European tour; the next time he saw Vanderlyn he intended to request that at least one copy be made of the original. Burr also planned to ask Vanderlyn to copy more Renaissance masterworks for his private collection; he especially wanted paintings of *putti*, or the little winged angels that typically accompanied portraits of the Madonna, signifying celestial love, or if with reclining Venuses, their presence represented carnal love. Vanderlyn had already copied some of the masterpieces which Napoleon had brought back from his campaigns and had installed in the Louvre, renamed the Musée Napoleon in 1803. Burr often reflected on his family's strong spiritual background (the Presbyterian divine Jonathan Edwards, for example, being his grandfather), which his political enemies of course never mentioned. For that reason and more, he especially admired the copy Vanderlyn made for him after Raphael's *Sleeping Jesus*, or the *Sommeil de Jesus*, as it was titled in its latest home, the new Musée Napoleon.[5] Burr was especially eager to see first-hand Vanderlyn's historical painting *Caius Marius Amid the Ruins of Carthage*, the critical success of which the American newspapers had roundly celebrated.

Interlude in Rome: Vanderlyn's History Painting *Caius Marius Amid the Ruins of Carthage*

Vanderlyn had traveled to Rome in late 1805 and had painted a larger than life history painting titled *Caius Marius Amid the Ruins of Carthage*, completing it in the fall of 1807.[6] The painting ostensibly depicted the reversed fortunes of the Roman military commander Marius (157–86 BC), who plotted his revenge while in political exile amidst the fallen ruins of the ancient city of Carthage (Rome's traditional enemy). The famous tale from classical history, however, also had compelling parallels to contemporary situations and events, as we shall see.

Vanderlyn exhibited *Marius* to critical acclaim in Rome and soon after returned to Paris. There he met with Denon, who only half-jokingly was also called the "Eye of Napoleon," because he was always searching for art that would promote the reputations of France and its emperor.[7] The Academy professors and critics in Rome had spoken; now Denon wanted to see the talented American "Wanderlyn," as the Italians pronounced his name, tout de suite. During their meeting, Denon carefully examined the painting *Marius* and probed Vanderlyn as to its likely meaning, all the while suspecting that what he saw would flatter the emperor, whose admiration for the Roman military commander was no secret to those within his inner circle. Denon's collateral duties as musée director included acting as gatekeeper and filter, so that he was always searching for the most intriguing entries to include in the biennial Salons. Although Vanderlyn was reluctant to explain the painting's meaning, and handily recalled several Renaissance masters' examples to politely excuse himself, Denon remained suitably impressed.

So too was Napoleon, who personally awarded Vanderlyn a prestigious gold medal for the painting during his official visit to the Salon in the fall of 1808.[8] According to Vanderlyn, the emperor stopped his entourage and, pointing to *Marius* hanging on the walls amidst thousands of entries, exclaimed, "Give the medal to that one!" Napoleon wished to purchase *Marius* for France's national collection, but Vanderlyn demurred, as he intended to exhibit the painting in America.

The gold medal, which featured a portrait of Napoleon on one side and the date of the Salon on the reverse, was one of the few badges of merit available to foreigners according to recent imperial decree.[9] It seems likely, to judge by Vanderlyn's theme and sculptural model for *Marius*—promptly selected by the academy professors for the next Grand Prix competition—that had Vanderlyn been French rather than American, he might well have been among those artist colleagues and friends who received a Cross of the Legion of Honor at that very same Salon. This badge of merit was crafted by Napoleon and was the First Empire's most prestigious award. But was Vanderlyn inducted into the Legion of Honor despite his foreign status?

The praise from Rome along with Denon's approbation played a large role in bringing Vanderlyn a unique award in May of 1808. This was his induction, according to a beautiful hand-drawn, illustrated and signed certificate found among the artist's papers, into Paris's exclusive and secret society of artists—called the Order of the Rose Cross and Pelican—a subset of the Chevaliers de la Croix de Paris and a fraternal organization within the Legion of Honor. The Chevalier de la Croix emblem on Vanderlyn's certificate, along with a recently discovered membership list in the archives of Paris, allows the link to be made for the first time. That the artists' Order of the Rose Cross and Pelican shared fraternal bonds with the Freemasons seems likely, to judge by the cryptic symbols surrounding the certificate's margins.[10]

The artist-members included Cross of the Legion of Honor recipients and upper echelon Academicians like the Duke of Parma, a leading statesman within Napoleon's regime. Born Jean Jacques Régis de Cambacérès (1753–1824), he served as one of the order's most high-ranking officers.[11] Each member identified his rank according to a symbol drawn beside his name. Vanderlyn's illustrated membership certificate, with its attendant red seal and ribbon, shows that his emblem was a cross with a single bar (other signatories' crosses had up to five bars). The membership roster from 1809–1810 lists him as "Jean Vanderlyn, rue d'Assas, 72, et à New York," with the cross symbol appearing beside his name. This only-surviving membership list along with Vanderlyn's certificate provides compelling proof that Vanderlyn was a member of Napoleon's Legion of Honor, notwithstanding the official proscription for nomination that barred foreigners.[12]

The ultimate meaning of the painting was further complicated when the artist attached a provocative title to it, thereby linking the work to the double-edged sword which was the symbiotic legacies of the American and French revolutions. Vanderlyn correctly surmised that the controversial subject would spur debate and thus advance one of his goals. In focusing on the story of Marius, and giving the painting the title *Caius Marius Amid the Ruins of Carthage* (1807), Vanderlyn was deliberately contributing his opinion to an ongoing conversation about history paintings, with Marius as the narrative's protagonist or antagonist. These earlier paintings, chiefly exhibited when the French monarchy's powers were waning, elicited a crescendo of speculation and critical debate in Paris just as transatlantic conversations were parsing the successes and failures of both the American and French revolutions. For some, the figure of Marius prefigured the rewards of revolution; for others, he was an omen of civil discord and national collapse.

To many contemporaries who carefully scrutinized the painting, Marius' story also seemed to allude to the modern day Caesar-Napoleon (i.e., Burr), and the latter's so-called western expedition. Alarmists framed the venture as a means for the former Vice President to wreak revenge on President Thomas Jefferson. The newspapers first sensationalized the "plot" by regaling readers with rumors in the summer of 1805. Vanderlyn, however, also received inside information from Nicholas Biddle, whose relative Nancy Biddle was married to General James Wilkinson (Burr's alleged co-conspirator). While the newspapers galvanized public hysteria by re-visiting rumors in circulation since the 1780s that claimed Wilkinson was in the pay of the Spanish and a traitor to the fledgling Republic, Nicholas, whose father Charles was a confidant of Burr's kept his friend Vanderlyn apprised of facts via letters and also during a visit to Rome when they walked together in the ruin-strewn *campagna*. Thus, Vanderlyn was a unique witness to unfolding events.

Beginning his composition in 1806 (or in the midst of the so-called Burr Conspiracy), Vanderlyn finished his larger-than-life oil painting in the fall of 1807 (or in the aftermath following Burr's controversial acquittal). Still unresolved was the moral credibility of the revolution allegedly perpetrated by Burr and his associates (the legal ends already having been examined during the trial). For although acquitted, many still assumed Burr was guilty of plotting disunion and was set free due to a mere technicality in the law that Judge John Marshall exploited and directed the jury to observe during their deliberations.

Other contemporaries who scanned *Marius*, its setting, and its ancillary objects were confident that the painting alluded to Napoleon and his martial and political exploits. Certainly, Vanderlyn's painting was conceived during a time when ongoing relations between Napoleonic France and Rome, also called the "City of Artists" and the "Eternal City," were fraught with tension, and had been since the 1790s. In 1797, Napoleon threatened the Papal States with invasion. To avert the disaster, the Treaty of Tolentino was signed, a condition of which stipulated that one hundred prized works of art and five times as many manuscripts be transferred from the Vatican's collection to Paris.

Despite the treaty, the French occupied Rome briefly between 1798 and 1799 before being forced out by the royalist Neapolitans and their British allies; however they returned to occupy Rome between 1809 and 1814. Even between 1799 and 1809, Rome did not rest, for French-occupied territories encircled the city as the former Papal States, one by one, succumbed to Napoleon and his empire. Great Britain and Europe's combined might and successive coalitions could do nothing to stop the Machiavellian French "sphinx," as counterrevolutionaries liked to call him. An allegory gaining currency depicted France as a Herculean rapist of other nations' cultural treasures.

Souring relations, too, was that many clergy and Pope Pius VII resented Napoleon's meddling with, and belittling of, their religion. Napoleon insisted they were superstitious, and he made multiple attempts to undermine their collective authority. Among other outrages, Napoleon demanded oaths of loyalty, confiscated church properties, and banned the worship of saints.

Pius vowed that although Napoleon was emperor of France, he would never be "Emperor in Rome." In retaliation Napoleon declared the pope a madman, and in 1809 gave orders for his arrest, deportation, and incarceration at Savona, while the entire papal archives were to be inspected and removed to Paris. But rather than weaken the pope's influence, the bad treatment made him a martyr. Thus Napoleon's vaunted reputation as a revolutionary "liberator" was further weakened and he was increasingly considered to be a tyrannical upstart.

As a way to legitimize the confiscations, in 1803 Napoleon made moves to further boost the prestige of French art and the reputations of the new custodians of the wartime trophies. To wit, the French Academy in Rome was ordered to vacate its quarters and relocate to the more conspicuous and prestigious Villa Medici. Affiliated French archaeologists, ostensibly to make amends for the transfer of the artworks to Paris, busied themselves by trying to save certain Roman monuments from vandalism and deterioration. Although an ambitious project, many viewed it with suspicion and denied any altruistic ends. A catty comment by the admittedly biased British visitor John Chetwood Eustace, who came to Rome in 1802, illustrates the mood: "The French under the pretext of beautifying the city, but in reality to discover and seize the treasures of art still supposed to be buried under its ruins, have commenced several excavations, and of course made some discoveries."

Vanderlyn, whose friends in Rome included many Englishmen (and one who tried, albeit unsuccessfully, to purchase *Marius* for the British national collection) relished the wit and irony in such statements. On the other hand, as an artist Vanderlyn's enthusiasm for the artworks and antiquities that remained in Rome and for those already transferred to the Louvre could not rightly be contained. Thus, our artist was caught in a quandary. The hot seat that lately seemed to be his constant abode was uncomfortably studded with political thorns. For Vanderlyn and many others forcefully argued that only in Rome could artists, regardless of their nationality, be at ease. His reasoning was spot-on, for by tradition all artists were welcomed in Rome. There they were encouraged to study the antiquities and Renaissance paintings—a precious invitation at a time when most art collections were strictly private, or, at best, difficult to gain access to.

Such was the case with Great Britain's national museum, housed in Montague House and opened on January 15, 1759. Napoleon's answer to the British (France's traditional enemy), the creation of the Musée Napoleon (present day Louvre), would signal a watershed moment by giving true access to everyone. Of course the museum, named in his honor, was a prize jewel in the imperial crown he would don, to the consternation of many, by 1804.

The American Napoleon

Burr's happy news as written in his journal could be misconstrued (and most popular historians have), as an endorsement of Napoleon and his militant, freebooting ways. The truth was, Burr's opinion of the emperor—in line with many of his Democratic-Republican contemporaries—had dramatically changed over the years. In 1802, Burr was in Charleston and gave Theodosia's father-in-law, William Alston, a bust of the First Consul.[13] A firm friend of liberty, Alston displayed Napoleon's bust on his mantle. Too, Napoleon was nominated as an honorary member of the Academy of the Fine Arts in New York. Burr, as a founding member, and Vanderlyn, as the academy's cultural attaché, proudly took part in garnering Napoleon's letter of consent and his symbolic support.

But Napoleon alarmed admirers when in 1799 he overturned the Directory, France's governmental body, and later installed himself as First Consul. His credibility as a true friend of liberty was further eroded when in 1804, he crowned himself Emperor of the French, snatching the crown from Pope Pius VII's hands because he hesitated, or refused, to place it on Napoleon's head.[14] At 53, Burr was described as resembling an "American Napoleon" by one female admirer at the Weimar court. Seven years earlier, Vanderlyn's profile portrait of Burr had matched in remarkable ways the bust of Napoleon given to Alston. Was the resemblance intentional or was it a clever foil? Would Burr soon meet his alleged doppelgänger?

Vanderlyn's 1810 portrait of Burr, a collaborative piece undertaken following their belated reunion, was brought to life in the artist's atelier in Paris. It reveals that Henriette von Knebel of Weimar was not exaggerating. The profile portrait from 1810 is similar to Vanderlyn's 1802 portrait but departs from it in intriguing ways.[15] The resemblance to Napoleon is clear: the sharp piercing eyes, the strong Roman nose, the thin lips, the closely cropped dark hair. Yet portraits of Napoleon painted during this same time reveal that his formerly taut soldier's body had gone slack; by contrast Burr was fit. Grey streaks in Burr's once-raven hair make him look not old or weary, but at once mature, suave, and sage. A thin squiggle from the portraitist's brush enhanced Napoleon's reputation as cynical and cruel; Burr's slightly upturned lips implied his wit. Whereas Napoleon is often shown with bent back, Burr's posture is natural and relaxed, yet alert. Multiple Doric columns, symbols of strength and rectitude, stand on a classical portico in the background. On the horizon dark storm clouds are forming. Burr's luxurious black coat resembles a classic judicial robe; behind him a lush red curtain is pulled back.

The ensemble, a collaborative effort and tentatively discussed before Vanderlyn's brush brought the canvas to life, recollects a time and notable role played by Burr while Vice President to President Thomas Jefferson. In this scenario, the columns and red curtain refer to the controversial impeachment trial of Federalist judge Samuel Chase in 1805. Despised by the president, Judge Chase, his friends and allies insisted, was the victim of political persecution. Were the tables of justice to be overturned? Both parties watched with bated breath as Vice President Burr, who insisted on decorum, presided over the trial.

During impeachment investigations it was whispered that Jefferson remained confident that Burr, whom he believed was in his pocket, would remain loyal to party and help tilt the scales of justice against Chase. Jefferson's latest young artist-devotée, Rembrandt Peale, attended the trial in anticipation of executing a grand history painting that would lionize the Jeffersonian Republicans and make a national spectacle of Chase. But Burr angered Republicans—and delighted Federalists—when he chose to preside over the trial in an even-handed manner, thereby elevating blind justice over party affiliation. When the Senate found Chase not guilty, Burr followed up with an impromptu departing speech, the gist of which astonished the assembled Congress.

It was his last act as vice president, and Burr meant to impress upon those gathered before him the novel experiment that was America's judicial system. Pausing for a moment for effect, Burr continued: it must be stressed, he said, that our framers' aspirations included that our courts work impartially and with justice for all. These earnest closing remarks temporarily dumbfounded Congress but Burr said no more, preparing instead for his final exit. Several members watched respectfully as he closed the congressional doors behind him; some wept while others tried to capture the Vice President's unwritten parting words on paper.[16] Rembrandt Peale quietly scotched his national history painting idea, his proposed subject-villain having been publicly vindicated.

Vanderlyn's 1810 portrait is not, however, a simple gloss on one important event—the Chase trial—in Burr's life. Visual clues within the portrait hint that more is at stake; perhaps a moral lesson will be the ultimate takeaway. Certainly the gathering storm clouds in the background of Burr's portrait suggest another, related and ominous, event: his trial for treason two years later in Richmond, Virginia. During the summer of 1807, Burr played a decisive role in his own defense. The tables were turned and now he, instead of Chase, faced heinous allegations. Moreover, Burr's plight was compounded by the specter of public execution. That was to be the fate of the "American Napoleon," as Burr was sometimes called in the press, had he been found guilty.

Vanderlyn's portrait may implicitly draw parallels between Burr's and Napoleon's physical similarities, but at the same time, subtle visual clues make counterclaims. Elements like the symbolic Doric columns, with their square bases, plinths, and moldings, are suggestively juxtaposed near the attentive Burr. They hint of divergent personalities and ideologies at a crossroads; if one pivots toward a system of checks and balances, the other endorses the unleashing of executive powers and privileges. If one embraces liberty, the other mocks the notion.

The neatly aligned Doric columns in Burr's 1810 portrait immediately recall a striking architectural antecedent at play in Vanderlyn's earlier and most celebrated history painting, *Caius Marius Amid the Ruins of Carthage*.

Sleeping Venuses and Parisian Violets

In 1810, Burr entered a Paris where Napoleon and his advisors were behind doors, plotting a diplomatic alliance between France and Austria, ruled by Emperor Francis I.[17] The civil and religious marriage between Napoleon and Francis's daughter, the Archduchess Marie-Louise, would take place on April 1 and 2, 1810. The marriage processional would advance through the Grande Galerie of the Musée Napoleon, with the religious ceremony culminating in the museum's Salon Carré. The French neoclassical painter Jacques-Louis David, mentor to Vanderlyn, would capture the moment in a panoramic painting replete with the museum's cultural war trophies and distinguished guests (including members of the American expatriate community like John Armstrong) in the background.

The symbolic locale of the wedding, where Napoleon's sculptural and framed captives would prominently surround him, would not escape the astute Vanderlyn and Burr. The Archduchess Marie-Louise, the classical sculpture called the *Sleeping Cleopatra/Ariadne* (said to be the "bride" of the pope), Raphael's *Transfiguration* (1520), Veronese's *Marriage at Cana* (1563), Correggio's *Jupiter and Sleeping Antiope with Cupid* (1525), and others; all were war trophies to Napoleon's way of thinking. Burr's strategy would thus include appealing to the emperor's geopolitical aspirations, his erstwhile reputation as the protector of liberty, and, last but not least, his pride in being a connoisseur of the arts and his vaunted reputation as the "savior" of the confiscated works.

Burr recorded his arrival in Paris, France, on February 16, 1810. He did not try to contact Vanderlyn, believing that his former protégé had abided by his plan to revisit Rome, Italy, to continue his studies of the celebrated antiquities and paintings still remaining in the "City of Seven Hills." Instead, Burr immediately set out to rekindle former relationships with Count Constantin Volney and Pierre Auguste Adet. Burr had forged friendly and political alliances with both of these French representatives to America during the mid–1790s. Diplomatic relations between France and America had weakened under Washington's and Adams' presidential administrations; Burr and Adet had hoped that by working together, they could reinvigorate those fraternal bonds. Their dreams and schemes were ambitious and included the settlement and liberation of British North America (present-day Canada) at their nexus.

Burr's reunion with his Parisian friends and former political allies was animated, but while the tête-à-tête with Adet was recorded in his journal its substance was not—a smart decision should the journal fall into the bureaucratic hands of Napoleon's censors. A lesser known but equally important catalyst sparked Burr's trip to Paris, besides receipt of the news concerning Napoleon's new liberation venues and revived war with Spain: Burr's own revived scheme, vis-à-vis the annexation of British North America to the United States. The timing was auspicious, as Napoleon was also dusting off old plans to oust the British from these former French possessions. The parameters of "X" were elastic; Burr welcomed their expansion to accommodate points south *and* north.

According to the Canadian historian Frank Murray Greenwood, Napoleon would fully subscribe to this new development.[18] In this scenario, the oft-cited mysterious hostage-like status by Napoleon's agents that Burr endured once in Paris becomes understandable, for soon after his arrival the French emperor had the Duc de Cadore engage his latest political prisoner in writing a prospectus of his revived plan for invading British North America.[19] Like Burr's current prospectus, his earlier plan concerning British North America had yoked financial, humanitarian, and political concerns together.

Burr would soon notice (and grasp why) the American expatriate community in Paris shunned him. Still, he would scoff at former friends who now ignored him, and balk at the recent newspaper editorials that accused him of being a man with no country due to his own indiscretion and fidelity to none. In sum, his accusers would allege that because Burr could find no backing for his "western expedition" in London, he seamlessly turned to her traditional enemy, Paris. This versatile strategy for backing his venture was cited as proof of Burr's continuing treachery.

The writers of these columns intentionally left out a key factor generally known to Burr's entrepreneurial contemporaries but forgotten today. For this reason, modern-day biographers have unwittingly repeated these misleading allegations. But during America's formative years, banks as they are known today did not exist; therefore businessmen, inventors, and other speculative concerns typically turned first to London for financial backing. If that failed, they would next try their luck at Paris or vice-versa. Robert Fulton, Joel Barlow, and Ira Allen were notable examples relying on this financial model; Burr's method was thus conventional and in no way treacherous, desperate, or even revolutionary.[20] Another ingredient in the recipe for funding often included a humanitarian element, especially if the project or invention in some way involved the amelioration of perceived universal foes or woes. Burr's project neatly encompassed each of these elements.

John Trumbull's "Mistake"

Burr's interest in liberating British North America had its origins even before the tumultuous 1790s. His study of the area began during the Revolutionary War while serving under General Montgomery during the patriot siege of Quebec. The American rebels tried, albeit unsuccessfully, to conquer Canada in late 1775. Among those troops were several key figures who, years later, refused to give up the dream; they included Burr, the hero of the doomed attack on Quebec. Burr's role in trying to retrieve the fallen body of General Richard Montgomery, who was fatally wounded during the siege, was immortalized in 1777 by Hugh Henry Brackenridge in his poem titled "The Death of General Montgomery, in Storming the City of Quebec: A Trajedy."

The patriotic effort to liberate Canada lingered in the public imagination long after the death of Montgomery, partly because the Americans were so close to successfully achieving their goal.[21] The tragic though patriotic saga also attracted the attention of American artist John Trumbull in early 1776 when Matthias Ogden—who was ordered by General Benedict Arnold to carry the news about Montgomery's fall to General George Washington—arrived in camp.[22] As an aide-de-camp to Washington, Trumbull would have heard about the news firsthand from Ogden's verbal report. In addition, Trumbull's duties at that time included not only drawing plans of the enemy's positions, but also reporting, perhaps using the artist's language of the brush, on the condition of the troops returning to Quebec from the campaign.[23] Thus there can be no doubt that the patriot siege of Quebec and its historical details—the soldier's individualized but worn "uniforms," their injuries, and the like—captured the artist's imagination.

It comes as no surprise to learn, then, that Trumbull chose the siege to include in his series of history paintings commemorating America's Revolutionary War and its heroes. The composition was the second painting in his series, and Trumbull's title was *The Death of General Montgomery Before the Battle of Quebec*. Completed in 1786, the complex work cleverly paid tribute to Trumball's erstwhile teacher's (Benjamin West) earlier watershed history painting titled *The Death of General Wolfe Before the Battle of Quebec* (1770).

In Trumbull's painting, Montgomery's lifeless body falls into the arms of a soldier, whom contemporaries would have identified as Captain Aaron Burr. The young volunteer soldier became a national hero when he risked his own life to retrieve his general's fallen body from the driving snow. In the painting, the exact circumstances of Montgomery and his troops' sacrifice for their country are transformed into an earthly model of piety, sacrifice, and virtue, for the central group consisting of Montgomery and Burr "quotes" another famous sculpture and chapter from Biblical history. The sculptural model referred to in Trumbull's painting (following West's precedent) is Michelangelo's *Pièta*, in which the Virgin Mary holds the broken, tortured body of her son Jesus after he has been taken down from the Roman cross. Artistic "quotes" such as this upheld a venerable tradition in late eighteenth-century aesthetic theory and practice; as devices they worked to solicit the empathy of viewers for the subject and actors pictured in the painting.

Citing well-known classical and Renaissance artistic precedent was one way that history painters—like Trumbull and his younger contemporary Vanderlyn—effectually signaled to audiences that the contemporary subject depicted on their canvas was not simply an image detailing a current event. "Grand Manner" history painting received its name due to the large and intricate scale of the canvases used for illustrating the historical subjects. In utilizing these and other devices, history painters elevated their subjects and signaled to viewers that the scenes were deserving of their empathy and were fit subjects for intellectual and moral contemplation.

Remarkably, the proverbial fly in the ointment did not surface until some two decades after the event at Quebec, when Trumbull belatedly issued a key to the painting that claimed to identify the participants. In Burr's place, Trumbull identified Matthias Ogden, the messenger of the news to General Washington's camp. Trumbull, when pressed for answers, cited artistic license and only a partial knowledge of the historical circumstances. In light of Trumbull's altered political position during the 1790s, however, this explanation rang hollow and did not satisfy the curiosity of his contemporaries like William Dunlap. Burr's supporters were vexed but not surprised by Trumbull's "mistake." By that time, Trumbull the Federalist, it was well known, worshiped Alexander Hamilton and was the political protégé of John Jay, both of whom were political adversaries of Burr.

Redux: Burr's "Trojan Horse" Strategy

Around the same time that the Trumbull "key" controversy arose, Burr and Adet were joining forces in planning their peaceful "revolution" of British North America.[24] A frequent guest at Burr's Richmond Hill mansion, Adet's portrait was painted by Vanderlyn. In turn, Adet supplied Vanderlyn with letters of introduction to influential Parisians who could help advance his career once in the metropolis.

The success of Burr's portion of the Canadian scheme was contingent upon a modern-day Trojan horse ruse. It worked along similar lines to a plan Burr had proposed earlier for providing clean water to the city of New York: the formation of a corporation called the Manhattan Company. The prospectus for the Manhattan Company included a small provision that resulted, to the Federalist-Hamiltonians' horror, in the establishment of a bank that served the interests of clients other than America's Federalist elite—who were being served by Hamilton's Bank of the United States and the Bank of New York.[25]

This time, however, the Trojan horse was a community of German immigrants headed by the artist and land speculator William Berckzy. Financed by the "German Company," a corporation founded by Burr and several other investors, the immigrants planned to take advantage of free land in Canada offered by the British authorities to anyone who would come and settle it. The German Company looked upon the immigrant community's resettlement as a plum land investment: once the land grants became official, then Berckzy would repay the investors by giving them a large share of the land grants, which they could flip and sell for a large profit.[26]

The formation of the German Company followed on the heels of even earlier plans with revolution and Canadian land speculations at their base. These projects involved Burr's close friends and business associates, including Charles Williamson and Timothy Green (both of whom would be involved in the later "western expedition"). Into this mix came Asa Danforth, who allegedly worked in tandem with Burr and other Albany interests to annex the area around York (present-day Toronto). The combined efforts of the entrepreneur-revolutionaries were stymied, however, when Robert Liston, British envoy to the U.S., caught wind of their covert operations. Writing on November 1, 1797, to Lord Grenville, the British foreign minister, Liston highlighted a warning he had recently received, one relayed by an anonymous American sympathetic to Great Britain. "There exists," Liston wrote, "a project for the purchase of extensive territory in Upper Canada of which the leading though not ostensible members are men of high-flying democratic sentiments who would rejoice to see an independent Republic established in Canada in the room of the present Colonial and Monarchical Government."[27]

At the head of this conspiracy, continued Liston, was Aaron Burr and his associates Elias Boudinot and the governor of New York, George Clinton. Liston was also aware of the movements of Constantin Volney, who earlier that summer had helped orchestrate the plot for conquering Canada. He would return to Paris to report on "measures for the operation" to the Directory, the provisional government of France, which had promised to bankroll the movement.

Borderlines Blurred: Vanderlyn's Pendant Paintings of Niagara Falls

Between 1801 and 1803, Vanderlyn returned to America for a brief visit and in the process became a participant in the Canadian scheme. Already proclaimed as America's leading portraitist by his erstwhile teacher Gilbert Stuart, Vanderlyn was besieged with requests from clients. Burr, however, also provided Vanderlyn in the autumn of 1801 with a fit "historical" subject: Niagara Falls. In arming his protégé with a letter of introduction to Thomas Morris (another business associate and former U.S. senator of New York's western district), Burr neatly established Vanderlyn as his official proxy. Morris in turn provided the artist with several letters of introduction. These enabled him to travel into Canada without incident and without being turned back by British sentries.

Vanderlyn's views were thus completed on the British side of Niagara Falls, but the sites they represented would have worked like a clarion call to anyone even faintly familiar with ongoing patriotic reports that aimed to expunge the British from—or to "revolutionize"—Canada. The two large paintings correctly envisioned the falls from both the British and the American sides, eliminating for all intents and purposes any indications of the contested border dividing the two hostile nations. Significantly, Vanderlyn also eliminated all signs of civilization from his views, although the British side, from where he painted the scenery, was already heavily settled, according to extant contemporary accounts. The views thus aimed to please two parties with disparate or combined goals: those interested in settling Canada's virgin lands, or those interested in dissolving the border currently dividing the British side of the Niagara from the American side.

Vanderlyn used tiny figures in the foreground of the falls to establish their panoramic breadth, but the figures were not simply "stock" characters; they were given distinguishing characteristics.[28] For example, in the oil painting titled *A View of the Western Branch of the Falls of Niagara, Taken from Table Rock* (1801), smartly dressed gentlemen nervously peer over the projecting rock while another converses with an Indian of statuesque Apollonian proportions—a handsome, tan, and muscular man. This Native American who wears traditional clothing may represent Burr's friend, the Mohawk chief Joseph Brant. He gesticulates and points to objects and lands surrounding the falls. His gentleman companion may well be Vanderlyn, who as Burr's agent not only would be gathering statistics from Brant concerning potential land sales, but also intelligence the Mohawk would provide the artist with concerning the surrounding borderlands. Brant would also relate the Indians' dissatisfaction with the Delphic promises tendered to them by the British authorities, including reneging on important treaty points such as allowing the Indians to sell their own lands.

Vanderlyn's pendant view of Niagara Falls titled *A Distant View of the Falls of Niagara,*

Including Both Branches with the Island, and Adjacent Shores, Taken from the Vicinity of the Indian Ladder (1801) suggestively shows the dividing of Niagara Falls as the river rushes around Iris Island (later called Goat Island). Significantly, while the island was within U.S. territory, it divided the falls into those located on the Canadian and the American sides. The title was a subtle way to call attention to a border that many Americans wished would disappear and thereby seamlessly unite the two territories. In letters and published circulars, Vanderlyn was careful to stress the falls' geographical accuracy as shown in his paintings. This was the sort of information needed by anyone contemplating surveying the area or wishing to cross the border undetected.

The second part of the Burr-directed Niagara Falls project involved having engravings made of Vanderlyn's pendant paintings so that copies could easily be circulated among art lovers, budding revolutionaries, and capitalist cognoscenti—all of whom watched with bated breath for the impending fate of the falls and the surrounding borderlands. The engravings after Vanderlyn's pendant paintings subsequently were completed under his supervision in Paris and London in editions of two hundred. The bulk of these engravings were then shipped back to America and to the law offices of Roger Strong, Burr's law partner and business associate.

Did Vanderlyn act as Burr's puppet or did he act on his own agency? The historical record shows that he conducted himself as an equal partner in the project. Too, Vanderlyn's own unrequited fascination with capturing the scenic beauty of Niagara Falls and problematic border relations continued unabated; in 1841, for example, he submitted a large-scale painting of the falls to that year's Salon in Paris. The title references the most recent attempt by American patriots to annex Canada to the United States and the ensuing diplomatic fallout between the two nations: *View Taken of Niagara River in Upper Canada; This View Shows the Spot Where the Steam Boat Caroline Was Set on Fire*. The plot failed before it even got started, with the conspirators camping on Goat Island, situated on the American side. Under cover of night, British troops crossed the border and set fire to, then set adrift the steamship *Caroline*, where more conspirators allegedly were sleeping. As the steamship engine exploded and became a floating torch, nearing the deadly falls, any hopes for the vandalism remaining a covert act were dashed. Spectators on the Niagara River banks witnessed the fireworks, then recounted what they saw to newspaper editors anxious to capitalize on the ensuing international diplomatic furor.[29]

Aaron Burr and the Napoleonic Subplot in Vanderlyn's *Caius Marius Amid the Ruins of Carthage*

Burr wrote on February 23 that he learned from the "celebrated" U.S. captain Nathan Haley ("the first American I have seen"), that Vanderlyn was in Paris (not Rome) and "hunting me down." The captain wrote down and handed to Burr Vanderlyn's address—71, Rue de Vaugirard. Haley may also have told Burr about the beautiful, detail-filled portraits Vanderlyn had painted of himself and his wife. The portraits were pendants, meaning that they, like Vanderlyn's portraits of Burr and Theodosia from 1802, were to hang beside each other as a paired unit.

Burr carried Theodosia's portrait with him around Paris, as he had earlier in England and other points on the Continent. It remained unframed so Burr could unroll the oil-on-canvas portrait whenever he wanted to "introduce" people to his daughter. Remarkable conversations are recorded in his journal whereby not only Burr but also his friends held discussions and engaged in repartee with "Theodosia." With the portrait, Burr could also instantly transport himself to a semi-imaginary plane. There he could envision and review the day's events and his ruminations about them with his absent daughter. Was Burr unusual in staging conversations with Theodosia's portrait? Not at all. This was a cultural conceit inherited from classical antiquity, whereby an absent person's portrait was understood to stand in absentia for their physical self, whether the loved ones be separated geographically or by death.

Burr adopted the same ritual conceit in writing to the absent Theodosia in his journal, although we can be certain that key passages were never meant for her perusal. These included, no doubt, entries detailing his sexual escapades with prostitutes. Soon to join him in this enterprise was his friend and protégé Vanderlyn, with the rendezvous giving birth to an impromptu verbal and written code whereby their favorite consorts, for example, were referred to as "the violets." Employing the code in the letters they exchanged the following year, Burr and Vanderlyn also discussed the subject and progress of Vanderlyn's great mythological history painting (then underway on the artist's easel) titled *Ariadne Abandoned by Theseus on the Island of Naxos*. Nearby the sleeping, naked, and recently ravished Ariadne, violets—the flowers that were a critical detail within Napoleon's supporters' haberdashery—grow in luxurious clumps beside a forest stream.

Devised as a pendant for his earlier *Caius Marius Amid the Ruins of Carthage*, the story depicted in *Ariadne* was a well-known tale about moral deceit and political treachery from mythological history. The story shown in *Marius*—a cautionary tale about vanity and overweening ambition—was a famous chapter from classical history. Both stories aimed to edify their audiences and served as mnemonic devices for instilling universal or moral lessons. In this way they offered adults a moral template for contemplation, much like Aesop's fables taught children how to quickly tell right from wrong. Moreover, the individual subjects and narratives of each painting were to be understood as united thematically—and according to then-current art theory, typically pointed to a contemporary topic of debate.

A similar phenomenon was recognized as the charge animating religious triptychs. Each of three hinged panels might depict individual stories from biblical history, but it was understood that a predominant theme or lesson provided the metaphorical glue that bound them together. For this reason, Renaissance religious paintings were scrutinized for meaning in the same way that history paintings were, especially as so many masterpieces had been removed from dimly lit churches in Italy and hung in the brightly lit halls of the Louvre in Paris. This was an important pastime that Burr and Vanderlyn would share together in the days to come.

The Many Threads of Ariadne's Clue

Burr found Vanderlyn's calling card in his lodgings. He had tried earlier to find his protégé, but when he called at 71, Rue de Vaugirard, no one knew who Vanderlyn was. "Could Vanderlyn, too, have turned rascal?" he sadly confided in his journal. But Captain Haley, it turned out, was slightly mistaken: Vanderlyn lived at 72, Rue de Vaugirard, which was about a half-mile from 71! Burr set out once again to find Vanderlyn, and soon he and

Vanderlyn were joyfully clasping and greeting one another. Breakfast chez Vanderlyn followed (Vanderlyn's supposed poverty while in Paris is belied by his ability to maintain a private residence in addition to an atelier and servant who cooked and cleaned), and then Burr was given a guided tour of the atelier, which was filled with paintings and drawings, including the tentative outlines of what would become *Ariadne* leaning on the great easel. And at last, Burr was able to feast his eyes on *Marius*. He wrote of it: "An hour looking at [Vanderlyn's] pictures. *Marius on the Ruins of Carthage* obtained the gold medal in 1808. I see nothing in that line to exceed it."

Burr also saw Vanderlyn's copies of original paintings that were on view at the Musée Napoleon, including Corregio's *Jupiter and Sleeping Antiope with Cupid*.[30] In the painting, Antiope and a cupid sleep together in the woods; a lustful Jupiter is stealthily lifting up her garment and intends to ravish her at any minute. This painting, so beautiful it astonished those who saw it, gave Burr ideas about cupid's role and others concerning political cupidity that might help his protégé. We might also imagine that he asked right there on the spot to have a copy of that particular cupid made for his own collection.

The two friends then headed directly to the Musée Napoleon, with Vanderlyn excitedly pointing out all of the trophies brought to the museum by Napoleon's conquests. Vanderlyn would have discussed Raphael's *Transfiguration* with Burr in front of the massive painting, as all admirers of art did when first encountering it in the halls of the Musée Napoleon. It was the first time the canvas could be studied in the light, as it had been removed from its original dark and inaccessible church altar setting. Vanderlyn would have pointed out how the Renaissance master combined several seemingly random Biblical miracle stories, compressing them into a single narrative about Jesus' triumph over those who ridiculed and threatened him; three centuries later Raphael's biblical rebus remained a matter of keen intellectual debate.

Burr was especially impressed with the scale of the museum, and he noted the names of several ancient sculptures recently removed from the Vatican's collection: the Apollo Belvedere, the Laocoön (which, notably, had formed the sculptural model for Vanderlyn's 1804 painting *The Massacre of Jane McCrea*). Finished soon after Vanderlyn returned from his 1801–1803 hiatus in the U.S., the painting was exhibited at the Salon of 1804 near the busts of his friends Robert Fulton and Joel Barlow by the French neoclassical sculptor Houdon. *Jane McCrea* was the first painting in a series by Vanderlyn to focus on a nationalist theme, revived almost as a religion in Napoleonic France. This was, simply put, the "treachery of the British," or "Carthage," as the island and its inhabitants were also called.

Vanderlyn and Burr would thereafter often visit the Musée Napoleon, and also the sculpture gardens of the Palace of Versailles outside Paris. Vanderlyn would memorialize the latter site in his panorama *The Palace and Gardens of Versailles*. According to local tradition in Kingston, where he completed the panels for this painting by 1819, the portraits of celebrities and his friends from Paris were inserted along with his own. The well-dressed man sporting a viewing lens-eyepiece and scanning the landscape—and his prospects—may represent Burr, the visionary revolutionary and "projector," as he liked to call himself. "Projectors" were otherwise known in the eighteenth-century as inventors, speculators, and entrepreneurs, or they were a happy combination of all three bents.

Vanderlyn would have discussed Veronese's *The Wedding at Cana* with Burr, which was also, like the bulk of the masterpieces in the Musée Napoleon, a war trophy from 1797, taken from the Benedictine monastery San Giorgio Maggiore in Venice despite its massive size. Vanderlyn was so taken with Veronese's masterpiece that, with time, he gained a certain reputation. A few decades later, fellow artist Thomas Pritchard Rossiter would paint Vanderlyn seated and playing a guitar (an invention, as Vanderlyn was not a musician) in *A Studio Reception, Paris* (1841).[31] The invention was a way for Vanderlyn to be identified. It also figuratively allowed him to tip his hat or pay tribute to his Venetian artist-hero, Veronese. The famous Venetian similarly had depicted himself, à la mise-en-scène, in *The Wedding at Cana* with a viola da gamba (a bowed string instrument), next to the instrument-playing artists Titian and Bassano.[32]

Vanderlyn soon introduced Burr to his friends, including the artist known today only as "Hernandez" and the artist and dentist of exceptional repute, inventiveness, and entrepreneurial talent whom they called "Fonzi."[33] Vanderlyn's paramour was also part of this close-knit circle. Burr claimed that this Venus, whom we know only as "the beautiful D.C.," was the most beautiful woman he had ever seen. We know what she looked like, however, because she agreed to pose for the head, neck, arms and hands of *Ariadne*, and she likely posed for the rest or "John is a booby," wrote Burr in his journal.

Vanderlyn also brought Burr to the residence of "Madame Fenwick," where Vanderlyn's portrait of her rested on the drawing room mantel.[34] Burr subsequently enjoyed many "tête-à-têtes" with her; Madame Fenwick's husband Joseph is rarely mentioned by either Burr or Vanderlyn; his successful speculative and business partnership with John Mason of Virginia probably led to long absences. Joseph Fenwick was a merchant of fine Bordeaux wines, and this may account for that vintage being Vanderlyn's favorite. The discovery of fine wines was another favorite pastime of the friends while Burr was in Paris.

Burr described Madame Fenwick in letters to Theodosia, declaring that she was her intellectual equivalent. Both Vanderlyn and Burr agreed on this remarkable point and also that Madame Fenwick's keen intellect *and* unique skin tone matched Theodosia's exactly. She therefore became a model for Vanderlyn, whom Burr charged with making at least two copies after his original portrait of Theodosia from 1802.

Also of note is the fact that it was Madame Fenwick who arranged for Burr's adoption of "Aaron Columbus Burr."[35] Surviving letters suggest that he was born around 1800 and may have been named in honor of the Fenwicks' own son, Columbia Franco Fenwick. Madame Fenwick also holds the honor of being the last person to see Vanderlyn before he took the stage to Le Havre; she wrote that she may have caused him to miss his ship, as she did not want him to leave. Vanderlyn's ship almost symbolically arrived in the U.S. on Thanksgiving Day 1815. Vanderlyn carried several letters and gifts from Madame Fenwick to recipients in America.

A surviving sketchbook of Vanderlyn's, today in a private collection, is filled with sketches of the Parisian countryside, the estate of Draveil, (residence of the fabulously wealthy American expatriate Daniel Parker), ancient statuary—likely from Versailles and the Musée Napoleon—and also many preliminary sketches of sleeping Venuses done as the artist grappled with a fit feminine subject to complement and inform the meaning of his painting *Marius*.[36] There are notes about current art theory, which according to Burr's journal the friends enjoyed reading aloud to each other (probably as they sipped fine Bordeaux wines); in particular, Burr mentioned Burke's influential 1757 essay *Sublime and the Beautiful*.[37] There are also personal reflections about artist contemporaries and their struggles. The contents suggest that this very same sketchbook was Vanderlyn's constant companion while Burr was visiting Paris.

Soon after arriving in the metropolis, Burr became uncomfortably aware that Napoleon did not want his guest to leave. Burr was asked to submit letters and prospectuses of "X," and most likely the emperor found Burr to be a handy prisoner but one to be kept at bay until Napoleon could resolve mounting diplomatic and wartime problems. The emperor's incredible martial luck, it seems, was on the wane. Burr complained to his journal that he was a prisoner in Paris and soon would be without a sous, the French equivalent of an American penny. Moreover, the American diplomatic community did not want him to reenter the U.S. and worked against his prospects in having a passport granted. They had entered into a "combination" against him, Burr wrote in his journal. Some of the same individuals treated Vanderlyn just as shabbily. Vanderlyn noted that former friends now crossed to the other side of the street when they saw him approaching, and they no longer tipped their hats to him.

Burr's spirits remained high, however, and he made good use of his time in trying to help Vanderlyn by promoting his protégé to Denon and other people of influence. He also hoped to capitalize on Vanderlyn's ability to speak Dutch. Burr had renewed old business relations and was expecting contracts from the Holland Land Company, the firm which could help bankroll his scheme once back in New York. Vanderlyn discovered that he could not read the dialect, but found a fellow Dutchman who could. Burr also gave power of attorney privileges to Vanderlyn so that he could tie up loose ends once he managed to escape the metropolis and purview of Napoleon's agents. Ultimately, Burr hoped his Holland Land Company venture would be profitable and pay for both of their passages back to America. This, unfortunately, would not be the case.

Burr's tenure in Paris partially coincided with the artist Rembrandt Peale's first of two visits to Paris (we met Rembrandt above as an artist-spectator at the trial of Chase). Rembrandt hoped to persuade Denon and ultimately Napoleon to purchase his father's history painting for France's national collection. His father called his painting about the first scientific dig in New York the "Mammoth Picture," and father and son hoped that their contacts with prominent scientists at the National Institute would help promote their venture. Along with collecting prominent scientists' portraits, Rembrandt was a visitor to Vanderlyn's studio, where both drew the models the artist employed.

Vanderlyn found most of his models in the vicinity of the Palais Royal, where prostitutes who doubled as models were plentiful. For Vanderlyn and Burr, watching the women was a sort of muse; but Burr noted that for Vanderlyn the hunt for models was almost an obsession. Vanderlyn hired numerous prostitute-models, Pygmalion-like, in his quest to capture the goddess-like beauty of the mythological Ariadne now that he had decided on an appropriate subject. Another entrepreneurial angle was at play in having a beautiful nude goddess for display, and Rembrandt and Vanderlyn together discussed the various venues for this venture. They were inspired by the entrepreneurial success of the Swedish-American artist Adolph Ulrich Wertmüller, who exhibited his mythological history painting *Danaë Receiving Jupiter in a Shower of Gold* (1787) in Philadelphia during the 1790s to great critical and financial success. The nude in America, although a commonplace in France, created a scandal. Wertmüller, however, was able to deftly sidestep the pitfalls and hence capitalize on the fallout. Vanderlyn and Rembrandt, who dreamed of acquiring "riches and fame" with their work, were of course duly impressed with the possibilities the genre offered.

As the Salon of 1810 approached, Rembrandt suddenly returned home as Vanderlyn readied his esquisse, or drawing of his proposed subject, for entry.[38] The details and theme he and Burr discussed together, with Burr often consulting with Denon and in the process managing to impress the sophisticated museum director with his broad knowledge of art and its history.

The boastful Rembrandt's sudden return, Vanderlyn had smirked, was prompted by his belated realization that his own artistic powers were not as good as his "puffs" suggested. "Puffs" in eighteenth-century lingo were self-made boasts; they were puffs because they consisted more of hot air than fact, and Rembrandt's own father acknowledged that his son wrestled with the sin of excessive pride. Nonetheless, Burr and Vanderlyn could overlook Rembrandt's occasional faults because he had plenty of other good qualities to counteract the bad. For example, at much risk to his own reputation, he cheerfully carried Burr's letters across the Atlantic at a time when the American officials in Paris decreed that no one could lawfully do so.

How did Vanderlyn resolve his history-painting quandary and settle upon Ariadne as a fit subject? The answer partly lies in Burr's reaction to *Marius*, to which we shall return below. Another facet of the riddle comes alive in Vanderlyn's sketchbook, the pages of which are filled with sketches of reclining female figures. Vanderlyn was already well acquainted with the ancient and Renaissance "Sleeping Venus" formulas; his painting after Correggio's *Antiope* was his way of thinking about the literary narratives that were attached to such mythological or classical subjects.

In Vanderlyn's work from Rome, more clues can be found. As a veiled expression of the current political situation and its impact on the cultural landscape, Vanderlyn drew the triumphal *Arch of Titus* (c. 82 AD) in 1806 or 1807 in situ, or on the spot where it stood in Rome. In the drawing, the arch is the focal point, but the more controversial sculptural panels inside the arch are what fascinates, as the artist was careful to provide glimpses of each panel. Vanderlyn understood the principle that sometimes "by saying less, more is revealed." These panels depicted, and celebrated, a Roman victory from the classical past that had poignant parallels to modern times. The arch and its panels impacted Vanderlyn in at least two powerful, interlocking ways and so are worth reviewing here.

The first reason is that the French archaeologists in Rome made a point of prioritizing their studies of this arch among all the other Roman examples, because Napoleon wanted it to be the model for his own triumphal arch—the Arc de Triomphe—to be erected in Paris as a monument to his victory over the Third Coalition at Austerlitz (1805). It was this victory, followed by those at Jena (1806) and Friedland (1807) that spelled the eventual downfall of Rome and her allies in 1809.

The second reason is that the panels inside the arch, both of which can be glimpsed in Vanderlyn's drawing, depict the triumphal parade in Rome following Titus's siege of Jerusalem (70 AD). In one panel, Roman soldiers carry and flaunt booty taken from the temple at Jerusalem, including a candelabra with seven branches, what may be the Ark of the Covenant, and captives who now would be Roman slaves. In the pendant panel, Titus rides in a chariot, with the goddesses of Rome and Victory escorting his entourage, while being besieged by worshipful Roman citizens. Although the French archaeologists claimed that in conserving the arch they were paying partial restitution to the Italians for the national treasures they removed during the 1790s, the selection of Titus's arch with its panels about triumphal parades and booty surely provoked their ire, for particularly galling to the Vatican and the citizens of Rome was Napoleon's similar triumphal entry into Paris in 1798, replete with chariots bearing the treasures demanded during the Treaty of Tolentino including sculptures and paintings such as the sculptural group *Laocoön*, *Apollo Belvedere*, the bust of *Brutus*, and *Reclining Cleopatra/Ariadne*. Notably, Vanderlyn would "cite" these antiquities and others in his most ambitious history paintings.

Vanderlyn's and Burr's meetings with Denon would have made impressions upon them both, for he was not called the "Eye of Napoleon" for naught. Denon's artistic scope was broad, and somehow he managed to remain calm in the face of the international storm brewing due to a majority of the civilized world's cultural treasures being removed to the museum. As Vanderlyn and Burr debated the stakes involved, an idea was formulating in the artist's mind. He had already coyly alluded to the controversy in his *Marius* painting; now the theme needed to carry through to his pendant painting, and the Vatican *Cleopatra* (reidentified as *Ariadne* by Napoleon's cultural agents) provided the perfect sculptural model. The theme needed to promote Napoleon; but on the other hand, for those viewers who looked more closely, yet another, contradictory, narrative was alluded to.

In brief, Vanderlyn's *Marius* and *Ariadne* at their surface levels paid tribute to Napoleon's vaunted reputation as France's Hercules and as liberator of the arts. Vanderlyn flattered the emperor by modeling his subjects after some of his most prized war trophies. These were the Vatican's *Reclining Cleopatra/Ariadne* and in the *Marius* painting, the sculptural references pointing to the national collection's sculpture of *Marius*, depicted seated among the ruins of Carthage. Lost today, this sculpture held great resonance for Napoleon. Following Vanderlyn's award of the gold medal for his painting in 1808, the academy professors would select it as the model to be replicated for the 1810 Grand Prix competition.[39] Subsequently, Vanderlyn's friend Jean-Pierre Cortot would win the competition.[40]

For the head of *Marius*, Vanderlyn made no bones about whom his *Marius* referenced to, for he substituted for the head of the (unlocated) *Marius* the Vatican bust of *Brutus*. The bust's appeal to Napoleon was widely known; during the processional leading from Rome to Paris in 1798, he insisted it lead the way.[41] The historical Brutus's appeal lay in his reputation as the savior of liberty, a notion to which Napoleon and his promoters subscribed and which in effect also served as a "puff" for the modern Brutus-Napoleon.

The overarching theme that Napoleon and his adherents such as Denon would have found irresistible, however, was the pendant paintings' references to France's traditional enemy, Great Britain. Beginning with Vanderlyn's *Jane McCrea* from 1804, which cited a recent incident of British treachery, each of his most ambitious historical productions thematically emphasized Napoleon's dream to crush John Bull. The "island" was also called Carthage, a reference to classical Rome's traditional enemy, Carthage. And if Marius literally sat among the ruins of Carthage, plotting his revenge against Rome, so too did Ariadne represent France as betrayed by Theseus (read Great Britain). With a tiara in her hair and scantily clad in red, white, and blue garments, Ariadne in Vanderlyn's painting became a shorthand allegory of Liberty betrayed.

A general idea about the seriousness of this sentiment can be gathered by the actions of Denon following the rupture of the Treaty of Amiens. The treaty temporarily brought peace to the two traditional enemies between 1801 and 1803. Foreign visitors to the Louvre/Musée Napoleon flocked to see the galleries during the interim. They were amazed to

214   Appendix B: Aaron Burr and John Vanderlyn (by Katherine Woltz)

see, for the first time in history, works of art arranged by school and chronologically. In the case of the sculpture collection, the director arranged them thematically. The British artist Joseph Farington, for example, counted some 2,500 visitors one day when he visited; the majority of those visitors were British. But Napoleon had all the foreign visitors expelled from the museum when the treaty ended, and Denon underscored nationalist sentiment when he had the Bayeux Tapestry installed as a reminder of that particular victory from 1066. Moreover the emperor initiated a competition. The sculptural subject was William the Conqueror, and the winning entry was to be installed in a visible area in Paris.[42]

But Vanderlyn, trained by profession and also by his membership in the Order of the Rose Cross and Pelican to value the authority of symbolism, offered an alternate narrative for those who chose to look more carefully. For example, critics of Napoleon would have recognized the sculptural sphinx atop the helmet at Marius's feet; the sphinx was used by counterrevolutionaries in prints and text to allude to controversies associated with his Egyptian campaign, but also it referred to the two-faced, unpredictable personality that was Napoleon's.

In the *Ariadne* canvas, viewers familiar with the myth of Ariadne would notice that

Ariadne Asleep on the Island of Naxos by John Vanderlyn. Burr saw the painting, begun in 1809, in progress at Vanderlyn's home/studio and praised the model's beauty. Vanderlyn completed the painting by 1814. Oil on canvas, 68½ in. × 87 in. (174.0 cm × 221.0 cm) (courtesy Pennsylvania Academy of the Fine Arts, Philadelphia, gift of Mrs. Sarah Harrison, Joseph Harrison, Jr., Collection.

she sleeps not in an arid landscape but a lush, wooded island. Slight changes such as this signaled to viewers to look and think more critically about the subject; the lush island and smaller adjacent island, for example, would be recognized by contemporaries as emblematic of the Continent and the British Isles. Ariadne, in her guise as Liberty, would identify the nation within the Continent as France. But because *Ariadne* was modeled after a celebrated "captive" sculpture—the Vatican *Reclining Cleopatra/Ariadne*—other viewers, sympathetic to nations that had lost their cultural treasures to Napoleon, might read her tragic abandonment by her erstwhile lover Theseus as an allegory of Napoleon's ravishing of other nations' cultural treasures, whereby Theseus stands in for Napoleon and Ariadne's fate stands in for the fate of the captive works of art as a group.

Sketch for Ariadne (1809–1912) by John Vanderlyn. While the finished painting is a masterpiece, Vanderlyn here was grappling with the anatomy. He was the first American artist to study in Paris and the first to exhibit a painting with a nude subject in America. Charcoal heightened with white on toned paper, 17-⅝ in. × 23 in. (44.7675 cm × 58.42 cm) (courtesy Pennsylvania Academy of the Fine Arts, Philadelphia, gift of the International Business Machines Corporation Collection).

When Burr first laid eyes on *Marius* in Vanderlyn's atelier, however, he saw something entirely different. He of course realized what contemporaries might (and did) see in Vanderlyn's composition. This was the historical figure of Marius as an allegorical referent to Burr and his alleged vengeful actions against the Jeffersonian administration during his "western expedition." Indeed, this remains the conventional interpretation of the painting today. But to impose a rhetorical question, would Vanderlyn portray his friend and patron in such an unflattering light? More likely, Vanderlyn's primary goal was to portray the Burrite point of view in his chef d'oeuvre, *Marius*.

Indeed, the more the painting is scanned for metaphorical meaning, the more facile in spirit does the "Burr as *Marius*" interpretation become. The fate of Burr, however, who was nearly broken in the hands of his political enemies, appears to be a narrative woven into the background tapestry of objects that is Vanderlyn's *chef d'oeuvre inconnu*. We can examine portions of the painting to find these referents from the ground up. In the midst of the ruin-filled landscape of Carthage, broken aqueducts, symbolic of the collapse of classical technological might, are strewn throughout the campagna. Their age is suggested by the fissures breaking their once-smooth surfaces and also by the vegetation which threatens to cover and then bury them in the ground. For more astute contemporaries, these objects would suggest much more than simple, common ruins. They might, for example, recall how Burr's political adversaries tried to undermine his project for bringing water into Manhattan.

The classical temple with six columns on the hill behind the seated figure of Marius has stumped art historians who have tried, albeit unsuccessfully, to identify the structure.

But for contemporaries familiar with Burr's trial, the structure closely replicates the Virginia State Capital, designed by Thomas Jefferson and patterned after the Maison Carrée in France. Richmond, like Rome, was a designated "City of Seven Hills," and Vanderlyn places his architectural ruin high on an escarpment overlooking Carthage. But unlike the Virginia State Capital or Maison Carrée, the columns of Vanderlyn's classical palace have one column that has fallen down, a time-honored symbol of governmental corruption. Not by accident, the fallen column in the painting of *Marius* is in contrast to the upright columns that Vanderlyn depicts in his 1810 portrait of Burr, discussed above.

Another object pointed out by contemporaries, and which Vanderlyn refused to explain, was the tiny red fox in the distant background. Upon close inspection, the fox's head is turned, and it is looking directly at the back of Marius. Vanderlyn insisted that he included the fox because one appeared among the ruins as he and his companions, Nicholas Biddle or the artist Washington Allston perhaps, were walking in the *compagna*. "The incident," he insisted, "caused me to introduce the fox into the composition." The problem was, no one believed him. Most contemporaries believed the fox, with its reputation for Machiavellian political chicanery, stood in for Burr. But for the Burrites, a better candidate was at hand.

Following the fox clue, observers may have asked Vanderlyn why Marius, who was known to have varicose veins at this time of his life as he was getting older, was depicted as a man in the prime of life. The Roman military man who elevated himself in society by his own efforts rather than by noble birth and who initiated a series of military reforms, of course was the perfect foil for Napoleon. But in America, the military commander whose reputation was tarnished by Machiavellian maneuvers and known for military reform was none other than General James Wilkinson.

Vanderlyn introduced another element in his positioning of Marius, a detail lovers of art such as Burr would have grasped. This use of artistic license was his "quoting" of the Vatican *Belvedere Torso*. A fragment of the original sculpture, it featured a muscular man's torso, the figure seated with a bit of animal skin peeping out beneath him. This led to the figure's being identified as Hercules (yet another mythological figure with whom Napoleon was identified). But a character flaw that Marius shared with General James Wilkinson was vanity; and Wilkinson's vanity and pompous nature led to the Burrites' belittlement of him, especially during Burr's trial in Richmond. As part of his flamboyant haberdashery, Wilkinson was infamous for owning a spectacular leopard-skin saddle "blanket," while his personalized military uniform underscored his pompous nature.

Yet a more direct allusion to Wilkinson as a modern-day Hercules was made by Alexander Hamilton, with whom Wilkinson had joined forces in the 1790s in order to secure his position as head of the American military and to initiate a series of military reforms: "Whenever the Government appears in arms it ought to appear like a *Hercules* and inspire respect by a display of strength."[43] Wilkinson, a man loyal to no one except himself, next abandoned his Hamiltonian-Federalist sympathies and attached himself to the new Jeffersonian administration, but not until the time was right.

And as Vanderlyn's friend Washington Irving noted, at Burr's trial no one was more vain, deceptive, or Machiavellian than Wilkinson. It was a point that all the Burrites insisted upon. In the final analysis, Vanderlyn's *Marius* was a painting with many interrelated narrative threads. But for the Burrites, the figure of Marius most closely represented Wilkinson, who framed Burr as a conspirator in a series of alarming letters to President Jefferson. Wilkinson's betrayal of Burr surmounted all of the machinations against Burr perpetrated by his political enemies combined, as Vanderlyn suggested in the ancillary elements of his painting. And how did *Ariadne* relate to the Burrite narrative at work in *Marius*? If we think of plan "X" as Burr's strategy for establishing liberty in royalist geographical points both south and north, then Ariadne's betrayal by Theseus becomes Burr's betrayal by Wilkinson. For in the final analysis, Burr's intentions were good; but Wilkinson had plotted and carried out for decades the means for betraying America and her hard-won liberties to the Spanish royalists.

In concluding our narrative, the question as to what may have gone through Burr's mind when he first saw *Marius* returns full circle. For one, he knew that he did not have to explain himself to Vanderlyn, as he had to others during his European tour. His protégé's older half brother, Dr. Pieter Vanderlyn, had been the "trusted messenger" who carried letters between New York and Kingston for Burr and his political associate and friend Peter Van Gaasbeek. Although Van Gaasbeek died in 1798 and Dr. Pieter Vanderlyn in 1802, their faith in Burr lived on in Vanderlyn.

The portrait painter Gilbert Stuart (who gave Vanderlyn painting tips and instructions) had done a good thing when he brought the penurious plight of the young Vanderlyn to Burr's attention in early 1795. And Van Gaasbeek played his part too, respectfully showing Burr's letter to Vanderlyn. In it, Burr had written in the third person to Van Gaasbeek, begging him to show the youth the letter and allow him to "rescue genius from obscurity" by allowing him (Burr) to "remove that obstacle" by becoming Vanderlyn's patron. For these reasons and more, Burr never doubted that Vanderlyn's *Marius* painting a profound statement for setting the political and historical records straight.

Perhaps Burr's expansive knowledge of art so impressed Denon it caused him to intercede on his behalf with Napoleon. Regardless, Denon's help, combined with that tendered by the Duc de Bassano, allowed Burr to receive his passport for returning to the U.S. A series of letters followed, exchanged between Burr (in Amsterdam) and Vanderlyn (in Paris). The substance of these letters have to do with Vanderlyn's forwarding more of Fonzi's dental prostheses to Burr, the purchase of sundry items available only in France, and, of course, discussions of the copies of Theodosia's portrait and the "Violets." To wit, Burr scolded Vanderlyn from Amsterdam on September 1, 1811: "Your letter of the 26th was received and that of the 27th this morning. I can't help pitying you a little for the Violette affair. You deserve however to be castrated, you rascal! To descend from Venus to a yahoo! Oh if I were there I would endeavor to inspire La Belle with the idea of a *douce* Vengeance (sweet vengeance)." Vanderlyn's paramour "La Belle D.C." was thus referred to as a Venus. This gives us further clues that, indeed, she did consent to pose for "the whole" figure of Ariadne, as Burr had hoped.

The reader may wonder why Burr was so anxious as to the state of Theodosia's unfinished portrait-copy. Clues lie in the pendant formula replicated earlier in a pendant-portrait watch cherished by Burr. This watch, today in a private collection, suggests a related collaboration between Burr and Vanderlyn, or Theodosia's and Burr's pendant portraits from 1802. The watch, when opened, reveals two portraits in which the sitters, Aaron Burr and his wife Theodosia Bartow Prevost Burr, face each other as if in the midst of a conversation.[44] This same convention was followed in Vanderlyn's 1802 pendant portraits of Burr and his daughter, Theodosia. Burr likely asked Vanderlyn to update the watch-model formula, whereby the portrait of his deceased wife would be replaced by his daughter.

Following the marriage of Burr and Theodosia Prevost on July 2, 1782, their friend Governor William Livingston wrote to congratulate the couple, adding this adage: "May Love be the Time Piece in Your Mansion, and Happiness its Minute Hand." It is within the realm of possibility that Burr's pendant-portrait watch is an intimate expression of this verse, a private innuendo that the couple preserved by having their pendant portraits painted on the dial of a pocket watch. In the same way, Vanderlyn's pendant portraits of Burr and his daughter recreated the conversation piece format at work in the watch portraits.

Burr, who like Vanderlyn was so attuned to the telling details within art, may have asked his protégé why he made such a flattering allegorical portrait of *Marius*; for if he represented Wilkinson, it was well known that, despite the general's flamboyant ways, he was nonetheless pudgy with thinning hair, to judge by Charles Willson Peale's portrait of him from the 1790s. Would any contemporaries catch the link between Marius and Wilkinson? Certainly the newspapers did not compare Burr to Marius's fate at Carthage (except for one lone Federalist voice).[45] On the other hand, the historical Marius's military reforms were known to all schoolchildren, as were Wilkinson's contemporary military reforms, which attracted attention because they were so very unpopular. A hallmark of conceit occurs when certain people, such as Napoleon or Wilkinson, hold flattering images of themselves in their minds' eye. This vision, of course, is typically at odds with the truth. And in thinking of that, Burr smiled to himself each time he viewed his protégé Vanderlyn's celebrity history painting, *Marius Amid the Ruins of Carthage*.

Chapter Notes

Preface
1. Italo Calvino, *Hermit in Paris: Autobiographical Writings*, trans. Martin McLaughlin (New York: Random House, 2003), 168.

One
1. Aaron Burr to Joseph Alston, March 22, 1805, in Matthew L. Davis, *Memoirs of Aaron Burr*, Vol. 2 (New York: Harper & Bros., 1836), 365.
2. Frederic Smoler interview with Gordon Wood, "The Radical Revolution," *American Heritage* 43, no. 8 (1992), http://www.americanheritage.com/content/radical-revolution.html (accessed August 25, 2014).
3. Roger G. Kennedy, *Burr, Hamilton, and Jefferson: A Study in Character* (New York: Oxford, 2000), 8.
4. Milton Lomask, *Aaron Burr: The Conspiracy and Years of Exile, 1805–36* (New York: Farrar Straus Giroux, 1982), 299.
5. Theodosia Burr Alston to Aaron Burr, May 31, 1809, in Mark Van Doren, ed., Correspondence of Aaron Burr and his Daughter Theodosia (New York: Covics-Friede, 1929), 299.
6. James Parton, *The Life and Times of Aaron Burr* (New York: Mason Brothers, 1858), 162–163.
7. Ibid., 165.

Two
1. William K. Bixby, ed., *The Private Journal of Aaron Burr*, Vol. 1 (Rochester: Genesee Press, 1903), note at 277.
2. Lady Mary Loyd, trans., *New Letters of Napoleon I: Omitted from the Edition Published Under the Auspices of Napoleon III* (New York: Appleton, 1897), passim.
3. Paul Gautier, *Madame De Staël Et Napoléon* (Paris: Plon, 1903), 236.
4. Buckner F. Melton, Jr., *Aaron Burr: Conspiracy to Treason* (New York: John Wiley & Sons, 2002), 209.
5. Aaron Burr to Joseph Alston, July 18, 1804, in Matthew L. Davis, *Memoirs of Aaron Burr*, Vol. 2, 327.
6. Bixby, *Journal of Aaron Burr*, Vol. 1, vi–vii.
7. Dominic Sandbrook, "Pistols at Dawn," *the Telegraph*, June 11, 2009, http://www.telegraph.uk/culture/books/bookreviews/5506794/Pistols-at-Dawn.html (accessed August 25, 2014).

Three
1. Countess d'Aulnoy, "La Biche Au Bois," published 1697, http://www.lescontesdefees.fr/contes-et-auteurs/mme-d-aulnoy/la-biche-au-bois/.
2. "Natural Goodness—Connoisseurs Delight in Roussillon's Sweet Wines," *France* (Summer 1997), 4.

Four
1. James H.S. McGregor, *Paris from the Ground Up* (Cambridge, MA: Belknap Press of Harvard University Press, 2009), 234.
2. William L. Chew III, "Life Before Fodor and Frommer: Americans in Paris from Thomas Jefferson to John Quincy Adams," *French History* 18, no.1, 43.
3. William Lee, *A Yankee Jeffersonian: Selections from the Diary and Letters of William Lee of Massachusetts, Written from 1796–1840*, Mary Lee Mann, ed. (Cambridge, MA: Harvard University Press, 1858), 19.
4. Jefferson to John Banister, Jr., October 15, 1785, in *The Papers of Thomas Jefferson*, Vol. 8, Julian Boyd et al., eds. (Princeton, NJ: Princeton University Press, 1950), 636–637.
5. H.W. Small, *A History of the Town of Swan's Island*, 2nd ed. (Maine, 1937), 20–30, www.swansisland.org/small/pdf.
6. Dorothy Simpson, *The Maine Islands in Story and Legend* (J.B. Lippincott, 1960; reprint, Nobleboro, ME: Blackberry, 1987), 183–187.
7. "Russell, Jonathan," in *Biographical Directory of the U.S. Congress*.
8. Lawrence S. Kaplan, "Jonathan Russell and the Capture of the Guerrier," *William and Mary Quarterly* 24, no. 2, third series (April 1967), 284–287.
9. Richard Grady, "Mendon Congressman Planned Extravagant Welcome for Revolutionary War Hero" (July 24, 2012), Mendon, Massachusetts Web site.
10. James Landale, *The Last Duel: A True Story of Death and Honour* (New York: Canongate, 2006), 156.
11. http://blog.britishnewspaperarchive.co.uk/2012/08/24/the-first-duel-fought-in-hot-air-balloons-paris-1808/.
12. Alistair Horne, *The Seven Ages of Paris* (New York: Alfred A. Knopf, 2004), 165–166.
13. Claude-Isabelle Brelot, "La Noblesse Reinventée," *Nobles De Franche-Comte De 1814 a 1870: Annales, Histoire, Sciences Sociales* 2, no. 4 (1996), 808–811.

14. Pierre Duyre, "Les Chevaliers Dans La Noblesse Imperial," *Revue d'Histoire Modern Et Contemporaine* 17, no. 3 (1970), 671–679.
15. Johannes Willms, *Paris, Capital of Europe: From the Revolution to the Belle Epoque*, trans. Eveline L. Kanes (New York: Holmes and Meier, 1997), 104–105.
16. J.F. Bernard, *Talleyrand: A Biography* (New York: G. Putnam's Sons, 1973), 278–281.
17. *Mémoires Du Duc De Rovigo, Pour Servir À L'histoire De L'empereur Napoléon*, Project Gutenberg, www.gutenberg.org/ebooks/20108.
18. Gisela Bergstrasser, "Duke Emmerich Joseph Von Dalberg as a Collector of Drawings," *Master Drawings* 22, no. 1 (Spring 1984), 28–43, 115–121.
19. www.napoleon-empire.net/personnages/maret.php, pp.1–4 and www.1789–1815.com/maret.htm.
20. Philip Mansel, *The Court of France, 1789–1830* (New York: Cambridge University Press, 1988), 83–86.
21. www.paulfrasercollectibles.com/News/Napoleon's-signed-kremlin-letter, 1–2.
22. Helmut De Terra, *Humboldt: The Life and Times of Alexander Von Humboldt, 1769–1859* (New York: Alfred A. Knopf, 1955), 190–209.
23. L. Kellner, *Alexander Von Humboldt* (New York: Oxford University Press, 1963), 79ff.
24. Harvey Levenstein, *Seductive Journey: American Tourists in France from Jefferson to the Jazz Age* (University of Chicago Press, 2000), 47.

Five

1. Aaron Burr to Theodosia Burr Alston, April 22, 1809, and Theodosia Burr Alston to Aaron Burr, August 1, 1809, in *Correspondence of Aaron Burr and His Daughter Theodosia*, Mark Van Doren, ed. (New York: Covics-Friede, 1929), 291–292, 305–306.
2. Ibid., v.
3. Gordon S. Wood, *Revolutionary Characters* (New York: Penguin, 2007), 232; Gordon S. Wood, *Empire of Liberty: A History of the Early Republic* (New York: Oxford, 2010), 101.
4. Basil Willey, *The English Moralists* (New York: Anchor, 1967), 265.
5. Dr. Vincenzo Guerini, *The Life and Works of Giuseppangelo Fonzi* (New York: Lea & Febiger, 1925), 25–31.
6. *Actes, Societé Francaise D'histoire De L'art Dentaire* (2013), 18, www.biusante.parisdescartes.fr/sfhad/vol18/2013.
7. Colin Jones, "The King's Two Teeth," muse.jhu.edu/journals/history_workshop_journal/v065/65.jones.o1.html, pp1/9–7/9.
8. Javier Sanz, and Miguel A. Lopez-Bermejo, and Micheline Ruel-Kellermann, "Giuseppangelo Fonzi (1768–1840): La Vie Et l'Oeuvre D'un Illustre Dentist," *Actes, Societé Francaise D'histoire De L'art Dentaire* 12 (2007), 15–19.
9. Jeremy Bentham, *The Works of Jeremy Bentham*, "Published Under the Superintendence of His Executor, John Bowring," 11 vols. (Edinburgh: William Tait, 1838–1843), Vol. 10, 432, http://oll.libertyfund.org/titles/2085 (accessed May 31, 2014).
10. Mary-Jo Kline, ed., *Political Correspondence and Public Papers of Aaron Burr*, 2 vols. (Princeton University Press, 1983), Vol. 2, 1108, 1115–16.
11. John Kukla, *A Wilderness So Immense: The Louisiana Purchase and the Destiny of America* (New York: Knopf, 2003), 254–257.
12. Paul D. Evans, *The Holland Land Company* (Buffalo Historical Society, 1924), is the source for the discussion of HLC, and Appendix II contains quotations of the company's share prices on the Amsterdam Stock Exchange.

Six

1. Michael Broers, *Europe Under Napoleon, 1799–1815* (New York: Arnold, 1996), 193.
2. John E. Crowley is emeritus professor of history at Dalhousie University and the author of *The Invention of Comfort: Sensibility and Design in Early Modern Britain and Early America* (Baltimore: Johns Hopkins University Press, 2001) and *Imperial Landscapes: Britain's Global Visual Culture, 1745–1820* (Yale University Press, 2011).
3. James Woodforde, *The Diary of a Country Parson: The Reverend James Woodforde*, John Beresford, ed., Vol. 4 (London, 1926–31), 245.
4. Benjamin Thompson, "Of Chimney Fire-Places" [1796], *Collected Works of Count Rumford*, Sanborn C. Brown, ed. (Cambridge, MA: Belknap Press of Harvard University Press, 1968–70), quoted Vol. 2, 239.
5. Franklin to Lord Kames, February 28, 1768, in *Writings of Benjamin Franklin*, Albert Henry Smyth, ed., Vol. 5 (New York: Macmillan, 1907), 107–110, quoted 107.
6. Thomas Malthus, "An Essay on the Principle of Population: The Sixth Edition (1826), with Variant Readings from the Second Edition (1803)," in *The Works of Thomas Robert Malthus*, E.A. Wrigley, and David Souden, eds. Vol. 3 (London: Pickering & Chatto, 1986), 466–468.
7. Cristina Barreto, and Martin Lancaster, *Napoleon and the Empire of Fashion, 1795–1815* (Milano, Italy: Skira, 2010), 101.
8. C. William Sangster, *Umbrellas and Their History*, 1871, Project Gutenburg.
9. http://blogs.loc.gov/loc/2014/02/george-washingtons-philadelphia-household-1793–1794.
10. http://fr.wikisource.org/wiki/Auteur:Jacques_Barbeu_du_Bourg.
11. Al Saguto made top boots for the Smithsonian to go on the manikin with George Washington's uniform. "A Shoemaker's Son Is a Prince Born," he quotes. He is the resident historian of shoemaking at Colonial Williamsburg.
12. The *Merveilleuses* (feminine), and *Incroyables* (masculine) were, during the Directory period, young people who shocked the public by their eccentric outfits and their allure.
13. An authority on French fashion history and jewelry, Claudette Joannis has written many books, including *Sarah Bernhardt* and *Jewels in the Louvre*. She has been a curator at both the Louvre and Malmaison and bears the title of *Conservateur En Chef Du Partrimoine*.
14. Rembrandt Peale, "Letters from Paris," *Portfolio*, Vol. 3 (September 1810; reprint, Philadelphia), 1874–75.

15. Captain Jean-Roche Coignet, *The Note-Books of Captain Coignet, Soldier of the Empire, 1799–1816* (Novato, CA: Presidio Press, 1989), 104–105.

Seven

1. M.E. Ravage, *Empress Innocence: The Life of Marie-Louise* (New York: Alfred A. Knopf, 1931), 155.
2. Marie-Louise Biver, *Le Paris De Napoléon* (Paris: Librairie Plon, 1963), 193–194.
3. Ravage, 155.
4. Henry Haynie, *Paris Past and Present* (New York: Frederick A. Stokes, 1902), 111.
5. Marrinan, 282.
6. Sebastien Mercier, *Le Nouveau Paris* (Paris: Fuchs, C. Pougens, C.-F. Cramer, "AN VII," 1793; reprint, Paris: Mercure de France, 1994), 381; in Marrinan, 382.
7. L.P., *Voyage Descriptive Et Historique* 2 (1814), 99–100; in Davidson, 287.
8. Livingston to Mother, December 12(?), 1801, papers in William L. Chew III, "Life Before Fodor and Frommer," 42–43.
9. Brian N. Morton, *Americans in Paris: An Anecdotal Street Guide* (Ann Arbor, MI: Olivia & Hill, 1984), 191.
10. Francois Robichon, "Le Panorama, Spectacle De L'histoire," *Le Mouvement Social*, no. 131 (April–June 1985), 65–67.
11. Kirkpatrick Sale, *The Fire of His Genius* (New York: Free Press, 2001), 74–80; John S. Morgan, *Robert Fulton* (New York: Mason/Charter, 1977), 54–80.
12. Henry W. Dickinson, *Robert Fuller: Engineer and Artist, His Life and Works* (New York: John Lane, 1913), 70.
13. "Lettre Du Citoyen Robert, Conservateur Des Tableau Du Museum National, Au Citoyen Fulton, Sur Le Panorama Nouvellement Établi Au Jardin Des Capucines," *Moniteur Universel*, September 8, 1799.
14. Steven Connor, *Dumbstruck: A Cultural History of Ventriloquism* (New York: Oxford University Press, 2000), 197, 211–213.
15. Duchess d'Abrantes (Madame Junor), *Memoirs of Napoleon, His Court and Family*, Vol. 2 (New York: D. Appleton, 1854), 284–286.
16. Jessica Riskin, "The Defecating Duck, or, the Ambiguous Origins of Artificial Life," reprinted from *Critical Inquiry* 29, no.4 (Summer 2003), by the University of Chicago.
17. Christopher Hibbert, *Napoleon: His Wives and Women* (New York: Norton, 2002), passim.
18. http://just vienna.com/imperial-days/born-onto-a-throne-the-son-of-napoleon-and-marie-louise.
19. Octave Aubry, *The King of Rome: Napoleon II, "L'aiglon"* (Philadelphia: J.B. Lippincott, 1932), passim.
20. Anthony Sutcliffe, *Paris: An Architectural History* (New Haven, CT: Yale University Press, 1993), 67.
21. Horne, 178.
22. Chew, "From Romanticism to Realism: American Tourists in Revolutionary France," in *Selected Papers* (2002), 49.
23. John Quincy Adams, *The Diaries of John Quincy Adams*, "A Digital Collection," Massachusetts Historical Society, www.masshist.org/jqadiaries/, March 28, 1815.

24. Charles de Clary-Aldringen, *Trois Mois À Paris, Lors Du Mariage De l'Empereur Napoleon 1er Et De l'Archduchesse Marie-Louise* (Paris: Plon-Nourrit, 1914), 57, in Michael Marrinan, *Romantic Paris: History of a Cultural Landscape, 1800–1850* (Stanford University Press, 2009), 75.
25. Horne, 85.
26. Priscilla Ferguson, *Paris as Revolution: Writing the Nineteenth-Century City* (Berkeley: University of California Press, 1997), 58.
27. Robin Nagle, *Picking Up* (New York: Farrar Straus, 2013), 94.
28. Victor Hugo, *Les Miserables*, trans. Julie Rose (New York: Random House, 2008), 1040.
29. *Ibid.*, 1034.

Eight

1. William I. Chew III, "John Quincy Adams: American Tourist in Paris, 1815," *Napoleonica: La Revue*, no.18 (2013), 119.
2. David McCullogh, *The Greater Journey: Americans in Paris* (New York: Simon & Schuster, 2011), 51.
3. Anthony Sutcliffe, 68.
4. Peter Hicks, *Napoleon and the Theatre*, www.napoleon.org/en/reading_room; original German version, *Was Fur Ein Theater!: Kronungen Und Spektakel in Napoleonischer Zeit*, Dominik Gugel, and Christina Egli, eds. (Frauenfeld, Stuttgart, Vienna: Verlag Huber, 2003), 109–115.
5. Horne, 193.
6. William Lee, to Mrs. Susan Pee, February 10, 1810, in *William Lee: A Yankee Jeffersonian; Selections from the Diary and Letters of William Lee of Massachusetts Written from 1796–1840*, Mary L. Mann, ed. (Cambridge, MA: Harvard University Press, 1958).
7. Marvin Carlson is Sidney E. Cohn Professor of Theater and Comparative Literature at the Graduate Center of the City University of New York. His commentaries on two famous stage actors are based on an extract from the first chapter of his seminal book, *The French Stage in the Nineteenth Century* (1972).
8. Marvin A. Carlson, *The French Stage in the Nineteenth Century* (Methuen, NJ: Scarecrow Press, 1972), 47.
9. Denise Z. Davidson, "Making Society 'Legible': People-Watching in Paris After the Revolution," *French Historical Studies* 28, no. 2 (Spring 2005), 13.
10. Michele Root-Bernstein, *Boulevard Theater and Revolution in Eighteenth Century Paris* (Ann Arbor: University of Michigan Research Press), 100–101.
11. Olivier Bernier, *The Eighteenth Century Woman* (New York: Doubleday, 1981), 102.
12. Horne, 194.
13. Quoted in David Chaillou, *Napoleon Et l'Opéra* (Paris: Fayard, 2004), 174.
14. Judith Chazin-Bennahum, *Dance in the Shadow of the Guillotine* (Carbondale: Southern Illinois University Press, 1988), 30.
15. E. Delecluze, *Louis David: Son Ecole Et Son Temps, Paris, 1855*, in Lorenz Eitner, *Neoclassicism and Romanticism, 1750–1850*, Vol. 2 (Englewood Cliffs, NJ: Prentice-Hall, 1970), 9, 207.
16. David M. Lubin, Charlotte C. Weber Professor of Art at Wake Forest University, is the author of sev-

eral books on American visual culture. This extract draws from passages in his *Picturing a Nation: Art and Social Change in Nineteenth-Century America* (Yale University Press, 1994).

17. Horne, *Seven Ages of Paris*, 180.
18. Ibid.
19. Walter Benjamin, "On the Concept of History," *Gesammelten Schriften* 1, no. 2, (Frankfurt am Main: Suhrkamp Verlag, 1974), translation by Dennis Redmond, 2001.
20. Andrew McClellan, *Inventing the Louvre: Art, Politics, and the Origins of the Modern Museum in Eighteenth-Century Paris* (New York: Cambridge University Press, 1994), 6.
21. John Scott, *A Visit to Paris in 1814* (London: 1816), 246ff, in Lorenz Eitner, *Neoclassicism and Romanticism, 1750–1850*, Vol. 2 (London: Prentice Hall, 1971), 12.
22. William T. Oedel, "After Paris: Rembrandt Peale's Apollodorian Gallery," *Wintherthur Portfolio* 27, no. 1 (Spring 1992), 3.
23. Carla Hesse, *Publishing and Cultural Politics in Revolutionary Paris, 1789–1810* (Berkeley: University of California Press, 1999), 236.
24. This is based on passages from *Revolution and the Antiquarian Book: Reshaping the Past, 1780–1815* (Cambridge University Press, 2011), kindly reworked for the authors by Kristian Jensen, head of Arts and Humanities at the British Library.
25. William L. Chew III, "From Romanticism to Realism: American Tourists in Revolutionary France," in *The Consortium on the Revolutionary Era, 1750–1850; Selected Papers, 2000*, Donald D. Horward, and Michael F. Pavkovic, and John K. Severn, eds. (Florida State University: Institute on Napoleon and the French Revolution, 2002).
26. Alfred Fierro, *Historical Dictionary of Paris* (Lanham, MD: Scarecrow, 1998), 41.
27. Ehrlich Blake, *Paris on the Seine* (New York: Athenaeum, 1962), 213–214.
28. Edouard Fournier, *Histoire Du Pont Neuf* (Paris: Dentu, 1862), in Uzanne, 18.
29. Octave Uzanne, *The Book-Hunter in Paris: Studies Among the Bookstalls and the Quays* (London: Elliot Stock, 1893), 40.
30. Ibid., 47.
31. Aaron Burr to Christoph Daniel Ebeling, December 5, 1809.
32. Marie Sponberg Pedley, "The Map Trade in Paris, 1650–1825," *Imago Mundi* 33 (1981), 41.

Nine

1. Ian Kelly, *Cooking for Kings: The Life of Antonin Careme, the First Celebrity Chef* (New York: Walker, 2003), 47.
2. Giles MacDonogh, *Palate in Revolution: Grimod De La Reynière and the "Almanach Des Gourmands"* (London: Robin Clark, 1987), 18.
3. William H. Ukers, *All About Coffee* (New York: Tea & Coffee Trade Journal, 1935), passim.
4. Joan DeJean, *The Essence of Style: How the French Invented High Fashion, Fine Food, Chic Cafes, Style, Sophistication, and Glamour* (New York: Free Press, 2005), 139.

5. Jean-Paul Sartre, *Being and Nothingness: A Phenomenological Essay on Ontology*, Hazel E. Barnes, trans. (New York: Washington Square, 1956), 41–42.
6. Michael Warner, "Franklin and the Letters of the Republic," *Representations*, no. 16 (University of California Press, Autumn 1986), 116.
7. Denise Z. Davidson, "People-Watching in Paris," 290.
8. Joan de Jean, *The Essence of Style*, 140–142.
9. W. Scott Haine, *The World of the Paris Café: Sociability Among the French Working Class, 1789–1914* (Baltimore: Johns Hopkins University Press, 1996), 16.
10. Ibid., 24.
11. Ibid., 212.
12. Marie-Henri Beyle (de Stendhal), *The Red and the Black*, C.K. Scott Moncrieff, trans., Vol. 2 (New York: Modern Library, 1926), 144.
13. Lee, *Yankee*, 30.
14. Washington Irving to Andrew Quoz, July 21, 1804, *Letters*, Vol. 1, 1802–1823, R.M. Alderman, et al., eds. (Boston: Twayne, 1978), 34.
15. Theodosia to Aaron Burr, February 14, 1811, Burr, 140.
16. Giles MacDonogh is a British author and journalist. This passage is based on his book *A Palate in Revolution: Grimod De La Reynière and the "Almanach Des Gourmands"* (London: Robin Clark, 1987).
17. Rebecca Spang, *The Invention of the Restaurant: Paris and Modern Gastronomic Culture* (Cambridge, MA: Harvard University Press, 2000), 175.
18. Susan Pinkard, *A Revolution in Taste: The Rise of French Cuisine, 1650–1800* (New York: Cambridge University Press, 2009), 241.
19. Priscilla Parkhurst Ferguson is a professor of sociology at Columbia University and the author of *Accounting for Taste: The Triumph of French Cuisine* (University of Chicago Press, 2004).
20. Jeri Quinzio is a historian of food and author of *Of Sugar and Snow: A History of Ice Cream Making* (University of California Press, 2009) and *Food on the Rails: The Golden Era of Railroad Dining* (Rowman & Littlefield, 2014).
21. Steven Mennell, *All Manners of Food: Eating and Taste in England and France from the Middle Ages to the Present* (Champaign: University of Illinois Press, 1995), 145.
22. Nathan Schachner, *Aaron Burr: A Biography* (New York: Frederick A. Stokes, 1937), 121.

Ten

1. Denise Z. Davidson, "Making Society 'Legible': People-Watching in Paris After the Revolution," 266.
2. Ibid., 273.
3. Ibid., 286.
4. Michelle Maskiell, "Consuming Shawls and Empires, 1500–2000," *Journal of World History* 13, no. 1 (Spring 2002), 39.
5. *Journal Des Dames Et Des Modes* 7, no. 36 (March 22, 1803).
6. David McCullough, *The Greater Journey: Americans in Paris* (New York: Simon & Schuster, 2011), 26.
7. http://beq.ebookgratuits.com/balzac/Balzac_06_Une_Double_Famille.pdf, 5–6.

8. Priscilla Parkhurst Ferguson, *Paris as Revolution: Writing the Nineteenth-Century City* (Berkeley: University of California Press, 1994), 57.
9. Honoré de Balzac, *A Harlot's Progress*, Vol. 1, ch. 21, *La Comédie Humaine*, George Saintsbury, ed. (New York: Macmillan, MDCC CXCVI), www.archive.org/stream/comdiehumainee17balcuoft/.
10. A. Roger Ekirch, *At Day's Close: Night in Times Past* (New York: W.W. Norton, 2005), 88.
11. Wolfgang Schivelbusch, *Disenchanted Night: The Industrialization of Light in the Nineteenth Century*, Angela Davies, trans. (Berkeley: University of California Press, 1988), 95.
12. Craig Koslofsky, *Evening's Empire: A History of the Night in Early Modern Europe* (New York: Cambridge University Press, 2011), 171–176.
13. Brian Bowers, *Lengthening the Day: A History of Lighting Technology* (New York; Oxford: Oxford University Press, 1998), 28.
14. Willms, 134.

Eleven

1. Barbara Taylor, and Sarah Knott, *Women, Gender and the Enlightenment* (New York: Palgrave Macmillan, 2007), 47.
2. Ibid.
3. Nancy Isenberg, *Fallen Founder: The Life of Aaron Burr* (New York: Penguin, 2007), 383.

Twelve

1. William St. Clair, *The Godwins and the Shelleys* (New York: W.W. Norton, 1989), 499.
2. Ibid., 500.
3. P.I. Jacob, *Curiosités De l'Histoire Du Vieux Paris* (Paris: Adolphe Delahays, 1858), 17.
4. Clare A. Lyons, *Sex Among the Rabble: An Intimate History of Gender and Power in the Age of Revolution, Philadelphia, 1730–1830* (Chapel Hill: University of North Carolina Press, 2006), 245.
5. Nancy Isenberg, *Fallen Founder: The Life of Aaron Burr* (New York: Penguin, 2008), 233–234.
6. Jonathan van Meter, "Julia Louis-Dreyfus in the Present Tense: Her Transformational Turn on Veep," New York, December 9, 2013, 34.
7. Morris's journal entry of 3 June March 1789, Diary, 1: 104ff, in Richard Brookhiser, *Gentleman Revolutionary: Gouverneur Morris, the Rake Who Wrote the Constitution* (New York: Free Press, 2003).
8. Stendhal, *Stendhal on Love*, trans. Sophie Lewis (Hesperus Press, 2009; c1822), 95.
9. Historian John Kukla is the author of *Mr. Jefferson's Women* (Knopf, 2008) and *Patrick Henry* (Simon & Schuster, 2015).
10. Brookhiser, *Gentleman Revolutionary*, 117.
11. Jill Harsin, *Policing Prostitution in Nineteenth-Century Paris* (Princeton, NJ: PUP, 1985), 6.
12. Letter of Adele Valois to Zelie Lebeuf, September 21, 1821, quoted in Davidson, "People-Watching in Paris," 292.
13. Lyons, *Sex Among the Rabble*, 248.
14. Washington Irving, to Alexander Beebee, 3 August 1805, in *Letters*, ed. Ralph M. Aderman et al. (Boston: Twayne, 1978), Vol. 1, 199ff.
15. Alain Corbin, "Backstage," in *A History of Private Life*, Vol. 4, *from the Fires of Revolution to the Great War*, Michelle Perrot, ed., Arthur Goldhammer, trans., (London: Belknap, 1994), 589.
16. Lyons, *Sex Among the Rabble*, 248.
17. Thomas A. Foster, *Sex and the Founding Fathers: The American Quest for a Relatable Past* (Philadelphia: Temple University Press, 2014), 167.
18. Bertrand Russell, *History of Western Philosophy* (New York: Simon & Schuster, c1945, 1972), 677.
19. Walter Jackson Bate, *From Classic to Romantic* (Cambridge: Harvard University Press, 1946), 163.
20. Isenberg, *Fallen Founder*, 79.
21. Mary Wollstonecraft, *An Historical and Moral View of the Origin and Progress of the French Revolution and the Effect It Has Produced in Europe*, Vol. 1 (London: St. Paul's Church Yard, 1794), 452–453.
22. Joan B. Landes, *Women and the Public Sphere in the Age of the French Revolution* (Ithaca, NY: Cornell University Press, 1988).

Fourteen

1. Matthew L. Davis, ed., *The Private Journal of Aaron Burr*, Vol. 2 (New York: Harper & Brothers, 1838), 238–39.

Epilogue

1. W.H. Shelton, *The Jumel Mansion: Being a Full History of the House on Harlem Heights Built by Roger Morris Before the Revolution* (Boston: Houghton Mifflin, 1916), 191.

Appendix A

1. James Parton, *The Life and Times of Aaron Burr* (New York: Houghton, 1858).

Appendix B (by Katherine Woltz)

1. I thank the Luce/ACLS Foundation, the Robert H. Smith International Center for Jefferson Studies, the Dupont Foundation, the University of Virginia Graduate School of Arts and Sciences for fellowships and travel awards; also thank you to Joyce Zucker, Wint Aldrich, Avery Smith, Robert Slater, Barbara Westbrook Duffy, Deana Preston, Lisa Bruck, Rich Goring, Christine Lindsay, and Charles Hickman for their inestimable help.
2. In 1786 the American artist John Trumbull (1756–1843) completed his painting *The Death of General Montgomery in the Attack on Quebec, December 31, 1775*. Trumbull made a key to identify the participants in the siege but not until 1798, twelve years after he finished the painting. During that interval he had served as secretary to John Jay during negotiations for "Jay's Treaty" in London (1794–1796) and afterwards was appointed one of the commissioners to resolve the

articles attendant in the treaty. Trumbull's key used artistic license and substituted, for example, Matthias Ogden for Aaron Burr, the patriot who caught his general's body as it fell from the explosion which killed him. See fns. 21–23.

3. John Vanderlyn, *Portrait of Theodosia Burr Alston* (1802; Yale University Art Gallery); John Vanderlyn, *Portrait of the Artist* (1800; Metropolitan Museum of Art). The Yale portrait of Theodosia may not be the original portrait from 1802; the original portrait's present whereabouts, or if it still exists, remains unknown. Vanderlyn made several copies after the original for Burr and other family members.

4. Each of these letter discoveries enabled more details of Burr's Paris sojourn and his relationship with John Vanderlyn to come to light (this footnote is an excerpt from the public lecture/Powerpoint presentation, and exhibition of key letters discussed, presented by me at the Senate House State Historic Site, Kingston, NY, Sept. 25, 2008). The first cache was discovered by Charles Page Carter on September 20, 1886. Included were two letters written by Burr to Van Gaasbeek, which enabled the story of Burr's patronage of Vanderlyn to be told. A third letter from Burr to Van Gaasbeek revealed that Vanderlyn's older half brother, Dr. Pieter Vanderlyn, was a trusted member of the Burr–Van Gaasbeek political circle and ran letters between the two men. A fourth important letter to Van Gaasbeek was not dated or signed. On its verso is written "Private Instructions." Partially in code, Carter wrongly assumed the author was Burr, as it discussed strategies to help Burr win the presidential election of 1796 (but Carter assumed it discussed the presidential election of 1800). This cipher letter is not included in the Aaron Burr Papers edited by Klein and Ryan (1983), likely because the handwriting cannot be pinned to Burr.

I found a related set of letters while searching for correspondence between Livingston and Vanderlyn. This set, consisting of three Van Ness letters, to my knowledge, had never been published. They are in the Edward Livingston Papers, Rare Books and Special Collections, Firestone Library, Princeton University, in the folder marked "William Peter Van Ness (1778–1826)." The dates are as follows: February 2, 1801; July 22, 1802; August 21, 1802.

The relevance of the Carter cipher letter to the three Van Ness letters is as follows: Van Ness, writing on February 2, 1801, to Edward Livingston, hoped to convince him that with a little back-room dealing he could help put Burr into the presidential seat for the 1800 election. "The election of Col. Burr is at present the wish of the Republicans at Albany," wrote Van Ness before detailing the election strategy. Once Jefferson won the election, Van Ness, eager to retrieve the damning letter, wrote to Livingston on July 22, 1802, pretending that someone else had written the letter of February 2, 1801. The third letter, written on August 21, 1802, flatly requested that Livingston return the February 2, 1801, letter. But, all three letters remained with Livingston.

Both the Senate House unsigned, undated letter with cipher found by Carter and the three Van Ness letters at Princeton, in my opinion, show how other people conspired to put Burr into the presidential seat, likely without his knowledge or consent. As for the Carter cipher letter, analysis of the handwriting leads to the conclusion that it was not authored by Aaron Burr. The Burr autograph, letter, and ephemera collector Judge Brian D. Hardison, author of *Burriana* (Grolier Club, 2012), kindly examined the handwriting. He, too, concluded that the handwriting was not Burr's. Remnants of Carter's original discovery are today in the collection of the Senate House State Historic Site. The four Carter letters discussed above are as follows: Anonymous coded and undated letter to Peter Van Gaasbeek (torn into two parts; the written section is archive #2973–153 and the other section with the code and list is #2973–154). The Burr to Van Gaasbeek letter (November 12, 1796) is #2973–143; the patronage letter, which consists of a letter written by Burr to Van Gaasbeek (June 21, 1795), is #SH 1975 696A; the insert meant for Vanderlyn's perusal with the same date is #SH 1976 696B).

A second cache of Burr-Vanderlyn letters was discovered by Albert Malloy (Kingston); a third by the 1940s found in a barn (Kingston). Fourth set: letters of Vanderlyn and his French paramour (Iabelle D.C.?), but burned c. 1915 to "preserve the artist's reputation." The trunk in which Vanderlyn kept letters for his biographers was donated to the Senate House. Its contents sadly were scattered; the Huntington Library, however, owns the set exchanged between Amsterdam and Paris / Burr and Vanderlyn.

5. Known today as the *Madonna of the Veil* or the *Madonna of Loreto* (circa 1513; Musée Condé, Chantilly). The dual symbolism of the veil may have appealed to Vanderlyn and Burr: Mary's veil recalls conventional imagery that prefigures the shroud, but Raphael fills the scene with beauty, light, and serene ambiance so that Mary, shielding the sleeping baby Jesus with her veil, optimistically hints of Christ's future resurrection and victory over his enemies.

6. John Vanderlyn, *Caius Marius Amid the Ruins of Carthage* (1807; M.H. de Young Memorial Museum of San Francisco). For illustration, see https://art.famsf.org/john-vanderlyn/caius-marius-amid-ruins-carthage-49835.

7. Napoleon appointed Dominique Vivant Denon (1747–1825) as director of the Louvre in November 1802; Denon resigned the post in 1815 once the royalists had regained power. The Louvre's name was changed to the Musée Napoléon in 1803 and then to the Musée Royale in 1814 when King Louis XVIII and the royalists entered Paris and exiled Napoleon. Napoleon was first exiled to the island of Elba in the Mediterranean and then, after escaping and regaining power for "100 Days" in 1815, he was exiled for good by the British to the island of St. Helena, off the coast of Africa. There he died in 1821, in his will significantly leaving to the dramatist Antoine-Vincent Arnault (1766–1834), "the author of *Marius*, one-hundred thousand francs." Arnault's *Marius à Minturne* was first performed in Paris in 1791.

8. According to the October 24, 1808, edition of the *Paris Moniteur, Journal de l'Empire*, 16 entries from the Salon held in 1808 received gold medals.

9. Vanderlyn's gold medal is missing today. The painting was allegedly purchased from Vanderlyn by his fellow townsman Leonard Kip (1826–1906) for $350.

10. The symbols' meanings have yet to be determined.

11. Jean Jacques Regis de Cambacérès (1753–1824). Napoleon made him Duke of Parma in 1808. The duke was a former admirer of Napoleon, but Cambacérès' views toward him were altered when he turned the French Consulate into an empire in 1804.

12. Vanderlyn's certificate is among his papers at the Senate House State Historic Site, Kingston, New York. The membership list for the Paris Order of the Chevaliers de la Croix (1809–1810) is the only one known to exist. It resides in the archives of the Musée de la Franc-Maçonnerie, Paris. I thank Dr. Pierre Mollier, directeur du département Bibliothèque-Archives-Musée du Grand Orient de France, for his help and expertise. Dr. Mollier states that many leading First Empire artists, such as the Musée Napoleon secretary Joseph Lavallée and Academian Cambacérès, were Freemasons. The use of coded symbols was one way in which members could communicate with each other about politically sensitive topics and thus escape Napoleon's censors.

13. According to letters exchanged between Burr and Vanderlyn around this time, they were to travel to Charleston together. Vanderlyn may have brought Burr's bust of Napoleon from Paris.

14. Pope Pius VII (1742–1823), birth name Barnaba Niccolò Maria Luigi Chiaramonti.

15. John Vanderlyn, *Portrait of Aaron Burr* (1810; New York Historical Society).

16. Vanderlyn's contemporary Rembrandt Peale attended the Chase trial; he hoped to do a large-scale history painting after watching the proceedings. For reasons unexplained, he abandoned the project after Chase was acquitted.

17. Born Franz Joseph Karl (1768–1835). As Francis II he was the last emperor of the Holy Roman Empire, which was dissolved in 1806 after Napoleon defeated the Third Coalition at Austerlitz. Francis despised Napoleon, and the expedient marriage of his daughter Marie-Louise to the French emperor was a bitter pill to swallow. In 1804, as Francis I, he founded Austria and was its first emperor. Thereafter the first *Doppelkaiser* (double emperor) in history ruled the Austrian Empire until his death in 1835.

18. Frank Murray Greenwood, *Legacies of Fear: Law and Politics in Quebec in the Era of the French Revolution* (Toronto: University of Toronto Press, 1993), 195; 312; fn 8.

19. Jean-Baptiste de Nompère de Champagny (1756–1834), appointed the first Duc de Cadore by Napoleon and chosen to succeed Tallyrand as France's minister of foreign affairs between August 1807 and April 1811. Various accounts have Talleyrand or the Duc de Cadore gave Burr the gift of an ornamental ring engraved with the image of a phoenix rising. The story of the phoenix rising from the ashes derives from ancient Greek mythology and commonly references a heroic person who has successfully overcome personal adversity. Burr's ring was last seen during the latter half of the nineteenth-century; its location today is unknown.

20. For Barlow and Fulton, see Richard Buel, Jr., *Joel Barlow: American Citizen in a Revolutionary World* (Baltimore: Johns Hopkins University Press, 2011), 272–73; for Ira Allen see T.S. Webster, "Ira Allen in Paris, 1800, Planning a Canadian Revolution," *Report of the Annual Meeting of the Canadian Historical Association* 42, no. 1 (1963), 74–80.

21. Notably, the efforts of Montgomery and his men were sobering to the British. In London, statesman and author Edmund Burke captured public sentiment when he mocked the lethargic movements of the British army, comparing them to Montgomery's men, who "in one campaign conquered Two-thirds of Canada."

22. Nancy Isenberg, *Fallen Founder: The Life of Aaron Burr* (Viking, 2007), 19–32.

23. Jules David Prown, "John Trumbull as History Painter," in Helen A. Cooper, *John Trumbull: The Hand and Spirit of a Painter* (Yale University Art Gallery, 1982): 54; fn. 11; Helen A. Cooper, ibid., "John Trumbull: A Life," entry for the year 1776, 3.

24. See Alan Taylor, "A Northern Revolution of 1800? Upper Canada and Thomas Jefferson," in James Horn, Jan Ellen Lewis, and Peter S. Onuf, eds., *The Revolution of 1800: Democracy, Race, and the New Republic* (Charlottesville: University of Virginia Press, 2002), 383–409; Lillian F. Gates, "Roads, Rivals and Rebellions: The Unknown Story of Asa Danforth, Jr.," *Ontario History* 76, no. 3 (September 1984), 233–54; Jean-Pierre Wallot, *Intrigues Françaises Et Americaines Au Canada, 1800–1802* (Montreal: Editions Lemeac, 1965), 112–17.

25. See Gerard T. Koeppel, *Water for Gotham: A History* (Princeton: Princeton University Press, 2000), 70–101. Today's Chase Bank is the financial descendant of Burr's Manhattan Company.

26. Rosemarie L. Tovell, *Berczy* (National Gallery of Canada, 1991); A.J.H. Richardson and Helen I. Cowan, "William Berczy's Williamsburg Documents," *Rochester Historical Society Publications* 20 (1942), 141 ff.

27. Wallot, *Intrigues Françaises*, 112–117.

28. The fate of Vanderlyn's original pendant views is unknown but many engravings survive. An exception is the oil on canvas titled *A View of the Western Branch of the Falls of Niagara, Taken from Table Rock* (begun in the fall of 1801); its style does closely resemble Vanderlyn's work from this time. Vanderlyn's two views were last observed, in 1807, hanging on the walls of the New York Library. *A View of the Western Branch* today is in the collection of Historic New England, Boston, Massachusetts. Vanderlyn's engravings after the original views are reproduced in John Davis Hatch, "John Vander Lyn's Prints of Niagara Falls," *Antiques* 138, no. 6 (December 1990), 1252–61. Recently a panoramic oil study of Niagara Falls by Vanderlyn was discovered and underwent conservation analysis and restoration. Today it resides in the Crystal Bridges Museum of American Art, Bentonville, Arkansas, and is reproduced in Katherine Woltz, "The Genius of John Vanderlyn, Kingston-Born Painter," *Kaatskill Life* 26, no. 3 (Fall 2011), 10–23.

29. Kenneth R. Stevens, *Border Diplomacy: The Caroline and McLeod Affairs in Anglo-American-Canadian Relations, 1837–1842* (Tuscaloosa: University of Alabama Press, 1989).

30. Today Vanderlyn's copy after Correggio's *Jupiter and Sleeping Antiope with Cupid* is in the collection of the Century Association, New York. Correggio's painting is currently titled *Venus, Satyr and Cupid* and remains in the Louvre, Paris.

31. Thomas Pritchard Rossiter (1818–1871). *A Studio Reception, Paris* is in the collection of the Albany Institute of History and Art, Albany, New York; Woltz, "The Genius of John Vanderlyn," 10–23.

32. *Ibid.*

33. Hernandez's identity unfortunately remains uncertain. "Fonzi" is Giuseppangelo Fonzi (1768–1840), who made advances in dentistry with his porcelain dentures and novel means to prevent patients' gums from bleeding. Aaron Burr became his devoted client and friend, having Vanderlyn purchase dental items for him from Fonzi even after Burr left Paris for the United States.

34. Her portrait by Vanderlyn is unlocated today.

35. Aaron Columbus Burr, according to letters I am translating and putting into context, was probably born around 1800 and died in 1882. Nineteenth-century popular historians suggested he was an illegitimate child of Burr's, conceived during Burr's European tour, which they mistakenly thought was underway by 1808. For that reason, Aaron Columbus Burr's birth date was given as 1808. Once in the U.S., Burr paid for the young man's education, helped him hone his English writing skills, and found suitable custodians for him.

36. The owners of this sketchbook (circa 1810) graciously allowed me to document it but prefer to remain anonymous.

37. Edmund Burke, *The Origin of Our Ideas of the Sublime and the Beautiful* (London, 1757).

38. The 1810 Salon catalogue entries list Vanderlyn's *Ariadne* but not that it was only an *esquisse*. This has been a great source of confusion to Vanderlyn scholars who were unfamiliar with some of the Salon entry methods.

39. Handwritten Grand Prix subject and rules announcement for the category of sculpture (1810), found in the Archives Nationales, Paris, France.

40. Jean-Pierre Cortot (1787–1842), winner of the Grand Prix competition for sculpture, 1810, based on his copy of the sculpture *Marius Amid the Ruins of Carthage* (today unlocated). For illustration see first edition of Charles Paul Landon, "Annales du Musee…" (Paris, 1810). Copy in Library of Congress.

41. For the symbolism associated with the 1798 processional, see Diana Rowell, *Paris: The New Rome of Napoleon I* (A and C Black, 2012), 146; Andrew McClellan, *Inventing the Louvre* (University of California Press, 1994), 114–23; Marie-Louise Blumer, "Catalogue des Peintures Transportées d'Italie en France de 1796 a 1814," *Bulletin de la Société de l'Histoire et l'Art Français*, 2nd fasc. (1936), 244–348; and Marie-Louise Blumer, "La Commission pour la Recherche des Objets de Sciences et Arts en Italie (1796–1797)," *La Révolution Française* 87 (January–March 1934), 62–88; (April–June 1934), 124–50; (July–September 1934), 222–59.

42. For Denon's response to the rupture of the Peace of Amiens, see Gabriel Vauthier, "Denon et le Gouvernement des Arts sous le Consulat," *Annales Révolutionnaires* 4 (1911), 355–56.

43. Alexander Hamilton quoted in Andro Linklater, *An Artist in Treason: The Extraordinary Double Life of General James Wilkinson* (Bloomsbury, 2010), 185.

44. While researching the Burr family portraits between 1880 and 1920, Dr. John Stillwell was informed that the pendant-portrait watch was in the possession of a descendant of Anthony Bowrowson (Burr's chef at Richmond Hill) and that he had seized the watch for a debt owed him by Burr. Stillwell was further told that the portraits represented Theodosia Bartow Prevost Burr (left) and her daughter Theodosia Burr (right) and that the portraits were painted circa 1790. I disagree, for if Stillwell's information was correct, then Burr's daughter, Theodosia, born June 21, 1793, would have been 7 years old in 1790. The woman on the right is full-bosomed, while the person on the left appears to be a man dressed in a gentleman's or officer's coat fashionable at that time. My guess is that the woman on the right represents Burr's wife, Theodosia Bartow Prevost Burr. The man on the left would be Burr, especially given the man's curly hair. Stuart's portrait from 1794 reveals that Burr's unshorn hair was curly, or at least wavy. The portraits likely were painted in 1782, on the occasion of the Burrs' marriage. If so, then Governor William Livingston's adage equating eternal devotion with an instrument that keeps time—to wit, "may love be the time piece in your mansion, and happiness its minute hand"—would be a fitting memento for the couple to associate with a watch preserving their portraits. The dynamics of the paired portraits made it the perfect "conversation piece."

45. I thank James Lewis for this newspaper reference.

Bibliography

Adams, John Quincy. *The Diaries of John Quincy Adams*. A Digital Collection. Massachusetts Historical Society. www.masshist.org/jqadiaries/.

Aubry, Octave. *The King of Rome, Napoleon II, "L'aiglon."* Philadelphia: J.B. Lippincott, 1932.

Bentham, Jeremy. *The Works of Jeremy Bentham.* "Published Under the Superintendence of His Executor, John Bowring." Edinburgh: William Tait, 1838–1843. 11 vols. http://oll.libertyfund.org/titles/2085.

Bergeron, Louis. *France Under Napoleon*. Translated by R.R. Palmer. Princeton, NJ: Princeton University Press, 1981.

Bergstrasser, Gisela. "Duke Emmerich Joseph Von Dalberg as a Collector of Drawings." *Master Drawings* 22, no.1 (Spring 1984).

Bernard, J.F. *Talleyrand: A Biography*. New York: G.P. Putnam's Sons, 1973.

Bernier, Olivier. *The Eighteenth Century Woman*. New York: Doubleday, 1981.

_____. *Lafayette: Hero of Two Worlds*. New York: E.P. Dutton, 1983.

Barreto, Cristina, and Martin Lancaster. *Napoleon and the Empire of Fashion, 1795–1815*. Milano, Italy: Skira, 2011.

Biver, Marie-Louise. *Le Paris De Napoléon*. Paris: Librairie Plon, 1963.

Blake, Ehrlich. *Paris on the Seine*. New York: Athenaeum, 1962.

Bonaparte, Napoléon. *New Letters of Napoleon I, Omitted from the Edition Published Under the Auspices of Napoleon III*. Translated by Lady Mary Loyd. New York: Appleton, 1897.

Brelot, Claude-Isabelle. "La Noblesse Reinventée." *Nobles De Franche-Comte De 1814 À 1870: Annales. Histoire, Sciences Sociales* 2, no. 4 (1996).

Broers, Michael. *Europe Under Napoleon, 1799–1815*. New York: Arnold, 1996.

Buckner, F. Melton, Jr. *Aaron Burr: Conspiracy to Treason*. New York: John Wiley & Sons, 2002.

Burr Aaron. *Memoirs of Aaron Burr*. Edited by Matthew L. Davis. 2 vols. New York: Harper & Bros., 1836.

_____. *Political Correspondence and Public Papers of Aaron Burr*. 2 vols. Edited by Mary-Jo Kline. Princeton, NJ: Princeton University Press, 1983.

_____. *The Private Journal of Aaron Burr*. Edited by William K. Bixby. 2 vols. Rochester: Genesee Press, 1903.

Burr, Aaron, and Theodosia Burr Alston. *Correspondence of Aaron Burr and His Daughter Theodosia*. Edited by Mark Van Doren. New York: Covics-Friede, 1929.

Carlson, Marvin A. *The French Stage in the Nineteenth Century*. Methuen, NJ: Scarecrow Press, 1972.

Chaillou, David. *Napoleon Et l'Opera*. Paris: Fayard, 2004.

Chateaubriand, Francois de. *Mémoires D'outré-Tombe*. Translated by A.S. Kline, 2005. http://www.poetryintranslation.com/PITBR/Chateaubriand/Chathome.htm.

Chazin-Bennahum, Judith. *Dance in the Shadow of the Guillotine*. Carbondale: Southern Illinois University Press, 1988.

Chew, William L., III. "Americans in France During the Revolution and Napoleon." *Napoleonic Scholarship*, no. 4 (November 2011).

_____. *From Romanticism to Realism: American Tourists in Revolutionary France, the Consortium on the Revolutionary Era, 1750–1850, Selected Papers*, 2000.

_____. "John Quincy Adams: American Tourist in Paris, 1815." *Napoleonica: La Revue*, no. 18 (2013).

_____. "Life Before Fodor and Frommer: Americans in Paris from Thomas Jefferson to John Quincy Adams." *French History* 18, no.1.

_____. "'Straight' Sam Meets 'Lewd' Louis: American Perceptions of French Sexuality, 1775–1815." In *Revolutions and Watersheds: Transatlantic Dialogues, 1775–1815*. Edited by W.M. Verhoeven and Beth Dolan Kautz. Atlanta: Rodopi, 1999.

Coignet, Jean-Roche. *The Note-Books of Captain Coignet, Soldier of the Empire, 1799–1816*. Novato, CA: Presidio Press, 1989.

Connor, Steven. *Dumbstruck: A Cultural History of Ventriloquism*. New York: Oxford University Press, 2001.

D'Abrantes, la Duchesse de (Madame Junot). *Memoirs of Napoleon, His Court and Family*. New York: D. Appleton, 1873.

Davidson, Denise Z. "Making Society 'Legible': People-Watching in Paris After the Revolution." *French Historical Studies* 28 (2005).

De Terra, Helmut. *Humboldt: The Life and Times of Alexander Von Humboldt, 1769–1859*. New York: Alfred A. Knopf, 1955.

DeJean, Joan. *The Essence of Style: How the French Invented High Fashion, Fine Food, Chic Cafés, Style, Sophistication, and Glamour*. New York: Free Press, 2005.

Dickinson, Henry W. *Robert Fuller, Engineer and Artist: His Life and Works*. New York: John Lane, 1913.

Duyre, Pierre. "Les Chevaliers Dans La Noblesse Impériale." *Revue d'Histoire Modern Et Contemporaine* 17, no. 3 (1970).

Eitner, Lorenz. *Neoclassicism and Romanticism, 1750–1850*. Englewood Cliffs, NJ: Prentice-Hall, 1970.

Evans, Paul D. *The Holland Land Company*. Buffalo, NY: Buffalo Historical Society, 1924.

Ferguson, Priscilla Parkhurst. *Paris as Revolution: Writing the Nineteenth-Century City*. Berkeley: University of California, 1997.

———. "Reading City Streets." *French Review* 61, no. 3 (February 1988).

Fierro, Alfred. *Historical Dictionary of Paris*. Lanham, MD: Scarecrow Press, 1998.

Foster, Thomas. "Reconsidering Libertines and Early Modern Heterosexuality: Sex and American Founder Gouverneur Morris." *Journal of the History of Sexuality* 22, no. 1 (January 2013).

———. *Sex and the Founding Fathers: The American Quest for a Relatable Past*. Philadelphia: Temple University Press, 2014.

Fournier, Edouard. *Histoire Du Pont Neuf*. Paris: Dentu, 1862.

Gaehtgens, Thomas W. *Napoleon's Arc De Triomphe*. Gottingen: Vandenhoeck & Ruprecht, 1974.

Gautier, Paul. *Madame De Staël Et Napoléon*. Paris: Plon, 1903.

Grady, Richard. "Mendon Congressman Planned Extravagant Welcome for Revolutionary War Hero." July 24, 2012. Mendon, Massachusetts, Web site.

Guerini, Vincenzo. *The Life and Works of Giuseppangelo Fonzi*. New York: Lea & Febiger, 1925.

Haynie, Henry. *Paris Past and Present*. New York: Frederick A. Stokes, 1902.

Hesse, Carla. *Publishing and Cultural Politics in Revolutionary Paris, 1789–1810*. Berkeley: University of California Press, 1999.

Hibbert, Christopher. *Napoleon: His Wives and Women*. New York: Norton, 2002.

Hicks, Peter. *Napoleon and the Theatre*. www.napoleon.org/en/reading_room. Original German version: *Was Fur Ein Theater!: Kronungen Und Spektakel in Napoleonischer Zeit*. Edited by Dominik Gugel and Christina Egli, Frauenfeld, Stuutgart, Vienna: Verlag Huber, 2003.

Hillam, Christine, ed. *Dental Practice in Europe at the End of the 18th Century*. New York: Rodopi, 2003.

Hoffmann-Axthelm, Walter. *History of Dentistry*. Translated by H.M. Koehler. Chicago: Quintessence, 1981.

Horne, Alistair. *The Seven Ages of Paris*. New York: Alfred A. Knopf, 2004.

Howard, Donald D., Michael F. Pavkovic and John K. Severn. Florida State University, Institute on Napoleon and the French Revolution. *Consortium on Revolutionary Europe, 1750–1850*, selected papers, 2002.

http://blogs.loc.gov/loc/2014/02/george-washingtons-philadelphia-household-1793-1794.

http://fr.wikisource.org/wiki/Auteur:Jacques_Barbeu_du_Bourg.

http://just vienna.com/imperial-days/born-onto-a-throne-the-son-of-napoleon-and-marrie-louise.

Hugo, Victor. *Les Miserables*. Translated by Julie Rose. New York: Random House, 2008.

Jefferson, Thomas. *The Papers of Thomas Jefferson*. Edited by Julian P. Boyd, et al., Vol. 8. Princeton, NJ: Princeton University Press, 1950.

Jensen, Kristian. *Revolution and the Antiquarian Book: Reshaping the Past, 1780–1815*. New York: Cambridge University Press, 2011.

Jones, Colin. *The King's Two Teeth*. muse.jhu.edu/journals/history_workshop_journal/v065/65.jones.o1.html, pp1/9–7/9.

Kaplan, Lawrence S. "Jonathan Russell and the Capture of the Guerrier." *William and Mary Quarterly* 24, no. 2 (April 1967). Third Series.

Kellner, L. *Alexander Von Humboldt*. New York: Oxford University Press, 1963.

Kennedy, Roger G. *Burr, Hamilton, and Jefferson: A Study in Character*. New York: Oxford, 2000.

Kukla, Jon. *Mr. Jefferson's Women*. Richmond, VA: Alfred A. Knopf, 2007.

———. *A Wilderness So Immense: The Louisiana Purchase and the Destiny of America*. New York: Knopf, 2003.

Landale, James. *The Last Duel: A True Story of Death and Honour*. New York: Canongate U.S., 2006.

Lee, William. *William Lee, a Yankee Jeffersonian: Selections from the Diary and Letters of William Lee of Massachusetts Written from 1796–1840*. Edited by Mary L. Mann. Cambridge, MA, 1958.

"Lettre Du Citoyen Robert, Conservateur Des Tableau Du Museum National, Au Citoyen Fulton, Sur Le Panorama Nouvellement Établi Au Jardin Des Capucines." *Moniteur Universel*. September 8, 1799.

Lomask, Milton. *Aaron Burr: The Conspiracy and Years of Exile, 1805–36*. New York: Farrar Straus Giroux, 1982.

Malthus, Thomas. "An Essay on the Principle of Population: The Sixth Edition (1826) with Variant Readings from the Second Edition (1803)." In *The Works of Thomas Robert Malthus*. Edited by E.A. Wrigley and David Soudens. London, 1986.

Mansel, Philip. *The Court of France, 1789–1830*. New York: Cambridge University Press, 1988.

Marrinan, Michael. *Romantic Paris: History of a Cultural Landscape, 1800–1850*. Stanford, CA: Stanford University Press, 2009.

Massachusetts Historical Society. *Knox Papers: Swan to Knox, March 29, 1788*.

McClellan, Andrew. *Inventing the Louvre: Art, Politics, and the Origins of the Modern Museum in Eighteenth-Century Paris*. New York: Cambridge University Press, 1994.

McCullogh, David. *The Greater Journey: Americans in Paris*. New York: Simon & Schuster, 2011.

McGregor, James H.S. *Paris from the Ground Up*. Cambridge, MA: Belknap Press of Harvard University Press, 2009.

Melton, Buckner F., Jr. *Aaron Burr: Conspiracy to Treason*. New York: John Wiley & Sons, 2002.

Morgan, John S. *Robert Fulton*. New York: Mason/Charter, 1977.

Morrisey, Robert. *The Economy of Glory: From Ancien Régime France to the Fall of Napoleon*. Translated by Teresa Lavender Fagan. Chicago: University of Chicago Press, 2013.

Morton, Brian N. *Americans in Paris: An Anecdotal Street Guide*. Ann Arbor, MI: Olivia & Hill, 1984.

"Natural Goodness—Connoisseurs Delight in Roussillon's Sweet Wines." *France* (Summer 1997).

Oedel, William T. "After Paris: Rembrandt Peale's Apollodorian Gallery." *Wintherthur Portfolio* 27, no. 1 (Spring 1992).

Parmet, Herbert S., and Marie B. Hecht. *Aaron Burr: Portrait of An Ambitious Man*. New York: Macmillan, 1967.

Parton, James. *The Life and Times of Aaron Burr*. New York: Mason Brothers, 1858.

Peale, Rembrandt. "Letters from Paris." *Portfolio of an Artist* (September 1810). Philadelphia: H. Perkins, 1839.

Pedley, Marie Sponberg. "The Map Trade in Paris, 1650–1825." *Imago Mundi* 33 (1981).

Quynn, Dorothy Mackay. "The Art Confiscations of the Napoleonic Wars." *American Historical Review* 50, no. 3 (April 1945).

Ravage, M.E. *Empress Innocence: The Life of Marie-Louise*. New York: Alfred A. Knopf, 1931.

Rémuat, Madame De. *Memoirs*. Translated by Mrs. Cashel Hoey and John Lillie. New York: D. Appleton, 1880.

Rice, Howard C. Rice. "James Swan: Agent of the French Republic, 1794–1796." *New England Quarterly* 10, no. 3 (September 1937).

Riskin, Jessica. "The Defecating Duck, Or, the Ambiguous Origins of Artificial Life." Reprinted from *Critical Inquiry* 29, no. 4 (Summer 2003) in 2003 by the University of Chicago.

Roberts, Andrew. *Napoleon: A Life*. New York: Viking, 2014.

Robichon, Francois. "Le Panorama, Spectacle De L'histoire." *Le Mouvement Social*, no. 131 (April–June 1985).

Root-Bernstein, Michele. *Boulevard Theater and Revolution in Eighteenth Century Paris*. Ann Arbor, MI: Umi Research Press, 1984.

Rovigo, Le Duc de. *Mémoires Du Duc De Rovigo, Pour Servir À l'Histoire De l'Empereur Napoléon*. Project Gutenberg. www.gutenberg.org/ebooks/20108.

Russell, Jonathan. *Biographical Directory of the U.S. Congress*. Washington D.C.: Government Printing Office, 1913.

Sale, Kirkpatrick. *The Fire of His Genius: Robert Fulton and the American Dream*. New York: Free Press, 2001.

Sandbrook, Dominic. "Pistols at Dawn." *Telegraph*, June 11, 2009. http//www.telegraph.uk/culture/books/bookreviews/5506794/Pistols-at-Dawn.html (accessed August 25, 2014).

Sangster, C. William. *Umbrellas and Their History*. Project Gutenburg.

Sanz, Javier, Miguel A. Lopez-Bermejo and Micheline Ruel-Kellermann. "Giuseppangelo Fonzi (1768–1840): La Vie Et l'Oeuvre D'un Illustre Dentiste." *Actes: Societé Francaise D'histoire De L'art Dentaire* 12 (2007).

Simpson, Dorothy. *The Maine Islands in Story and Legend*. J.B. Lippincott, 1960; reprnt., Nobleboro, ME: Blackberry, 1987.

Small, H.W. *A History of the Town of Swan's Island*. 2nd ed. Maine, 1937. www.swansisland.org/small/pdf.

Smoler, Frederic. "The Radical Revolution." *American Heritage* 43, no. 8 (1992). http://www.americanheritage.com/content/radical-revolution.html (accessed August 25, 2014).

Sutcliffe, Anthony. *Paris: An Architectural History*. New Haven, CT: Yale University Press, 1993.

Thompson, Benjamin. "Of Chimney Fire-Places" [1796]. In *Collected Works of Count Rumford*. Edited by Sanborn C. Brown. Cambridge, MA, 1968–70.

Uzanne, Octave. *The Book-Hunter in Paris: Studies Among the Bookstalls and the Quays*. London: Elliot Stock, 1893.

Van Laun, Henri. *The French Revolutionary Epoch: Being a History of France from the Beginning of the First French Revolution*. New York: Cassell Petter & Galpin, 1878.

Willey, Basil. *The English Moralists*. New York: Anchor, 1967.
Williams, Kate. *Ambition and Desire: The Dangerous Life of Josephine Bonaparte*. New York: Ballantine, 2014.
Willms, Johannes. *Paris, Capital of Europe: From the Revolution to the Belle Époque*. Translated by Eveline L. Kanes. New York: Holmes and Meier.
Wood, Gordon S. *Empire of Liberty: A History of the Early Republic*. New York: Oxford, 2009.
———. *Revolutionary Characters*. New York: Penguin, 2007.
Woodforde, James. *The Diary of a Country Parson: The Reverend James Woodforde*. Edited by John Beresford. London, 1926–1931.
www.napoleon-empire.net/personnages/maret.php.
www.paulfrasercollectibles.com/News/Napoleon's-signed-kremlin-letter.
www.1789–1815.com/maret.htm.
Yorke, James. "Percier and Fontaine: Propagators of the Empire Style of Architecture in Europe." The Consortium on Revolutionary Europe, 1750–1850; Proceedings, 1989, to Commemorate the Bicentennial of the French Revolution, 1990.

Index

Numbers in **_bold italics_** indicate pages with photographs.

Aaron Burr Legion 193, 194
Abrantes, Laure Junot, duchesse d' 90
Achaintre 123
Adams, Abigail 113, 141
Adams, John 23, 46, 47, 139, 164, 189
Adams, John Quincy 29 99, 103
Adet, Pierre-Auguste 202, 203
Alberg, duc d' 13, 14, 30, 138, 183, 220, 227
Alexander, Czar 34, 35, 64, 76, 93, 105
Allen, Ira 203
Allston, Washington 216
Alston, Aaron Burr 17, 44, 63, 174, 183, 186, 189
Alston, Joseph 111, 189
Alston, Theodosia Burr 195, 197
Alston, William 200
Allegory of France 199; as Hercules 213; as Liberty 213; as Rome vs Carthage 213
Amiens, Treaty of 82, 92, 214, 226
Ancient Sculpture: Apollo Belvedere 213; Belvedere Torso 215–216; bust of Brutus 213; Laocoön 213; seated Marius 213; Sleeping Cleopatra/Ariadne 202, 213;
Ariadne Asleep on the Island of Naxos 115–117, 171–172, 208–215
Arietty 87
Anne of Cleves, Queen 17
Apparel: men's 60–62, 67, 70, **_71_**, 72–74, 76; women's 70–72, 142–143, 168
Arc de Triomphe 33, **_79_**–81, 94, 212, 228
Argand Lamp 150–151
Athenée des Arts 49, 50
Aulnoy, Marie Comtesse d' 18
Austerlitz, battle of 97, 105, 212, 225; bridge **_96_**, 97, 100
automatons 90–91

baiser fatal 175
balloons 30, 111, 219
balls 89, 90
Balzac, Honoré de 92, 129, 137, 140, 146–149
Barlow, Joel 209
Barbeau-Dubourg, Jacques 66
Barlow, Joel 203
Barrault, Jean-Louis 87
Bassano, duc de 12, 14, 38–39, 182, 184–186
baths 30, 91, 159, 173, 162, 173
Beaumarchais, Pierre-Augustin Carol de 104
bees 89
"La Belle DC" 217
La Belle Limonadiere 136
Bellerophon 36
Benjamin, Walter 118, 146
Bentham, Jeremy 6–7, 52, 105
Berckzy, William 205
Berg, Grand Duchess of 90
Bernadotte, Jean Baptiste Jules 92
Bernard, J.F. 35
Bernier, Olivier 41
Berthier, Louis-Alexander, Prince de Wagram 62
Biddle, Charles 199
Biddle, Nancy 199
Biddle, Nicholas 199, 215–216
Billiards 74, 87, **_130_**, 150
Bixby, William 8, 162–163
Blake, Ehrlich 121
Blennerhassett, Harman 192
Blennerhassett, Margaret 192
Boilly, Louis-Léopold 77, 115
Bonaparte, Jérome-Napoléon 11–12
Bonaparte, Joseph-Napoléon 34, 35, 41, 182, 188–189
Bookbuying 52, 57, 83, 84, 86, 93, 103, 119–123
Boots 62, **_66_**, 66–70, 73, 107, 143, 169, 170
Bosio, Jean-Francois 70
Boulevard des Crimes 87

Bourbons 22, 34–35, 39, 91–92, 117, 168
Bourrienne, Louis de 47
Bourse 129
Bowers, Brian 151
Brackenridge, Hugh Henry 204
Brant, Joseph 206
Breguet, Abraham-Louis 63
Brignole-Sale, Pellina Marcheradi 37
Broers, Michael 57
Brongiart, A.T. 94
Bruneseau, Pierre-Emmanuel 101
Burello, Valerio 49
Burns, Robert 21
Burr, Aaron: 196; arrives in Paris 202; Burr, Aaron Columbus 210, 226n35; as Caesar-Napoleon 199, 201, 201; and Chase trial 201; death 194–195; as flaneur/projector in Vanderlyn's panorama of Versailles 209; Manhattan Company 205, 215–216; as Marius 218; pendant portrait watch 217–218, 226n44; Richmond Hill mansion 205; ring 225n19; trial at Richmond 202; Western Expedition 199; Vanderlyn's c. 1810 portrait 201–202; Vanderlyn's 1802 pendant portrait of Burr and daughter Theodosia 224n3
Burr, Aaron Columbus 210
Burr, Samuel Engle, Jr. 53
Burr, Theodosia: as daughter 28, 43–44, 110, 114, 158, 169, 179, 189; gifts for 44, 55, 57, 63, 83, 86; portraits **_8_**, 18
Burr, Theodosia Bartow Prevost 153, 164, 217–218

Cabinet des Modes 70
Cadore, duc de 12, 30, 34, 35, 203, 217, 225n19
Cafés 36, **_78_**, 84, 126–131, **_134_**, **_136_**

231

Index

Caius Marius Amid the Ruins of Carthage 197–200
Cambacérès, Duke of Parma 198
Canada 203–207, 225
Canning, George 15
cannons 73, 95–98
Canova, Antonio 117
Carcel Lamp 151
Careme, Antoinin 139
Carlson, Marvin 106–107
Carné, Marcel 111
Carriages 22, 28, 35, 46, 73, 91, 110, 122, 129, 143, 144–148 **147**
Carrousel **33**, 94
Carter, Charles Page 224n4
Castro, de 171
Cemeteries 97, 100
Chalgrin, J.F.T. 94
Champagny, Jean-Baptiste de 34–35
Chappy, Jean-Luc 31
Charleston *see* South Carolina
Chase, Justice Samuel 6, 201
Chateaubriand 41
Chazin-Bennahum, Judith 114
Checkers 173
Chemant, Nicolas Dubois de 50
Chess 36, 85, 128
Chew, William L. 23, 24
Chimneys *see* Fireplaces
Cicero 132
Cigars 20, 21, 90, 135, 146, 173, 174, 184
Clecy, Hélène de 48
Clinton, George 206
Clough, Captain 27
Cockades 23
Coffee 57; drinking 86, 125–129, 132, 136–139, 150, 170; making 18, 99, 124
Coignet, Jean-Roch 74
Comfort 158–159
Compiègne 76, 182
Concorde, Place de la 42, 77, 96, 145
Congress of Vienna 37
Constitution 29
Continental System 54
Cooper, James Fenimore 119
Corneille, Pierre 104
Correggio: *Jupiter and Sleeping Antiope with Cupid* 202
Cortot, Jean-Pierre 213; 226n39, 226n40
Cradle, imperial 32, 33
Crowley, John E. 58–60
Customs 187

Dahlberg, Emmerich Joseph von 36–37
Danforth, Asa 205
Darwin, Charles 40
David, Jacques-Louis: and *Coronation* painting 202
David, Jean-Louis **71**, 90, 98, 114–115, 146, 202
Davidson, Denise Z. 142
Davis, Matthew L. 155, 185, 191

Denon, Dominique-Vivant Baron 99, 118, 146, 182, 184, 197–198, 213, 214, 217
Dibdin, Thomas Frognel 120
Dickinson, Charles 15
Diderot 167, 177
"The Digestive Duck" 91
Dogs 76, **77**, 88, 91, 111, **144**
Double standard 165–166, 173
Draveil: estate 210
Druon, Maurice 76
Duchesnois, Catherine 105, 108
Duels 6, 14, 15, 30, 129–130
Dunlap, William 205
Duyre, Pierre 31

Edwards, Jonathan 195, 197
Edwards, Ogden 195
Election (1800) 5, 6, 164, 189
Elephant sculpture **98**
Les Enfants du Paradis 87
Enghien, duc d' 36
Epinay, Madame 155
Erie Canal 56
Eustice, John Chetwood 199
Exceptionalism, American 24

Farington, Joseph 214
Fenwick, Catherine 17, 19, 22, 64, 156, 159–160, 186?, 210
Fenwick, Columbia Franco 210
Fenwick, Joseph 135, 210
Ferguson, Priscilla 133
Fesch, Cardinal **82**
Festivities 73, 80, 82
Firefighters 97, 101, 151
Fireplaces 7, 17–21, 57–60, 65, 69, 70, 124, 178
Fireworks 74, 77, 80, 90, 109, 207
Flahaut, Adelaide de 34
Flavell, Julie 5
Floods 100
Fontaine, Pierre-Francois-Léonard 80, 94, 96
Fontainebleau 39
Fonzi, G.A. **48**; chez 46, 64, 88, 111, 138, 159; dentistry 50–51; friendship with Burr 46–50, 73, 86, 90, 148
Food *see* Meals
Foster, Thomas A. 172
Foster's Wharf 27
Fouché, Joseph 35–36, 39, 87, 151
Fountains 78, 98–100
Fox, 199; 215–216
Francis I 202
Franklin, Benjamin: in London 167; in Paris 23, 29, 62, 66, 87, 250, 276; science of 18, 59, 119, 150
Franz, Duke of Reichstadt *see* King of Rome
Freemasonry 198
Fulton, Robert 88, 203, 209
fumistes 18–20

Galerie des modes et costumes Francois 70
Gambling 34, 35, 78, 86–87, 132, 150
Games 77, 90
Garsault, Francois Alexandre de 68
Gay-Lussac, Joseph Louis 40
Genlis, Madame de 123
George, Marguerite-Josephine 108
George Eastman Institute 49
German Company 205
Godwin, William 150, 162
Gothenburg 60
Göttingen 196
Grand Manner Painting 204
Grande Armée 36, 39, 73, 129
Grandpre, Monsieur de 30
La Grange-Blénau 41–42
Green, Timothy 205
Grenville, Lord 205
Grisettes see Prostitutes
Grolier Club 7
Guerini, Vincenzo 49
Guidebooks 123, 136, 148
Gutters *see* Sanitation

Haines, W. Scott 129
Hair: men's **2**, 57, 62, 104, 201; women's 72, 143, 158, 176, 213
Haley, Capt. Nathan 207
Hamburg 11, 15, 41, 44, 47, 87, 107, 155
Hamilton, Alexander 10, 14, 32, 205, 216; 1804 duel 5–6, 15, 29, 106, 159
Hats 57, 61–62
Health 132, 156, 166, 176, 178
Heligoland 43
Henrietta Maria, Queen 84
Henry VIII 17
Hicks, Elias 130
Holbein, Hans 17
Holland 38, 41, 122, 149
Holland Land Company 10, 54–56, 185, 211
Horne, Alistair 61
Houbigant 143
Hugo, Victor **98**, 101
Huguenin, Julie 178
Humboldt, Alexander von 29, 39–41
Humors, theory of 166–167

Ice cream 78, 87, 135–138 **134**, **136**
Iéna 97
Incroyables 68, 140, 220
Institut National 39, 40, 51, 123
Invalides 74, 88, 97, 145
Irving, Washington 23, 130, 215–216
Isabey, Jean-Baptiste 72, 89, 90, 105
Isenberg, Nancy 55, 165, 175, 191
Italy 34, 66, 94, 103, 117, 118, 202, 208

Index

Jackson, Andrew 15
Jardin des Plantes 39, **96**
Jay, John 205, 224*n*2
Jefferson, Thomas: architect of the Virginia state capitol 215–216; election 5–7; lifestyle 58–59, 62, 135; Maison Carrée as inspiration 215–216; in Paris 23, 25, 29, 49, 85, 97, 123; presidency 40, 165, 194, 199, 217; relations with women 124, 164–166, 176; travel 2
Jensen, Kristian 120
Jones, Colin 22, 49
Jones, John Paul 2
Josephine, Empress: fashions 64, 71, 77, 143, 168; Napoleon and 72, 76, 82–83, 91, 108
Journal des dames et des modes 70
journal-making 7–8
Jumel, Eliza 188

Kames, Lord (Henry Home) 60
Keats, John 152
Kegel, Sabine 62–64
Kennedy, John F. 157
Kennedy, Roger G. 192
Keynes, John 56
King of Rome 22, 32, **34**, 74, 91–92
Kingston, NY 196
Kneble, Henriette Von 201
Knox, Henry, Gen. 26
Koslofsky, Craig 150
Kukla, John 166

"La Belle DC" 217
Lafayette, Adrienne 41, 42
Lafayette, Marquis de 28–29, 41–42, 75, 97
Lafon, Pierre 106
Lancers of the Guard 73
Landis, Joan B. 175
Lang, Andrew 18
La Notre, André 94
Latin Quarter 40
Lavoisier, Antoine 150
Lee, William 24–25, 105
Legion of Honor 198
Leipzig, Battle of 37
L'Enfant, Pierre Charles 74
Le Pique, Monsieur 30
Le Sueur, Jean-Francois 113
Legion of Honor 31, 35, 41, 74
Lighting: exterior 97, 149–151, 168; interior 7, 58, 59, 80, 89, 104, 105, 171
Liston, Robert 205
Livingston, William 54, 87, 212, 218
Loans 27, 44, 185
Lodgings 19–20, 57, 148
Lost in Translation (Eva Hoffman) 3
Louis XIII 84
Louis XIV 84, 100, 109, 125, 150

Louis-Benoit 113
Louis-Philippe 39, 84, 85
Louisiana Purchase 53
Louvre Museum: 71, **80**–82, 114–119, 195, 197, 199–200; Burr at 183–184; as Musée Napoléon 197; name change 119
Lubin, David M. 115–117
Ludewig, Grand Duke of Hesse 37
Luxembourg Palace 65, 84
Luxury items 27, 63, 83–84, 138
Lyons, Claire 172

MacDonogh, Giles 125, 131
MacMillan, Harold 157
Madeleine, Church of 93
Madison, Dolley 28, 158
Madison, James 28, 45, 158, 164
Maine 26–27
Male bonding 172–173
Malloy, Albert 224*n*4
Malmaison 104
Malthus, Thomas 60
Manchester-Liverpool railway 18
Mansel, Philip 38
Maps 29, 101, 123, 148
Maret, Hugues-Bernard *see* Duc de Bassano
Marie Antoinette, Queen 105, 143, 169
Marie-Louise, Queen 33, 35, 74, 76, 83; fashions 71, 77; marriages 24–25, 38, 79–80, **82**, 91
Marie-Thérèse (daughter of Louis XVI) 38
Marius, as historical figure 197, 217
Marly 100
Marrinan, Michael 85
Mars, Mademoiselle 108
Marshall, John 199
McClellan, Andrew 118–119
McCullough, David 5, 146
McGregor, James H.S. 22
McRae, Alexander 13–14
Meals 21, 124–135 155–156
Mendon, Massachusetts 29
Mercier, Sébastien 85, 123
Merino sheep 28, 42
Merveilleuses 20*n*, 70
Mésangère, Pierre de la 70
Mexican plan, Burr's 6, 11, 38, 40, 52–53, 56–57, 196
Militarism 22, 74, **80**
Mirrors 27, 93, 126–128, 136, 171
Moitte, Madame 71
Moliere (Jean-Baptiste Poquelin) 30
Mollerat, Jean-Baptiste 51
Moncrieffe, Margaret 191
Le Moniteur Universel 38
Monroe, James 45, 54, 164, 188
Montesquieu 30
Montgomery, Gen. Richard 203–204, 224*n*2
Montmorency 88, 158, 175–176, 180

Morris, Gouverneur 27, 34, 85, 97, 163–165, 167, 169
Morris, Thomas 206
Mulard, Henri-François 143

Napoleon **33**, **89**, 69–108 passim, 113–132, 139–148 passim, 164, 167, 169, 175, 197, 203, 211–216; Burr and 2–3, 11–12, 53–54; bust 200, 225*n*13; will and playwright Antoine Vincent Arnault 225*n*7
Napoleon III 12
National Assembly 38, 41, 117
Nautilus 88
naval power 53–54
Necker, Jacques 128
Neipperg, Adam Albert, Count van 92
New Orleans 53
New York: 1–7, 10–12, 23, 30, 44–45, 101, 135, 139, 141
newspapers 15–16, 36, 38, 130
Niagara Falls 206
Noah, Mordecai M. 114
nobility, French 23, 30–32
Notre-Dame 77, 80, 145
Nudity in art 23

Ogden, Matthias 204, 205
Ohio 6, 15, 53, 192
Olsen, Mimi Vang 192
Ombres chinois (shadow puppets) 90
O'Pecko, Paul 187
Orleans, Louis Philippe Joseph d' 84
Orleans, Philippe I, duc d' 78, 84
Ourcy Canal 57, 99

Paine, Thomas 3
Palais Royal 77, 78, 83, **78**, **83**; entertainment 17, 58, 86–89, 103, 128–132, 169; history 84–85
Panoramas 87–91, 90, 209?
Parades *see* festivities
Paris in 1810 72–73, 76 92–102, 196
Paris Opera 23, 42, 104, 109, 112–114
Parker, Daniel 210
Parvenus 22, 92, 103
Passports 11–14, 43, 87 182–186
Pavilion of Peace 78
Peale, Charles Willson 40; and "Mammoth Picture" 211
Peale, Rembrandt 23, **61**, 73, 201, 211–212
Pepys, Samuel 179
Percier, Charles 80, 94–96
Performances: indoor 103–114; outdoor 87–91, **144**, 145–146
Perfume 27, 143, 169
Poland 38, 40, 151
Police: activities 80, 85, 97, 121,

138, 168; Burr and 11–12, 185; heads 13, 35–36, 39, 87, 149; spying 38, 42, 129, 159
Pont Neuf 122
Pope Pius VII 199, 201
The Prince (Machiavelli) 32, 199, 216
Princeton University 5
Pont Neuf 122
Portugal 38
Prostitutes 2, 23, 25, 77, 85–**86**, **93**, 142, 162–177
Prussia 36–40 passim, 76, 97, 118
Public spaces 142
Puppets 87, 90, 109, 145

Quebec 194, 203
Quinzio, Jeri 134–138

Randolph, David Meade 45
Raphael: *Sleeping Jesus* 197, 224n5; *Transfiguration* 202
Raymond, J.A. 94
Récamier, Madame 168
Reign of Terror 41
Remusat, Comte de 108, 109, 113
Restaurants 20–1, 41, 57, 78, 84–86, 90, 99, 128, 131–140, 148
Reynie, Nicholas de la 150
Reyniere, Grimod de la 125
Richelieu, Cardinal 84, 109
Richmond Hill 32
Richmond, VA 6
Rigaud, Hyacinthe 50
Robespierre, Maximilien 27, 128, 145
Rome 197
Root-Bernstein, Michele 112
Rosseau, Brenda 61
Rossiter, Thomas Pritchard 21, 158
Rousseau, Jean-Jacques 87, 132, 158, 167, 174–176, 180–181
Roussillon 20–21, 124, 150
Roux, Louis 12–13, 53–54
Rovigo, duc d' 13, 35, 36
Rowlandson, Thomas **136**
Rumford, Benjamin Thomas, Count of 18–19, 59
Russell, Bertrand 174–175
Russell, Jonathan 14, 185

Saint-Cloud, Chateau de 76
Saint-Lambert, marquis de 176
Sainte-Beuve, Charles-Augustin 100
Sainte Pélagie 28, 64, 146
Sally 27
Le Salon Carré 24, **77**, **80**, 81
Sanitation 58, 100–102
Sartre, Jean-Paul 127, 172
Savary *see* Rovigo
Schiller, Friedrich 37
Schivelbusch, Wolfgang 150
Schonbrunn Castle 38
Seine **122**

Sensibilité 174–175
Sèvres 92, 97
Sewers *see* Sanitation
Sexual escapades (Burr's) 162–177
Shakespeare, William 104, 107
Shaving 62
Shelley, Percy 162
Shockoe Hill (Richmond, Virginia) 85
Shoes 62, **67**, 68–69, **143**, **149**
Shopping 63, 65, 83–85
Siege of Quebec 194, 204
Sieyes, Abbé 41
Signs **67**, 140
Sleeping 44, 58, 153, 182
Smoking 16
Sons of Liberty 26
South Carolina 43, 45, 62, 88, 100, 195, 200
Spain 35
Spang, Rebecca L. 133
Sphinx 199
Spitzweg, Carl **19**
Splatterdashes 69
Stael, Madame de 36
Stanton, Elisabeth Brandon 192
Staten Island 195
Steamship *Caroline* 207
Stendahl (Marie-Henri Beyle) 61, 91, 129
Stephenson, George 18
Stocks 54–56
Stowe, Harriet Beecher 192
Streets: cleaning 144; numbering of 26
Strong, Roger 207
Stuart, Gilbert 217
Sugar 20, 57, 124–126, 137, 139, 152, 170, 173–174
Sugarplums 138–139
Suleiman Aga 125
Sully, Thomas **9**
Sutcliffe, Anthony 93
Suvorov, Count Alexander 67
Swartout, Sam 188
Swediaur, Francois-Xavier 158

Talleyrand-Périgord, Charles Maurice de (Prince) 32, 34–36, 39, 41, 92, 139, 142, 225n19
Talma 42, **60**, 104–107
Teeth 47–51
Temple Prison 38
Tennis 30
Thayer, James 88
Theaters 8, 103–113
Tightrope 87, 109, 111
Tilset, Treaties of 34–35, 76, 93
Tissot, Samuel Auguste David 166
Titus, Arch of 212
Tivoli Garden 90
Tourists 23, 97, 114–119, 141, 147
Toys: 17; imperial 91–92
Translations 7, 16, 66, 137, 185
Treason trial 5, 6, 56
Treaty of Tolentino 199, 213

Triumphal entry into Paris 1798, 213
Trumbull, John 203, 204, 205, 224n2
Tuileries **25**, 30, **33**, 77, **80**, 82, 91, 94, 96–97, 115, 141–142, 145

Umbrellas 64–66, **65**
Uniforms 62, 69, 74

Valjean, Jean 101–102
Valkenaer 22, 138
Valley Forge, battle of 74
Vanderbilt, Cornelius 195
Vanderlyn, John 64, 88; *Ariadne Abandoned by Theseus on the Island of Naxos* 208–209, 213–215, 217; called "Wanderlyn," by Italian critic 197; copy after Correggio's *Jupiter and Sleeping Antiope with Cupid* 226n30; drawing of the *Arch of Titus* 212; esquisse of 212; friendship with Aaron Burr 26; gold medal 198, 225n8, 225n9; initiate into the Order of the Rose Cross and Pelican 198, 225n12; *Marius Amid the Ruins of Carthage* 197–198, 202, 207, 209, 213, 215, 217–218; *Massacre of Jane McCrea* 209, 213; model of 171–172; paintings 23, 49, 88–89, 115–117, 172–173, 194–218; paintings and engravings of Niagara Falls 206–207; Palace and Gardens of Versailles 209; pendant portraits of Burr and daughter Theodosia 217–218; power of attorney for Burr 211; at Salon of 1808 197; self-portrait 195
Vanderlyn, Dr. Pieter 217
Van Doren, Mark 44
Van Gaasbeek, Peter 217
Vaucanson, Jacques de 90
Vendome Column 94–**95**, 96
Ventriloquism 87, 89
Venus 197
Veronese, Paolo 202, 210
Versailles 30, 63, 89, 97, 100, 105, 118, 150, 168, 209–210
Vienna 37, 76, 91–92, 100, 118
Vigilant 121, 185
Vignon, Pierre 94
Vinegar: 101, 158; Burr's scheme 39, 46, 51–52, 100, 124
Virginia State Capital 199
Vivant-Denon *see* Denon, Dominique-Vivant, Baron
Volney, Comte de [Constantin Francois de Chasseboeuf] 110, 202, 206
Voltaire [Francois-Marie Arouet] 87, 104, 132, 167, 176

waistcoats 17, 61, 72
walking 67, 141–151, **143**

Washington, George 42, 50, 66, 75, 135, 204
watches **45**, 55, 61–64, 85–86, 217
water 10, 20, 29, 57, 99–102
Waterloo, battle of 32, 34, 36, 99, 118
weather 7, 17–18, 20, 122, 158
wedding of Napoleon and Marie-Louise **24–25**, 76–77, 79–8, **81, 82**, 91, 100
Wellington, Arthur Wellesley, 1st Duke of 64, 118
Wertmüller, Adolph Ulrich 211
West, Benjamin 204
Western venture *see* Mexico
Wilkinson, Gen. James 199, 215–216
Willey, Basil 45
Williamson, Charles 205
Willms, Johannes 31, 76
wine 124, 210
Wirt, William 192
Wolfe, Gen. James 66
Wollstonecraft, Mary 85, 116–117, 152–153, 170, 181
Woltz, Katherine 88–89
Women 152–161
Woodforde, James 58

"X" plan 52–54, 196, 203, 211; 217

www.ingramcontent.com/pod-product-compliance
Lightning Source LLC
Chambersburg PA
CBHW081551300426
44116CB00015B/2841